Amsterdam

written and researched by

Martin Dunford, Phil Lee and Karoline Densley

Contents

The Golden Age colour section following p.160

Architecture in Amsterdam colour section following p.240

◁◁ The Grachtengordel at night ◁ Café culture in Amsterdam

Introduction to

Amsterdam

Capital of the Netherlands, Amsterdam enjoys most of the advantages of a large city but not too many of the disadvantages; it's relatively small, it has a good transport system so it doesn't take forever to get from place to place, and – thanks to its canals – many parts of the centre are peaceful and relatively uncongested. The canals, too, make Amsterdam special, with the city's characteristic tall, gabled houses reflected in their black-green waters.

All considered, it's a unique and beautiful city; whether you're touring its elegant waterways, sipping a beer in one of its old cafés, or dodging the trams on Dam Square, you'll know that you couldn't be anywhere else in the world.

Amsterdam is also defined by its people and by its recent history; the city has a youthful feel and a friendly, welcoming attitude towards visitors that has been shaped by the liberal counterculture of the last four decades. It's no longer the hippy haven it once was, and in fact, in the last few years the city has been more or less absorbed into the slick mainstream of the rest of Europe. But some things haven't changed, and it's hard not to feel drawn by its vibrant, open-air summer events, by the cheery intimacy of its cafés, and by the Dutch facility with languages; just about everyone you meet in Amsterdam will be able to speak good-to-fluent English, and often more than a smattering of French and German too.

△ Leliegracht

Amsterdam is, however, far from being as cosmopolitan a city as, say, London or Paris; despite the huge numbers of immigrants from the former colonies in Surinam and Indonesia, as well as from Morocco and Turkey, to name but a few, almost all live and work outside the centre and can seem almost invisible to the casual visitor. Indeed, there is an ethnic and social homogeneity in the city centre that seems to counter everything you may have heard about Dutch integration. It's a contradiction that is typical of Amsterdam. The city is world-famous as a place where the possession and sale of cannabis are effectively legal – or at least decriminalized – and yet for the most part Amsterdammers can't really be bothered with the stuff. Well-publicized events of recent years, like the murder of radical film director Theo van Gogh, point to a city – and a society – that is less at ease with itself than you might have thought. And while Amsterdam is renowned for its tolerance towards all styles of behaviour (its policy on prostitution is also world-renowned), a primmer, more conventional big city, with a more mainstream dress sense, would be hard to find. Indeed, if anything, the city is trying to reinvent

> **The city has a youthful feel and a friendly, welcoming attitude towards visitors**

itself these days and attract a more upmarket kind of tourist, a little less focused on smoking and drinking. In recent years, a string of hardline city mayors has embarked on a generally successful policy of squashing Amsterdam's image as a counterculture icon and depicting it instead as a centre for business and international high finance. Almost all of the inner-city squats, which once defined local people-power, are gone or legalized, and coffee-shops have been forced to choose between selling dope or alcohol; if only

So much to see, so little time...

Amsterdam is perfect for short breaks: it's small, so you can amble about almost everywhere and see pretty much everything; there are very few must-see sights, so you don't have to spend half your time feeling guilty about the cultural icons you should be visiting; and there are literally hundreds of enticing bars, cafés and restaurants where you can take the weight off your feet between points of interest. The itineraries below are to give you an idea of how to plan your time. Mostly designed around key sights, they cover everything from a flying visit to a full week in the city. Follow them to the letter by all means – but don't be afraid to dip in and out either; they can be used as rigidly, or as flexibly, as you like.

Two days
Dam Square • Koninklijk Paleis • Red Light District • Oude Kerk • Rijksmuseum Van Gogh Museum • Leidseplein • Grachtengordel South • Museum Van Loon/Museum Willet-Holthuysen • Rembrandtplein

Three days
As above, plus:
Westerkerk • Anne Frank Huis • Brouwersgracht • Western docklands

Five days
As above, plus:
Rembrandthuis • Waterlooplein • Verzetsmuseum • Artis Zoo • Tropenmuseum • Heineken Experience • De Pijp • Vondelpark • Museumtramlijn • Amsterdamse Bos • Amsterdam ArenA

Seven days
As above, plus:
Stedelijk Museum • Esnoga • Joods Historisch Museum • Eastern docklands • Zeeburg • Haarlem • Keukenhof Gardens

▽ Centraal Station

for economic reasons, many have switched to the latter. The cityscape, too, is changing, with large-scale urban development on the outskirts and regeneration within.

Nevertheless, Amsterdam remains a casual and intimate place, and Amsterdammers themselves make much of their city and its attractions being *gezellig*, a rather over-used Dutch word roughly corresponding to a combination of "cosy", "lived-in" and "warmly convivial". Nowhere is this more applicable than in the city's unparalleled selection of **drinking** places, whether you choose a traditional brown café or one of a raft of newer, more stylish bars. The city boasts dozens of excellent **restaurants** too, with great Indonesian options and a host of increasingly adventurous Dutch establishments. As for

cultural attractions, the city holds its own in contemporary European film, dance, drama and music; it harbours several top-notch jazz venues, as well as the Concertgebouw, home to one of the world's leading orchestras, and the state-of-the-art Muziekgebouw, the city's new, prestigious venue for opera and orchestral music. The club scene is relatively restrained, although a wealth of **gay bars** and clubs partly justifies Amsterdam's claim to be the "Gay Capital of Europe".

Where to go

he city's layout is determined by a web of canals radiating out from a historical core to loop right round Amsterdam's compact centre, which takes about forty minutes to stroll from one end to the other. Butting up to the River IJ, the **Old Centre** spreads south from **Centraal Station** bisected by the Damrak and its continuation, the Rokin, the city's main drag; en route is the Dam, the main square. The Old Centre remains Amsterdam's commercial heart, as well as the hub of its bustling street life, and also holds myriad shops, bars and restaurants. The area is also home to the **Red Light District**, just to the east of the Damrak, and contains dozens of fine old buildings, most memorably the Oude Kerk, the Amstelkring and the Koninklijk Paleis.

△ Brouwersgracht

The Old Centre is bordered by the first of the major canals, the Singel, whose curve is mirrored by those of the Herengracht, Keizersgracht and Prinsengracht – collectively known as the **Grachtengordel**, or "Girdle of Canals". These waterways were part of a major seventeenth-century urban extension and, with the interconnecting radial streets, form the city's distinctive web shape. This is Amsterdam's most delightful area, full of the handsome seventeenth- and eighteenth-century canal houses, with their decorative gables, and narrow, dreamy canals that most people associate with the city; a well-worn image perhaps, but one that is still entirely authentic. Here you'll also find perhaps the city's most celebrated attraction, the **Anne Frank Huis**, the house in which the young Jewish diarist hid away during the German occupation of World War II, now a poignant reminder of the Holocaust.

▽ Skating on Amsterdam's canals

Immediately to the west of the Grachtengordel lies the **Jordaan**, one-time industrial slum and the traditional heart of working-class Amsterdam, though these days almost entirely gentrified. The same applies to the adjacent **Western docklands**, although the origins of this district are very different; the artificial islands of the Westerdok were dredged out of the river to create extra wharves and shipbuilding space during the seventeenth century, and only in the last few decades has the shipping industry moved out.

On the other side of the centre is the **Old Jewish Quarter**, home to a thriving Jewish community until the German occupation of World War II. Postwar development laid a heavy hand on the quarter, but nonetheless there are a couple of significant survivors, principally the **Esnoga** (Portuguese Synagogue) and the **Joods Historisch Museum** (Jewish Historical Museum). The adjacent Plantagebuurt is greener and more suburban, but it does possess one excellent museum, the **Verzetsmuseum** (Resistance Museum); the neighbouring **Eastern docklands**, in particular Zeeburg, is another formerly industrial area now undergoing rapid renewal.

Amsterdam's **Museum Quarter** contains, as you might expect, the city's premier art museums, principally the **Rijksmuseum** with its wonderful collection of Dutch paintings, including several of Rembrandt's finest works, and the excellent **Van Gogh Museum**, which holds the world's largest collection of the artist's work. Both lie just a stone's throw from the city's finest park, the **Vondelpark**.

Finally, the residential suburbs – or **Outer Districts** – spreading beyond Singelgracht – are relatively short of attractions – notable exceptions being the wooded parkland of the **Amsterdamse Bos** and the **Amsterdam ArenA,** home to the city's celebrated football team, Ajax.

Talk to Amsterdammers about visiting other parts of their country and you may well be met with looks of amazement. Ignore them. The Netherlands is a small nation, and the Dutch have an outstanding public transport system: an integrated network of trains and buses that makes a large and varied slice of the country easily visitable. Consequently, the choice of possible **day-trips** is extensive; the towns of **Haarlem** and **Alkmaar**, the old Zuider Zee ports of **Marken** and **Volendam**, and the pretty town of **Edam** are all worth a visit – not to mention the much-touted **Keukenhof Gardens**, which are at their best, not surprisingly, during spring and early summer.

When to go

A msterdam enjoys a fairly standard, temperate **climate**, with warm summers and moderately cold and wet winters. The weather is certainly not severe enough to make very much difference to the city's routines. That said, high summer – roughly late June to August – sees the city packed to the gunnels and parts of the centre almost overwhelmed by the tourist throng, whereas spring and autumn are not too crowded and can be espe-

> Spring and autumn can be especially beautiful, with mist hanging over the canals

cially beautiful, with mist hanging over the canals and low sunlight beaming through the cloud cover. At any time of the year, but particularly in summer, try to book your accommodation ahead of time.

Average daily temperatures (°C) and monthly rainfall (mm)

	Jan	Feb	Mar	Apr	May	June	July	Aug	Sept	Oct	Nov	Dec
Min°C	1.2	0	3.7	4.8	8.2	12	13.5	13	10.9	7.7	4.8	3.5
Max°C	5.1	6.4	8.5	12.6	16.8	19.2	21	21	18.3	14	8.8	6.7
mm	78	43.6	89.3	39.3	51.2	60.1	63.4	60	80.1	104.7	76.4	72.3

20

things not to miss

It's not possible to see everything Amsterdam has to offer on a short trip – and we don't suggest you try. What follows, in no particular order, is a subjective selection of the city's highlights, from elegant canal-side architecture and vibrant markets to outstanding art collections and traditional bars – all arranged in colour-coded categories to help you find the very best things to see, do and experience. All entries have a page reference to take you straight into the guide, where you can find out more.

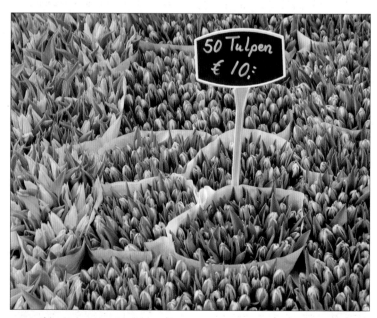

50 Tulpen
€ 10:

01 Bloemenmarkt Page **82** • Masses of colourful blooms for sale, including – of course – tulips.

02 **The Begijnhof** Page 52 • The fourteenth-century Begijnhof is one of the quietest and prettiest corners of the city centre.

03 **The Eastern docklands** Page **107** • The city's most resurgent district, with some of its coolest bars and restaurants, and landmark contemporary architecture.

04 **Indonesian food** Page **180** • Fill up on Amsterdam's ethnic food speciality.

11

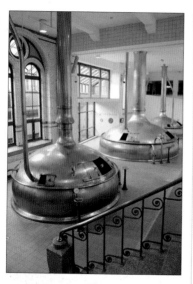

05 **The Heineken Experience** Page **128** • Although this is no longer a working brewery, the compensation is an excellent museum devoted to the art of brewing – with a few beers thrown in along the way.

06 **Cycling** Page **27** • Get around the city like a local by renting a bike for the day.

07 **Koninklijk Paleis** Page **47** • Co-opted by the Dutch royals but originally Amsterdam's town hall, this building speaks volumes about the city during the Golden Age.

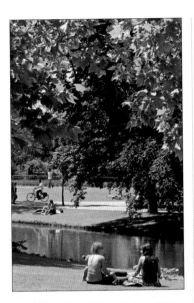

08 The Vondelpark Page 124 •
The leafy Vondelpark, with its ponds, footpaths and colony of parrots, is the city's most attractive park.

09 Proeflokaalen Page 182 •
Served ice-cold, jenever, the Dutch version of gin, is the nation's favourite spirit, and these "tasting-houses" are the traditional places to sample it in its various flavours.

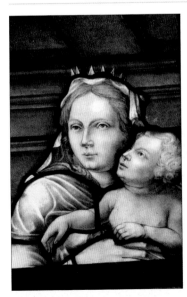

10 Oude Kerk Page 56 • The city's
oldest and most venerable church, slap-bang in the middle of the Red Light District.

11 The Grachtengordel
Page 63 • The elegant bends and handsome canal houses of the city's seventeenth-century extension are what makes the city unique.

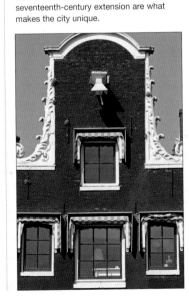

12Concertgebouw Page **123** • One of the finest concert halls in Europe, attracting some of the biggest names in classical music and opera.

13Anne Frank Huis
Page **68** • The museum created in the secret annexe – home to Anne Frank and her family for two years during World War II – is the city's most moving sight.

14The Jordaan Page **85** • The Jordaan holds many of the city's most diverting secondhand and bric-a-brac shops – and some of its prettiest canals.

Red Light District
Page **55** • It's too steeped in the art of titillation to be truly shocking these days, but Amsterdam's Red Light District is still the real thing – and a big attraction in its own right.

16 **Coffeeshops** Page **202** • Nowhere else in the world can you smoke high-quality dope in such comfortable – and legal – surroundings.

18 **Brown Cafés**
Page **181** • Amsterdam is famous for its brown cafés – dark, cosy and very traditional.

17 **Van Gogh Museum** Page **120** • The world's most comprehensive collection of the artist's work – simply unmissable.

19 **Rijksmuseum** Page **114** • The city's greatest museum – featuring everything from paintings to furniture and applied arts – is currently undergoing restoration, but you can still see the best of its paintings in the Philips Wing.

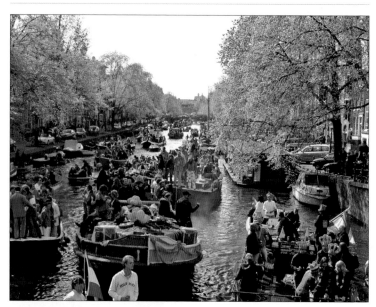

20 **Queen's Day** Page **259** • Amsterdammers let their hair down on Queen's Day (Koninginnedag), the city's biggest and wildest municipal knees-up.

Basics

Basics

Getting there

UK travellers are spoilt for choice when it comes to deciding how to get to Amsterdam. There are plenty of flights, from all over the UK, and taking the train through the Channel Tunnel is just as easy – not much cheaper but almost as quick. Bus travel is probably the most affordable option, and by car, deals for drivers on ferry routes into Dutch and Belgian ports are particularly competitive. From North America and Canada the main decision is whether to fly direct – easy enough as Schiphol is a major international air travel hub, served by dozens of short- and long-haul airlines – or to route via London, picking up a budget flight onwards from there. From Australia and New Zealand, all flights to Amsterdam require one or two stops on the way; from South Africa, direct flights are available.

Flights from the UK and Ireland

Amsterdam is one of the **UK**'s most popular short-haul destinations, and you'll find loads of choice – in carriers, flight times and departure airports. Aside from the major full-service carriers (KLM, British Airways and BMI), there are plenty of no-frills airlines operating flights to Amsterdam, including easyJet, BMIbaby and Thomsonfly, as well as a few business-oriented, smaller carriers such as VLM.

Flights to Amsterdam's **Schiphol Airport** (pronounced skip-oll) take roughly an hour from London, or ninety minutes from Scotland and the north of England. There's a good number of daily flights out of **London** – Heathrow, Gatwick, Stansted, Luton and London City – plus nonstop flights from many of the UK's **regional airports**, including Birmingham, Bournemouth, East Midlands, Cardiff, Coventry, Southampton, Norwich, Liverpool, Manchester, Leeds-Bradford, Doncaster-Sheffield, Humberside, Newcastle, Teesside, Edinburgh, Glasgow and Aberdeen.

Whichever route you choose, it's hard to say precisely what you'll pay at any given time: the **price** depends hugely on when you book and when you fly, what offers are available – and how lucky you get. However, flying to Amsterdam with one of the **low-cost airlines** between April and September, you'll pay around £100 return travelling at convenient times at the weekend, including taxes, as opposed to £150 with one of the **full-service carriers**. Weekday travel will cost £50–60 with a budget carrier, £100 or

so with a full-service airline. If you want more flexibility with your ticket you'll pay more, as you will if you book at the last minute – economy return tickets from London to Amsterdam can cost anything up to £400. All carriers offer their lowest prices online.

Flying to Amsterdam from **Northern Ireland**, the most economical option is with easyJet out of Belfast International (fares are around £130). From the **Republic of Ireland**, Aer Lingus flies six times daily to Amsterdam from Dublin and twice daily from Cork, for a minimum €175–200 return, depending on the season, with fares rising to €450 or more at peak times.

Flights from the US and Canada

Amsterdam's Schiphol Airport is among the most popular and least expensive gateways to Europe from **North America and Canada**, and finding a convenient and good-value flight is rarely a problem. **Direct flights** are operated by KLM/Northwest, Continental and Singapore Airways; many more fly **via London** and other European centres – and are nearly always cheaper because of it.

Virtually every region of the US and Canada is well served by the major airlines. KLM and Northwest, which operate a joint service, offer the widest range of flights, with direct or one-stop flights to Amsterdam from eleven US cities, and connections from dozens more. From elsewhere in the US, the Dutch charter firm Martinair flies year-round from **Miami** and **Orlando** direct to Amsterdam. Singapore Airlines and United

19

also fly direct to Amsterdam from **Chicago**, while Delta operates from **Atlanta** and Continental from **Houston**.

Booking far enough in advance, you should be able to find a **fare** between April and September for $600–800 return from New York (flight time 8hr 10min), $800 from Atlanta (10hr), and around $1000 from Chicago (8hr) or LA (10hr 30min), though booking less than a couple of weeks in advance can push these prices up considerably.

From **Canada**, KLM flies direct to Amsterdam year-round from **Vancouver** (9hr 45min) and from **Toronto** (7hr 10min). Between April and October, Martinair flies from Toronto, Vancouver (10hr 30min), **Edmonton** (11hr) and **Calgary** (11hr). There

are also plenty of one-stop options via Frankfurt, London and Paris. **Fares** from Toronto go for around Can$1200, from Vancouver around Can$1500.

Flights from Australia, New Zealand and South Africa

There are **no direct flights** to the Netherlands from **Australia and New Zealand**: all involve at least one stop. Singapore Airways and Malaysian offer the most direct routes out of **Sydney** (stopping in Singapore and Kuala Lumpur respectively). Thai, Austrian and Qantas all have two stops (Bangkok/Frankfurt, Kuala Lumpur/Vienna and Singapore/Frankfurt). Flights from **Christchurch** go via Sydney and London and from

Fly less – stay longer! Travel and climate change

Climate change is the single biggest issue facing our planet. It is caused by a build-up in the atmosphere of carbon dioxide and other greenhouse gases, which are emitted by many sources – including planes. Already, flights account for around 3–4 percent of human-induced global warming; that figure may sound small, but it is rising year on year and threatens to counteract the progress made by reducing greenhouse emissions in other areas.

Rough Guides regard travel, overall, as a global benefit, and feel strongly that the advantages to developing economies are important, as are the opportunities for greater contact and awareness among peoples. But we all have a responsibility to limit our personal "carbon footprint". That means giving thought to how often we fly and what we can do to redress the harm that our trips create.

Flying and climate change

Pretty much every form of motorized travel generates CO_2, but planes are particularly bad offenders, releasing large volumes of greenhouse gases at altitudes where their impact is far more harmful. Flying also allows us to travel much further than we would contemplate doing by road or rail, so the emissions attributable to each passenger are greater. For example, one person taking a return flight between Europe and California produces the equivalent impact of 2.5 tonnes of CO_2 – similar to the yearly output of the average UK car.

Less harmful planes may evolve but it will be decades before they replace the current fleet – which could be too late for avoiding climate chaos. In the meantime, there are limited options for concerned travellers: to reduce the amount we travel by air (take fewer trips, stay longer!), to avoid night flights (when plane contrails trap heat from Earth but can't reflect sunlight back to space), and to make the trips we do take "climate neutral" via a carbon offset scheme.

Carbon offset schemes

Offset schemes run by **climatecare.org**, **carbonneutral.com** and others allow you to "neutralize" the greenhouse gases that you are responsible for releasing. Their websites have simple calculators that let you work out the impact of any flight. Once that's done, you can pay to fund projects that will reduce future carbon emissions by an equivalent amount (such as the distribution of low-energy light bulbs and cooking stoves in developing countries). Please take the time to visit our website and make your trip climate neutral.

www.roughguides.com/climatechange

Wellington via Melbourne or Sydney and London. One further option is to pick up a cheap ticket to **London**, and then continue your journey to Amsterdam with one of the no-frills budget airlines (see p.22).

From **South Africa**, KLM offers **direct flights** to Amsterdam, with services from Cape Town and Johannesburg. South African Airways offers indirect flights via London and Frankfurt; Lufthansa via Frankfurt; and Virgin Atlantic via London.

Fares from Sydney are around A$1800, from Melbourne A$2000 and from Auckland A$2400. A return flight from Christchurch or Wellington will set you back around NZ$2700. Flights with KLM from Cape Town cost around R7400; from Johannesburg, R8200. Indirect flights via London or Frankfurt cost around R8000.

By train

The simplest and quickest way to travel to Amsterdam by **train** is to take the **Eurostar** service from London nonstop to Brussels. At the time of going to press, trains depart from London Waterloo (2hr 15–30min); from November 2007, trains will leave from St Pancras International station (1hr 50min) in central London and from Ebbsfleet International station (1hr 40), off Junction 2 of the M25. Trains arrive at Bruxelles-Midi station (Brussel-Zuid in Dutch), from where plenty of fast trains – including the **Thalys** high-speed services (ⓦ www.thalys.com) – head on to Amsterdam (around 2hr 30min). The total **journey time** from London is around six hours, and Eurostar can arrange a through ticket from any point in the UK.

A standard return **fare** to Amsterdam costs around £150, but special deals are common-place, especially in the low season; and you can also sometimes reduce costs by accepting certain ticket restrictions. Book through Rail Europe or directly through the Eurostar website (for both, see p.23).

The Dutch Railways website ⓦ www.ns.nl can give full **timetable** details (in English) of trains from stations in the UK to any station in the Netherlands, including **ferry times**.

A longer – but cheaper – **rail-and-ferry route**, the Dutchflyer, is available through Stena Line in conjunction with One Railway. The journey operates twice daily (morning and late afternoon) from London's Liverpool Street station to Harwich (1hr 40min) and connects with the rapid ferry crossing to the Hook of Holland, or Hoek van Holland (3hr 40min), from where fast trains head on to Amsterdam (1hr 35min). Total **journey time** from London is around eight hours.

Prices from London start at £50 return for an Apex fare, which must be booked at least a week in advance; the return journey needs to be made within one month. A standard open return costs £90, or £72 with a young person's railcard. With an **overnight sailing**, fares start at £110. Tickets are available from One Railway (see p.23) and larger main-line stations, or you can book online with Dutch-flyer direct (see p.23).

By bus

Travelling by **long-distance bus** is generally the cheapest way of reaching Amsterdam from the UK, but it is very time-consuming: the journey from London to Amsterdam takes twelve hours or more. **Eurolines** (see p.23) operates three services daily (8am, 8pm & 10pm) from London to Amsterdam, all using Eurotunnel. A standard **fare** is £52 return (under-26s and over-60s pay £49) though promotional return fares can be snapped up for much less. The lesser-known **Anglia Lines** (see p.23) operates a daily coach service between London Victoria and central Amsterdam, via Brussels, which leaves once daily at 2.30pm and costs just £38 return (£34 if you're under 26) if booked seven days in advance. The journey takes around nine hours.

By car

To reach Amsterdam by **car** or by **motorbike**, you can either take a **ferry**, or – preferable for its hassle-free crossing – Eurotunnel's **shuttle-train** through the **Channel Tunnel**. Note that Eurotunnel only carries cars (including occupants) and motorbikes, not cyclists or foot passengers. Amsterdam is roughly 370km from the Eurotunnel exit in Calais.

There are up to four shuttle trains per hour (only one per hour midnight–6am), taking 35min (45min for some night departure times), and you must check in at Folkestone at least 30min before departure. It's possible to turn up and buy your **ticket** at the tollbooths (exit the M20 at junction 11a), though it's a good idea to book in advance through the website (see opposite) at busy times.

Fares depend on the time of year, time of day and length of stay (the cheapest ticket is for a day-trip, followed by a five-day return); it costs less to travel between 10pm and 6am, while the highest fares are reserved for weekend departures and returns in July and August. Prices are charged per vehicle; short-stay savers between April and October for a car start at around £110. If you wish to stay more than five days, a standard return costs from around £130, while a "Flexiplus" fare, which entitles you to change your plans at the last minute, costs more still. Some special offers are usually also available.

Three operators run **ferries** from the UK direct to ports in the Netherlands, and all offer year-round services. The fastest **route** is with Stena Line, which sails from Harwich in Essex to the Hook of Holland; the journey time is 6 hours 15 minutes, but you can take a super-fast daytime service which does the journey in just 3hr 40min; travelling at night always takes longer and you have to book a cabin. P&O North Sea Ferries operate from Hull to Rotterdam (11hr). DFDS Seaways sails once daily from Newcastle (North Shields) to IJmuiden (14hr), half an hour's drive from Amsterdam.

Aside from the options direct to Dutch ports, you might want to consider the ferry routes to **Belgium** and **France**. P&O sail once a day from Hull to Zeebrugge in Belgium (14hr 30min), while Norfolkline operates a year-round service from Dover to the French border town of Dunkerque (2hr).

Fares vary hugely, depending on when you leave, how long you stay, if you have a car, and number of passengers. Discounts for students and under-26s are available.

Airlines and agents

Online booking

Ⓦ www.expedia.co.uk (in UK) Ⓦ www.expedia .com (in US) Ⓦ www.expedia.ca (in Canada)
Ⓦ www.lastminute.com (in UK)
Ⓦ www.opodo.co.uk (in UK)
Ⓦ www.orbitz.com (in US)
Ⓦ www.travelocity.co.uk (in UK)

Ⓦ www.travelocity.com (in US) Ⓦ www .travelocity.ca (in Canada) Ⓦ www.zuji.com.au (in Australia) Ⓦ www.zuji.co.nz (in New Zealand)

Airlines

Aer Lingus UK ☎ 0870/876 5000, Republic of Ireland ☎ 0818/365 000, Ⓦ www.aerlingus.com.
Air Canada Canada ☎ 1-888-247-2262, Ⓦ www .aircanada.ca.
Air France UK ☎ 0870/142 4343, US ☎ 1-800/237-2747, Canada ☎ 1-800-667-2747, Ⓦ www.airfrance. com.
Air New Zealand Australia ☎ 13 24 76, New Zealand ☎ 0800/737 000, Ⓦ www.airnz.co.nz.
American Airlines US ☎ 1-800-433-7300, Ⓦ www. aa.com.
bmi UK ☎ 0870/607 0555 or ☎ 0870/607 0222, Ireland ☎ 01/407 3036, US ☎ 1-800/788-0555, Ⓦ www.flybmi.com.
bmibaby UK ☎ 0871/224 0224, Republic of Ireland ☎ 1890/340 122, Ⓦ www.bmibaby.com.
British Airways UK ☎ 0870/850 9850, Republic of Ireland ☎ 1890/626 747, US & Canada ☎ 1-800/ AIRWAYS, Australia ☎ 1300/767 177, New Zealand ☎ 09/966 9777, Ⓦ www.ba.com.
Cathay Pacific US and Canada ☎ 1-800/538-2942, Australia ☎ 13 17 47, New Zealand ☎ 09/379 0861, Ⓦ www.cathaypacific.com
Continental Airlines US & Canada ☎ 1-800/523-3273, Australia ☎ 02/9244 2242, New Zealand ☎ 09/308 3350, Ⓦ www.continental.com.
Delta US & Canada ☎ 1-800/221-1212, Australia ☎ 1300/302 849, New Zealand ☎ 09/9772232, Ⓦ www.delta.com
easyJet UK ☎ 0905/821 0905, Republic of Ireland ☎ 0870/600 0000, Ⓦ www.easyjet.com.
KLM (Royal Dutch Airlines)/Northwest/KLM UK ☎ 0870/507 4074, Republic of Ireland ☎ 1850/747 400, US & Canada ☎ 1-800/225-2525, Australia ☎ 1300/303 747, New Zealand ☎ 09/921 6040, SA ☎ 11/961 6767, Ⓦ www.klm.com, Ⓦ www.nwa.com.
Lufthansa US ☎ 1-800/3995-838, Canada ☎ 1-800/563-5954, Australia ☎ 1300/655 727, New Zealand ☎ 0800-945 220, SA ☎ 0861/842 538, Ⓦ www.lufthansa.com.
Malaysia Airlines US ☎ 1-800/5529-264, Australia ☎ 13 26 27, New Zealand ☎ 0800/777 747, Ⓦ www. malaysia-airlines.com.
Martinair US ☎ 1-800/627-8462, Canada ☎ 1-416-364-3672, Ⓦ www.martinair.com.
Qantas US and Canada ☎ 1-800/227-4500, Australia ☎ 13 13 13, Ⓦ www.qantas.com; New Zealand ☎ 0800/808 767 or 09/357 8900, Ⓦ www .qantas.co.nz.
Ryanair UK ☎ 0871/246 0000, Republic of Ireland ☎ 0818/303 030, Ⓦ www.ryanair.com.

Singapore Airlines US ☎1-800/742-3333, Canada ☎1-800-663-3046, Australia ☎13 10 11, New Zealand ☎0800/808 909, SA ☎11/880 8560 or 11/880 8566, ⓦwww.singaporeair.com.
South African Airways SA ☎11/978 1111, ⓦwww.flysaa.com.
Thai Airways US ☎1-212/949-8424, Australia ☎1300/651 960, New Zealand ☎09/377 3886, ⓦwww.thaiair.com.
Thomsonfly UK ☎0870 1900 737, ⓦwww.thomsonfly.com.
United Airlines US ☎1-800/UNITED-1, Australia ☎13 17 77, ⓦwww.united.com.
Virgin Atlantic US ☎1-800/821-5438, Australia ☎1300/727 340, SA ☎11/340 3400, ⓦwww.virgin-atlantic.com.
VLM Airlines UK ☎020/7646 0757, ⓦwww.flyvlm.com.

Agents and operators

ebookers UK ☎0800/082 3000, Republic of Ireland ☎01/488 3507, ⓦwww.ebookers.com. Low fares on an extensive selection of scheduled flights and package deals.
North South Travel UK ☎01245/608 291, ⓦwww.northsouthtravel.co.uk. Friendly, competitive travel agency, offering discounted fares worldwide. Profits are used to support projects in the developing world, especially the promotion of sustainable tourism.
STA Travel UK ☎0871/2300 040, US ☎1-800/781-4040, Australia ☎134 STA, New Zealand ☎0800/474 400, SA ☎0861/781 781, ⓦwww.statravel.com. Worldwide specialists in independent travel; also student IDs, travel insurance, car rental, rail passes, and more. Good discounts for students and under-26s.
Trailfinders UK ☎0845/058 5858, Republic of Ireland ☎01/677 7888, Australia ☎1300/780 212, ⓦwww.trailfinders.com. One of the best-informed and most efficient agents for independent travellers.

Rail contacts

Dutchflyer UK ☎08705 455455, ⓦwww.dutchflyer.co.uk.
European Rail UK ☎020/7387 0444, ⓦwww.europeanrail.com.
Europrail International Canada ☎1-888/667-9734, ⓦwww.europrail.net.
Eurostar UK ☎0870/518 6186, outside UK ☎0044/12336 17575, ⓦwww.eurostar.com.
One Railway UK ☎0845 600 7245, ⓦwww.onerailway.com.
Rail Europe UK ☎0870/837 1371, US ☎1-877/257-2887, Canada ☎1-800/361-RAIL, ⓦwww.raileurope.co.uk, ⓦwww.raileurope.com/us.

Bus contacts

Anglia Lines UK ☎0870/608 8806, ⓦwww.eurobusexpress.co.uk.
Eurolines UK ☎0870/580 8080, ⓦwww.nationalexpress.com/eurolines.

Ferry companies

DFDS Seaways UK ☎0870/252 0524, ⓦwww.dfdsseaways.co.uk.
Eurotunnel UK ☎0870/535 3535, ⓦwww.eurotunnel.com.
Norfolkline UK ☎0870/870 1020, ⓦwww.norfolkline.com.
P&O Ferries UK ☎0870/598 0333, ⓦwww.poferries.com.
Stena Line UK ☎0870/570 7070, Northern Ireland ☎0870/520 4204, Republic of Ireland ☎021/427 2965, ⓦwww.stenaline.co.uk.

Channel tunnel

Eurotunnel UK ☎0870/535 3535, ⓦwww.eurotunnel.com.

Arrival

Arriving in Amsterdam by train and plane could hardly be easier. Schiphol, Amsterdam's international airport, is a quick and convenient train ride away from Centraal Station, the city's international train station, which is itself just a ten-minute metro ride from Amstel Station, the terminus for long-distance and international buses. Centraal Station is also the hub of Amsterdam's excellent public transport network, whose trams, buses and metro combine to reach every corner of the city and its suburbs.

By air

Amsterdam's international airport, **Schiphol** (℗0900/7244 7465, Ⓦwww.schiphol.nl), is located about 15km southwest of the city centre. It's one of the busiest airports in Europe, and one of the best-organized, with an efficient **transfer** system to the city and indeed the rest of the country. Arriving passengers are channelled through to a large and well-signposted plaza, which has all the **facilities** you would expect – car rental desks, banks, exchange offices, left-luggage facilities, ATMs and a VVV (tourist office) with accommodation booking service, as well as a Netherlands Railways ticket office and access to the **rail station**.

Trains run from the airport's rail station to Amsterdam's **Centraal Station** every ten minutes during the day and every hour at night (midnight–6am); the journey takes 15–20 minutes and costs €3.60 one-way, €6.20 return; there's a 50c surcharge if you buy from the ticket office rather than the ticket machines. **Hotel shuttles** are another option; the Connexxion service (℗038/339 4741, Ⓦwww.schipholhotelshuttle.nl), departs from the designated bus stop outside the Arrivals hall every thirty minutes (on the half-hour) from 6am to 9pm at a cost of €12 one-way, €19 return. The route varies with the needs of the passengers it picks up at the airport, but buses take about thirty minutes to get from the airport to the city centre. Tickets are available from the Connexxion desk in the Arrivals Hall. There are also plenty of **taxis**;

the fare from Schiphol to most parts of the city centre is €40–45.

By train and bus

Amsterdam's **Centraal Station** (CS) has regular connections with key cities in **Germany**, **Belgium** and **France**, as well as all the larger towns and cities of the Netherlands. Amsterdam also has several suburban train stations, but these are principally for the convenience of commuters. Centraal Station has just enjoyed a much-needed facelift and has lots of **facilities**, including left-luggage lockers and a staffed left-luggage office (see p.33). There's also a **VVV** (tourist office) on platform 2 and a second directly across from the station entrance, plenty of ATMs and a GVB exchange office, more shops than you can shake a stick at, and lots of places to eat too, including a good and atmospheric restaurant-café, *Restaurant 1e Class*, open all day on platform 2 (see p.188). For all rail enquiries contact **NS** (Netherlands Railways; international enquiries ℗0900/9296; domestic enquiries ℗0900/9292; Ⓦwww.ns.nl).

Eurolines' (see p.23) long-distance, international **buses** arrive at **Amstel Station**, about 3.5km to the southeast of Centraal Station. The metro journey to Centraal Station takes about ten minutes. Anglia Lines' (see p.23) buses arrive at Centraal Station, well placed for everything the city has to offer.

Getting around

Almost all of Amsterdam's leading attractions are clustered in or near the city centre, within easy walking – and even easier cycling – distance of each other. For longer jaunts, the city has a first-rate public transport system, run by the GVB, comprising trams, buses, a smallish metro system and four passenger ferries across the River IJ to the northern suburbs (see p.139). Centraal Station is the hub of the system with a multitude of trams and buses departing from outside on Stationsplein, which is also the location of a metro station and a GVB public transport information office.

Tickets

The most common type of **ticket**, valid for all forms of GVB transport, is the **strippenkaart**, a card divided into strips: fold your *strippenkaart* over to expose the number of strips required for your journey and then insert it into the on-board franking machine. Amsterdam's public transport system is divided into **zones**, and one person making a journey within one zone costs two strips. The "Centre" zone covers the city centre and its immediate surroundings (well beyond Singelgracht), and thus two strips will cover more or less every journey you're likely to make. If you travel into an additional zone, it costs three strips, and so on. More than one person can use the same *strippenkaart*, as long as the requisite number of strips is stamped. After franking, you can use any GVB tram, bus

Water transport

Cruising along Amsterdam's **canals** might not be the fastest way of getting from A to B – but it's certainly picturesque. The following options give you the freedom to hop on and off as you please; for **guided tours**, see p.37.

  Canal Bus (☏020/623 9886, ⓦwww.canal.nl) operates on three circular routes – coloured green, red and blue – which meet at various points: at the jetty opposite Centraal Station beside Prins Hendrikkade; on the Singelgracht opposite the Rijksmuseum; and by the Stadhuis on Waterlooplein. There are fourteen stops in all and together they give easy access to all the major sights. Boats leave from the jetty opposite Centraal Station every half an hour or so during high season between 9.50am and 7.25pm, and a day ticket for all three routes, allowing you to hop on and off as many times as you like, costs €17 per adult, €11 for children (4–12 years old); it's valid until noon the following day and entitles the bearer to small discounts at several museums. Two-day passes cost €28.50.

  Museumboot (☏020/530 1090, ⓦwww.lovers.nl) calls at seven jetties located at or near many of the city's major attractions. It departs from opposite Centraal Station (every 30min; 10am–5pm) and a come-and-go-as-you-please day ticket costs €15, children €13 (4–12 years old).

  Canal Bikes (☏020/626 5574, ⓦwww.canal.nl) are four-seater pedaloes which take a lifetime to get anywhere but are nevertheless good fun, unless – of course – it's raining. You can rent them at four central locations: on the Singelgracht opposite the Rijksmuseum; on the Prinsengracht outside the Anne Frank Huis; on Keizersgracht at Leidsestraat; and behind Leidseplein. Rental prices per person, per hour are €7 (3–4 people) or €8 (1–2 people), plus a refundable deposit of €50. They can be picked up at one location and left at any of the others; opening hours are daily 9am–6pm, till 9.30pm in July and August.

and the metro for up to one hour. At the time of writing, a two-strip *strippenkaart* costs €1.60 and a three-strip €2.40; you can buy these on the bus or tram. However, you're better off buying tickets in advance, from tobacconists, the GVB, the VVV and metro stations; a fifteen-strip costs €6.70 and a 45-strip €19.80.

You can opt instead for a **dagkaart** (day ticket), which gives unlimited access to the GVB system for up to a maximum of three days. Prices are €6.30 for 24 hours, €10 for 48 hours and €13 for 72 hours.

Finally, note that the GVB tries hard to keep **fare-dodging** to a minimum and wherever you're travelling, and at whatever time of day, there's a reasonable chance you'll have your ticket checked. If you are caught without a valid ticket, you risk an on-the-spot fine of €35.

By tram, bus and metro

The city centre is crisscrossed by **trams**. Two of the more useful are trams #2 and #5, which link Centraal Station with Leidsestraat and the Rijksmuseum every ten minutes or so during the day. Get on trams via the front door (where the ticket machine is located) and off through the rear doors. **Buses** are mainly useful for going to the outskirts, and the same applies to the **metro**, which has

just two city-centre stations, Nieuwmarkt and Waterlooplein.

Trams, buses and the metro operate daily between 6am and midnight, supplemented by a limited number of **nightbuses** (*nachtbussen*), which run roughly every half hour from midnight until 7am. All tram and bus stops display a detailed **map** of the network. For further details on all services, head for the main **GVB information office** (Mon–Fri 7am–9pm, Sat & Sun 8am–9pm; ☎0900/8011, ⊛www.gvb.nl) on Stationsplein; the website has a useful journey planner. The GVB's free, English-language *Tourist Guide to Public Transport* is very helpful, and it also provides free **transport maps** too; you will also find a map of the city's tram, metro and bus routes at the back of this book.

By bike

One of the most agreeable ways to explore Amsterdam is by **bicycle**. The city has an excellent network of designated **cycle lanes** (*fietspaden*) and for once cycling isn't a fringe activity – there are cyclists everywhere. Indeed, much to the chagrin of the city's taxi drivers, the needs of the cyclist often take precedence over those of the motorist, and by law, if there's a collision it's always the driver's fault.

Amsterdam addresses

For the uninitiated, Amsterdam **addresses** can be a little confusing. Addresses are written as, for example, "Kerkstr. 79 II", which means the second-floor apartment at Kerkstraat 79. The ground floor is indicated by **hs** (*huis*, house) after the number; the basement is **sous** (*sousterrain*). In some cases, especially in the **Jordaan**, where streets have the same name, to differentiate between them, **1e**, **2e**, **3e** and even occasionally **4e** are placed in front; these are abbreviations for *Eerste* (first), *Tweede* (second), *Derde* (third) and *Vierde* (fourth). Many **side streets** take the name of the main street they run off, with the addition of the word *dwars*, meaning "crossing"; for instance, Palmdwarsstraat is a side street off Palmstraat. Furthermore, and for no apparent reason, some dead-straight cross-streets change their name – so that, for example, in the space of about 300m, 1e Bloemdwarsstraat becomes 2e Leliedwarsstraat and then 3e Egelantiersdwarsstraat.

As for boats, **T/O** (*tegenover*, or "opposite") in an address shows that the address is a boat: hence "Prinsengracht T/O 26" would indicate a boat to be found opposite Prinsengracht 26.

The main Grachtengordel canals begin their numbering at Brouwersgracht and increase as they progress anticlockwise. By the time they reach the Amstel, Herengracht's house numbers are in the 600s, Keizersgracht's in the 800s and Prinsengracht's in the 900s.

Bike **rental** is straightforward, with lots of rental outlets (*fietsenverhuur*) in central Amsterdam. Among the best are: Bike City at Bloemgracht 70 (℡020/626 3721, ⓦwww. bikecity.nl; daily 9am–6pm); Damstraat Rent-a-Bike at Damstraat 20–22 (℡020/625 54029, ⓦwww.bikes.nl; daily 9am–6pm); and Macbike, which has branches at Centraal Station (Eastpoint), Stationsplein, Mr Visserplein 2 and Wteringschans 2 (℡020/620 0985, ⓦwww.macbike.nl; daily 9am–5.45pm). Most places charge around €4 an hour, €6 for three hours, €7–10 per day or 24 hours, €18 for three days and €30–35 for a week for a standard bike; 21-speed cycles cost about half as much again. Everyone asks for some type of security, usually in the form of a cash deposit (some will take credit card imprints) and/or passport.

Finally, if you want to **buy** a bike, a well-worn boneshaker will set you back about €100, maybe less, while €150 and up should get you a fairly decent secondhand machine; see p.222 for a list of recommended **bike shops**. Never buy a bike from someone off the street or in a bar as it will almost certainly have been stolen. Bike **theft** is in fact a real problem, so make sure you have a good lock – they can be bought cheaply at the city's flea market (see p.236) among other places. For useful **cycling terms** in Dutch, see p.301.

By car

The centre of Amsterdam is geared up for trams and bicycles rather than **cars** as a matter of municipal policy. Pedestrianized zones as such are not extensive, but motorists still have to negotiate a convoluted one-way system, avoid getting boxed onto tramlines and steer around herds of cyclists.

Driving into the city is strongly discouraged by the authorities; parking your car in the outer suburbs and entering the city by tram or metro is a better idea. If you do take your car into the centre, you'll find that on-street **parking** is very limited – with far too many cars chasing too few spaces – and can be quite expensive. Every city-centre street where parking is permitted is metered between 9am and at least 7pm every day, sometimes until midnight. The standard **rate** is €3.20 for one hour, around €26 for the

day (9am–7pm) and €17 or so for the evening in the city centre (7pm–midnight). An entire day's parking (9am–midnight) costs just short of €40, and you can buy a ticket for the whole week for a little over €150. Tickets are available from meters if you are paying by the hour, or from **Stadtoezicht** offices around town – call ℡020/5530333 for details of the nearest one to you. If you overrun your ticket, you can expect to be clamped by eager traffic wardens, and thereafter, if you don't follow the instructions posted on your windscreen promptly (and pay a fine of around €100), your vehicle will soon be heading off to the municipal pound – and it will cost you a further €150 to get it back. The good news is that signs on all the main approach roads to Amsterdam indicate which of the city's car parks have spaces. **Car parks** in the centre charge comparable rates to the metered street spaces. Some of the most central 24-hour car parks are: Amsterdam Centre (Prins Hendrikkade 20; €3.40 per hour); De Bijenkorf (Beursplein/Damrak; €3.40 per hour, €50 per day); De Kolk (NZ Voorburgwal/NZ Kolk; €3.80 per hour, €40 per day); Muziektheater (Waterlooplein, under City Hall; €3.20 per hour, €34 per day). Those on the outskirts are a good deal less expensive and are invariably but a short journey from the centre by public transport. Finally, note that some of the larger **hotels** either have their own parking spaces or offer special deals with nearby car parks.

Car rental agencies

Adams Rent-a-Car Nassaukade 345–346 ℡020/685 0111, ⓦwww.adamsrentacar.nl.
Avis Nassaukade 380 ℡020/683 6061, ⓦwww.avis.com.
Budget Overtoom 121 ℡0900/1576, ⓦwww.budget.com.
Diks Autoverhuur Van Ostadestraat 278–280 ℡020/662 3366, ⓦwww.diks.net.
Europcar Overtoom 197 ℡020/683 2123, ⓦwww.europcar.com.
Hertz Overtoom 333 ℡020/612 2441, ⓦwww.hertz.com.

Taxis

Due to the various obstacles that Amsterdam motorists face, **taxis** are not as much use as they are in many other cities. They are, however, plentiful: there's a taxi **rank** on Stationsplein outside Centraal Station, and other ranks are liberally distributed across the city centre; they can also be hailed on the street. If all else fails, call ☎020/677 7777. **Fares** are metered and are reasonably high, but distances are small; the trip from Centraal Station to the Leidseplein, for example, will cost around €12, €2 more to Museumplein – and fares go up by about fifteen percent late at night.

The media

English-speakers will find themselves quite at home in Amsterdam, as Dutch TV broadcasts a wide range of British programmes, and English-language newspapers from around the world are readily available.

Newspapers and magazines

British newspapers are on sale at most newsagents on the day of publication, for around €4. Current issues of UK and US **magazines** are widely distributed too, as is the *International Herald Tribune*.

Of the **Dutch newspapers**, *NRC Handelsblad* is a right-of-centre paper that has perhaps the best news coverage and a liberal stance on the arts; *De Volkskrant* is a progressive, leftish daily; the popular right-wing *De Telegraaf* boasts the highest circulation figures in the country and has a well-regarded financial section; *Algemeen Dagblad* is a right-wing broadsheet; while the middle-of-the-road *Het Parool* ("The Password") and the news magazine *Vrij Nederland* ("Free Netherlands") are the successors of underground Resistance newspapers printed during wartime occupation. The Protestant *Trouw* ("Trust"), another former underground paper, is centre-left in orientation with a focus on religion.

Bundled in with the weekend edition of the *International Herald Tribune* is **The Netherlander**, a small but useful business-oriented review of Dutch affairs in English. For events listings in English, see Tourist information (p.36).

Television and radio

Dutch **TV** isn't the best, but English-language programmes and films fill up a fair amount of the schedule – and they are always subtitled, never dubbed. Many bars and most hotels have at least two of the big pan-European **cable and satellite** channels – including MTV, CNN and Eurosport – and most cable companies also give access to a veritable raft of foreign television channels, including Britain's BBC1 and BBC2, National Geographic, Eurosport and Discovery, and a host of Belgian, German, French, Spanish, Italian, Turkish and Arabic stations, some of which also show un-dubbed British and US movies. Other Dutch and Belgian TV channels – cable and non-cable – regularly run English-language movies with Dutch subtitles.

Dutch **radio** has numerous stations catering for every niche. Of the **public service stations**, Radio 1 is a news and sports channel, Radio 2 plays AOR music, Radio 3 plays chart music and Radio 4 classical, jazz and world music. Of the **commercial stations**, some of the main nationwide players are Radio 538, Veronica, Sky Radio and Noordzee FM, and pretty much all play chart music. The one-time stalwart of the squatter movement, Radio Honderd, which is only available in and around Amsterdam, at 99.3FM, offers a wide-ranging playlist from world dance to electronica. Jazz Radio, at 99.8FM, speaks for itself. The Dutch Classic FM, at 101.2FM, plays mainstream classical music, with jazz after 10pm.

There's next to no **English-language programming**, apart from the overseas-targeted Radio Netherlands (@www.rnw.nl), which broadcasts Dutch news in English, with articles on current affairs, lifestyle issues, science, health and so on, and the BBC World Service (@www.bbc.co.uk/worldservice), which broadcasts pretty much all day in English on 648kHz (AM) around Amsterdam; it also occupies 198kHz (long wave) and 101.3 (FM) – as do the Voice of America (@www.voa.gov) and Radio Canada International (@www.rcinet.ca), whose frequencies are listed on their respective websites.

Travel essentials

Crime and personal safety

Though Amsterdam is relatively untroubled by crime in comparison with other European cities, there is nevertheless more street crime than there used to be, and it's advisable to be on your guard against **petty theft**; secure your belongings in a locker when staying in hostel accommodation, and never leave any valuables on view in a car. On the street, beware of the distraction ploys that petty thieves can try, such as someone asking for directions while an accomplice puts their hand in your bag; if you're in a crowd be wary of people moving too close to you. Be cautious when using **ATM**s, especially late at night, and be wary of suspicious devices fitted around the card slot. If you're on a **bike**, make sure it is well locked up; bike theft and resale is a major industry here – as is the usual mobile phone theft – keep your network provider's number handy in case you have to bar your phone.

If you are robbed, you'll need to go to a **police station** to report it, not least because your insurance company will require a police report; remember to make a note of the report number – or, better still, ask for a copy of the statement itself. Don't expect a great deal of concern if your loss is relatively small – and don't be surprised if the process of completing forms and formalities takes ages. If your credit card is stolen, report the theft immediately to your card company (see p.34 for contact details).

As for **personal safety**, it's generally possible to walk around most parts of the city without fear of harassment or assault, but wherever you go at night it's always better to err on the side of caution. In particular, Amsterdam's **Red Light District** can have an unpleasant, threatening undertow (although the crowds of people act as a deterrent), as can the area around **Centraal Station** and certain quiet parts of **De Pijp**. In general, try not to wander around looking lost. Using **public transport**, even late at night, isn't usually a problem, but if in doubt take a taxi.

If you're **detained** by the police, you don't automatically have the right to a phone call, although in practice they'll probably phone your consulate for you – not that consular officials have a reputation for excessive helpfulness (particularly in drug cases). If your alleged offence is a minor matter, you can be held for up to six hours without questioning; if it is more serious, you can be

In an **emergency** – police, fire or ambulance – call ☏112. ☏0900/8844 is the number to call if it's not an emergency; they'll give you the details of the nearest city-centre police station. There are police stations at the following locations: NZ Voorburgwal 104; Beursstraat 33; Elandsgracht 117; Marnixstraat 148; Lijnbaansgracht 219; Prinsengracht 1109; Ferdinand Bolstraat 190.

Drugs

Thousands of visitors come to Amsterdam just to get stoned. This is the one Western country where the purchase of **cannabis** is de-criminalized, and the influx of people drawn to the country by this fact creates problems: many Amsterdammers, for instance, get mightily hacked off with "drug tourism". The Dutch government's attitude to soft drugs is more complex than you might think: the use of cannabis is tolerated but not condoned, resulting in a rather complicated set of rules and regulations that can be safely ignored as long as you buy very small amounts for **personal use** only – which means possession of up to 30g and sales of up to 5g per purchase in coffeeshops, though in practice this is pretty relaxed, and many places will happily sell you much more than this (as they will space cakes, although these are also technically illegal).

Current **prices** per gram of hash and marijuana range from €10 for low-grade stuff up to €25 for top-quality hash and as high as €40 for really strong grass. Buy in bulk, or sell to other people, and you become liable under Dutch criminal law. Outside of **coffeeshops** (see pp.202–203 for a selection), it is permitted to smoke in some bars, though you should always ask first; and you should never, ever buy dope on the street – if you do, you'll likely become a magnet for some pretty unsavoury characters, plus you may find yourself not buying dope at all; in any case there's really no need with the delights on offer in the city's many coffeeshops.

Needless to say, the one thing you shouldn't attempt to do is take any form of cannabis out of the country. A surprising number of people think (or claim to think) that if it's bought in Amsterdam it can be taken back home legally; this story won't wash with **customs** officials and drug enforcement officers, who will happily add your stash to the statistics of national drug seizures, and arrest you into the bargain.

As far as **other drugs** go, the Dutch law surrounding magic mushrooms is that you can legally buy and possess any amount so long as they are fresh, but as soon as you tamper with them in any way (dry or process them, boil or cook them), they become as illegal as crack. Despite the existence of a lively and growing trade in cocaine and heroin, possession of either could mean a stay in one of the Netherlands' lively and ever-growing jails. Ecstasy, acid and speed are as illegal in the Netherlands as they are anywhere else.

---

detained for up to 24 hours. For details of foreign embassies and consulates, see opposite.

Travellers with disabilities

Despite its general social progressiveness, the Netherlands is only just getting to grips with the requirements of people with **mobility problems**. In Amsterdam and most of the other major cities, the most obvious difficulty you'll face is in negotiating the cobbled streets and narrow, often broken pavements of the older districts, where the key sights are often located. Similarly, provision for people with disabilities on **public transport** is only average, although improving – many new buses, for instance, are now wheelchair-accessible. And yet,

while it can be difficult simply to get around, practically all **public buildings**, including museums, theatres, cinemas, concert halls and hotels, are obliged to provide access, and do.

Places that have been certified **wheelchair-accessible** now bear an International Accessibility Symbol (IAS). Bear in mind, however, that a lot of the older, narrower **hotels** are not allowed to install lifts, so check first. If you're planning to use the Dutch **train network** during your stay and would appreciate assistance on the platform, phone the Bureau Assistentieverlening Gehandicapten (Disabled Assistance Office) on ☏030/235 7822 at least three hours before your train departs, and there will be someone to meet and help you at the station (office open daily 7am–11pm). NS, the

Netherlands Railways association, publishes information about train travel for people with disabilities online at ⓦwww.ns.nl and in various leaflets, stocked at main stations.

Travellers with a pre-existing medical condition are sometimes excluded from **insurance policies**; read the small print carefully. Ask your doctor for a medical certificate of your fitness to travel as some insurance companies insist on it.

Electricity

The Dutch electricity supply runs at 220v AC. British equipment needs only a plug adaptor; American apparatus requires a transformer and an adaptor.

Entry requirements

Citizens of the UK, Ireland, Australia, New Zealand, Canada and the US do not need a **visa** to enter the Netherlands if staying for three months or less. However, you do need a **passport** valid for at least six months after your arrival, a **return airline ticket** and/or funds deemed to be sufficient for your stay. Travellers from **South Africa** staying less than three months do need to obtain a tourist visa through the Dutch embassy (see below) before they leave for the Netherlands; for stays of longer than three months, an Authorisation for Temporary Residence (ATR) is required.

For longer stays, EU nationals are required to get hold of a **resident's permit** (MVV permit), obtainable from your Dutch Embassy at home or in Amsterdam at the Vreemdelingenpolitie (Foreign Police), Johan Huizingalaan 757 (☎020/559 6300, ⓦwww .immigratiedienst.nl).

Non-EU and **new EU** members who intend to stay beyond three months must apply for a temporary residence permit (a "VTV") within three days of their arrival. Go to the Aliens Police office (*Vreemdelingenpolitie*) armed with your birth certificate and proof that you have the funds to finance your stay, a fixed address, and health insurance. For further information, visit the Ministry of Foreign Affairs website ⓦwww.minbuza.nl.

EU and non-EU members who intend to work will need a **work permit**; employers should apply for this on your behalf. The exceptions to this rule are the work schemes

set up for Australian, New Zealand and Canadian citizens aged 18–30, who can stay for up to 12 months in the Netherlands on a **"Working Holiday Scheme"**, provided you can convince the authorities that your main priority is holidaying, not working. For further information, contact the Dutch embassies in Canberra, Wellington, Ottawa or London.

Wherever you're from, a good source of information if you're planning a **long-term stay** in Amsterdam is a non-profit organization called **Access** (Herengracht 472, second floor, ☎020/423 3217, ⓦwww. access-nl.org). They operate a very useful English-language information line on everything from domestic services to legal matters, as well as running courses on various aspects of Dutch administration and culture.

Dutch embassies abroad

Australia 120 Empire Circuit, Yarralumla, ACT 2600 ☎02/6220 9400, ⓦwww.netherlands.org.au.
Canada 350 Albert St #2020, Ottawa, ON, K1R 1A4 ☎613/237 5030, ⓦwww.netherlandsembassy.ca.
Ireland 160 Merrion Rd, Dublin 4 ☎01/269 3444, ⓦwww.netherlandsembassy.ie.
New Zealand PO Box 480, Ballance/Featherston St, Wellington ☎04/471 6390, ⓦwww .netherlandsembassy.co.nz.
South Africa 210 Queen Wilhelmina Ave, New Muckleneuk, Pretoria ☎012/425 4500, ⓦwww .dutchembassy.co.za.
UK 38 Hyde Park Gate, London, SW7 5DP ☎020/ 7590 3200, ⓦwww.netherlands-embassy.org.uk.
USA 4200 Linnean Ave NW, Washington, DC 20008 ☎202/244 5300, ⓦwww.netherlands-embassy .org.

Embassies and consulates in the Netherlands

Australia Carnegielaan 4, 2517 KH The Hague ☎070/310 8200, ⓦwww.netherlands.embassy. gov.au.
Canada Sophialaan 7, 2514 JP The Hague ☎070/311 1600, ⓦwww.canada.nl.
Ireland Dr Kuijperstraat 9, 2514 BA The Hague ☎070/363 0993, ⓦwww.irishembassy.nl.
New Zealand Carnegielaan 10, 2517 KH The Hague ☎070/346 9324, ⓦwww.nzembassy.com.
South Africa Wassenaarseweg 40, 2596 CJ The Hague ☎070/392 4501, ⓦwww.zuidafrika.nl.
UK Lange Voorhout 10, 2514 ED The Hague

☏070/427 0427, ⓦwww.britain.nl; Consulate-General: Koningslaan 44, PO Box 75488, 1070 AL Amsterdam ☏020/676 4343.
USA Lange Voorhout 102, 2514 EJ The Hague ☏070/310 2209, ⓦwww.usemb.nl; Consulate General: Museumplein 19, 1071 DJ Amsterdam ☏020/575 5309.

Gay and lesbian travellers

Amsterdam is one of the top **gay** destinations in Europe: attitudes are tolerant, bars are excellent and plentiful, and support groups and facilities are unequalled. The national organization for gay men and women, **COC** (ⓦwww.coc.nl), dates from the 1940s and is actively involved in gaining equal rights for gays and lesbians, as well as informing society's perceptions of homosexuality. The national HQ is in Amsterdam, at Rozenstraat 14 (Mon–Fri 9am–5pm; ☏020/626 8300); it can offer help, advice and information on events around the city.

For more help and advice contact Amsterdam's **Gay and Lesbian Switchboard** on ☏020/623 6565. Gay legislation in the Netherlands is streets ahead of the rest of the world; same-sex marriage and adoption by same-sex partners were legalized in 2001, and within six months over two thousand couples had tied the knot. The age of consent is 16.

Consider timing your visit to coincide with **Amsterdam Pride** (ⓦwww.amsterdam-gaypride.nl) on the first weekend in August, **Queen's Day** on April 30 or **Leather Pride** (ⓦwww.leatherpride.nl) in late October and November. For more information on gay festivals and events, as well as gay accommodation and nightlife, see Chapter Twelve.

Health

As a member of the European Union, the Netherlands has free reciprocal health agreements with other member states. **EU citizens** are entitled to free treatment within the Netherlands' public healthcare system on production of a European Health Insurance Card (**EHIC**), which you can obtain by picking up a form at the post office, calling ☏0845 606 2030, or applying online at ⓦwww.dh.gov.uk; allow up to 21 days for delivery. The EHIC is free of charge and valid for at least three years, and it basically entitles you to the same treatment as an insured person in The Netherlands. **Australians** are able to receive treatment through a reciprocal arrangement with Medicare (check with your local office for details).

In an **emergency** phone ☏112. If you're reliant on free **treatment** within the EU health scheme, try to make this clear to the ambulance staff, and, if you're whisked off to hospital, to the medic you subsequently encounter. If possible, it's a good idea to hand over a photocopy of your EHIC on arrival at the hospital to ensure your status is clearly understood. As for describing symptoms, you can be pretty sure that someone will speak English. Without an EHIC you won't be turned away from a hospital, but you will have to pay for any treatment you receive and should therefore get an official receipt, a necessary preamble to the long-winded process of trying to get at least some of the money back.

You can get the address of an **English-speaking doctor** from your local pharmacy, tourist office or hotel. The 24-hour medical helpline **Central Medical Service** (☏0900/5032042 premium line) can give general advice about medical symptoms and let you know the details of duty doctors. If you're entitled to free treatment under EU health agreements, double-check that the doctor is both working within, and regarding you as a patient of, the public health care system. Bear in mind, though, that even within the EU agreement you may still have to pay a significant portion of the prescription charges (although senior citizens and children are exempt). Most private health insurance policies don't help cover prescription charges either, and although the "excesses" are usually greater than the cost of the medicines, it's worth keeping receipts just in case.

The main **hospitals** (*ziekenhuis*) are: Academic Medical Centre (AMC; Meibergdreef 9, ☏020/566 9111), Onze Lieve Vrouwe Gasthuis (1e Oosterparkstraat 279, ☏020/599 9111) and Sint Lucas Ziekenhuis (Jan Tooropstraat 164, ☏020/510 8911).

Minor ailments can be remedied at a drugstore (*drogist*). These sell non-prescription drugs as well as toiletries, tampons, condoms and the like. A **pharmacy** or

Rough Guides travel insurance

Rough Guides has teamed up with Columbus Direct to offer you **travel insurance** that can be tailored to suit your needs. Products include a low-cost **backpacker option** for long stays; a **short break option** for city getaways; a typical **holiday package option**, and others. There are also annual **multi-trip** policies for those who travel regularly. Different sports and activities (trekking, skiing, etc) can usually be covered if required. See our website (🌐 www.roughguidesinsurance.com) for eligibility and purchasing options. Alternatively, UK residents should call ☎ 0870/033 9988; Australians should call ☎ 1300/669 999 and New Zealanders should call ☎ 0800/55 9911. All other nationalities should call ☎ +44 870/890 2843.

apotheek (usually open Mon–Fri 9.30am–6pm, but often closed Mon mornings) also handles prescriptions; centrally located pharmacies include Dam Apotheek (Damstraat 2, ☎ 020/624 4331), Lairesse Apotheek (De lairessestraat 40, ☎ 020/662 1022) and Apotheek Koek, Schaeffer & Van Tijen (Vijzelgracht 19, ☎ 020/623 5949). There aren't any 24-hour pharmacies, but the Afdeling Inlichtingen Apotheken helpline (☎ 020/694 8709; 24hr) will supply addresses of ones that are open late.

Dental treatment is not within the scope of the EU health agreement; enquire at the local tourist office or your hotel reception for an English-speaking dentist.

Insurance

Even though **EU** health care privileges apply in the Netherlands, you'd do well to take out an **insurance policy** before travelling to cover against theft, loss, illness or injury. A typical policy usually provides cover for the loss of baggage, tickets and – up to a certain limit – cash or cheques, as well as cancellation or curtailment of your journey. Many policies can be chopped and changed to exclude coverage you don't need: sickness and accident benefits can often be excluded or included at will. If you need to make a **claim**, you should keep all receipts, and in the event you have anything stolen, you must obtain an official statement from the police.

Visitors planning **longer stays** (at least three months) are required by Dutch law to take out private health insurance. Taking out private insurance means the cost of items not within the scope of the EU scheme, such as dental treatment and repatriation on medical grounds, will be covered.

Non-EU residents, apart from Australians, will need to insure themselves against all eventualities, including medical costs. In the case of major expense, the more worthwhile policies promise to sort matters out before you pay rather than after, but if you do have to pay upfront, make very sure that you always keep full doctors' reports, signed prescription details and all receipts.

Internet

Most of the city's better hotels now offer Internet access. If you have a wireless-enabled laptop, the wi-fi service Hotspot Amsterdam (🌐 www.hotspotamsterdam.com) covers much of the centre and gives you ten days' Internet access for €10; you sign up and pay by credit card online.

There are **Internet cafés** dotted around the centre; easyInternetcafé at Damrak 33 (daily 9am–10pm) has 144 PCs and reasonable rates.

Laundry

Larger hotels generally provide a laundry service, though this tends to be expensive. The city's best **self-service laundry** is Clean Brothers, Kerkstraat 56 (Grachtengordel south; daily 7am–9pm), charging €4 for a wash and dry. They also do service washes, dry-cleaning, ironing, and so on. Other laundries are to be found at: Elandsgracht 59 (Jordaan and Western docklands) and Warmoesstraat 30 (Old Centre).

Left luggage

There's a staffed left-luggage desk in the basement of **Schiphol Airport**, between Arrivals halls 1 and 2 (daily 7am–10.45pm), as well as left-luggage lockers. Small items cost roughly €3 per day, medium €4, large €5 and very bulky items €7.50; the maximum storage time is seven days. At **Centraal Station**, you'll find coin-operated left-luggage lockers (daily 7am–1pm), as well as a staffed left-luggage office (daily 7am–11pm). Small coin-operated lockers cost €3.70 for 24 hours, the larger ones €5.90. Luggage left at the staffed office costs €8 per item.

At train stations outside of Amsterdam, left-luggage lockers cannot currently be used without a Dutch debit card.

Libraries

The main **public library**, Centrale Bibliotheek, is at Prinsengracht 587, just north of Leidsegracht (Mon 1–9pm, Tues–Thurs 10am–9pm, Fri 10am–7pm, Sat 10am–5pm; Oct–March also Sun 1–5pm).

Lost property

For items lost on the **trams**, **buses** or **metro**, contact GVB Head Office, Prins Hendrikkade 108–114 (Mon–Fri 9am–4pm; ☎020/460 5858). For property lost on a **train**, go to the Gevonden Voorwerpen office at Centraal Station, Stationsplein 15 (☎020/557 8544). After five days all unclaimed property goes to the **Central Lost Property Office** at 2e Daalsedijk 4, Utrecht (☎030/235 3923). If you lose something in the **street** or **park**, try the police lost property office at Stephensonstraat 18 (Mon–Fri noon–3.30pm; ☎020/559 3005). **Schiphol Airport**'s lost and found desk is in the Arrivals Hall (daily 7.45am–4.15pm; ☎020/601 2443).

Mail

The Netherlands has an efficient **postal system**. Post offices are plentiful and mostly open Monday to Friday 8.30am to 5pm, though some big-city branches also open on Saturday from 8.30am to noon. The central post office is at Singel 250 (Mon–Fri 9am–6pm, Sat 10am–1.30pm). **Stamps** are sold at a wide range of outlets including many shops and hotels. **Postboxes** are everywhere, but be sure to use the correct slot – the one labelled *overige* is for post going outside the immediate locality.

Maps

The **maps** in this guide should be more than adequate for most purposes, but if you need one on a larger scale, or with a street index, then pick up *The Rough Guide Map to Amsterdam*, which has the added advantage of being waterproof and rip-proof. This marks all the key sights as well as the location of many restaurants, bars and hotels. If you want a map covering the outer suburbs as well, the best bet is the **Falk** map of Amsterdam (1:15,000). Other options include the city maps sold by the **VVV**, which come complete with a street index, and the handily compact, spiral-bound street atlases produced by Falk (Suburbs: 1:12,500; centre 1:7500).

Money

The **currency** of the Netherlands – like much of the rest of the EU – is the **euro** (€), divided into 100 cents. At the time of writing the exchange rate was €1.33 to $1 and €0.68 to £1. There are **notes** of €500, €200, €100, €50, €20, €10 and €5, and **coins** of €2, €1, 50c, 20c, 10c, 5c, 2c and 1c. Euro coins feature a common EU design on one face, but different country-specific designs on the other, but no matter what the design, all euro coins and notes are legal tender in all of the following countries as well as the Netherlands: Austria, Belgium, Finland, France, Germany, Greece, Ireland, Italy, Luxembourg, Portugal and Spain.

The Netherlands is a **cash** society; as a general rule, people prefer to pay for most things with notes and coins. However, **debit cards** are becoming increasingly popular, and most shops and restaurants accept these and credit cards. You can use many Visa, Mastercard and UK debit cards (within the Cirrus, Plus or Maestro systems) to withdraw cash from ATMs – often the quickest and easiest way of obtaining money. There are dozens around the city and they give instructions in a variety of languages.

In the event that your credit card is lost or stolen, call ☎020/504 8000 for American Express (☎0800/022 0100 for traveller's cheques); ☎0800/022 5821 for Mastercard; ☎0800/022 3110 for Visa. See p.29 for how to report a crime.

Dutch **banks** and **post offices** usually offer the best deals on changing money. Banking hours are Monday to Friday 9am to 4pm, with a few big-city banks also open Thursday until 9pm or on Saturday morning; all are closed on public holidays (see below). Outside these times, changing money is rarely a problem; there's a nationwide network of **GWK exchange offices**, which are open late every day, and at Amsterdam Centraal Station and Schiphol Airport, 24 hours a day. GWK offers competitive rates and charges reasonable commissions, but some other agencies do not, so be cautious. VVV tourist offices also exchange money, as do most hotels and campsites and some hostels, but their rates are generally poor.

Opening hours and public holidays

The Dutch weekend fades painlessly into the working week with many smaller shops and businesses, even in Amsterdam, staying closed on **Monday mornings** until noon. Normal **opening hours** are, however, Monday to Friday 8.30/9am to 5.30/6pm and Saturday 8.30/9am to 4/5pm, and many places open late on Thursday or Friday evenings. **Sunday** opening is becoming increasingly common.

Most **restaurants** are open for dinner from about 6 or 7pm, and though many close as early as 9.30pm, a few stay open past 11pm. **Bars, cafés and coffeeshops** are either open all day from around 10am or don't open until about 5pm; all close at 1am during the week and 2am at weekends. **Nightclubs** generally open their doors from 11pm to 4am during the week, though a few open every night, and some stay open until 5am at the weekend. A handful of **night**

shops – *avondwinkels* – stay open into the small hours or round the clock. Note that many **supermarkets** are shut on Sundays.

Museums, especially those that are state-run (such as the Rijksmuseum), tend to follow a pattern: closed on Monday, open Tuesday to Saturday from 10am to 5pm, and on Sundays from 1 to 5pm, although things are slowly changing in favour of seven-day opening. Though closed for Christmas and New Year, state-run museums adopt Sunday hours on the remaining public holidays, when most shops and banks are closed. **Galleries** tend to be open from Tuesday to Sunday from noon to 5pm. Precise opening hours are quoted throughout the guide.

Public holidays (*Nationale feestdagen*) provide the perfect excuse to take to the streets. The most celebrated of them all is **Queen's Day** – *Koninginnedag* – on April 30, which is celebrated throughout the Netherlands but with particular gusto in Amsterdam. The rest are as follows: New Year's Day, Good Friday, Easter Sunday and Monday, Liberation Day (May 5), Ascension Day, Whit Sunday and Monday (seven weeks after Easter), and Christmas (December 25 and 26).

Phones

The **international phone code** for the Netherlands is 31. Numbers prefixed ☏0800 are free; those prefixed ☏0900 are premium-rate – a (Dutch) message before you're connected tells you how much you will be paying for the call, and you can only call them from within the Netherlands. **Phone cards** can be bought at many outlets, including post offices, tobacconists and VVV offices, and in several denominations, beginning at €5. However, **phone boxes** are

---

Calling home from abroad

Note that the **initial zero** is omitted from the area code when dialling the UK, Ireland, Australia and New Zealand from abroad.
UK international access code + 44 + city code.
Republic of Ireland international access code + 353 + city code.
US and Canada international access code + 1 + area code.
Australia international access code + 61 + city code.
New Zealand international access code + 64 + city code.
South Africa international access code + 27 + city code.

provided by different companies and their respective phone cards are not mutually compatible; **KPN** phones (and cards) are the most common. The cheap-rate period for **international calls** is between 8pm and 8am during the week and all day at weekends.

There is a good coverage for **mobile phone networks** all over the Netherlands. You need to use a mobile with 900 and 1800 MHz bands. Pre-paid SIM cards are available in telephone shops (on the Rokin and around Kalverstraat) and in some supermarkets.

To speak to the **Operator** (domestic and international), cal ☎0800 0410; for **Directory Enquiries**, dial ☎0900 8008 (domestic), ☎0900 8418 (international).

The Dutch **phone directory** is available (in Dutch) at ⊛www.detelefoongids.nl.

Time

Amsterdam, and indeed the whole of The Netherlands, is on **Central European Time** (CET) – one hour ahead of London, six hours ahead of New York, nine hours ahead of Los Angeles and eight hours behind Sydney. **Daylight saving** operates from the end of March to the end of October.

Tipping

Tipping isn't quite as routine a matter as it is in the US or even in the UK. However, these days you are expected to leave something if you have enjoyed good service – up to around ten percent of the bill should suffice in most **restaurants**, while hotel **porters** and **taxi drivers** may expect a euro or two on top of the fare.

Tourist information

Information on Amsterdam is easy to get hold of, either before you leave from the **Netherlands Board of Tourism**, by phone or post or via the Internet – the NBT's all-encompassing website, ⊛www.holland.com, highlights upcoming events and is strong on practical information.

For information about **what's on**, there's either the VVV (see box) or the **Amsterdam Uitburo**, the cultural office of the city council, housed in a corner of the Stadsschouwburg theatre on Leidseplein (daily 10am–6pm, Thurs until 9pm; ☎0900/0191). You can get advice here on anything remotely cultural, as well as tickets and copies of listings magazines. Amongst the latter, there's a choice between the AUB's own monthly *Uitkrant*, which is comprehensive and free but in Dutch, or the VVV's *Day by Day in Amsterdam*. Alternatively, the newspaper *Het Parool*'s Wednesday entertainment supplement, *Uit en Thuis*, is one of the most up-to-date reference sources.

Various **tourist passes** are available. The VVV's much-touted **Amsterdam Card** provides free and unlimited use of the city's public transport network, a complimentary canal cruise and free admission to the bulk of the city's museums and attractions. It costs €33 for one day, €43 for two consecutive days and €53 for three – again consecutive – days. Altogether it's not a bad deal,

---

The VVV

Once in Amsterdam, any of the city's tourist offices, the **VVV**s (pronounced "fay-fay-fay"), will be able to help with practical information.

There's a VVV on platform 2 at Centraal Station (Mon–Sat 8am–8pm, Sun 9am–5pm); a second, main one directly across from the main station entrance on Stationsplein (daily 9am–5pm); and a third on Leidsestraat, just off the Leidseplein (daily 9am–5pm). These three offices share one premium-rate **information line** on ☎0900/400 4040, and a **website**: ⊛www.visitamsterdam.nl. They offer **advice and information** and sell a range of **maps** and guidebooks as well as **tickets** and passes for public transport. They also take in-person bookings for canal cruises and other organized **excursions**, sell theatre and concert tickets, and operate an extremely efficient **accommodation reservation service** for just €3 plus a refundable deposit which is subtracted from your final bill – especially useful in high season when finding accommodation isn't always easy.

Guided tours

No one could say the Amsterdam tourist industry doesn't make the most of its **canals**, with a veritable armada of glass-topped **cruise boats** shuttling along the city's waterways, offering everything from quick hour-long excursions to fully-fledged dinner cruises. There are several major operators which occupy the prime pitches – the jetties near Centraal Station on Stationsplein, beside the Damrak and on Prins Hendrikkade. **Prices** are fairly uniform, with a one-hour tour costing around €10 per adult, €6 per child (4–12 years old), and around €25 (€15) for a two-hour cruise at night. The big companies also offer more **specialized boat trips** – dinner cruises from around €50, literary cruises, and most notably the weekly Architecture Cruise run by Lovers (☎020/530 1090, ⓦwww.lovers.nl; €19.50/14.50). All these cruises – and especially the shorter and less expensive ones – are extremely popular, and long queues are common throughout the summer. There are also plenty of tours on dry land, from guided **cycle rides** to a meander around the city **on foot**. A selection is given below, but if you have a specific interest – Dutch art, for example – it's well worth asking at the **VVV** to see what's on offer.

Tour operators

Mee in Mokum Keizersgracht 346 ☎020/625 1390. Guided walking tours of the old centre and the Jordaan provided by long-time Amsterdam residents. Tours run four or five times weekly; €3 per person. Advance reservations required.

Reederij P. Kooij on the Rokin, beside the Queen Wilhelmina statue ☎020/623 3810, ⓦwww.rederijkooij.nl. One way of avoiding the tour queues is to head for the first-rate Reederij P. Kooij, which offers a standard range of day and night cruises at competitive prices. Also has a (more crowded) jetty opposite Centraal Station on Stationsplein, and by Leidseplein.

Urban Home & Garden Tours ☎020/688 1243, ⓦwww.uhgt.nl. Three-hour tours (April–Oct) that explore a number of the city's canal houses and gardens, guided by landscape gardeners and art historians. Tours are held Fri, Sat and Sun, and cost €25 (the fee includes refreshments). Cash only, no credit cards.

Yellow Bike Tours Nieuwezijds Kolk 29, off Nieuwezijds Voorburgwal ☎020/620 6940, ⓦwww.yellowbike.nl. Three-hour guided cycling tours around the city (two daily April to mid-Oct) that cost €19.50 per person, including the bike. Other tours – of the Jordaan, Red Light District, etc – available. Advance reservations required.

---

but you have to work fairly hard to make it worthwhile. It's available from any branch of the VVV. An alternative if you're staying for more than a couple of days is the **Museumkaart** (museum card), which gives free entry to most museums in the whole of the Netherlands for a year; it costs €30 (€15 if you're 24 or under), plus a one-off fee of €4.95. Full details, including online ordering, are at ⓦwww.museumjaarkaart.nl, or you can purchase one at any participating museum.

The **I Amsterdam** pass (ⓦwww.iamsterdamcard.com) – which serves as a public transport pass and an entrance ticket to all the major museums, and offers discounts at restaurants and attractions – is available in 24hr, 48hr and 72hr versions, costing €33,

€43 and €53 respectively. A free canal boat ride is included in the price. You can buy it online, or at any VVV.

Concessionary rates are applied at every city sight and attraction as well as on the public transport system. Rates vary, but usually seniors (65+) get in free or for a discounted price, while children of 5 and under get in for free; family tickets are common too.

Netherlands Board of Tourism offices

UK PO Box 30783, London WC2B 6DH ☎020/7539 7950, ⓔinfo-uk@holland.com.
USA 355 Lexington Ave, New York, NY 10017 ☎1-212-370-7360, ⓔinformation@holland.com
There are no offices in Australia or New Zealand.

Canada 14 Glenmount Court, Whitby, Ontario L1N 5M8 ⊤ 905 666 5960, ⊕ jzandboer@holland.com.

Tourist offices and government sites

Australian Department of Foreign Affairs
Ⓦ www.dfat.gov.au, Ⓦ www.smartraveller.gov.au.
British Foreign & Commonwealth Office Ⓦ www
.fco.gov.uk.

Canadian Department of Foreign Affairs Ⓦ www
.dfait-maeci.gc.ca.
Irish Department of Foreign Affairs Ⓦ www
.foreignaffairs.gov.ie.
New Zealand Ministry of Foreign Affairs Ⓦ www
.mft.govt.nz.
South African Department of Foreign Affairs
Ⓦ www.dfa.gov.za
US State Department Ⓦ www.travel.state.gov.

The City

The City

The Old Centre

msterdam's most vivacious and arguably most touristy district, the **Old Centre** is an oval-shaped tangle of narrow streets and picturesque canals that is confined in the north by the River IJ and to the west and south by the Singel, the first of several canals that once girdled the entire city. Given the dominance of **Centraal Station** on most transport routes, this is almost certainly where you'll arrive. Immediately outside, **Stationsplein** is home to the main tourist and transport information offices – a busy maelstrom of buskers and bicycles, trams and tourists. From here, a stroll across the bridge will take you onto the **Damrak**, which divided the **Oude Zijde** (Old Side) of the medieval city to the east from the smaller **Nieuwe Zijde** (New Side) to the west. It also led – and leads – to the heart of the Old Centre, **Dam Square**, which is overseen by two of the city's most impressive buildings, the **Koninklijk Paleis** (Royal Palace) and the **Nieuwe Kerk** (New Church). **Rokin** runs south from Dam Square, parallel to pedestrianized **Kalverstraat**, which is the city's prime mainstream shopping street. Sightswise, the main targets in this area are the secluded **Begijnhof**, a circle of dignified old houses originally built to house a semi-religious community in the 1340s, and the **Amsterdams Historisch Museum**.

Nowadays, much of the Oude Zijde is taken up by the city's notorious **Red Light District**, which stretches across Warmoesstraat and the two canals – **Oudezijds Voorburgwal** and **Oudezijds Achterburgwal** – that formed the heart of medieval Amsterdam. There's a prevailing seediness in the Red Light District that inevitably dulls its many architectural charms, but there are still one or two signs that you are in what is the city's most historic quarter: the delightful **Amstelkring**, a clandestine Catholic church dating from the seventeenth century, and the charming Gothic architecture of the **Oude Kerk**, not to mention the relatively unpretentious beauty of the canals themselves (if you can block out the prevailing neon).

The sleazy atmosphere decreases the further east you go, towards **Nieuwmarkt**, a large and unassuming square that marks the start of **Kloveniersburgwal**, a large and stately canal that effectively marks the border of the Red Light District. Further east, another canal, Groenburgwal, is one of the most beguiling parts of the Old Centre, with a medley of handsome old houses lining what is one of its prettiest stretches of water.

Some history

Amsterdam's **Old Centre** follows the core of the original city, its narrow streets and canals confined to the north by the River IJ and the harbour, and to the west and south by the Singel, which used to form the boundary of the old port. This was where Amsterdam began, starting out as a humble **fishing village** at

THE OLD CENTRE

River IJ

0   200 m

N

Passenger Ferries

DE RUIJTERKADE

Centraal Station

Hofje Van Brienen

Open

STATIONS-PLEIN

Centraal Station

GVB

PRINS HENDRIKKADE

Luthersekerk

Crowne Plaza Hotel

St Nicolaaskerk

In 't Aepjen

Schreierstoren

OOSTERDOKSKADE

PRINS HENDRIKKADE

Damrak

Beurs

Amstelkring

Prostitution Info Centre

RED LIGHT DISTRICT

BEURSPLEIN

Oude Kerk

Scheepvaarthuis

PRINS HENDRIKKADE

Magna Plaza

Nieuwe Kerk

De Bijenkorf

Condomerie Het Gulden Vlies

Waag

RAADHUISSTRAAT

Koninklijk Paleis

DAM

War Memorial

NIEUW-MARKT

Nieuwmarkt

Montelbaanstoren

Madame Tussaud's

Hash Museum

Oude Schans

Vrankrijk

Kleine Trippenhuis

Trippenhuis

No 69

'ome Jan'

Oostindisch Huis

Nieuwmarkt

Pintohuis

Gassan Diamonds

No 83

Spinhuis

Zuiderkerk & Zuidertoren

Amsterdams Historisch Museum

No 92

No 91 Galerie Mokum

Agnietenkapel

RUSLAND

RAAMGRACHT

Wilhelmina Statue

University of Amsterdam

Rembrandthuis

Begijnhof

Huis op de Drie Grachten

Oudemanhuispoort

OLD JEWISH QUARTER

Allard Pierson Museum

SPUI

Waterlooplein

Nos 141–147

Hotel Doelen

STAAL STRAAT

Rasphuis

MUNTPLEIN

Hotel de l'Europe

Amstel

Muziektheater

Esnoga

Leidseplein

KONINGSPLEIN

Munttoren

Bloemenmarkt

AMSTEL

Waterlooplein

Joods Historisch Museum

the marshy mouth of the River Amstel before the local lord gave it some significance by building a castle here in 1204. Sixty years later, the Amstel was dammed – leading to the name "Amstelredam" – and the village began to flourish as a **trading centre**, receiving its municipal charter from a new feudal overlord, the Count of Holland, in about 1300. Thereafter, the city developed in stages, each of which was marked by the digging of new **canals** to either side of the main canal linking the River IJ with Dam Square, along today's Damrak. The city grew at first around the canals of today's Red Light District and after that on the other side of the Damrak.

Time and again the wooden buildings of medieval Amsterdam went up in smoke, until finally, after a particularly severe fire in 1452, timber was banned in favour of brick and stone – and it's these handsome **canal houses** of the seventeenth and eighteenth centuries that provide the Old Centre with most of its architectural high points.

Damrak and the Nieuwe Zijde

Running from Centraal Station to Dam Square, the **Damrak** was a canal until 1672, when it was filled in; up until then it had been the medieval city's main nautical artery, with boats sailing up it to discharge their goods right in the centre of town on the main square. Thereafter, with the docks moved elsewhere, the Damrak became a busy commercial drag, as it remains today, and Dam Square became the centre of municipal power. To the west of the Damrak lies the Old Centre's **Nieuwe Zijde**, whose outer boundary was marked in the 1500s by a defensive wall, hence the name of its principal avenue, **Nieuwezijds Voorburgwal** ("In Front of the Town Wall on the New Side"). The wall disappeared as the city grew, and in the nineteenth century the canal that ran through the middle of the street was earthed in, leaving the unusually wide thoroughfare that you see today. This area was, however, badly mauled by the developers in the 1970s and – give or take a scattering of old canal houses on Nieuwezijds Voorburgwal – there's no great reason to linger.

Centraal Station and around

With its high gables and cheerful brickwork, the neo-Renaissance **Centraal Station** is an imposing prelude to the city. At the time of its construction in the 1880s, it aroused much controversy because it effectively separated the centre from the River IJ, source of the city's wealth, for the first time in Amsterdam's long history. There was controversy about the choice of architect too; the man chosen, **Petrus J.H. Cuypers**, was Catholic, and in powerful Protestant circles there were mutterings about the vanity of his designs (he had recently completed the Rijksmuseum) and their unsuitability for Amsterdam. In the event, the station was built to Cuypers' design, but it was to be his last major commission; thereafter he spent most of his time building parish churches.

At the time of writing the station was dominated by building works on the city's new north–south transport link; once they're complete, expect a much spruced-up building and open space beyond.

Outside the station, **Stationsplein** is a messy open space, edged by ovals of water, packed with trams and dotted with barrel organs and chip stands, with

---

Wal

As befits a country that has spent so much of its time keeping the sea at bay, the Dutch word **wal** (wall or embankment) is used in all sorts of colloquialisms, including *tussen wal en schip raken*, literally ending up between wall and ship – that is, not knowing what to do – and *aan lager wal raken* – to end up at a lower wall, meaning someone's bad fortune was beyond their control. Or you might try *van de wal in de sloot* – basically the equivalent of going from the frying pan to the fire.

THE OLD CENTRE | Damrak and the Nieuwe Zijde

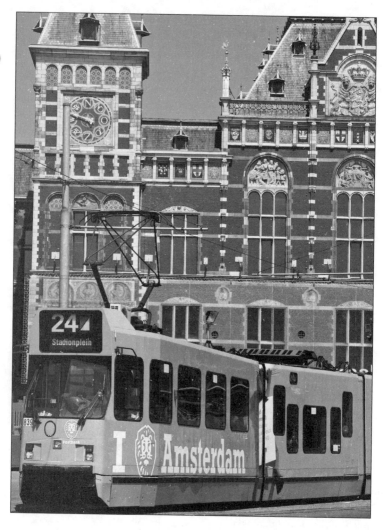

△ Centraal Station

street performers completing the picture in the summer. Across the water, to the southeast on Prins Hendrikkade, rise the twin towers and dome of **St Nicolaaskerk** (Mon & Sat noon–3pm, Tues–Fri 11am–4pm; free), the city's foremost Catholic Church, dedicated to the patron saint of sailors – and of Amsterdam. Like the station, it dates back to the 1880s; the cavernous interior holds some pretty dire religious murals, mawkish concoctions only partly relieved by swathes of coloured brickwork. Above the high altar is the **crown** of the Habsburg Emperor Maximilian, very much a symbol of the city and one you'll see again and again. Amsterdam had close ties with Maximilian; in the late fifteenth century he came here as a pilgrim and stayed on to recover from an illness. The burghers funded many of his military expeditions and, in return, he let the city use his crown in its coat of arms – a practice which, rather surprisingly, survived the seventeenth-century revolt against Spain.

Just along from St Nicolaaskerk, at the top of the Geldersekade canal, is the squat **Schreierstoren** (Weepers' Tower), a rare surviving chunk of the city's medieval wall. Originally, the tower overlooked the River IJ and it was here that women gathered to watch their menfolk sail away, though like many good stories this is apparently apocryphal: "Schreierstoren" refers to the sharp angle – the "schreye" – at which it was built, rather than the weeping women. Nonetheless, an old and weathered stone **plaque** inserted in the wall is a reminder of all those supposed sad farewells, and another – much more recent – plaque recalls the departure of Henry Hudson from here in 1609. On this particular voyage Hudson stumbled across the "Hudson" river and an island the locals called Manhattan. The colony that grew up there became known as New Amsterdam, a colonial possession that was only renamed New York after the English seized it in 1664. These days the Schreierstoren houses a small café with a terrace overlooking the canal.

In the opposite direction from the St Nicolaaskerk, it's a few metres to the end of **Zeedijk**, which was originally just that – a dyke to hold back the sea; it now girdles the north end of the Red Light District. Not so long ago this narrow thoroughfare was the haunt of drug addicts, and very much a no-go area at night. But it's been spruced up and now forms a lively route through to Nieuwmarkt, on the eastern edge of the Red Light District, as well as being the main hub of Amsterdam's small but growing Chinatown. Its seaward end is home to a couple of the oldest bars in the city and there are any number of Chinese, Thai and Vietnamese foodie treats as you make your way further down.

Damrak

From Stationsplein, **Damrak**, a broad, unenticing avenue lined with tacky restaurants, bars and bureaux de change, slices south into the heart of the city, first passing an inner harbour crammed with the bobbing canal cruise boats of Amsterdam's considerable tourist industry. Just beyond the harbour at Damrak 277 is the imposing bulk of the **Beurs**, the old Stock Exchange (opening hours and admission depend on exhibitions; guided tours can be arranged on ⓣ020/620 8112; ⓦwww.beursvanberlage.nl) – known as the "Beurs van Berlage" – a seminal work designed at the turn of the twentieth century by the leading light of the Dutch Modern movement, **Hendrik Petrus Berlage** (1856–1934). Berlage re-routed Dutch architecture with this building, forsaking the historicism that had dominated the nineteenth century, and whose prime practitioner had been Cuypers (see p.43). Instead he opted for a style with cleaner, heavier lines, inspired by the Romanesque and the Renaissance, but with the minimum of ornamentation – and in so doing anticipated the Expressionism that swept northern Europe from 1905 to 1925. The Beurs has long since lost its commercial function and nowadays hosts concerts and holds exhibitions on modern art and design, but the building is still the main event, from the graceful exposed ironwork and shallow-arched arcades of the main hall through to a fanciful frieze celebrating the stockbroker's trade. If the Beurs is closed, stop by the *Café Beurs van Berlage* that fronts onto Beursplein around the corner (see p.188) for a coffee, and admire the tiled scenes of the past, present and the future by the twentieth-century Dutch artist Jan Toorop.

Just southwest of the Beurs, the enormous department store **De Bijenkorf** (see p.228) – literally "beehive" – extends south along the Damrak. Amsterdam's

△ View of Damrak from the Beurs

answer to Harrods, De Bijenkorf posed all sorts of problems for the Germans when they first occupied the city in World War II. The store was a Jewish concern, so the Nazis didn't really want their troops shopping here, but it was just too popular to implement a total ban. The bizarre solution was to prohibit German soldiers from shopping on the ground floor, where the store's Jewish employees were concentrated, as they always had been, in the luxury goods section.

The Nieuwe Zijde

Running parallel to, and west of, the Damrak, **Nieuwezijds Voorburgwal** kicks off with the **Crowne Plaza Hotel** at no. 5, formerly the Holiday Inn, built on the site of an old tenement building called **Wyers**. The 1985 clearance of squatters from Wyers ranks among the more infamous of that decade's anti-squatting campaigns, involving a great deal of protest (and some violence) throughout the city. The squatters had occupied the building in an attempt to prevent yet another slice of the city being converted from residential to business use. They were widely supported by the people of Amsterdam, but they couldn't match the clout of the American hotel company and riot police were sent in; construction of the hotel followed soon after.

From the hotel, it's a short walk along Hekelveld and a right turn down Kattengat to the **Lutherse Kerk**, a round, seventeenth-century edifice whose copper dome gives this area its nickname, **Koepelkwartier** ("Copper quarter"). Church domes are a rarity in Amsterdam, but this one was no stylistic peccadillo; until the late eighteenth century, only Dutch Reformed churches were permitted the (much more fashionable) bell towers, so the Lutherans got stuck with a dome. It's a grand, self-confident building, seen to best advantage from the Singel canal, but it has been dogged by bad luck; in 1882 the interior was gutted by fire and, although it was repaired, the cost of maintenance proved too high for the congregation, who decamped in 1935. After many years of neglect, the adjacent *Renaissance Hotel* bought the church, turning it into a conference centre.

Doubling back to Nieuwezijds Voorburgwal, you soon reach the triangular open space of **Nieuwezijds Kolk**, where the angular, glassy and ultramodern building on the corner is testament to the recent large-scale construction work that has transformed the area. When the underground car park was being dug here, workers discovered archeological remains dating back to the thirteenth century; this turned out to be the castle of the "Lords of Amstel", which, it is thought, had occupied the site when it was open marshland, even before the Amstel was dammed. The square is anchored by a quaint brick, gabled building, but the series of pedestrianized alleys that link Nieuwezijds Voorburgwal to the Damrak to the south of Nieuwezijds Kolk are without much charm. Consequently, it's better to stay on Nieuwezijds Voorburgwal as it heads south, its trees partly concealing a series of impressive canal houses, though these fizzle out as you approach Dam Square.

Dam Square

Situated at the heart of the city, **Dam Square** gave Amsterdam its name – it was here, in the thirteenth century, that the River Amstel was dammed; the fishing village that grew around it became known as "Amstelredam". Boats could sail down the Damrak into the square, and unload right in the middle of the village, which soon prospered by trading herring for Baltic grain. In the early fifteenth century, the building of Amsterdam's principal church, the **Nieuwe Kerk**, followed by the town hall (now the Royal Palace), formally marked Dam Square as Amsterdam's centre.

Today it's an open and airy but somehow rather desultory space, despite – or perhaps partly because of – the presence of the main municipal **war memorial**, a prominent stone tusk adorned by bleak, suffering figures and decorated with the coats of arms of each of the Netherlands' provinces (plus the ex-colony of Indonesia). The memorial was designed by **Jacobus Johannes Pieter Oud** (1890–1963), a De Stijl stalwart who thought the Expressionism of Berlage much too flippant.

The Amsterdam branch of **Madame Tussaud's** waxworks is on Dam Square too, at no. 20 (daily 10am–6.30pm, July and Aug open till 9pm; last entry 1hr before closing; €19.95, children aged 5–15 €14.95; ⓦ www.madametussauds .nl); although it has a few Dutch celebs you won't necessarily know, most of its models are either international stars, royalty, or Dutch footballers like Johann Cruyff.

The Koninklijk Paleis

Dominating Dam Square is the **Koninklijk Paleis** (Royal Palace, July & Aug daily 11am–5pm, and occasionally at other times during the year too; ⓣ020/620 4060; €4.50, €6.50 with audio tour; ⓦ www.koninklijkhuis.nl), although the title is deceptive, given that this vast sandstone structure was built as the city's Stadhuis (Town Hall), and only had its first royal occupant when Louis Bonaparte moved in during the French occupation (1795–1813).

From Town Hall to Royal Palace

At the time of the building's construction in the mid-seventeenth century, Amsterdam was at the height of its powers. The city was pre-eminent amongst

Dutch towns, and had just resisted William of Orange's attempts to bring it to heel. Predictably, the council craved a **residence** that was a declaration of the city's municipal power and opted for a startlingly progressive design by **Jacob van Campen**, who proposed a Dutch rendering of the classical principles revived in Renaissance Italy. Initially, there was opposition to the plan from the council's Calvinist minority, who pointed out that the proposed **Stadhuis** would dwarf the neighbouring Nieuwe Kerk (see p.49), an entirely inappropriate ordering, so they suggested, of earthly and spiritual values. However, when the Calvinists were promised a new church spire (it was never built) they promptly fell into line and in 1648 work started on what was then the largest town hall in Europe, supported by no less than 13,659 wooden piles driven into Dam Square's sandy soil – a number every Dutch schoolchild remembers by adding a "1" and a "9" to the number of days in the year. The poet Constantijn Huygens called the new building "The world's Eighth Wonder / With so much stone raised high and so much timber under".

The Stadhuis received its **royal designation** in 1808, when Napoleon's brother Louis, who had recently been installed as king, commandeered it as his residence. Lonely and isolated, Louis abdicated in 1810 and hightailed it out of the country. Afterwards, possession of the palace became something of a sore point between the Royal family and the city; the initial compromise kept the building as royal property on condition that the royals stayed here for part of the year, but the Oranges almost universally failed to make much of an appearance. This irritated many Amsterdammers, and in the 1930s the Oranges offered the city fifteen million guilders to build a new city hall in return for a new agreement, which allowed them to use the Palace whenever they wanted, with ownership passing to the state (as distinct from the city); the new town hall, on Waterlooplein (see p.98), was finally completed in the 1980s. Nowadays the Dutch royals live down in the Huis ten Bosch, near the Hague, and only use the Royal Palace for state occasions.

The building

The **exterior** of the palace is very much to the allegorical point: twin tympani depict Amsterdam as a port and trading centre, the one at the front presided over by Neptune and a veritable herd of unicorns. Above these panels are representations of the values the city council espoused – at the front, Prudence, Justice and Peace, to the rear Temperance and Vigilance on either side of a muscular, globe-bearing Atlas. One deliberate precaution, however, was the omission of a central doorway – just in case the mob turned nasty (as they were wont to do) and stormed the place.

The **interior** also proclaims the pride and confidence of the Golden Age, principally in the lavish **Citizen's Hall**, an extraordinarily handsome, arcaded marble chamber where the enthroned figure of Amsterdam looks down on the earth and the heavens, which are laid out at her feet in three circular, inlaid marble maps, one each of the eastern and western hemispheres, the other of the northern sky. Other allegorical **figures** ram home the municipal point: flanking "Amsterdam" to left and right are Wisdom and Strength, and the reliefs to either side of the central group represent good governance: on the left is the god Amphion, who plays his lyre to persuade the stones to pile themselves up into a wall, and to the right Mercury attempts to lull Argos to sleep – stressing the need to be vigilant. All this is part of a good-natured and witty symbolism that pervades almost all of the building: cocks fight above the entrance to the Commissioner of Petty Affairs; **Ferdinand Bol**'s painting in the Burgomasters' Council room depicts an unsuccessful attempt to bribe and then frighten (with the elephant trumpeting behind the curtain) a Roman consul; and a medallion above the door of the Bankruptcy Chamber shows the *Fall of Icarus*, surrounded by marble carvings depicting hungry rats scurrying around an empty money chest and nibbling at unpaid bills. In the Magistrates' Court is a second Bol **painting**, *Moses the Lawgiver*, depicting Moses descending from Mount Sinai with the Ten Commandments, but most of the paintings displayed in the palace are of little distinction.

The decorative whimsy fizzles out in the **High Court of Justice** at the front of the building, close to the entrance. Inside the consciously intimidating chamber, the judges sat on the marble benches flanked by heavyweight representations of Righteousness, Wisdom, Mercy and so forth as they passed judgement on the hapless criminal in front of them; possibly even worse, the crowd on Dam Square could view the proceedings through the barred windows, almost always baying for blood. They usually went home contented; as soon as the judges had passed the death sentence, the condemned were whisked up to the wooden scaffold attached to the front of the building and promptly dispatched.

Magna Plaza

Behind the Royal Palace, on Nieuwezijds Voorburgwal, you can't miss the old neo-Gothic post office of 1899, now converted into the **Magna Plaza** shopping mall (Mon 11am–7pm, Tues–Sat 10am–7pm, Thurs 10am–9pm, Sun noon–7pm; ⓦ www.magnaplaza.nl) – a grand affair that makes an attractive setting for the numerous clothing chains that now inhabit its red-brick interior. It certainly was a great place to buy stamps, but the post office building was never very popular despite its whimsical embellishments, which continued the town's tradition of plonking towers on every major building partly as a matter of civic pride, and partly to contribute to the city's spiky skyline. The architect responsible, a certain C.G. Peters, took a surprising amount of flack for his creation, which was mocked as "postal Gothic".

The Nieuwe Kerk

Vying for importance with the Royal Palace is the adjacent **Nieuwe Kerk** (opening hours and admission vary with exhibitions, but usually daily 10am– 6pm; ☎020/638 6909, ⓦ www.nieuwekerk.nl). Despite its name (literally "new church"), it's an early fifteenth-century structure built in a late flourish of the Gothic style, with a forest of pinnacles and high, slender gables. Badly damaged by fire on several occasions, and unceremoniously stripped of most of its fittings by the Calvinists, the **interior** is a hangar-like affair of sombre demeanour, whose sturdy compound pillars soar up to support the wooden vaulting of the ceiling. Amongst a scattering of decorative highlights, look out for an extravagant, finely carved mahogany **pulpit** that was fifteen years in the making, a cleverly worked copper **chancel screen** and a flashy, Baroque **organ case**.

There's also the spectacularly vulgar **tomb** of Admiral Michiel de Ruyter (1607–76), complete with trumpeting angels, conch-blowing Neptunes and cherubs all in a tizzy. In a long and illustrious naval career **de Ruyter** trounced in succession the Spaniards, the Swedes, the English and the French, and his rise from deck hand to Admiral-in-Chief is the stuff of national legend. His most famous exploit was a raid up the River Thames to Medway in 1667 and the seizure of the Royal Navy's flagship, *The Royal Charles*; the subsequent Dutch crowing almost drove Charles II to distraction. De Ruyter was buried here with full military honours and the church is still used for state occasions; the coronations of queens Wilhelmina, Juliana and, in 1980, Beatrix, were all held here.

After the church, pop into the adjoining *'t Nieuwe Kafé*, which occupies one of the old ecclesiastical lean-tos and serves excellent coffee and delicious lunches and snacks.

Rokin, Kalverstraat and the Spui

Sandwiched between the Singel and **Rokin**, the southern part of the Old Centre is one of Amsterdam's busiest districts, mostly on account of pedestrianized **Kalverstraat**, a hectic shopping street. Taken as a whole, it's not a particularly engaging area, but it does have its moments, most enjoyably in the cloistered tranquillity of the **Begijnhof** and amongst the bars and cafés of the **Spui**. Here also is a brace of moderately diverting museums – the **Amsterdams Historisch Museum** and the archeological **Allard Pierson Museum**.

Rokin to Doelenstraat

The **Rokin** picks up where the Damrak leaves off, cutting south in a wide sweep that follows the former course of the River Amstel. The Rokin was the business centre of the nineteenth-century city, and although it has lost much of its prestige it is still flanked by an attractive medley of architectural styles incorporating everything from grandiose nineteenth-century mansions to more utilitarian modern stuff.

One initial highlight as you stroll south is the handsome Art Nouveau-meets-Art Deco Marine Insurance building at **no. 69**; others are the much earlier canal house at **no. 83** and the attractive stone mansion at **no. 91**. Across the street, at **no. 92**, is the Hajenius cigar shop with its flashy gilt interior, while a prominent equestrian **statue** of Queen Wilhelmina marks the spot where the Rokin hits the canal system. Born in The Hague, **Wilhelmina** (1880–1962) came to the throne in 1890 and abdicated in favour of her daughter, Juliana, 58 years later – a mammoth royal stint by any standard. After her retirement, she wrote *Lonely but not Alone*, which explored her strong religious beliefs, but her popularity was based on her determined resistance to the Germans in World War II, when she was the figurehead of the government-in-exile in London.

A few metres south, overlooking the canal at Oude Turfmarkt 127, the **Allard Pierson Museum** (Tues–Fri 10am–5pm, Sat & Sun 1–5pm; €5) is a good old-fashioned archeological museum in a solid Neoclassical building dating from the 1860s. Spread over two floors – and labelled in Dutch and English – it's not a large museum, but it has a wide-ranging collection of finds retrieved from Egypt, Greece and Italy. The particular highlight is the museum's Greek **pottery** with fine examples of both the black- and red-figured wares produced in the sixth and fifth centuries BC. Look out also for several ornate Roman **sarcophagi**, especially a whopper made of marble and decorated with Dionysian scenes, a very unusual wooden coffin from c.150 AD which is partly carved in the shape of the man held within, and Etruscan funerary urns and carvings, including an amazingly precise statue of a baby in swaddling clothes. Of the Egyptian artefacts on the ground floor, a model of a ship and its crew from the Middle Kingdom stands out – another funerary object, used to transport the soul of the dead to the afterlife.

Further south beyond the museum, **nos. 141–147 Oude Turfmarkt** are classic seventeenth-century canal houses, graced by bottle- and spout-shaped gables. Just past here, on Doelenstraat, the **Hotel de l'Europe** is one of the city's most luxurious and well-appointed places to stay, although the **Hotel Doelen** next door is perhaps of more historic interest, incorporating as it does the Kloveniers Tower, which was once the headquarters and meeting place of the company Rembrandt depicted in *The Night Watch*. No one knows for sure whether he painted *The Night Watch* here, but it certainly hung in the building at one time, and if you ask nicely in reception you can stroll up to see where it was, although – despite the tour groups that regularly trundle through – there's not much to look at beyond a crumbling red-brick wall and a bad photo of the painting.

Kalverstraat, the Spui and the Begijnhof

Running parallel to the Rokin to the west, **Kalverstraat**, a pedestrianized shopping street, curves north to Dam Square. The street has been a commercial centre since medieval times, when it was used as a calf market, and it was also here, in 1345, that the city witnessed the Miracle of the Host (see "The Oude Kerk" p.56) and became a route for pilgrims. There's not much to say about Kalverstraat – it really could be any European shopping street – but if you want to shop, and you're not looking for designer labels, this is the place to come.

A little way down Kalverstraat, workaday **Heiligeweg**, or "Holy Way", was once part of a much longer route used by pilgrims heading into Amsterdam and is still used for part of the Stille Omgang (Silent Procession, see p.259). Every other religious reference disappeared centuries ago, but there is one interesting edifice here: the fanciful gateway of the old **Rasphuis** (House of Correction) that now fronts a shopping mall at the foot of Voetboogstraat. The gateway is surmounted by a sculpture of a woman punishing two criminals chained at her

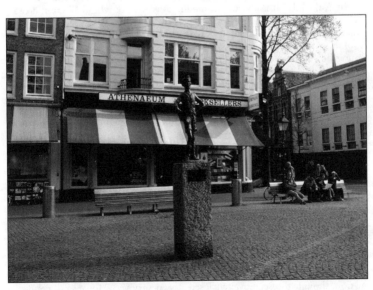

△ The Spui

Beguinages

One result of the urbanization of the Low Countries from the twelfth century onwards was the establishment of **beguinages** (*begijnhoven* in Dutch, *béguinages* in French) in almost every city and town. These were semi-secluded communities, where widows and unmarried women – the **Beguines** (*Begijns*) – lived together, the better to do pious acts, especially caring for the sick. In **construction**, beguinages follow the same general plan with several streets of whitewashed, terraced, brick cottages hidden away behind walls and gates and surrounding a central garden and chapel.

The **origins** of the Beguine movement are somewhat obscure, but it would seem that the initial impetus came from a twelfth-century Liège priest, a certain Lambert le Bègue (the Stammerer). The main period of growth came later with the establishment of dozens of new beguinages, like those in Ghent and Bruges in Belgium, and Breda and Amsterdam in the Netherlands. All were sponsored by the nobility and the later foundations – like the one here in Amsterdam – were established despite the opposition of the Papacy, which had declared them a potential source of heresy at the Council of Vienna in 1311.

Beguine communities were different from convents in so far as the inhabitants did not have to take vows and had the right to return to the secular world if they chose. At a time when hundreds of women were forcibly shut away in convents for all sorts of reasons (primarily financial), this element of choice made the communities an attractive proposition. In the Netherlands, the beguine movement was pretty much polished off by the Reformation – and the Calvinist assertion of the individual's need to have a direct relationship with God without the Church acting as intermediary; the convents closed down too. **Almshouses**, arguably the predecessors of state-subsidized housing, did something to fill the gap.

sides above the single word "Castigatio" (punishment). Beneath is a carving by Hendrick de Keyser showing wolves and lions cringing before the whip; the inscription reads: "It is a virtue to subdue those before whom all go in dread."

Cut up Voetboogstraat and you soon reach the **Spui**, whose west end opens out into a wide, tram-clanking square flanked by the appealing Athenaeum bookshop and a number of café-bars. In the middle is a cloying statue of a young boy, known as **'t Lieverdje** ("Little Darling" or "Loveable Scamp"), a gift to the city from a cigarette company in 1960. It was here in the mid-1960s, with the statue seen as a symbol of the addicted consumer, that the playful Sixties anarchist group, the **Provos**, organized some of their most successful *ludiek* (pranks).

From the Spui, you can proceed north towards the station along **Spuistraat**, a happening street, liberally sprinkled with bars and restaurants and the possessor of Amsterdam's last remaining **squat**, *Vrankrijk*. Or, by way of the fancy little gateway on the north side of the Spui, you can sneak into the **Begijnhof** (daily 10am–5pm; free), where a huddle of immaculately maintained old houses looks onto a central green, their backs to the outside world; if this door is locked, try the main entrance, just a couple of hundred metres north of the Spui on Gedempte Begijnensloot.

The Begijnhof was founded in the fourteenth century as a home for the Beguines – members of a Catholic sisterhood living as nuns, but without vows and with the right to return to the secular world (see box). The original medieval complex comprised a series of humble brick cottages, but these were mostly replaced by the larger, grander houses of today shortly after the Reformation, though the secretive, enclosed design survived. However, a couple of pre-Reformation buildings do remain, including the **Houten Huys**, at no. 34, whose wooden facade dates from 1477, the oldest in Amsterdam and erected before the city forbade the construction of timber houses as an essential precaution against fire. The **Engelse Kerk** (English Reformed Church), which takes up one side of the Begijnhof, is of medieval construction too, but it was taken from the Beguines and given to Amsterdam's English community during the Reformation. Plain and unadorned, the church is of interest for its carefully worked pulpit panels, several of which were designed by a youthful **Piet Mondriaan** (1872–1944), the leading De Stijl artist – although to see them you'll have to attend one of its services on Sundays at 10.30am. After they had lost their church, and in keeping with the terms of the *Alteratie* (see p.268), the Beguines were allowed to celebrate Mass inconspicuously in the clandestine Catholic **kapel** (Mon 1–6.30pm, Tues–Fri 9am–6.30pm; free), which they established in the house opposite their old church. It's still used today, a homely little place with some terribly sentimental religious paintings, one of which – to the left of the high altar – depicts the Miracle of the unburnable Host (see "The Oude Kerk" p.56).

The Amsterdams Historisch Museum

As you emerge from the east side of the Begijnhof, turn left onto narrow Gedempte Begijnensloot and it's 100m or so to the **Schuttersgalerij** – the Civic Guard Gallery. Here, an assortment of huge group portraits of the **Amsterdam militia**, ranging from serious-minded paintings of the 1540s through to lighter affairs from the seventeenth century, is displayed for free in a glassed-in passageway. They are interesting paintings – the pick are those by **Nicolaes Pickenoy** (1588–1650) – but the finest militia painting by a long chalk – Rembrandt's *The Night Watch* – is exhibited in the Rijksmuseum (see p.114).

The Schuttersgalerij is part of the **Amsterdams Historisch Museum** (entrances at Nieuwezijds Voorburgwal 357 & Kalverstraat 92, Mon–Fri 10am–5pm, Sat & Sun 11am–5pm; €6; ⓦwww.ahm.nl), which occupies the smartly restored but rambling seventeenth-century buildings of the municipal orphanage. The museum follows the city's development with a scattering of artefacts and a host of paintings from the thirteenth century onwards, but it's a slightly difficult collection to find your way around, and you need to pay close attention to the colour-coded signs that attempt to guide you through chronologically; the labelling at least is in English as well as Dutch.

Maps and paintings punctuate the galleries and record the growth of the city, starting with a lot of old **views of Amsterdam** back before the Golden Age, of which Cornelisz Anthonisz's 1538 *Bird's Eye View of Amsterdam,* in effect the oldest surviving plan of the city, stands out. There are paintings illustrating the country's former maritime prowess in Room 5, titled "Rulers of the Seas", and in Room 6 there is a view of Dam Square in the early seventeenth century that shows both the old and new town hall, while Room 7 has a rare cityscape by Jacob van Ruisdael that shows Dam Square and the harbour along Damrak. Room 10, "Social Care & Stern Discipline", examines the harsh paternalism of the city's merchant oligarchy, with paintings depicting the regents of several orphanages, self-contented bourgeoisie in the company of the grateful poor, while nearby Room 11, "**The Art of the Golden Age**", is distinguished by two paintings of the surgeons' guild at work – look out for Rembrandt's wonderful, if gruesome, *Anatomy Lesson of Dr Jan Deijman* – as well as Bartholomew van der Helst's *Governors and Governesses of the Spinhuis,* which

△ Amsterdams Historisch Museum

captures both the sternness of the institution (see p.59) and its daily routine going on behind them.

The museum doesn't just focus on the Golden Age, but dutifully and effectively records the **modern era** as well, starting with Breitner's *Dam Square* of 1898 and Jacob Maris's view of the *Schreierstoren*. Moving upstairs for the **twentieth century**, there is an inevitable focus on the war years and the Nazi occupation, including film footage of the city's liberation. Postwar material includes displays on the **CoBrA** art movement (see p.290) and Karel Appel's murals for the town hall (now decorating the city's *Grand Hotel* restaurant), the development of Schiphol Airport, the liberalization of dope and the rise of coffeeshops, and even a mock-up of an old brown café.

The Red Light District

The whole area to the east of Damrak, between Warmoesstraat, Nieuwmarkt and Damstraat, is the **Red Light District**, known locally as the "De Walletjes" ("Small Walls") on account of the series of low brick walls that contain its canals. The district stretches across the two narrow canals that marked the eastern part of medieval Amsterdam, **Oudezijds Voorburgwal** and **Oudezijds Achterburgwal**, with the far canal of **Kloveniersburgwal** forming its eastern boundary. The area is pretty seedy, although the legalized prostitution here has long been one of the city's most distinctive draws. It wasn't always so; the handsome facades of Oudezijds Voorburgwal in particular recall ritzier days, when this was one of the wealthiest parts of the city, richly earning its nickname the "Velvet Canal". The two canals, with their narrow connecting passages, are thronged with **"window brothels"** and at busy times the crass, on-street haggling over the price of various sex acts is drowned out by a surprisingly festive atmosphere – entire families grinning more or less amiably at the women in the windows or discussing the specifications (and feasibility) of the sex toys in the shops. Another feature are the hawkers who line the streets touting the peep shows and "live sex" within (and, unlike in London or New York, there actually is live sex within).

All in all, there's an undertow to the district that's not particularly pleasant, and with the added delights of the drug addicts that hang around during the day, you might not want to spend any longer here than is necessary. And don't even think about taking a picture of a "window brothel" unless you're prepared for some major grief from the camera-shy prostitutes. Dodging the dealers, the district also contains two prime attractions, the medieval **Oude Kerk** and the clandestine **Amstelkring** Catholic church.

Warmoesstraat

Soliciting hasn't always been the principal activity on sleazy **Warmoesstraat**. It was once one of the city's most fashionable streets, home to Holland's foremost poet, **Joost van den Vondel** (1587–1679), who ran his hosiery business from no. 110, in between writing and hobnobbing with the Amsterdam elite. Van den Vondel was a kind of Dutch Shakespeare; his *Gijsbrecht van Amstel*, a celebration of Amsterdam during its Golden Age, is one of the classics of Dutch literature, and he wrote regular, if ponderous, official verses, including well over a thousand lines on the inauguration of the town hall. Vondel had more than his share of hard luck too; his son frittered away the modest family fortune and he lived out his last few years as doorkeeper of the pawnshop on Oudezijds Voorburgwal known as "Ome Jan" (see p.59), dying of hypothermia at what was then the remarkable age of 92. Witty to the end, his own suggested epitaph ran: "Here lies Vondel, your grief withhold, for he hath suffered death from cold."

Vondel's Warmoesstraat house was knocked down decades ago, but the street does have two minor attractions – the **Condomerie Het Gulden Vlies**, at no. 141, which specializes in every imaginable design and make of condom, in sizes ranging from the small to the remarkable, and the **Prostitution Information Centre**, at Enge Kerksteeg 3, right by the Oude Kerk (Tues, Wed, Fri & Sat noon–7pm; ☎020/420 7328; ⊛www.pic-amsterdam.com), a legally recognized *stichting* or charitable foundation that was set up just over a decade ago (by an ex-prostitute, Mariska Majoor) to provide prostitutes, their clients and visitors with clear, dispassionate information about prostitution. It publishes the *Pleasure Guide* in Dutch and English, which bills itself as "an informative magazine about

Commercial sex in Amsterdam

Developed in the 1960s, The Netherlands' – and especially Amsterdam's – liberal approach to social policy has had several unforeseen consequences, the most dramatic being its international reputation as a centre for both drugs and **prostitution**. However, the tackiness of the Red Light District is just the surface sheen on what has been, at least recently, a serious attempt to address the reality of sex for sale, and to integrate this within a normal, ordered society. In Dutch law, prostituting oneself has long been legal, but the state had always drawn the line at brothels and soliciting in public. The difficulties this created for the police were legion, so finally, in 1996, a special soliciting zone was established and a couple of years later **brothels** were legalized in the hope that together these changes would bring a degree of stability to the sex industry. The authorities were particularly keen to get a grip on the use of illegal immigrants as prostitutes and also to alleviate the problem of numbers.

This legislation is partly the result of a long and determined campaign by the prostitutes' trade union, *De Rode Draad* ("The Red Thread"), which has improved the lot of its members by setting up new health insurance and pension schemes – and generally fighting for regular employment rights for prostitutes. Whether this has happened or not is debatable: the number of "window brothels" is limited, so a significant group of women ply their trade illicitly in bars and hotels. There are still lots of illegal immigrants in the Red Light District, and lots of pimps too. The **windows**, which are rented out for upwards of €100 a day, are less easy to control than registered brothels, and at least half of the District's prostitutes hand over at least some of their earnings to a pimp, who will usually be Dutch and often an ex-boyfriend.

If you want to know more, and to get an admittedly fairly tightly controlled, behind-the-scenes look at the Red Light District, you can take a tour with the Prostitution Information Centre – see pp.55–56 for details.

having a paid love-life", and even exhibits art by Mariska's artist father, and in its shop, "Wallenwinkel", sells books and pamphlets, and souvenirs of the Red Light District – postcards, fridge magnets, T-shirts and the like. It also runs hour-long **tours** of the Red Light District for €12.50 a person. All in all, it does a decent job of ridding prostitution of its seedy mystique.

The Oude Kerk

Just to the east of Warmoesstraat, bang in the middle of the Red Light District, is Amsterdam's most appealing church, the **Oude Kerk** (Mon–Sat 11am–5pm, Sun 1–5pm; Ⓦ www.oudekerk.nl), an attractive Gothic structure with high-pitched gables and finely worked lancet windows. There's been a church on this site since the middle of the thirteenth century, but most of the present building dates from a century later, funded by the pilgrims who came here in their hundreds following a widely publicized **miracle**. The story goes that, in 1345, a dying man regurgitated the Host he had received here at Communion, and when it was thrown on the fire afterwards, it did not burn. The unburnable Host was placed in a chest and installed in a long-lost chapel somewhere off Nieuwezijds Voorburgwal, before finally being transferred to the Oude Kerk a few years later. It disappeared during the Reformation, but to this day thousands of the faithful still come to take part in the annual **Stille Omgang**, a silent nocturnal procession terminating at the Oude Kerk and held in mid-March. The church is also regularly used for art displays and concerts.

The Protestants cleared the church of almost all of its ecclesiastical tackle during the Reformation, but its largely bare **interior** does hold several interesting features. These include some folksy misericords, a few faded vault paintings recovered from beneath layers of whitewash in the 1950s, and the unadorned memorial tablet of Rembrandt's first wife, Saskia van Uylenburg, beneath the smaller of the two organs. Much more diverting, however, are the three beautifully coloured **stained-glass windows** beside the ambulatory in what was once the Chapel of Our Lady. Dating from the 1550s, all three depict religious scenes – from left to right: the Annunciation, the Adoration of the Shepherds and the Assumption of the Virgin – and each is set above its respective donors. The characters are shown in classical gear with togas and sandals and the buildings in the background are firmly classical too, reflecting both artistic fashion and a belief that Greco-Roman detail was historically accurate. A fourth, rather different stained-glass window is located on the other side of the ambulatory. A secular piece of 1655, it features the Spanish king Philip IV ceding independence to a representative of the United Provinces (the Netherlands) under the terms of the Treaty of Munster of 1648, which wrapped up the Thirty Years' War. Like the earlier windows, the architectural backdrop is classical, but here it's to emphasize the dignity of the proceedings – and the king and the Dutch emissaries wear contemporary clothes.

Outside, the Oude Kerk **tower** is open weekends between April and September (1–5pm; €5) and offers predictably great views – in a city with relatively few such opportunities.

OZ Voorburgwal and the Amstelkring

The front of the Oude Kerk overlooks the northern reaches of **Oudezijds Voorburgwal**, whose imposing canalside houses are a reminder of its prosperous, seventeenth-century heyday. A few metres north of the church, at Oudezijds Voorburgwal 40, is the clandestine **Amstelkring** (Mon–Sat 10am–5pm, Sun 1–

△ The Red Light District

> ## Drug addicts in the Red Light District
>
> The police estimate that there are around a thousand hard-drug users in Amsterdam, who, as they put it, "cause nuisance", and there remain a few groups of **drug addicts** who hang around on the northern edge of the Red Light District. They are unlikely to molest strangers, but can still be a threatening presence. In fairness, though, the police have done their best to clean things up, and have dramatically improved the situation on the Zeedijk and Nieuwmarkt, which were once notorious for hard drugs, and at the canal bridge on Oude Hoogstraat, formerly nicknamed the "Pillenbrug" ("Pill Bridge"). Nonetheless, keep a close eye on your bag and wallet – the area is notorious for petty thievery.

5pm; €7, Ⓦwww.museumamstelkring.nl), which was momentarily the city's principal Catholic place of worship and is now one of Amsterdam's most enjoyable museums. Despite the reformation of 1578, the new regime treated its Catholics well, broadly speaking – commercial pragmatism has always outweighed religious zeal here – but there was a degree of discrimination; Catholic churches were recycled for Protestant use and their members no longer allowed to practise openly. The result was an eccentric compromise; Catholics were allowed to hold services in any private building providing that the exterior revealed no sign of their activities – hence the development of the city's **clandestine churches** (*schuilkerken*), amongst which the Amstelkring is the only one to have survived intact. Amstelkring, meaning "Amstel Circle", is the name of the group of nineteenth-century historians who saved the building from demolition.

The Amstelkring, more properly Ons Lieve Heer Op Solder ("Our Dear Lord in the Attic"), occupies the loft of a wealthy merchant's house and is perfectly delightful, with a narrow **nave** skilfully shoehorned into the available space. Flanked by elegant balconies, the nave has an ornately carved organ at one end and a mock-marble high altar, decorated with Jacob de Wit's mawkish *Baptism of Christ*, at the other. Even the patron of the church, one Jan Hartman, clearly had doubts about de Wit's efforts – the two spares he procured just in case are now displayed behind the altar. The rest of the house has been left untouched, its original furnishings reminiscent of interiors by Vermeer or de Hooch.

OZ Achterburgwal

A block across from OZ Voorburgwal, **Oudezijds Achterburgwal** is another pretty canal, but like its neighbour long despoiled by sleaze and tat. Stroll south for five minutes to reach the **Hash Marihuana Hemp Museum** at Oudezijds Achterburgwal 148 (daily 11am–10pm; €5.70, Ⓦwww.hashmuseum.com), which is still going strong despite intermittent battles with the police. As well as featuring displays on the various types of dope and numerous ways to smoke it, the museum has an indoor marijuana garden, samples of textiles and paper made with hemp, and pamphlets explaining the medicinal properties of cannabis. There's also a shop selling pipes, books, videos and plenty of souvenirs. Amsterdam's reliance on imported dope ended in the late 1980s with the growth of hydroponic growing techniques, whereby marijuana – and in particular a reddish variety bred in America, called "skunk" – was able to flourish under artificial lights without water. Nowadays over half the dope sold in the city's coffeeshops is grown in the Netherlands, and this place is positively evangelical about how to join in.

Across the canal, next door to Oudezijds Achterburgwal 185, at Spinhuissteeg 1, the **Spinhuis** was once a house of correction for "fallen women", who were put to work here on the looms and spinning wheels. Curiously, workhouses like this used to figure on tourist itineraries; for a small fee the public was allowed to watch the women at work, and at carnival times admission was free and large crowds came to jeer and mock. The justification for this was that shame was supposed to be part of the reforming process, but in fact the municipality unofficially tolerated brothels and the incarcerated women had simply been singled out for exemplary punishment. The Spinhuis has been turned into offices, but the old front door has survived intact, with an inscription by the seventeenth-century Dutch poet Pieter Corneliszoon Hooft: "Cry not, for I exact no vengeance for wrong but to force you to be good. My hand is stern but my heart is kind."

On the other side of the canal, the triangular parcel of land at the southern end of Oudezijds Achterburgwal is packed with university buildings, mostly modern or nineteenth-century structures built in the vernacular Dutch style. Together they form a pleasant urban ensemble, but the early seventeenth-century, step-gabled **Huis op de Drie Grachten** ("House on the Three Canals"), with its red shutters and mullion windows, stands out, sitting prettily on the corner of Oudezijds Achterburgwal and Oudezijds Voorburgwal. A few steps to the north, through an ornate gateway at Oudezijds Voorburgwal 231, is the **Agnietenkapel** (currently under restoration), originally part of a Catholic convent, but now owned by the university. Upstairs, the chapel has a good-looking, first-floor auditorium dating from the fifteenth century, formerly used for temporary exhibitions devoted to the university's history. Roughly opposite, just over the footbridge, the large brick and stone-trimmed building at Oudezijds Voorburgwal 302 has been known as **"Ome Jan"** ("Uncle John's") ever since the days when it was central Amsterdam's pawnshop. The poet **Vondel** (see p.55) ended his days working here, and a short verse above the fancy stone entranceway, which comes complete with the city's coat of arms, extols the virtues of the pawnshop – and the evils of usury. From "Ome Jan", it's a couple of hundred metres to the southern end of Oudezijds Voorburgwal, where the **Galerie Mokum** art shop (see p.22) uses the old Jewish nickname for the city.

Nieuwmarkt and around

The eastern reaches of the Red Light District peter out at cobbled **Nieuwmarkt**, a wide-open, sometimes druggy square that centres on the turreted **Waag**. It's within easy walking distance of a pleasant residential district situated between two canals – **Geldersekade** and **Oude Schans**, and lies at the end of the outermost of the three eastern canals of fifteenth-century Amsterdam, **Kloveniersburgwal** – a long, dead-straight waterway flanked by a string of dignified facades. Together these canals make for one of the most engaging parts of the city, especially at the southern end, where a small pocket of placid waterways and handsome old canal houses spreads over to neighbouring **Groenburgwal** – a narrow and almost impossibly pretty waterway.

Nieuwmarkt and Oude Schans

Nieuwmarkt was long one of the city's most important markets and the place where Gentiles and Jews from the nearby Jewish Quarter (see Chapter Four)

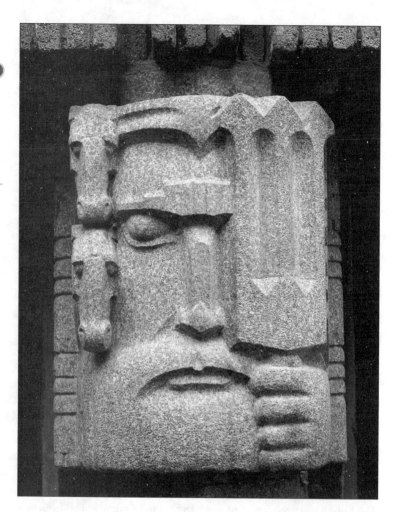

△ Carving on the Scheepvaarthuis

– just southeast along St Antoniebreestraat – traded. All that came to a traumatic end during World War II, when the Germans cordoned off the Nieuwmarkt with barbed wire and turned it into a holding pen. After the war, the square's old exuberance never returned and these days all that remains of its former trading is a small organic food **market** on Saturdays (9am–5pm).

The focus of the square, the sprawling, multi-turreted **Waag**, dating from the 1480s, has had a chequered history. Built as one of the city's fortified gates, Sint Antoniespoort, Amsterdam's expansion soon made it obsolete and the ground floor was turned into a municipal weighing-house, with the rooms upstairs taken over by the surgeons' guild. It was here that the surgeons held lectures on anatomy and public dissections, the inspiration for Rembrandt's *Anatomy Lesson of Dr Tulp*, displayed in the Mauritshuis Collection in The Hague. Abandoned by the surgeons and the weigh-masters in the nineteenth century, the building served as a furniture store and a fire station before falling into disuse, though it has recently been renovated to house a good café–bar and restaurant, *In de Waag* (see p.192).

Strolling along Recht Boomssloot from the northeast corner of Nieuwmarkt, it only takes a couple of minutes to reach the **Montelbaanstoren**, a sturdy tower dating from 1512 that overlooks the **Oude Schans**, a canal dug around the same time to improve the city's shipping facilities. The tower was built to protect the city's eastern flank but its decorative spire was added later, when the city felt more secure, by **Hendrick de Keyser** (1565–1621), the architect who did much to create Amsterdam's prickly skyline.

At the north end of the Oude Schans, turn left along busy Prins Hendrik-kade for the 300-metre amble to the **Scheepvaarthuis** (Shipping Building) an unusual edifice at no. 108, on the corner of Binnenkant. Completed in 1917, this is one of the flashiest of the buildings designed by the Amsterdam School of architecture, the work of a certain **Johann Melchior van der Mey** (1878–1949). An almost neurotically decorated edifice covered with a welter of detail celebrating the city's marine connections, the entrance is shaped like a prow and surmounted by statues of Poseidon and Amphitrite, his wife. Up above them are female representations of the four points of the compass, whilst slender turrets and Expressionistic carvings playfully decorate the walls. It's been empty for a while, but renovations are well underway to turn it into a luxury hotel.

Kloveniersburgwal

Heading south along Kloveniersburgwal from Nieuwmarkt, it's a short hoof to the **Trippenhuis** at no. 29, an overblown mansion complete with Corinthian pilasters and a grand frieze built for the Trip family in 1662. One of the richest families in Amsterdam, the Trips were a powerful force among the **Magnificat**, the clique of families (Six, Trip, Hooft and Pauw) who shared power during the Golden Age. One part of the Trip family dealt with the Baltic trade, another with the manufacture of munitions (in which they had the municipal monopoly), but in addition they also had trade interests in Russia and the Middle East, much like the multinationals of today. In the nineteenth century the Rijksmuseum collection was displayed here, but the house now contains the Dutch Academy of Sciences.

Almost directly opposite, on the west bank of the canal, the **Kleine Trippen-huis**, at no. 26 (now a lingerie shop), is by contrast one of the narrowest houses in Amsterdam, albeit with an attractively carved facade and a balustrade featuring centaurs and sphinxes. Legend has it that Mr Trip's coachman was so taken aback by the size of the new family mansion that he exclaimed he would be happy with a home no wider than the Trips' front door – which is exactly what he got; his reaction to his new lodgings is not recorded.

A few metres south, on the corner of Oude Hoogstraat, is the former headquar-ters of the Dutch East India Company, the **Oostindisch Huis**, a monumental red-brick structure with high-pitched gables and perky dormer windows, built in 1605 shortly after the founding of the company. It was from here that the Company organized and regulated its immensely lucrative trading interests in the Far East, importing shiploads of spices, perfumes and exotic woods (see box p.107). This trade underpinned Amsterdam's Golden Age; predictably, the people of what is now Indonesia, the source of most of the raw materials, received little in return. Nevertheless, despite the building's historic significance, the interior is of no interest today, being occupied by university classrooms and offices.

Continuing south, Kloveniersburgwal takes you into the student district, where the buildings here and along adjoining canals house the various departments of the **University of Amsterdam**. At the heart of this is the **Oudemanhuispoort** (Mon–Sat 10am–4pm), a covered passageway that leads between Kloveniersburgwal and OZ Achterburgwal. Now lined by secondhand book stalls, it was formerly part of an almshouse complex for elderly men – hence the unusual name. The buildings on either side are part of the university; their gardens provide a quiet place to rest between sights. Afterwards, you can either wander through the university's peaceful precincts, or, just beyond, cross the south end of Kloveniersburgwal to one of the prettiest corners of the city – a pocket of placid waterways and old canal houses that extends east to **Zwanenburgwal**. Cross the canal along **Staalstraat** and stop at the second of the two little swing bridges for one of the finest views in the city, down the slender **Groenburgwal** with the Zuiderkerk looming beyond.

Zuiderkerk

The **Zuiderkerk** (Mon–Fri 9am–4pm, Sat noon–4pm; free), dating from 1611, was the first Amsterdam church built specifically for the Protestants. It was designed by the prolific architect and sculptor, **Hendrick de Keyser** (see box p.71), whose distinctive – and very popular – style extrapolated elements of traditional Flemish design, with fanciful detail and frilly towers added wherever possible. The basic design of the Zuiderkerk is firmly Gothic, but the soaring tower (Zuidertoren) is a fine illustration of de Keyser's work, coming complete with balconies and balustrades, arches, urns and columns.

The **church** was deconsecrated in the 1930s, but it was here that the bodies of the dead were temporarily stored and piled up during the terrible winter of 1944–45. In the late 1980s, it was turned into a municipal information centre with displays on housing and the environment, plus temporary **exhibitions** revealing the city council's future plans; exhibits on roads and infrastructure changes attract considerable interest. The **tower**, which has a separate entrance, can be climbed during the summer (June–Sept Wed–Sat 2–4pm; €3) and from the top there are sweeping views over the city centre.

St Antoniesbreestraat

You can cut through from the Zuiderkerk to **St Antoniesbreestraat**, which once linked the city centre with the Jewish Quarter. Its huddle of shops and houses was mostly demolished in the 1980s to make way for a main road, but the plan was subsequently abandoned; the buildings that now line most of the street hardly fire the soul, even if the modern symmetries – and cubist, coloured panels – of the apartment blocks that sprawl along part of the street are at least visually arresting. One of the few survivors of all these municipal shenanigans is the **Pintohuis** (Mon & Wed 2–8pm, Fri 2–5pm, Sat 11am–4pm; free), at no. 69, which is now a public library. Easily spotted by its off-white Italianate **facade**, the mansion is named after Isaac de Pinto, a Jew who fled Portugal to escape the Inquisition and subsequently became a founder of the East India Company (see box p.107). Pinto bought this property in 1651 and promptly had it remodelled in grand style, with a facade interrupted by six lofty pilasters, which lead the eye up to the blind balustrade. The mansion was the talk of the town, even more so when de Pinto had the **interior** painted in a similar style to the exterior – pop in to look at the birds and cherubs of the original painted ceiling.

The Grachtengordel

The western reaches of medieval Amsterdam were once enclosed by the **Singel**, part of the city's protective moat, but this is now just the first of five canals that stretch right around the city centre, extending anticlockwise from Brouwersgracht to the River Amstel in a "girdle of canals", or **Grachtengordel**. This is without doubt the most charming part of Amsterdam, a lattice of olive-green waterways and dinky humpback bridges overlooked by street upon street of handsome seventeenth-century canal houses, almost invariably undisturbed by later development. Of the three main canals, **Herengracht** (Gentlemen's Canal) was the first to be dug, followed by **Keizersgracht** (Emperor's Canal), named after the Holy Roman Emperor and fifteenth-century patron of the city, Maximilian. Further out still is **Prinsengracht**, Princes' Canal, named in honour of the princes of the House of Orange.

It's a subtle cityscape – full of surprises, with a bizarre carving here, an unusual facade stone (used to denote name and occupation) there – and one where the **gables** overlooking the canals gradually evolved. The earliest, dating from the early seventeenth century, are crow-stepped gables, but these were largely superseded from the 1650s onwards by neck gables and bell gables, both named for the shape of the gable top. Some are embellished, many have decorative cornices, and the fanciest – which mostly date from the eighteenth century – sport full-scale **balustrades**. The plainest gables are those of former **warehouses**, where the deep-arched and shuttered windows line up to either side of loft doors that were once used for loading and unloading goods, winched by pulley from the street down below. Indeed, outside **pulleys** remain a common feature of houses and warehouses alike, and are often still in use as the easiest way of moving furniture into the city's myriad apartments.

The grandest Grachtengordel houses are concentrated along the so-called **De Gouden Bocht** – the Golden Bend – on Herengracht between Leidsestraat and the Amstel. Here, the architectural decorum – and arguably the aesthetic

This chapter covers the first four canals of the Grachtengordel – the Singel, Herengracht, Keizersgracht and Prinsengracht – as they sweep down from Brouwersgracht to the Amstel. For the purposes of this guide, the district has been split into two: **Grachtengordel west** and **Grachtengordel south** – divided at roughly the halfway point, Leidsegracht. There's no obvious walking route around the area – indeed you may prefer to wander around as the mood takes you – but the description given below goes from north to south, taking in all the highlights on the way. On all three of the main canals, **street numbers** begin at Brouwersgracht and increase as you go south.

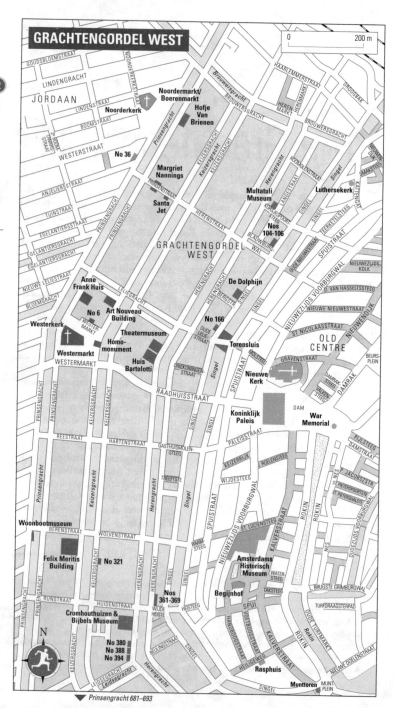

GRACHTENGORDEL WEST

0   200 m

GOUDSBLOEMSTRAAT

LINDENGRACHT

JORDAAN

LINDENSTRAAT

Noorderkerk

BOOMSTRAAT

WESTERSTRAAT

No 36

ANJELIERSTRAAT

TUINSTRAAT

EGELANTIERSSTRAAT

EGELANTIERSGRACHT

NIEUWE LELIESTRAAT

BLOEMGRACHT

Anne Frank Huis

No 6

Westerkerk

Westermarkt

WESTERMARKT

Homo-monument

Huis Bartolotti

Art Nouveau Building

Theatermuseum

Woonbootmuseum

BERENSTRAAT

Felix Meritis Building

No 321

HEESTRAAT

HARTENSTRAAT

RUNSTRAAT

Cromhouthuizen & Bijbels Museum

HUIDENSTRAAT

Nos 361–369

No 380
No 388
No 394

LEIDSEGRACHT

Noordermarkt/Boerenmarkt

Hofje Van Brienen

Margriet Nannings

Santa Jet

PRINSENSTRAAT

HERENSTRAAT

GRACHTENGORDEL WEST

De Dolphijn

HERENGRACHT

HERENGRACHT

No 166

OUDE LELIE-STRAAT

Torensluis

DRIEKONINGEN-STRAAT

RAADHUISSTRAAT

Koninklijk Paleis

GASTHUISMOLEN-STEEG

TREEFTSTE

WIJDESTEEG

WOLVENSTRAAT

RAAM-STEEG

WIJDE HEISTE

BRUUNGSTRAAT

Multatuli Museum

Nos 104–106

BRAUWBURG WAL

HAARLEMMERSTRAAT

Brouwersgracht

HAARLEMMERMARKT

DROOGBAK

BROUWERSGRACHT

IEREN MARKT

ROOMANNSTRAAT

Luthersekerk

SINGEL

KATTENGAT

SMAKSTEEG

BREEUWERS STRAAT

SPUISTRAAT

OUDE NIEUWSTRAAT

NIEUWEZIJDS KOLK

NIEUWEZIJDS VOORBURGWAL

D. VAN HASSELTSSTEEG

NIEUWE NIEUWESTRAAT

ST NICOLAASSTRAAT

OLD CENTRE

NIEUWENDIJK

BEURS-PLEIN

Nieuwe Kerk

GRAVENSTRAAT

DAM

War Memorial

DAMRAK STEEG

DAMRAK

VALKEN-STEEG

PUISTEEG

DAMSTRAAT

KEIZERRIJK

ROKLENSTEEG

ST JACOBSZSTN

ST PIETERSPOORTST

ST PIETERSHALTE

Amsterdams Historisch Museum

WATER-STEEG

Begijnhof

TAKSTEEG

SPUI

BRUGSTE GRIMBURGWAL

TURFDRAAGSTERPAD

DOEZELIJDS VOORBURGWAL

KALVERSTRAAT

ROKIN

ROKIN

NES

Rasphuis

OUDE TURNMARKT

NIEUWE DOELENSTRAAT

Munttoren

MUNT-PLEIN

N

64

Prinsengracht 681–693

vigour – of the seventeenth century are left behind for the overblown, French-influenced mansions that became popular with the city's richest merchants in the 1700s. Nevertheless, it is perhaps the district's overall atmosphere that appeals, rather than any specific sight, with one remarkable exception – the **Anne Frank Huis** (see p.68), where the young, and now internationally famous, Jewish diarist hid from the Nazis in World War II.

Expanding the city

The three main **Grachtengordel canals** – Herengracht, Keizersgracht and Prinsengracht – were dug in the seventeenth century as part of a comprehensive plan to extend the boundaries of a city no longer able to accommodate its burgeoning population. The idea was that the council would buy up the land around the city, dig the canals, and lease plots back to developers, thus increasing the size of the city from two to seven square kilometres. The plan was passed by the city council in 1607 and work began six years later, against a backdrop of corruption, with Amsterdammers in the know buying up the land they thought the city would soon have to purchase.

It was a monumental task, and the conditions imposed by the council were strict. The three **main waterways** were set aside for the residences and businesses of the richer and more influential Amsterdam merchants, while the **radial cross-streets** were reserved for more modest artisans' homes; meanwhile, immigrants, newly arrived to cash in on Amsterdam's booming economy, were assigned, albeit informally, the Jodenhoek (see Chapter Four) and the Jordaan (see Chapter Three).

In the Grachtengordel, everyone – even the wealthiest merchant – had to comply with a set of strict and detailed **planning regulations**. In particular, the council prescribed the size of each building plot – the frontage was set at thirty feet, the depth two hundred – and although there was a degree of tinkering, the end result was the loose conformity you can see today: tall, **narrow residences**, whose individualism is mainly restricted to the stylistic permutations amongst the gables. Even the colour of the front doors was once regulated, with choice restricted to a shade that has since become known as "Amsterdam Green" – still something of a rarity outside Holland. It took decades to complete the project, but by the 1690s it was all pretty much finished off – at a time, ironically, when Amsterdam was in economic decline.

In essence, the Grachtengordel is a tribute to the architectural tastes of the city's middle class, an amalgam of personal wealth and aesthetic uniformity – individuality and order – that epitomized Amsterdam's Protestant bourgeoisie in all its pomp.

Grachtengordel west

Stretching south from the Brouwersgracht to the Leidsegracht, **Grachtengordel west** boasts a fine selection of seventeenth-century canal houses. These are at their prettiest along **Herengracht** between Huidenstraat and Leidsegracht, and this is where you'll also find the **Bijbels Museum** (Bible Museum), home to an odd assortment of models of ancient Jewish temples. Nevertheless, easily the most popular attraction here is the **Anne Frank Huis**, on Prinsengracht, which is itself just a short stroll from the soaring architecture of the **Westerkerk**.

From Brouwersgracht to Prinsenstraat

Running east to west along the northern edge of the three main canals is **Brouwersgracht**, one of the most picturesque waterways in the city. Look down any of the major canals from here and you'll see the gentle interplay of water, barge, brick and stone that gives the city its distinctive draw. Strolling south from Brouwersgracht along the west side of **Prinsengracht**, past a huddle of houseboats, you soon reach the **Noorderkerk** (see p.87), a lugubrious pile on the edge of the Jordaan which oversees the **Noordermarkt**, the site of several markets, including a flea market (Mon 9am–1pm) and the Boerenmarkt, a farmers' produce market (Sat 9am–4pm). Just along the canal from the Noordermarkt, **Prinsengracht 36** has an especially well-proportioned – if attenuated – facade, its neck gable, pilasters and pediment dating from 1650.

Cross the canal at the bridge next to no. 36 and turn left for the **Hofje Van Brienen** (Mon–Fri 6am–6pm & Sat 6am–2pm; free), a brown-brick courtyard complex at Prinsengracht 85–133. Originally the site of a brewery, the *hofje* (see box p.85) was built as an almshouse in 1804 to the order of a certain Arnout van Brienen, who added a matching brick church (no entry) for good measure. A well-to-do merchant, van Brienen had locked himself in his own strongroom by accident and, in a panic, he vowed to build a *hofje* if he was rescued – he was and he did.

From the Hofje Van Brienen, it's the briefest of walks back to the first of the Grachtengordel's cross-streets, **Prinsenstraat** and its continuation **Herenstraat**, where the modest old tradesmen's houses now accommodate a string of knick-knack and clothes shops. Here you'll find a potpourri of handmade Latin American items at Santa Jet, Prinsenstraat 7, and designer clothes at Margriet Nannings, Prinsenstraat 6, 8 & 15.

The Multatuli Museum

Herenstraat opens out into the **Blauwburgwal**, a short and inordinately pretty slip of a canal, which had the misfortune to be hit by a bomb during the German invasion of 1940. The speed of the German victory meant that central Amsterdam was hardly damaged at all, but this incident alone cost 51 lives. From the Blauwburgwal, it's a quick gambol to Amsterdam's tiniest museum, the **Multatuli Museum**, just off the Herengracht at Korsjespoortsteeg 20 (Tues 10am–5pm, Sat & Sun noon–5pm; free; Ⓦ www.multatuli-museum.nl). This was the birthplace of **Eduard Douwes Dekker** (1820–87), Holland's most celebrated nineteenth-century writer and a champion of free thinking, who wrote under the pen name Multatuli. Dekker worked as a colonial official in the Dutch East Indies for eighteen years, becoming increasingly disgusted by the graft and corruption. He returned to Amsterdam in 1856 and spent the next four years encapsulating his East Indies experiences in the elegantly written satirical novel *Max Havelaar*, which enraged the Dutch merchant class, but is now something of a Dutch literary classic (see p.296). The museum's one room is filled with letters, first editions and a small selection of his furnishings, including the **chaise longue** on which he breathed his last.

From the Singel to Leliegracht

Slipping through to the Singel, turn right along the canal to reach **Singel 104–106**, twin mansions dating to the 1740s and equipped with the largest bell gables in the city – big but not especially attractive. Pushing on southwards, it's a short walk to the red-brick and stone-trimmed **De Dolphijn** (The Dolphin), at nos. 140–142. This was once home of Captain Banningh Cocq, one of the militiamen depicted in Rembrandt's *The Night Watch* (see p.119), but it takes its name from a late sixteenth-century Dutch grammar book written by the first owner, one Hendrick Spieghel. Nearby, **Singel 166** has the narrowest facade in the city – just 1.8m wide. It overlooks the **Torensluis**, easily the widest bridge in the Grachtengordel and decorated with a whopping bust of Multatuli.

Cut back along Oude Leliestraat and you soon reach **Leliegracht**, one of the tiny radial canals that cut across the Grachtengordel. It's a charming street, home to a number of bookshops and bars, and it also holds one of the city's finest examples of **Art Nouveau architecture** – the tall and striking building at the Leliegracht-Keizersgracht junction designed by Gerrit van Arkel in 1905. It was

The story of Anne Frank

The story of **Anne**, her family and friends, is well known. Anne's father, **Otto Frank**, was a well-to-do Jewish businessman who fled Germany in December 1933 after Hitler came to power, moving to Amsterdam, where he established a spice-trading business on the Prinsengracht. After the German occupation of the Netherlands, Otto – along with many other Jews – felt that he could avoid trouble by keeping his head down. However, by 1942 it was clear that this would not be possible; Amsterdam's Jews were isolated and conspicuous, being confined to certain parts of the city and forced to wear a yellow star, and roundups were increasingly common. In desperation, Otto Frank decided to move the family into the unused back rooms of their Prinsengracht premises, first asking some of his Dutch office staff if they would help him with the subterfuge – and they bravely agreed. The Franks went into hiding in July 1942, along with a Jewish business partner and his family, the van Pels (renamed the van Daans in the *Diary*). Their new "home" was separated from the rest of the building by a **bookcase** that doubled as a door. As far as everyone else was concerned, they had fled to Switzerland.

So began a two-year incarceration in the **achterhuis**, or rear house, and the two families were joined in November 1942 by a dentist friend, Fritz Pfeffer (the *Diary*'s Albert Dussel). Otto's trusted office staff continued working in the front part of the building, regularly bringing supplies and news of the outside world. In her diary Anne Frank describes the **day-to-day lives** of the inhabitants of the Secret Annex: the quarrels, frequent in such a claustrophobic environment, celebrations of birthdays, or of a piece of good news from the Allied Front; and of her own, slightly unreal, growing up (much of which, it's been claimed, was later deleted by her father).

In 1944, the atmosphere was optimistic; the Allies were clearly winning the war and liberation seemed within reach – but it wasn't to be. One day in the summer of that year, the Franks were **betrayed** by a Dutch collaborator; the Gestapo arrived and forced open the bookcase. The occupants of the Secret Annex were arrested and dispatched to Westerbork – the transit camp in the north of the country where all Dutch Jews were processed before being moved to Belsen or Auschwitz. Of the eight from the Annex, only Otto Frank survived; Anne and her sister died of typhus within a short time of each other in **Belsen**, just one week before the German surrender.

Anne Frank's **diary** was among the few things left behind in the Annex. It was retrieved by one of the family's Dutch helpers and handed to Otto on his return from Auschwitz. In 1947, Otto decided to publish his daughter's diary; since then, it has been translated into over sixty languages and sold literally millions of copies. The identity of the collaborator has never been confirmed.

67

originally the headquarters of a life insurance company, hence the two mosaics with angels recommending policies to bemused earthlings.

The Anne Frank Huis

In 1960, the Anne Frank Foundation set up the **Anne Frank Huis** (daily: mid-March to mid-Sept 9am–9pm; mid-Sept to mid-March 9am–7pm; closed Yom Kippur; €7.50, 10- to 17-year-olds €3.50, under-9s free; ☎020/556 7105, Ⓦwww.annefrank.org) in the premises on Prinsengracht where the young diarist and her family hid from the Germans during World War II. Since the posthumous publication of her diaries, Anne Frank has become extraordinarily famous, in the first instance for recording the iniquities of the Holocaust, and latterly as a symbol of the fight against oppression and especially racism, themes explored in a challenging exhibition seen at the end of a visit.

The **rooms**, also known as the Secret Annex or *achterhuis*, that the Franks occupied for two years, though stripped of furniture, still bear traces of their former occupants – such as the movie-star pin-ups in Anne's bedroom and the marks on the wall recording the children's heights. Remarkably, despite the number of visitors, there is a real sense of the personal here, and most find a visit to the Secret Annex a very moving experience. Video clips about the family in particular and the Holocaust in general provide some background information.

Anne Frank was only one of about 100,000 Dutch Jews who died during World War II, but this, her final home, provides one of the most enduring testaments to its horrors. Her diary has been a source of inspiration to many, including Nelson Mandela and Primo Levi.

Due to the popularity of the Anne Frank Huis, the queues can be on the long side; try to come early or late to avoid the crush – or book a slot online and skip the queue altogether.

The Westerkerk

Trapped in the *achterhuis*, Anne Frank liked to listen to the bells of the **Westerkerk** (April–Sept Mon–Fri 11am–3pm; free; Ⓦwww.westerkerk.nl), just along Prinsengracht, until they were taken away to be melted down for the German war effort. The church still dominates the district, its 85-metre **tower** (same hours; €5) – without question Amsterdam's finest – soaring graciously above its surroundings and offering panoramic views of the city centre from its balconies. On its top perches the crown of the Emperor Maximilian, a constantly recurring symbol of Amsterdam (see p.44) and the finishing touch to what was then only the second city church to be built expressly for the Protestants. The church was designed by **Hendrick de Keyser** (see box p.71) and completed ten years after his death in 1631. Its construction was part of the general enlargement of the city, but whereas the exterior is all studied elegance, the interior – as required by the Calvinist congregation – is bare and plain. Apart from the soaring stone columns and long windows, which allow the light to pour in, the only feature of note is the fancy wooden pulpit, where Protestant ministers once thundered away for hours on end.

The Westerkerk was also the last resting place of **Rembrandt**, though the location of his pauper's tomb is not known. Instead, a small memorial in the north aisle commemorates the artist, close to the spot where his son Titus was buried. Rembrandt adored his son – as evidenced by numerous portraits – and the boy's death dealt a final crushing blow to the ageing and embittered artist, who died just over a year later. During renovation of the church in the early

△ The Westerkerk

1990s, **bones** were unearthed that could have been those of Rembrandt – a possibility whose tourist potential excited the church authorities no end. Admittedly it was a long shot – paupers' tombs were usually cleared of their accumulated bodies every twenty years or so – but the obvious way to prove it was through a chemical analysis of the bones' lead content, expected to be unusually high if they were his, as lead was a major ingredient of paint. The bones were duly taken to the University of Groningen for analysis, but the tests proved inconclusive.

Westermarkt

Westermarkt, an open square in the shadow of the Westerkerk, contains two evocative statues. Just to the south of the church entrance, by Prinsengracht, is a small, poignant statue of **Anne Frank** by the gifted Dutch sculptor Mari Andriessen (1897–1979), who was also the creator of the dockworker statue

△ Anne Frank statue

outside Amsterdam's Esnoga (see p.100). The second piece, behind the church, beside Keizersgracht, consists of three pinkish granite triangles (one each for the past, present and future) of the **Homomonument**. The world's first memorial to persecuted gays and lesbians, commemorating all those who died at the hands of the Nazis, it was designed by Karin Daan and recalls the pink triangles the Germans made homosexuals sew onto their clothes during World War II. The monument has become a focus for the city's gay community and the site of ceremonies and wreath-laying throughout the year, most notably on Queen's Day (April 30), Coming-Out Day (Sept 5) and World AIDS Day (Dec 1). The monument's inscription, by the Dutch writer Jacob Israel de Haan, translates as "Such an infinite desire for friendship".

The French philosopher **René Descartes** (1596–1650) once lodged at Westermarkt 6, a handsome building with an attractive neck gable and fancy fanlight. Apparently happy that the Dutch were indifferent to his musings – and that therefore he wasn't going to be persecuted – he wrote "Everybody except me is in business and so absorbed by profit-making that I could spend my entire life here without being noticed by a soul", though this declaration may itself have been subterfuge; it's possible that Descartes was spying on the Dutch for the Habsburg King Philip II of Spain, a possibility explored in detail in A.C. Grayling's recent book entitled *Descartes: The Life and Times of a Genius*. In the event, Descartes spent twenty years in the Netherlands before accepting an invitation from Queen Christina to go to Stockholm in 1649. It turned out to be a poor choice; no sooner had he got there, than he caught pneumonia and died.

The Theatermuseum and Huis Bartolotti

A short walk from the Westermarkt, past the curving neo-Gothic terraces of **Raadhuisstraat**, is the enjoyable **Theatermuseum**, at Herengracht 168 (Mon–Fri 11am–5pm, Sat & Sun 1–5pm; €4.50; ⓦwww.tin.nl). The museum, which spreads over into the building next door, contains a diverting collection of theatrical bygones, from props through to stage sets, with a particularly good section devoted to puppets and puppetry. There is also a small display on modern Dutch theatre, featuring seminal stage sets; this adjoins the most unusual exhibit of all, the so-called **Chamber Theatre** of 1781. Built for the domestic delight of one of the city's richest merchants, one Baron van Slinge-landt, this miniature theatre – apparently the only one of its type to have survived in the whole of Europe – is equipped with a network of wooden handles by means of which the scenery can be changed and simple special effects introduced – cloudy skies, rolling seas and so forth. Currently, visitors can't have a go themselves, but there is a toy-town version in the same room, and you can twiddle away here to your heart's content.

The museum offers a lively programme of temporary exhibitions too, but just as interesting is the building itself, a classic canal house designed by **Philip Vingboons** (1607–78), arguably the most talented architect involved in the creation of the Grachtengordel. The house was built for Michael de Pauw, a leading light in the East India Company in the 1630s, its fetching sandstone facade a suitably grand preamble to an interior that sports a riot of flamboyant stucco work, verdant Italianate wall paintings and a splendid spiral staircase.

Next door, the **Huis Bartolotti**, at Herengracht 170–172 (no public access), is a tad older and a good deal flashier than its neighbour, its pirouetting facade of red brick and stone dotted with urns and columns, gargoyles and cherubs. The house is an excellent illustration of the Dutch Renaissance style: much more ornate than the typical Amsterdam canal house. The architect was **Hendrick de Keyser** (see box below), with a director of the West India Company, a certain Willem van den Heuvel, footing the bill. Van den Heuvel inherited a fortune from his Italian uncle and changed his name in his honour to Bartolotti – hence the name of the house.

Hendrick de Keyser

Born in Utrecht, the son of a carpenter, **Hendrick de Keyser** (1565–1621) moved to Amsterdam in 1591. Initially employed as an apprentice sculptor, de Keyser soon ventured out on his own, speedily establishing himself as one of the city's most sought-after sculptor-architects. In 1595 he was appointed the city's official stone-mason, becoming city architect too in 1612. His municipal commissions included three churches – the Zuiderkerk (see p.62), the Noorderkerk (see p.87) and the Westerkerk (see p.68) – and the upper storeys of the Munttoren (see p.82). His domestic designs were, however, more playful – or at least ornate – and it was here that he pioneered what is often called **Amsterdam Renaissance style**, in which Italianate decorative details – tympani, octagonal turrets, pilasters, pinnacles and arcades – were imposed on traditional Dutch design. The usual media were red brick and sandstone trimmings – as in the Huis Bartolotti.

71

South to the Woonbootmuseum and the Felix Meritis building

Between Westermarkt and Leidsegracht, the main canals are intersected by a trio of **cross streets**, which are themselves divided into shorter streets, mostly named after animals whose pelts were once used in the local tanning industry. There's Reestraat (Deer Street), Hartenstraat (Hart), Berenstraat (Bear) and Wolvenstraat (Wolf), not to mention Huidenstraat (Street of Hides) and Runstraat – a "run" being a bark used in tanning. The tanners are long gone and today these are all eminently appealing **shopping streets**, where you can buy everything from carpets and handmade chocolates to designer toothbrushes and beeswax candles.

Away from the side streets, back on the Prinsengracht, the **Woonbootmuseum** (Houseboat Museum; March–Oct Tues–Sun 11am–5pm; Nov–Feb Fri–Sun same hours; €3.25; ⓦ www.houseboatmuseum.nl), opposite Prinsengracht 296, is an old Dutch houseboat of 1914 that doubles as a tourist attraction with a handful of explanatory plaques about life on the water. Some 3000 barges and houseboats are connected to the city's gas and electricity networks. They are regularly inspected and there are strict controls to ensure their numbers don't proliferate.

From the boat, it's one block east along Berenstraat to the **Felix Meritis building**, at Keizersgracht 324. A Neoclassical monolith built in 1787, the mansion was built to house a science and arts society, which was the cultural focus of the city's upper crust for nearly one hundred years. Dutch cultural aspirations did not, however, impress everyone. It's said that when Napoleon visited Amsterdam the entire building was redecorated for his reception, only to have him stalk out in disgust, claiming that the place stank of tobacco. Oddly enough, it later became the headquarters of the Dutch Communist Party, but they sold it to the council who now lease it to the Felix Meritis Foundation (ⓦ www.felix.meritis.nl), which hosts a mixed bag of conferences and concerts (see p.215).

Keizersgracht 321 and Han van Meegeren

On the other side of the canal, **Keizersgracht 321** is in itself fairly innocuous, but this was once the home of the Dutch art forger **Han van Meegeren** (1889–1947). During the German occupation of World War II, Meegeren sold a "previously unknown" Vermeer to a German art dealer working for Herman Goering; what neither the agent nor Goering realized was that Meegeren had painted it himself. A forger *par excellence*, Meegeren had developed a sophisticated ageing technique in the early 1930s. He mixed his paints with phenol formaldehyde resin dissolved in benzene and then baked the finished painting in an oven for several hours; the end result fooled everyone, including the curators of the Rijksmuseum, who had bought another "Vermeer" from him in 1941.

The forgeries may well have never been discovered but for a strange sequence of events. In May 1945 a British captain by the name of Harry Anderson discovered Meegeren's "Vermeer" in Goering's art collection. Meegeren was promptly arrested as a collaborator and, to get himself out of a pickle, he soon confessed to this and other forgeries, arguing that he had duped and defrauded the Nazis rather than helping them – though he had, of course, pocketed the money. It was a fine argument and his reward was a short prison sentence – but in the event he died before he was locked up.

Herengracht 361–369 and the Cromhouthuizen

From Keizersgracht 321, double back to cut across Wolvenstraat, and turn right for **Herengracht 361–369**, a row of five houses, where you can compare and contrast the main types of **gable**: stepped at no. 361, bell at nos. 365 and 367 and neck at no. 369. Across the canal, at Herengracht 364–370, the graceful and commanding **Cromhouthuizen** consist of four matching stone mansions, embellished with tendrils, carved fruit and scrollwork, graced by charming little bull's-eye windows and capped by elegant neck gables. Built in the 1660s for one of Amsterdam's wealthy merchant families, the Cromhouts, the houses were designed by Philip **Vingboons** (1607–78), the most inventive of the architects who worked on the Grachtengordel during the city's expansion. As a Catholic, Vingboons was confined to private commissions – inconvenient no doubt, but at a time when Protestants and Catholics were at each other's throats right across Europe, hardly insufferable. Two of the houses have been adapted to hold the Bijbels Museum.

The Bijbels Museum

The lavish interiors of the Cromhouthuizen disappeared years ago, but the two buildings that now hold the **Bijbels Museum** (Bible Museum; Mon–Sat 10am–5pm, Sun 11am–5pm; €7.50; @ www.bijbelsmuseum.nl), at Herengracht 366-368, do still exhibit several decorative flourishes from their original function as homes for the rich. The best examples are on the ground floor behind the museum entrance, and comprise a striking spiral staircase and two painted ceilings of classical gods and goddesses by Jacob de Wit. You'll spot these at the end of a visit to the museum, which begins on Floor 3 (the top floor), where there's a large and detailed nineteenth-century model of the **Tabernacle**, the portable sanctuary in which the Israelites carried their holy of holies, the Ark of the Covenant. Attempts to reconstruct biblical scenes were something of a cottage industry in the Netherlands in the late 1800s, with scores of Dutch antiquarians beavering away, Bible in one hand and modelling equipment in the other, but the creator of this particular model, a Protestant vicar by the name of **Leendert Schouten** (1828–1905), went one step further, making it his lifetime's work. It was a good move; Schouten became a well-known figure and his model proved a popular attraction, drawing hundreds of visitors to his home. Schouten also assembled an interesting assortment of Middle Eastern **archeological finds** dating from the period when the Israelites were in exile in Egypt, and these are displayed on the third floor too.

Floor 2 sticks to a similar theme, with the main exhibit being a large and detailed model of Jerusalem's Temple Mount made at the end of the nineteenth century when Palestine was part of the Ottoman Empire. There are yet more models of the Temple on Floor 1, one at the time of Herod, another of when Solomon was king, and an outstanding collection of **antique Bibles** in the cellar. Arguably the most important of these Bibles is the official Statenvertaling (literally State's Translation), published in 1637. Key to the development of Dutch Protestantism, the Statenvertaling was the result of years of study by the leading scholars of the Netherlands, who returned to the original Greek and Hebrew texts for this translation; it sold by the cartload.

Herengracht 380–394

The gracious symmetries of the Cromhouthuizen contrast with the grandiose pretension of **Herengracht 380**, built in the style of a French chateau for a tobacco planter in 1889. Ornately decorated, the mansion's main gable is embellished with reclining figures and the bay window by cherubs, mythical characters and an abundance of acanthus leaves; it was also the first house in the city to be supplied with electricity. Roughly opposite, across the canal, is the only spot in Amsterdam where the houses come straight out of the water, Venice-like, without the intervention of a pavement.

Keeping to the west side of the canal, **Herengracht 388** is another handsome Philip Vingboons building, whilst **Herengracht 394**, the narrow house with the bell gable at the corner of Leidsegracht, bears a distinctive **facade stone** that illustrates the legend of the four Aymon brothers, who are depicted astride their steed. The subject of a popular medieval chanson, the legend is all about honour, loyalty and friendship, dynastic quarrels and disputes, revolving around the trials and tribulations of the horse. The long and rambling tale ends when the redoubtable beast repeatedly breaks free from the millstones tied around its neck and refuses to drown; the third time it comes to the surface, the brothers walk away, no longer able to watch the agonies of their animal. Assuming he's been abandoned, the horse cries out and promptly expires.

Leidsegracht

Herengracht 394 abuts the **Leidsegracht**, a mostly residential canal, lined with chic town houses and a medley of handsome gables. It's a tranquil scene – or at least it would be were it not for the flat-topped tour boats, which use the canal as a short cut, billowing out diesel fumes as they shunt into and out of Prinsengracht. An eighteenth-century wine merchant by the name of Paling would have welcomed the sight of a boat, when he slipped into the Leidsegracht on a dark November evening. Well known as one of the greediest men in Amsterdam, he could apparently shovel down seven pounds of beef, a leg of lamb and thirty herrings in one sitting. He also liked his wine, a weakness that prompted his early demise when he fell – or staggered – into the Leidsegracht.

Stroll out along Leidsegracht and turn left for **Prinsengracht 681–693**, where an exquisite set of seven neck gables – one for each of the provinces that originally broke away from the Habsburgs – comprises an especially harmonious ensemble that dates back to 1715. From here, it's an easy stroll to Leidseplein and Leidsestraat (see pp.76–77).

Grachtengordel south

Grachtengordel south holds many of the city's proudest and most touted mansions, clustered along **De Gouden Bocht** – the Golden Bend – the curve of Herengracht between Leidsestraat and the River Amstel. It's on this stretch that the merchant elite abandoned the material modesty of their Calvinist forebears, indulging themselves with lavish mansions, whose fancy facades more than hinted at the wealth within. In the late seventeenth and eighteenth centuries, this elite also forsook brick for stone and the restrained details of traditional Dutch architecture for pompous Neoclassicism, their defeat of the Spanish Habsburgs, allied with their commercial success, prompting them to compare themselves to the Greeks and Romans. In the event, it was all an illusion – the bubble burst when Napoleon's army arrived in 1793 – and, although the opulent interiors of two old mansions, the **Museum Willet-Holthuysen** and the **Van Loon Museum**, still

GRACHTENGORDEL SOUTH

Esnoga

JONAS DANIËL
MEIJERPLEIN

WEESPERSTRAAT

WATERLOOPLEIN

River Amstel

Muziektheater

Waterlooplein M

Amstel Sluizen

Magere Brug

Museum Willet-Holthuysen

AMSTEL

UTRECHTSESTRAAT

Schiller Hotel

REMBRANDT PLEIN

AMSTELSTRAAT

THORBECKE-PLEIN

Amstelveld

Amstelkerk

REGULIERSGRACHT

REGULIERSGRACHT

Frederiks Plein

WESTEINDE

OOSTEINDE

SARPHATISTRAAT

HUIDEKOPERSTRAAT

Muntoren

MUNT-PLEIN

Tuschinski

REGULIERS DWARSSTRAAT

Kattenkabinet

No 507

FOAM

Nos 508-510

Museum Van Loon

Bloemenmarkt

SINGEL

No 493

No 475

Nederlandsche Handelsmaatschappij

DE GOUDEN BOCHT

De Appel

GRACHTENGORDEL SOUTH

KEIZERSGRACHT

PRINSENGRACHT

NOORDERSTRAAT

VIJZELGRACHT

NIEUWE LOOIERSSTRAAT

FOKKE SIMONSZSTRAAT

WETERINGSCHANS

Lijnbaansgracht

Singelgracht

DEN TEXSTRAAT

NIC. WITSENSTRAAT

NICOLAAS WITSENKADE

STADHOUDERSKADE

Metz & Co.

KEIZERSGRACHT

KERKSTRAAT

VIJZELSTRAAT

NIEUWE SPIEGELSTRAAT

SPIEGELKWARTIER

PRINSENGRACHT

WETERINGDWARSSTR.

WETERINGSTRAAT

SPIEGELGRACHT

2e

1e

LEIDSESTRAAT

KEIZERSGRACHT

KERKSTRAAT

PRINSENGRACHT

Nos 681-693

Stadsschouwburg

LEIDSEDWARSSTRAAT

LANGE LEIDSEDWARSSTRAAT

KORTE LEIDSEDWARSSTRAAT

LEIDSE-PLEIN

American Hotel

MARNIXSTRAAT

LEIDSEKADE

LIJNBAANSGRACHT

ZIESENISKADE

Singelgracht

WETERINGSCHANS

STADHOUDERSKADE

Rijksmuseum

HOBBEMAKADE

RUYSDAELKADE

MUSEUM PLEIN

HOBBEMASTRAAT

MARNIXSTRAAT

LEIDSEKADE

STADHOUDERSKADE

ZANDPAD

VOSSIUSSTRAAT

SCHARP HUIS HOOFTSTRAAT

JAN LUIJKENSTRAAT

PIETER CORNELISZ HOOFTSTRAAT

PAULUS POTTERSTRAAT

Van Gogh Museum

VERMEERSTRAAT

MUSEUM QUARTER

N

0   200 m

give a flavour of those heady days, for the most part all that's left – albeit a substantial legacy – are the wonderful facades.

Grachtengordel south contains some rather less savoury areas too, where ill-considered twentieth-century development has blemished the city, especially in the seediness of the **Rembrandtplein** and the mediocrity of both Vijzelstraat and **Leidseplein**.

Leidseplein

Lying on the edge of the Grachtengordel, **Leidseplein** is the bustling hub of Amsterdam's nightlife, a somewhat cluttered and disorderly open space that has never had much architectural character. The square once marked the end of the road in from Leiden and, as horse-drawn traffic was banned from the centre at the time, it was here that the Dutch left their horses and carts – a sort of equine car park. Today, it's quite the opposite; relentless traffic made up of trams, bikes, cars and pedestrians gives the place a frenetic feel, and the surrounding side streets are jammed with bars, restaurants and clubs in a bright jumble of jutting signs and neon lights. It's not surprising, therefore, that on a good night Leidseplein can be Amsterdam at its carefree, exuberant best.

Leidseplein also contains two buildings of some architectural merit. The first is the grandiose **Stadsschouwburg**, a neo-Renaissance edifice dating back to 1894 that was so widely criticized for its clumsy vulgarity that the city council of the day temporarily withheld the money for decorating the exterior. Home to the National Ballet and Opera until the Muziektheater (see p.214) was

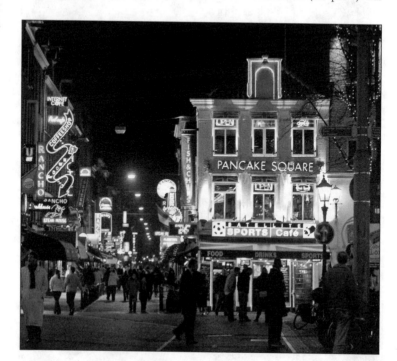

△ Leidseplein

completed on Waterlooplein in 1986, it is now used for theatre, dance and music performances (see p.214). However, its most popular function is as the place where the Ajax football team gathers on the balcony to wave to the crowds whenever they win anything – as they often do.

Close by, just off the square on Leidsekade, is one of the city's oddest buildings, the **American Hotel**, whose monumental and slightly disconcerting rendering of Art Nouveau comes complete with angular turrets, chunky dormer windows and fancy brickwork. Completed in 1902, the present structure takes its name from its demolished predecessor, which was – as the stylistic peccadillo of its architect, one W. Steinigeweg – adorned with statues and murals of North American scenes. Inside the present hotel is the *Café Americain*, once the fashionable haunt of Amsterdam's literati, but now a mainstream location for coffee and lunch. The Art Nouveau decor is still worth a peek – an artful combination of stained glass, shallow arches and geometric patterned brickwork.

Leidsestraat and the Spiegelkwartier

Heading northeast from Leidseplein is **Leidsestraat**, one of Amsterdam's principal shopping streets, comprising a long, slender gauntlet of fast food, fashion and shoe shops of little distinction. That said, the department store **Metz & Co**, at the junction with Keizersgracht, does occupy a good-looking stone building of 1891, its facade adorned by caryatids and topped by a distinctive corner dome. At the time of its construction, it was the tallest commercial building in the city – one reason why the owners were able to entice **Gerrit Rietveld** (1888–1964), the leading architectural light of the artistic movement De Stijl, to add a rooftop glass and metal showroom in 1933. The showroom has survived and is now a café offering an attractive view over the city centre; perhaps surprisingly, Rietveld designed just one other building in Amsterdam – the Van Gogh Museum (see p.20).

One block east of Metz & Co is Nieuwe Spiegelstraat, an appealing mix of shops and cafés, which extends south into Spiegelgracht to form the **Spiegelkwartier**. The district is home to the pricey end of Amsterdam's antiques trade and **De Appel**, a lively centre for contemporary art with well-presented, temporary exhibitions, at Nieuwe Spiegelstraat 10 (Tues–Sun 11am–6pm; €4; ⓦ www.deappel.nl).

De Gouden Bocht

Nieuwe Spiegelstraat meets the elegant sweep of Herengracht near the west end of the so-called **De Gouden Bocht** (The Golden Bend), where the canal is overlooked by a long sequence of double-fronted mansions, some of the most opulent dwellings in the city. Most of the houses here were extensively remodelled in the late seventeenth and eighteenth centuries. Characteristically, they have double stairways leading to the entrance, underneath which the small door was for the servants, whilst up above the majority are topped off by the ornamental cornices that were fashionable at the time. Classical references are common, both in form – pediments, columns and pilasters – and decoration, from scrolls and vases through to geometric patterns inspired by ancient Greece.

One of the first buildings to look out for on the north side of the canal – just across from (and to the west of) Nieuwe Spiegelstraat – is **Herengracht 475**, an extravagant stone mansion decorated with allegorical figures and surmounted by a slender balustrade. Typically, the original building was a much more modest

△ De Gouden Bocht

affair, dating from the 1660s, but eighty years later the new owner took matters in hand to create the ornate facade of today. Just along the canal to the east, **Herengracht 493** is similarly grand, though here the building is polished off with an extravagantly carved pediment. Further east along the canal, Herengracht 497 is, by comparison, rather restrained, but the interior has been turned into the peculiar **Kattenkabinet** (Cat Cabinet; Tues–Fri 10am–2pm, Sat & Sun 1–5pm; €5; Ⓦ www.kattenkabinet.nl), an enormous collection of art and artefacts relating to cats. They were installed by a Dutch financier, whose cherished moggy, John Pierpont Morgan (named after the American financier), died in 1984; feline fanatics will be delighted by the heartfelt tribute.

A hop, skip and a jump away, **Herengracht 507** is an especially handsome house, though not too grand, its Neoclassical pilasters, pediment, mini-balcony and double-stairway nicely balanced by its slender windows. It was once the home of Jacob Boreel, one-time mayor, whose attempt to impose a burial tax started a riot during which the mob ransacked his house. Opposite, at the corner of Vijzelstraat, is the monumentally incongruous Nederlandsche Handelsmaatschappij, a heavyweight structure with Expressionistic flourishes that dates back to 1923. Across Vijzelstraat and a few steps along the canal, the facades of **Herengracht 508–510** are worth close inspection; their neck gables, dating from the 1690s, sport sea gods which straddle dolphins and tritons – half-men, half-fish – whilst trumpeting through conch shells to pacify the oceans.

The Museum Willet-Holthuysen

The **Museum Willet-Holthuysen** (Mon–Fri 10am–5pm, Sat & Sun 11am–5pm; €5; Ⓦ www.museumwilletholthuysen.nl), near the Amstel at Herengracht 605, is billed as "the only fully furnished patrician house open to the public", which just about sums it up. The house dates from 1685, but the interior was remodelled by successive members of the coal-trading Holthuysen family until the last of the line, Sandra Willet-Holthuysen, donated her home and its contents to the city in 1895.

The museum entrance is through the old servants' door, leading into the basement, which holds a small collection of porcelain and earthenware. Up above are the family rooms, most memorably the **Blue Room**, which has been returned to its original, eighteenth-century Rococo splendour, a flashy and ornate style copied from France that Dutch merchants held to be the epitome of refinement and good taste. Other rooms have the more cluttered appearance of the nineteenth century – the Dining Room and the Ballroom being two cases in point.

The top floor exhibits the small fine and applied art collection assembled by Sandra's husband, Abraham Willet. There are Dutch ceramics, pewter and silverware here as well as four finely carved ivory pieces depicting the elements, made in Germany in the eighteenth century. Amongst the paintings, look out for a landscape by Willem Maris (1844–1910) and a distinctly smug self-portrait of Abraham at the age of 28.

At the back of the house lie the formal **gardens**, a neat pattern of miniature hedges graced by the occasional stone statue.

△ The Museum Willet-Holthuysen

The Amstel and the Magere Brug

Just east of Willet-Holthuysen, Herengracht comes to an abrupt halt beside the wide and windy **River Amstel**, which was long the main trade route into the Dutch interior – goods arriving by barge and boat were traded for the imported materials held in Amsterdam's many warehouses. Turning left here takes you to the Blauwbrug (Blue Bridge) and the Old Jewish Quarter (see Chapter Four), whilst in the opposite direction is the **Magere Brug** (Skinny Bridge), the most famous and arguably the cutest of the city's many swing bridges. Legend has it that the current bridge, which dates back to about 1670, replaced an even older and skinnier version, originally built by two sisters who lived on opposite sides of the river and were fed up with having to walk so far to see each other.

From the bridge, it's a few metres further south along the Amstel to the **Amstel sluizen**, the Amstel locks. Every night, the municipal water department closes these locks to begin the process of sluicing out the canals. A huge pumping station on an island out to the east of the city then starts to pump fresh water from the IJsselmeer into the canal system; similar locks on the west side of the city are left open for the surplus to flow into the IJ and, from there, out to sea via the North Sea Canal. The city's canal water is thus refreshed every three nights – though, what with three centuries of shopping trolleys, rusty bikes and general detritus, the water is only appealing as long as you're not actually in it.

Reguliersgracht and FOAM

From the Amstel sluizen, head west along the north side of Prinsengracht and you'll soon reach the small open space of the **Amstelveld**, popular for impromptu football games, with the seventeenth-century **Amstelkerk**, made of plain white wood, occupying one of its corners. It's here also that Prinsengracht intersects with **Reguliersgracht**, perhaps the prettiest of the three surviving radial canals that cut across the Grachtengordel – its dainty humpback bridges and green waters overlooked by charming seventeenth- and eighteenth-century canal houses.

Proceeding north up Reguliersgracht, turn left onto the north side of Keizersgracht for **FOAM**, at Keizersgracht 609 (Fotografiemuseum; Sat–Wed 10am–5pm, Thurs & Fri 10am–9pm; €7; ⓦwww.foam.nl), which offers a lively programme of photographic exhibitions, many of which have a local (and very modish) theme.

The Museum Van Loon

Across the canal from FOAM, the **Museum Van Loon**, at Keizersgracht 672 (Wed–Mon 11am–5pm; €6; ⓦwww.musvloon.box.nl), boasts the grandest canal house interior open to the public in Amsterdam. The first tenant of the property, built in 1672, was the artist Ferdinand Bol, who married an exceedingly wealthy widow and promptly hung up his easel for the rest of his days. The last owners were the van Loons, co-founders of the East India Company and long one of the city's leading families, though they came something of a cropper at the end of World War II. In 1884, one of the family, Hendrik, purchased this house for his son Willem, on the occasion of his marriage to Thora Egidius. Thora had friends and relatives in Germany and during the occupation she entertained them – unwisely, considering that several of her guests were high-ranking Nazi officials. After the war, allegations of collaboration besmirched Thora's reputation and an embarrassed Queen Wilhelmina fired Thora as her *dame du palais*, a position she had held since 1898; Thora died two months later.

The **interior** of the house has been returned to something akin to its eighteenth-century appearance, with oodles of wood panelling and fancy stucco work. Highlights include the ornate copper **balustrade** on the staircase, into which is worked the name "Van Hagen-Trip" (after the former owners of the house); the van Loons filled the spaces between the letters with fresh iron curlicues to prevent their children falling through. The top-floor landing has several pleasant **paintings** of Roman figures, and one of the bedrooms – the "painted room" – is decorated with a Romantic painting of Italy, depicting a coastal scene with overgrown classical ruins and diligent peasants. Such artistic conceits were a favourite motif with Amsterdam's bourgeoisie from around 1750 to 1820. The oddest items are the **fake bedroom doors**; the eighteenth-century owners were so keen to avoid any lack of symmetry that they camouflaged the real doors and created imitation, decorative replacements in the "correct" position instead. The other oddity is at the bottom of the garden, where the old **coach house** has *trompe l'oeil* windows; again, symmetry dictated that the building must have windows, but no self-respecting plutocrat wanted to be watched by his servants – hence the illusion.

Thorbeckeplein, Rembrandtplein and Reguliersbreestraat

Returning to Reguliersgracht, it's a couple of minutes' walk north to short and stumpy **Thorbeckeplein**, where an assortment of unexciting bars and restaurants flanks a statue of **Rudolf Thorbecke** (1798–1872), a far-sighted liberal politician and three-times Dutch premier whose reforms served to democratize the country in the aftermath of the European-wide turmoil of 1848.

Thorbeckeplein leads into **Rembrandtplein**, a dishevelled patch of greenery that was formerly Amsterdam's butter market. The square took its present name in 1876, and is today one of the city's nightlife centres, although its crowded restaurants and bars are firmly tourist-targeted. Rembrandt's **statue** stands in the middle, his back wisely turned against the square's worst excesses, including a platoon of life-size bronze statues copied from Rembrandt's most famous painting, *The Night Watch* (see p.119). Of the prodigious number of cafés and bars here, only the café of the *Schiller Hotel* at no. 26 stands out, with an original Art Deco interior lit by geometrical chandeliers and decorated with stained-glass windows.

The narrow streets edging Rembrandtplein aren't exactly peaceful either. The crumbling alleys to the north contain several of the city's raunchier gay bars, whilst **Reguliersbreestraat** is just supremely tacky. Nevertheless, tucked in among the slot-machine arcades, fast-food joints and sex shops is the city's most extraordinary cinema – the **Tuschinski**, at Reguliersbreestraat 26–28. Opened in 1921 by a Polish Jew, Abram Tuschinski, the cinema boasts a marvellously well-preserved Art Deco facade and interior, which also features coloured marble and a wonderful carpet, handwoven in Marrakesh to an original design. Tuschinski himself died in Auschwitz in 1942. The network of alleys behind the cinema was once known as **Duivelshoek** (Devil's Corner), and, although it's been tidied up and sanitized, enough backstreet seediness remains to make it a spot to be avoided late at night.

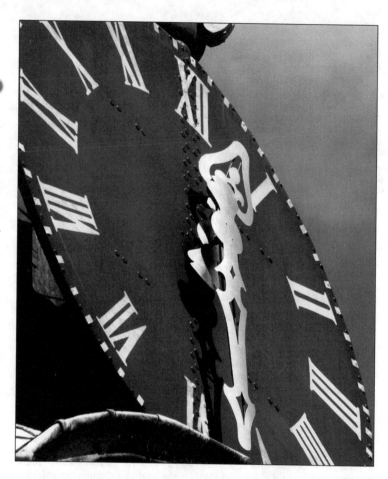

△ The Munttoren

The Munttoren and Bloemenmarkt

Reguliersbreestraat leads west to **Muntplein**, a dishevelled square where the sturdy **Munttoren** of 1480 was originally part of the old city wall. Later, it was adopted as the municipal mint – hence its name – a plain brick structure to which Hendrick de Keyser (see box p.71), in one of his last commissions, added a flashy **spire** in 1620. Metres away, on the southern bank of the Singel, lies the floating **Bloemenmarkt** (flower market; Mon–Sat 8.30am–5pm, though some stalls open on Sun), which is popular with locals and tourists alike. The market is one of the main suppliers of flowers to central Amsterdam, but its blooms and bulbs now share stall space with souvenir clogs, garden gnomes and delftware.

The Jordaan and Western docklands

L ying to the west of the city centre, the **Jordaan** (pronounced "yoar-darn") is a likeable and easily explored area of slender canals and narrow streets flanked by an agreeable mix of architectural styles, from modest, modern terraces to handsome seventeenth-century canal houses. Traditionally the home of Amsterdam's working class, with its boundaries clearly defined by the Prinsengracht to the east and the Lijnbaansgracht in the west, the Jordaan's character has been transformed in recent years by a middle-class influx, and the district is now one of the city's most sought-after residential neighbourhoods. Before then, and indeed until the late 1970s, the Jordaan's inhabitants were primarily stevedores and factory workers, earning a crust amongst the docks, warehouses, factories and boat yards that extended beyond **Brouwersgracht**, the Jordaan's northeastern boundary and nowadays one of Amsterdam's prettiest canals. Specific sights are few and far between, but nonetheless it's still a pleasant area to wander around.

The pint-sized **Scheepvaartsbuurt** (Shipping Quarter), part of the city's old industrial belt and now a mixed shopping and residential quarter, edges the Jordaan to the north, bisected by Haarlemmerstraat and its continuation Haarlemmerdijk. Just to the north lie the **Western docklands** or Westerdok, the oldest part of the sprawling complex of artificial islands that today sweeps along the south side of the River IJ, containing many of the city's maritime facilities. This patch of land was dredged out of the river to provide extra warehousing and dock space in the seventeenth century. The maritime bustle has pretty much disappeared here but, after a long period of neglect, the area is rapidly finding new life as a chichi residential quarter with smart apartments installed in its warehouses and its clutch of elegant canal houses revamped and reinvigorated, especially on **Zandhoek**. Finally, the working-class neighbourhood to the west of the Westerkanaal, which marks the limit of the Western docklands, is of interest for the **Het Schip** complex, a wonderful example of the Amsterdam School of architecture and, perhaps more importantly, an example of social housing at its most optimistic.

THE JORDAAN AND
WESTERN DOCKLANDS

The Jordaan

In all probability the **Jordaan** takes its name from the French word *jardin* ("garden"), since the area's earliest settlers were Protestant Huguenots, who fled here to escape persecution in the sixteenth and seventeenth centuries. Another possibility is that it's a corruption of the Dutch word for Jews, *joden*, who also sought refuge here. Whatever the truth, the Jordaan developed from open country – hence the number of streets and canals named after flowers and plants – into a refugee enclave, a teeming, cosmopolitan quarter beyond the pale of bourgeois respectability. Indeed, when the city fathers planned the expansion of the city in 1610, they made sure the Jordaan was kept outside the city boundaries. Consequently, the area was not subject to the rigorous planning restrictions of the main *grachten* – Herengracht, Keizersgracht and Prinsengracht – and its lattice of narrow streets followed the lines of the original polder drainage ditches rather than any municipal plan. This gives the district its distinctive, mazy layout, and much of its present appeal.

By the late nineteenth century, the Jordaan had become one of Amsterdam's toughest neighbourhoods, a stronghold of the city's industrial **working class**, mostly crowded together in cramped and unsanitary housing. Unsurprisingly, it was a highly politicized area, where protests against poor conditions were frequent, often coordinated by an influential and well-organized Communist Party. In the postwar period the slums were either cleared or renovated, but rocketing property prices in the wealthier parts of the city pushed middle-class professionals into the Jordaan from the early 1980s. This process of gentrification was at first much resented, but today the area is home to many young and affluent "alternative" Amsterdammers, who rub shoulders more or less affably with working-class Jordaaners with long-standing local roots.

Leidsegracht to Elandsgracht

The southern boundary of the Jordaan is generally deemed to be the **Leidsegracht**, though this is open to debate; according to dyed-in-the-wool locals the true Jordaaner is born within earshot of the Westerkerk bells, and you'd be hard-pushed to hear the chimes this far south. The narrow streets and canals just to the north of the Leidsegracht are routinely modern, but **Elandsgracht** does hold, at no. 109, the enjoyable indoor **De Looier antiques market** (daily 11am–5pm; closed Fri), which is good for picking up Dutch bygones, including tiles and ceramics, with a few stalls dealing in specialist wares such as silver trinkets or delftware. Footballophiles will also want to take a peek at the sports shop at Elandsgracht 96, where **Johan Cruyff** – star of Ajax in the 1970s and one of the greatest players of all time – bought his first pair of football boots.

> ## The Jordaan's hofjes
>
> One feature of the Jordaan's varied architectural pleasures is its **hofjes** – almshouses built around a central courtyard and originally occupied by the city's elderly and needy. There were – and are – *hofjes* all over the city (most famously the Begijnhof – see p.52), but there's a real concentration here in the Jordaan. Most date back to the seventeenth or eighteenth centuries, but the majority have been rebuilt or at least overhauled – and all are still lived in, often by those people they were originally built for. The Jordaan's most diverting *hofje* is the **Karthuizerhofje**, on Karthuizersstraat (see p.87).

Elandsgracht to Rozengracht

The streets immediately to the north of Elandsgracht are unremarkable, and easily the most agreeable route onwards is along the **Lijnbaansgracht** (Ropewalk Canal). This narrow canal threads its way round most of the city centre and here – in between Elandsgracht and Rozenstraat – its lapping waters are flanked by cobbled, leafy streets lined with old brick buildings. On **Rozenstraat** itself, at no. 59, is an annexe of the Stedelijk Museum (see p.109), the **Stedelijk Museum Bureau** (Tues–Sun 11am–5pm; free; Ⓦ www.smba.nl), which provides space for up-and-coming Amsterdam artists, with small-scale exhibitions, installations and occasional lectures and readings.

One block further north, **Rozengracht** lost its canal years ago and is now a busy and somewhat unattractive main road, though it was here at no. 184 that **Rembrandt** spent the last ten years of his life – a scrolled **plaque** set high into the wall distinguishes his old home. Rembrandt's last years were scarred by the death of his wife Hendrickje in 1663 and his son Titus five years later, but nevertheless it was in this period that he produced some of his finest work, including *The Return of the Prodigal Son*, which is displayed in the Hermitage, St Petersburg. Also dated to these years is *The Jewish Bride*, a touchingly warm and heartfelt portrait of a bride and her husband, completed in 1668 and now in the Rijksmuseum (see p.114). From Rozengracht, it's the shortest of walks to the Westerkerk and the Anne Frank Huis.

Rozengracht to Westerstraat

The streets and canals extending north from Rozengracht to Westerstraat form the heart of the Jordaan and provide the district's prettiest moments. Beyond Rozengracht, the first canal is the **Bloemgracht** (Flower Canal), a leafy waterway dotted with houseboats and traversed by dinky little bridges, its network of cross streets sprinkled with cafés, bars and quirky shops. There's a warm, relaxed community atmosphere here which is really rather beguiling, not to mention a clutch of fine old canal houses. Pride of architectural place goes

△ Bloemgracht

to **nos. 87–91**, a sterling Renaissance building of 1642 complete with mullion windows, three crowstep gables, brightly painted shutters and distinctive facade stones, representing a *steeman* (city-dweller), a *landman* (farmer) and a *seeman* (sailor). **Nos. 83–85** next door were built a few decades later – two immaculately maintained canal houses adorned by the bottleneck gables typical of the period.

From Bloemgracht, it's a few metres north to picturesque **Egelantiersgracht** (Rose-Hip Canal), where, at no. 12, **'t Smalle**, one of Amsterdam's oldest cafés, opened in 1786 as a *proeflokaal* – a tasting house for the (long-gone) gin distillery next door. In the eighteenth century, when quality control was erratic to say the least, each batch of *jenever* (Dutch gin) could turn out very differently, so customers insisted on a taster before they splashed out. As a result, each distillery ran a *proeflokaal* offering free samples, and this is a rare survivor. The café's waterside terrace remains an especially pleasant and popular spot to take a tipple (see p.186).

Moving on from here, a narrow cross street – 1e Egelantiersdwarsstraat and its continuation 1e Tuindwarsstraat and 1e Anjeliersdwarsstraat – runs north from **Egelantiersgracht** to workaday **Westerstraat**, a busy thoroughfare, which is home to the small but charming **Pianola Museum** (Sun 2–5pm; €5; Ⓦwww.pianola.nl), at no. 106, whose collection of pianolas and automatic music-machines dates from the beginning of the twentieth century. Fifteen have been restored to working order, and there are usually one or two playing throughout the afternoon, which are a delight to watch. These machines, which work on rolls of perforated paper, were the jukeboxes of their day, and the museum has a vast archive of over 15,000 rolls of music, some of which were "recorded" by famous pianists and composers – Gershwin, Debussy, Scott Joplin, Art Tatum and others. The museum runs a programme of pianola music concerts throughout the year (except July/Aug), where the rolls are played back on restored machines (exact times are listed on their website). Nearby, hidden behind a white doorway, is the largest of the Jordaan's *hofjes* (see box p.85), the **Karthuizerhofje**, Karthuizersstraat 89–171, a substantial courtyard complex established as a widows' hospice in the middle of the seventeenth century, though the present buildings are much more recent; it makes an appealing, peaceful diversion.

The Noorderkerk and the Noordermarkt

At the east end of Westerstraat, overlooking the Prinsengracht, is Hendrick de Keyser's **Noorderkerk** (Mon, Thurs & Sat 11am–1pm; free), the architect's last creation and probably his least successful, finished two years after his death in 1623. A bulky, overbearing brick building, it represented a radical departure from the conventional church designs of the time, having a symmetrical Greek cross floor plan, with four equally proportioned arms radiating out from a steepled centre. Uncompromisingly dour, it proclaimed the serious intent of the Calvinists who worshipped here in so far as the pulpit – and therefore the preacher – was at the centre and not at the front of the church, a symbolic break with the Catholic past. Nevertheless, it's still hard to understand quite how de Keyser, who designed such elegant structures as the Westerkerk, could have ended up designing this.

The **Noordermarkt**, the somewhat unimpressive square outside the church, contains a **statue** of three figures bound to each other, a poignant tribute to the bloody Jordaanoproer riot of 1934, part of a successful campaign to stop the government cutting unemployment benefit during the Depression;

△ Brouwersgracht Canal

you'll find the statue just in front of the church's west door. The inscription reads "The strongest chains are those of unity". The church also boasts a **plaque** honouring those Communists and Jews who were rounded up here by the Germans in February 1941. The square also hosts two of Amsterdam's best open-air **markets** (see p.236). There's a general household goods and flea market on Mondays (9am–1pm), plus a popular Saturday farmers' market, the **Boerenmarkt** (9am–4pm), a lively affair with organic fruit and vegetables, freshly baked breads and a plethora of oils and spices for sale. Cross an unmarked border, though, and you'll find yourself in the middle of a bird market, which operates on an adjacent patch at much the same time, and, if you're at all squeamish, is best avoided – the brightly coloured birds squeezed into tiny cages are not for everyone. Incidentally, the bustling *Lunchcafé Winkel*, beside the Noordermarkt at the corner with Westerstraat, sells huge wedges of home-made apple pie, which many Jordaaners swear is the best in town.

The Lindengracht and Brouwersgracht

Just to the north of the Noorderkerk, the **Lindengracht** ("Canal of Limes") lost its waterway decades ago, but has had a prominent role in local folklore since the day in 1886 when a policeman made an ill-advised attempt to stop an eel-pulling contest. Horrible as it sounds, **eel-pulling** was a popular pastime hereabouts: a live eel, preferably smeared in soap to make the entertainment last a little longer, was suspended from a rope strung across a canal. Teams took to their boats and tried to pull the poor creature off the rope, the fun being to see who would end up in the water; the winner came away with the eel – or at least a good piece of it. In 1886, the crowd unceremoniously bundled the policeman away, but when reinforcements arrived, the whole thing got out of hand and there was a full-scale **riot** – the Paling-Oproer ("Eel Uprising") – which lasted for three days and cost 26 lives.

The east end of the Lindengracht intersects with **Brouwersgracht**, which marks the northerly limit of both the Jordaan and the Grachtengordel (see also Chapter Two). In the seventeenth century, Brouwersgracht lay at the edge of Amsterdam's great harbour, one of the major arteries linking the open sea with the city centre. Thronged by vessels returning from – or heading off to – every corner of the globe, it was lined with storage depots and warehouses. Breweries flourished here too – hence its name – capitalizing on their ready access to shipments of fresh water. Today, the harbour bustle has moved way out of the centre to the northwest, and the **warehouses**, with their distinctive spout-neck gables and shuttered windows, have been converted into some of the most expensive apartments in the city. There's an especially fine, uninterrupted row of these warehouses at Brouwersgracht **172–212**, across the canal from the Lindengracht. You'll also find some handsome merchants' houses on the Brouwersgracht, as well as moored houseboats and a string of quaint little swing bridges, making it altogether one of the most classically picturesque canals in the whole of the city and a pleasant area for a stroll.

The Scheepvaartsbuurt and the Western docklands

Brouwersgracht is also the southern boundary of the **Scheepvaartsbuurt** – the Shipping Quarter – an unassuming neighbourhood which focuses on **Haarlemmerstraat** and its continuation **Haarlemmerdijk**, a long, rather ordinary thoroughfare lined with cafés and food shops, which once bustled with stevedores and working ships bound to and from Haarlem. In the eighteenth and nineteenth centuries, this district boomed thanks to its location between Brouwersgracht and the **Western docklands**, a narrow parcel of land dredged out of the River IJ immediately to the north and equipped with docks, warehouses and shipyards. The construction of these artificial islands took the pressure off Amsterdam's congested maritime facilities and was necessary to sustain the city's economic success. Stretching from the Western to the Eastern docklands, these riverside wharves functioned as Amsterdam's heartbeat until the city's shipping facilities began to move away from the centre, a process accelerated by the construction of Centraal Station, slap in the middle of the old quayside in the 1880s. The Western docklands hung on to some of the marine trade until the 1960s, but today – bar the odd small boatyard – industry has to all intents and purposes disappeared and the area is busy reinventing itself. There is still a vague air of faded grittiness here, but the old, forgotten warehouses – within walking distance of the centre – are rapidly being turned into bijou studios, and dozens of plant-filled houseboats are moored alongside the narrow streets.

Haarlemmerdijk and the Haarlemmerpoort

Before World War II the **Haarlemmerstraat** and its westerly extension **Haarlemmerdijk** were congested thoroughfares, but the trams that once ran here were rerouted and this is now a pleasant if unremarkable pedestrianized strip with bars, shops and cafés. The only architectural high point is the meticulously restored Art Deco interior of **The Movies** cinema (see p.218), near the west end of the street at Haarlemmerdijk 161. Just metres away, the busy Haarlemmerplein traffic junction sports the grandiose Neoclassical gateway, **Haarlemmerpoort**, built on the site of a medieval entrance to the city in 1840 for the new king William II's triumphal entry into the city. The euphoria didn't last long. William was a distinguished general, who had been wounded at Waterloo, but as a king he proved much too crusty and reactionary to be popular, only agreeing to mild liberal reforms after extensive rioting in Amsterdam and elsewhere.

The Western docklands

Proceeding north from the near (east) side of the Haarlemmerpoort, walk through the tunnel beneath the railway lines and then turn right along Sloterdijkstraat, which soon crosses the canal over onto **Galgenstraat** (Gallows Street), once the site of the municipal gallows, which were clearly visible to passing ships – to discourage potential law-breakers. Galgenstraat bisects the smallest of the Western docklands islands, diminutive **Prinseneiland**, a pleasing mix of houseboats, former warehouses and old canal houses, guarded by a pair of dainty little bridges.

Keep going straight along Galgenstraat, over the next canal, and then turn north up Grote Bickersstraat for the bridge over to another Western docklands island, **Realeneiland**, whose houseboats, ex-warehouses and mini-boatyards give it a distinctly nautical flavour. On the island, tiny, waterside **Zandhoek** once offered an uninterrupted view over the harbour and was long a favourite with the city's sea captains, who constructed a clutch of fine old canal houses along here in the seventeenth and eighteenth centuries. A number of them have survived and several are decorated with distinctive facade stones, including **De Gouden Reael**, at no. 14, whose stone sports a gold coin. Before Napoleon introduced a system of house numbers, these stones were the principal way that visitors could recognize one house from another, and many homeowners went to considerable lengths to make theirs unique. Jacob Real, the Catholic tradesman who owned this particular house, also used the image of a *real* – a

Spanish coin – to discreetly advertise his sympathies for the Catholic Habsburgs. The building now houses a very good café-restaurant (see p.198).

At the top of Zandhoek, cross over the canal and then turn left along Zoutkeetsgracht; another left turn, this time onto Planciusstraat, returns you to the pedestrian tunnel near the Haarlemmerpoort.

The Westerpark and Het Schip

Heading west from the Haarlemmerpoort along the main road, cross the canal, take the first right turn and on the other side of the road you'll come to the east entrance to the **Westerpark**, one of the city's smaller and – in terms of up-and-coming cultural centres – more enticing parks, running alongside a narrow sliver of canal. At the far end of the park you come across the old gas factory, the **Westergasfabriek**, a sprawling jumble of neo-Gothic buildings dating from the 1880s. Currently being developed as a complex for art and culture, it had a brief reincarnation as the city's prime venue for Acid House parties in the early 1990s.

On the north side of the park, before you reach Westergasfabriek, a pedestrian tunnel leads under the railway lines to **Zaanstraat**, the southern edge of a working-class neighbourhood that stretches north to the busy Spaarndammer Dijk boulevard. Taken as a whole, this part of the city is really rather glum, but hang a left on Zaanstraat and you soon reach Spaarndammerplantsoen, the site of **Het Schip**, a municipal housing block which is a splendid – and pristine – example of the Expressionistic Amsterdam School of architecture. Seven years in the making, from 1913 to 1920, the complex takes its name from its ship-like shape and is graced by all manner of fetching decorative details – from the intriguing mix-and-match windows to the wavy brick facades and ornamental sculptures of which the bulging "cigar" turret is its most self-indulgent. The architect responsible was **Michael de Klerk** (1884–1923), who also designed the two other housing blocks on Spaarndammerplantsoen, though Het Schip is easily the most striking. De Klerk reacted strongly against the influence of Berlage, whose style – exemplified by the Beurs – favoured clean lines and functionality, opting instead for much more playful motifs. De Klerk installed a post office in Het Schip and the interior, with its superb multicoloured tiling, has been restored and now serves as the small **Museum Het Schip** (Wed–Sun 1–5pm; €5; ⓦwww.hetschip.nl), which through the use of multimedia, short

△ Museum Het Schip

films and leaflets looks at the living conditions of the city's proletariat at the start of the twentieth century, relating it to the history of the Amsterdam School. The museum sells a pamphlet for self-guided tours explaining the architectural highlights of the complex, still used as social housing today. Half-hour guided tours (on request; €2.50) take you inside one of the restored residences and up to the turret, which serves no purpose other than that de Klerk thought it was aesthetically pleasing. Politically motivated, de Klerk and his architectural allies were eager to provide high-quality homes for the working class, though their laudable aims were often undermined – or at least diluted – by a tendency to overelaborate. For details of de Klerk's other major commission in Amsterdam, the De Dageraad housing project, see p.134.

Across the road from the museum, the pleasant *Lunchroom Het Schip* serves tasty light meals and often gets packed with tour groups. Het Schip is at the terminus of **bus** #22, which will whisk you back to Centraal Station in no time at all.

The Old Jewish Quarter and Eastern docklands

Once one of the marshiest parts of Amsterdam, the narrow slab of land between the curve of the River Amstel, Kloveniersburgwal and the Nieuwe Herengracht was the home of **Amsterdam's Jews** from the sixteenth century up until World War II. By the 1920s, this Old Jewish Quarter, aka the **Jodenhoek** ("Jews' Corner"), had become one of the busiest parts of town, crowded with tenement buildings and smoking factories, its main streets holding scores of open-air stalls, selling everything from pickled herrings to pots and pans. Sadly, the war put paid to all this and in 1945 the district lay derelict – and neither has postwar redevelopment treated it kindly. Its focal point, **Waterlooplein**, has been overwhelmed by a domineering town and concert hall, which caused much controversy at the time of its construction, and the once-bustling Jodenbreestraat is now bleak and very ordinary, with Mr Visserplein, at its east end, one of the city's busiest traffic junctions.

Picking your way round these obstacles is not much fun, but persevere – amongst all the cars and concrete are several moving reminders of the Jewish community that perished in World War II, most memorably the late seventeenth-century **Esnoga** (Portuguese synagogue), one of the city's finest buildings. Close by, four other synagogues have been merged into the fascinating **Joods Historisch Museum** (Jewish Historical Museum), celebrating Jewish culture and custom. There's a Rembrandt connection here too: in 1639, the artist moved into a house on the Jodenbreestraat and this has been restored as the **Rembrandthuis**, which, in addition to several period rooms, has a fine collection of the great man's etchings and features temporary displays of his paintings.

Immediately to the east of the Old Jewish Quarter lies the **Plantagebuurt**, a well-heeled residential area that's home to the city's botanical gardens, the **Hortus Botanicus**, as well as the **Artis Zoo** (see p.249) and the excellent **Verzetsmuseum** (Dutch Resistance Museum). From here, it's a short stroll southwest to **Hermitage Amsterdam**, an art gallery used for lavish temporary

WASMOES
STEEG

MARING
PAGGESTEEG

PRINS

HENDRIKKADE

St Nicolaaskerk

DAMRAK

Damrak

NIEUWE BRUGSTE

ZEEDIJK

OUDEZIJDS KOLK

GELDERSEKADE

PRINS HENDRIKKADE

OOSTERDOKSKADE

BRUGSTEEG

BIERSTEEG

RED LIGHT
DISTRICT

H HOEKSTEEG

GELDERSEKADE

KROME WAAL

Scheepvaarthuis

Prostitute
Information
Centre

WARMOESSTRAAT

VOORBURGWAL

OUDEZIJDS

Gelderse
steeg

WAALSTEEG

BUITEN BANT
AMMERSTRAAT

PRINS HENDRIKKADE

SCHIPPERSTR

Oosterdok

Oude Kerk

OUDEZIJDS ACHTERBURGWAL

OUDEZIJDS VOORBURGWAL

ZEEDIJK

NIEUWE

BINNENKANT

Waalseilandsgracht

KALKMARKT

MOLENSTE

Waag

GELDERSEKADE

NIEUWE

OUDE WAAL

OUDEZIJDS ACHTERBURGWAL

MONNIKENSTR

JONKERSTR

OOSTERSTRAAT

RIDDERSTRAAT

RECHT BOOMSSLOOT

OUDE SCHANS

Montelbaanstoren

STOOF
STEEG

Hash
Museum

BARNDESTEEG

BLOEDSTRAAT

NIEUWMARKT

KONINGSSTRAAT

KROMBOOMSSLOOT

RECHT BOOMSSLOOT

OUDE SCHANS

Rapen-

S. RAVENHEJE

PEPERSTRAAT

burgwal

RAPENBURG

KOESTRAAT

ST ANTONIESBREESTRAAT

OUDE SCHANS

OOSTERSE
KADE

BETHANIUNSTRAAT

Kleine
Trippenhuis

OUDE HOOGSTRAAT

KLOVENIERSBURGWAL

Nieuwmarkt

DIJKSTRAAT

Oude Schans

NIEUWE UILENBURGERSTRAAT

Oostindisch

Kloveniers-

NIEUWE HOOGSTRAAT

ZWANENBURGSTR

Nieuwmarkt

Pintohuis

Uilenburgergracht

ZANDSTR

Zuiderkerk

Gassan
Diamonds

VALKENBURGERSTRAAT

ANNE

FRANKSTRAAT

RAAMGRACHT

RAAMGRACHT

Rembrandthuis

VALKENBURGERSTRAAT

KLOVENIERSBURGWAL

GROENBURGWAL

TERWEESTRAAT

ZWANENBURGWAL

JODENBREESTRAAT

RAPENBURGERSTRAAT

Herengracht

GROENBURGWAL

Waterlooplein
Markt

NIEUWE HERENGRACHT

STAALSTRAAT

WATERLOOPLEIN

OLD JEWISH
QUARTER

Stadhuis

WATERLOOPLEIN

Mozes en Aaron Kerk

MR VISSERPLEIN

NIEUWE HERENGRACHT

Auschwitz
Monument

Jewish Memorial

"Stopera"

Waterlooplein

MUIDERSTRAAT

AMSTEL

Muziektheater

Esnoga

Dokwerker

PLANTAGE MIDDENLAAN

AMSTEL

Waterlooplein

WATERLOOPLEIN

NIEUWE AMSTELSTRAAT

Joods
Historisch
Museum

JONAS DANIËL
MEIJERPLEIN

Nieuwe

Hortus
Botanicus

AMSTELSTRAAT

BLAUWBRUG

NIEWE HERENGRACHT

HORTUSPLANTSOEN

WEESPERSTRAAT

PLANTAGE

REMBRANDT-
PLEIN

UTRECHTSESTRAAT

Museum Willet
Holthuysen

NIEWE HERENGRACHT

Hermitage
Amsterdam

HERENGRACHT

River Amstel

Amstelhof

Keizersgracht

HERENGRACHT

AMSTEL

NIEUWE KEIZERSGRACHT

NIEUWE KEIZERSGRACHT

NIEUWE

No 58

NIEUWE KERKSTRAAT

0   200 m

▲ *Muziekgebouw*

THE OLD JEWISH QUARTER AND EASTERN DOCKLANDS

▶ *Java Island*

PIET HEINKADE

DIJKSGRACHT

Stedelijk Museum

NEMO

OOSTERDOK

Oosterdok

N

De Amsterdam

Nederlands Scheepvaart-museum

ARCAM

KATTENBURGER-PLEIN

KATTENBURGERSTRAAT

K. BURGERKRUISSTR

OLIFANTSWERF

KATTENBURGERKADE

Kattenburgervaart

PRINS HENDRIKKADE

FOELIESTRAAT

NIEUWE FOELIESTRAAT

FOELIEDWARS-STRAAT

SCHIPPERSGRACHT

RAPENBURG

RAPENBURGER-PLEIN

KADIJKSPLEIN

BLIJ-ISPAD

KATTENBURGERGRACHT

WITTENBURGERKADE

BAKEN STRAAT

GROTE WITTENBURGERSTRAAT

PAREL STRAAT

KLEINE WITTENBURGERSTRAAT

POOLSTR.

WAGSAT

NIEUWEVAART

HOOGTE KADIJK

Nieuwevaart

Dutch East India Compound

LAAGTE KADIJK

ENTREPOTDOK

OVERHAALSGANG

WITTENBURGERGRACHT

Wertheim-park

PLANTAGEKADE

PLANTAGE DOKLAAN

PARKLAAN

Vakbondsmuseum

HENRI POLAKLAAN

Verzetsmuseum

Entrepotdok

ENTREPOTDOK

Museum Werf 't Kromhout

HOOGTE KADIJK

PLANTAGEBUURT

KERKLAAN

Artis Zoo

De Hollandsche Schouwburg

PLANTAGE

PLANTAGE

PLANTAGE MIDDENLAAN

PLANTAGE WESTERMANLAAN

PLANTAGE MUIDERGRACHT

PLANT LEPELLAAN

Plantage Muidergracht

ROETERSSTRAAT

NIEUWE PRINSENGRACHT

PLANTAGE MUIDERGRACHT

SARPHATISTRAAT

▶ *De Gooyer Windmill*

exhibitions of fine and applied art on loan from the Hermitage Museum in St Petersburg. Moving on from the Plantagebuurt, it's a short hop north to the reclaimed islands of the **Oosterdok**, dredged out of the River IJ to accommodate warehouses and docks in the seventeenth century; close by, the former postal sorting office now holds the contemporary art of the **Stedelijk Museum**.

The **Oosterdok** is one part of the Eastern docklands, a vast maritime complex that once spread right along the River IJ, stretching east from the Western docklands (see Chapter Three) to a clutter of nineteenth-century artificial islands that includes **Zeeburg**. Industrial decline set in during the 1880s, but Zeeburg is currently being redefined as a residential and leisure district, featuring funky bars, some startling modern architecture and several award-winning buildings.

The Old Jewish Quarter

Throughout the nineteenth century and up until the German occupation, the **Old Jewish Quarter** – the Jodenhoek – was a hive of activity, its main streets lined with shops and jam-packed with open-air stalls, where Jews and Gentiles traded in earnest. Fatefully, it was also surrounded by canals and it was these the Germans exploited to create the **ghetto** that foreshadowed their policy of starvation and deportation. They restricted movement in and out of the quarter by raising most of the swing bridges (over the Nieuwe Herengracht, the Amstel and the Kloveniersburgwal) and imposing stringent controls on every other access route. The Jews, readily identifiable by the yellow Stars of David they were obliged to wear, were not allowed to use public transport, ride bicycles or own telephones, and were placed under a rigorously imposed curfew. Meanwhile, roundups and deportations had begun shortly after the Germans arrived, and continued into 1945. By the end of the war, the Jodenhoek was deserted and, as the need for wood and raw materials intensified in the cold winter that followed, many of the houses were dismantled for fuel.

The Jodenhoek remained a neglected corner of the city well into the 1970s, when the battered remnants took another hit with the large-scale demolition that preceded the construction of the metro beneath Waterlooplein. By these means, the prewar Jodenhoek disappeared almost without trace, the notable exception being the imposing **Esnoga** (Portuguese Synagogue) and the four connected synagogues of the Ashkenazi Jews, now the **Joods Historisch Museum**. The district's other main sight is the **Rembrandthuis**, which features special exhibitions on the artist's work, life and times.

Jodenbreestraat and the Rembrandthuis

Jodenbreestraat, the "Broad Street of the Jews", was once the hub of Jewish activity in the city. Badly served by postwar development, this ancient thoroughfare is now short on charm, but in these unlikely surroundings, at no. 6, stands the **Rembrandthuis** (daily 10am–5pm; €8; ⓦ www.rembrandthuis.nl), an intriguing building whose intricate facade is decorated by pretty wooden shutters and a charming pediment. Rembrandt bought this house at the height of his fame and popularity, living here for over twenty years and spending a fortune on furnishings – an. expense that ultimately contributed to his bankruptcy (see box p.119). An inventory made at the time details the huge collection of paintings, sculptures and art treasures he had amassed, almost all of which were confiscated after he was declared insolvent and forced to move to a more modest house on Rozengracht in the Jordaan in 1658. The city council bought the Jodenbreestraat house in 1907 and has revamped the premises on several occasions, most recently in 1999.

△ The Rembrandthuis

A visit begins in the modern annexe, but you're soon into Rembrandt's old house, where a string of **period rooms** has been restored to something resembling their appearance when the artist lived here – the reconstruction being based on the inventory. The period furniture is appealing enough, especially the two dinky box-beds, and the great man's studio is surprisingly large and well lit, but the paintings that adorn the walls are mostly second-rate and none of them is actually a Rembrandt. The most interesting paintings are those by Rembrandt's master in Amsterdam, Pieter Lastman (1583–1633) – not because of their quality, but rather because their sheer mawkishness demonstrates just how far Rembrandt soared above his artistic milieu.

Beyond the period rooms, the rest of the Rembrandthuis is often given over to temporary exhibitions on the artist and his contemporaries. Here also, space permitting, is the museum's own collection of **Rembrandt's etchings**, as well as several of the original copper plates on which he worked. It's a large and varied collection, with the biblical illustrations usually attracting the most attention, though the studies of tramps and vagabonds are equally appealing.

Gassan Diamonds

From the Rembrandthuis, it's a couple of minutes' walk to the **Gassan Diamonds** factory (frequent guided tours daily 9am–5pm; 1hr; free; ℡020/622-5333, Ⓦwww.gassandiamonds.nl), which occupies a large and imposing brick building dating from 1897 on Nieuwe Uilenburgerstraat. Before World War II, many local Jews worked as diamond cutters and polishers, though there's little sign of the industry here today – Gassan being the main exception. Traditionally, the city's diamond workers were poorly paid and endured foul working conditions, but all this changed after the creation of the Diamond Workers' Association, the ANDB, at the end of the nineteenth century. Unionised, the diamond workers transformed their pay and conditions, becoming the vanguard of the working class under the leadership of the socialist rabbi **Henri Polak** (1868–1943). The ANDB also pushed education and did more to integrate the city's Jews into the mainstream than any other organization; predictably, the Germans made short work of the union during the occupation. **Tours** of the Gassan factory include a visit to the cutting and polishing areas as well as a gambol round the diamond jewellery showroom.

Waterlooplein

Jodenbreestraat runs parallel to the **Stadhuis en Muziektheater** (town and concert hall), a sprawling complex whose indeterminate modernity dominates **Waterlooplein**, a rectangular parcel of land that was originally swampy marsh. This was the site of the first Jewish Quarter, but by the late nineteenth century it had become an insanitary slum, home to the poorest of the Ashkenazi Jews. The slums were cleared in the 1880s and thereafter the Waterlooplein and its open-air market became the centre of Jewish life in the city. In the war, the Germans used the square to round up their victims, but despite these ugly connotations the Waterlooplein was revived in the 1950s as the site of the city's main **flea market** – and remains so to this day (Mon–Sat 9am–5pm; see also p.236), albeit on a much smaller scale. The market's reappearance in the 1950s was, as far as the city council was concerned, only a stopgap while they mulled over plans to entirely reinvent the depopulated Jodenhoek; for starters, whole streets were demolished to make way for the motorist – with Mr Visserplein, for example, becoming little more than a traffic intersection – and then, warming to their theme in the late 1970s,

The Jews in Amsterdam

From the late sixteenth century onwards, Amsterdam was a haven for refugee Jews escaping persecution throughout the rest of Europe. The **Union of Utrecht**, ratified in 1579, signalled the start of the influx. Drawn up by the largely Protestant northern Dutch provinces in response to the invading Spanish army, the treaty combined the United Provinces (later to become the Netherlands) in a loose federation, whose wheels could only be greased by a degree of religious toleration then unknown elsewhere across the Continent. Whatever the Protestants may have wanted, they knew that the Catholic minority (around 35 percent) would only continue to support the rebellion against the Spanish Habsburgs if they were treated well – the Jews benefited by osmosis and consequently immigrated here in their hundreds.

This **toleration** did, however, have its limits: Jewish immigrants were forced to buy citizenship; Christian-Jewish marriages were illegal; and, as with the Catholics, they were only allowed to practise their religion discreetly behind closed doors. A proclamation in 1632 also excluded them from most guilds – effectively withdrawing their right to own and run businesses. This forced them either to excel in those trades not governed by the guilds or introduce new non-guild trades into the city. Nonetheless, by the middle of the eighteenth century the city's Jewish community was active in almost every aspect of the economy, especially in bookselling, tobacco, banking and commodity futures.

The first major Jewish influx was of **Sephardic** Jews from Spain and Portugal, where persecution had begun in earnest in 1492 and continued throughout the sixteenth century. In the 1630s the Sephardim were joined in Amsterdam by hundreds of (much poorer) **Ashkenazi** Jews from German-speaking central Europe. The two groups established separate synagogues and, although there was no ghetto as such, the vast majority settled on and around what is now Waterlooplein, then a distinctly unhealthy tract of low-lying land that was subject to regular flooding by the River Amstel. Initially known as **Vlooyenburg**, this district was usually referred to as the **Jodenhoek**, or "Jews' Corner", though this was not, generally speaking, a pejorative term and neither did the Dutch eschew living here; Rembrandt, for instance, was quite happy to take up residence and frequently painted his Jewish neighbours. Indeed, given the time, the most extraordinary feature of Jewish settlement in Amsterdam was that it occasioned mild curiosity rather than outright hate, as evinced by surviving prints of Jewish religious customs, where there is neither any hint of stereotype nor discernible demonization.

The restrictions affecting both Jews and Catholics were removed during **Napoleon**'s occupation of the United Provinces, when the country was temporarily renamed the Batavian Republic (1795–1806). Freed from official discrimination, Amsterdam's Jewish community flourished and the Jewish Quarter expanded, nudging northwest towards Nieuwmarkt and east across Nieuwe Herengracht, though this was just the focus of a community whose members lived in every part of the city. In 1882, the dilapidated houses of the Jodenhoek were razed and several minor canals filled in to make way for **Waterlooplein**, which became a largely Jewish marketplace, a bustling affair that sprawled out along St Antoniesbreestraat and Jodenbreestraat.

At the turn of the twentieth century, there were around 60,000 Jews living in Amsterdam, but **refugees** from Hitler's Germany swelled this figure to around 120,000 in the 1930s. The disaster that befell this community during the **German occupation** is hard to conceive, but the bald facts speak for themselves; when Amsterdam was liberated, there were only 5000 Jews left and the Jodenhoek was, to all intents and purposes, a ghost town. At present, there are about 25,000 Jews resident in – and spread out across – the city, but while Jewish life in Amsterdam has survived, its heyday is gone forever.

the council announced the building of a massive new Waterlooplein town and concert hall complex. Opposition was immediate and widespread as it was feared the end result would be an eyesore, but attempts to prevent the building failed, and the Muziektheater opened in 1986, since when it has established an international reputation for the quality of its performances (see p.214). One of the story's abiding ironies is that the title of the protest campaign – "**Stopera**" – has passed into common usage to describe the whole complex.

Inside the "Stopera", amidst all the jaded concrete, there are a couple of minor attractions, beginning with the **glass columns** in the glass-roofed public passageway towards the rear of the complex. These give a salutary lesson on the fragility of the Netherlands; two contain water indicating the sea levels in the Dutch towns of Vlissingen and IJmuiden (below knee level), while another records the levels recorded during the 1953 flood disaster (way above head height). Down the stairs, a display indicates what is known as "Normal Amsterdam Level" (NAP), originally calculated in 1684 as the average water level in the River IJ and still the basis for measuring altitude above sea level across Europe. Metres away, in the Muziektheater's foyer, is a forceful and inventive **memorial** to the district's Jews, in which a bronze violinist bursts through the floor tiles.

Outside, at the very tip of Waterlooplein, where the River Amstel meets the Zwanenburgwal canal, there is a second memorial – a black stone **tribute** to the dead of the Jewish resistance; the inscription from Jeremiah translates as "If my eyes were a well of tears, I would cry day and night for the fallen fighters of my beloved people."

Mr Visserplein

Just behind the Muziektheater, on the corner of Mr Visserplein, is the **Mozes en Aaron Kerk**, a rather glum Neoclassical structure built on the site of a clandestine Catholic church in the 1840s. It takes its unusual name from a pair of facade stones bearing effigies of the two prophets that adorned the earlier building. Earlier still, the site was occupied by the house where the philosopher and theologian **Baruch Spinoza** was born in 1632. Of Sephardic descent, Spinoza's pantheistic views soon brought him into conflict with the elders of the Jewish community. At the age of 23, he was excommunicated and forced out of the city, moving into a small village where he survived by grinding lenses. After an attempt on his life, Spinoza moved again, eventually ending up in The Hague, where his free-thinking ways proved more acceptable.

Next door to the church, **Mr Visserplein** is a busy junction for traffic speeding towards the IJ tunnel. It takes its name from **Lodewijk Ernst Visser** (1871–1942), President of the Supreme Court of the Netherlands in 1939. He was dismissed the following year when the Germans occupied the country, and became an active member of the Jewish resistance, working for the illegal underground newspaper *Het Parool* ("The Password") and refusing to wear the yellow Star of David. He vehemently opposed the Nazi-appointed Judenrat (Jewish Council), publicly denouncing all forms of collaboration and arguing that the Dutch government should take responsibility for all Dutch citizens, Jew and Gentile alike. Visser died from a heart attack shortly after he was threatened with deportation to a concentration camp.

The Esnoga

Unmissable on the corner of Mr Visserplein is the brown and bulky brickwork of the **Esnoga** (Portuguese Synagogue; Sun–Thurs 10am–4pm & Fri 10am–3pm;

closed Yom Kippur; €6.50; ⓦ www.esnoga.com), completed in 1675 for the city's Sephardic Jews. One of Amsterdam's most imposing buildings, the central structure, with its grand pilasters and blind balustrade, was built in the broadly Neoclassical style that was then fashionable in Holland. It is surrounded by a courtyard complex of small outhouses, where the city's Sephardim have fraternized for centuries. Barely altered since its construction, the synagogue's lofty interior follows the Sephardic tradition in having the Hechal (the Ark of the Covenant) and tebah (from where services are led) at opposite ends. Also traditional is the **seating**, with two sets of wooden benches (for the men) facing each other across the central aisle – the women have separate galleries up above. A set of superb brass chandeliers holds the candles that remain the only source of artificial light. When it was completed, the synagogue was one of the largest in the world, its congregation almost certainly the richest; today, the Sephardic community has dwindled to just 250 families, most of whom live outside the city centre.

In one of the outhouses, a **video** sheds light on the history of the synagogue and of Amsterdam's Sephardim; the mystery is why the Germans left the building alone – no one knows for sure, but it seems likely that they intended to turn it into a museum once all of the Jews had disappeared.

Jonas Daniel Meijerplein

Next to the Esnoga, on the south side of its retaining outhouses, is **Jonas Daniel Meijerplein**, a scrawny triangle of gravel named after the eponymous lawyer, who in 1796, at the age of just 16, was the first Jew to be admitted to the Amsterdam Bar. It was here in February 1941 that around 400 Jewish men were forcibly loaded up on trucks and taken to their deaths at Mauthausen concentration camp, in reprisal for the killing of a Dutch Nazi during a street fight. The arrests sparked off the **February Strike** (Februaristaking), a general strike in protest against the Germans' treatment of the Jews. It was organized by the outlawed Communist Party and spearheaded by Amsterdam's transport workers and dockers – a rare demonstration of solidarity with the Jews whose fate was usually accepted without visible protest in all of occupied Europe. The strike was quickly suppressed, but is still commemorated by an annual wreath-laying ceremony on February 25, as well as by Mari Andriessen's statue the **Dokwerker** (Dockworker), here on Jonas Daniel Meijerplein.

The Joods Historisch Museum

Across the square, on the far side of the main road, the **Joods Historisch Museum** (Jewish Historical Museum; daily 11am–5pm; closed Yom Kippur; €7.50; ⓦ www.jhm.nl) is cleverly shoehorned into four adjacent Ashkenazi synagogues dating from the late seventeenth century. For years after the war these buildings lay abandoned, but they were finally refurbished – and connected by walkways – in the 1980s, to accommodate a Jewish resource centre and exhibition area. One highlight of a visit is the engaging display on Jewish life that occupies the main body of the capacious **Grote Synagogue**, which dates from 1671. This features a fine collection of religious silverware, plus all manner of antique artefacts illustrating religious customs and practices, alongside a scattering of paintings and portraits. In addition, the gallery up above holds a finely judged social history of the country's Jewish population, with an assortment of bygones, documents and paintings tracing their prominent role in a wide variety of industries, both as employers and employees, up until 1890.

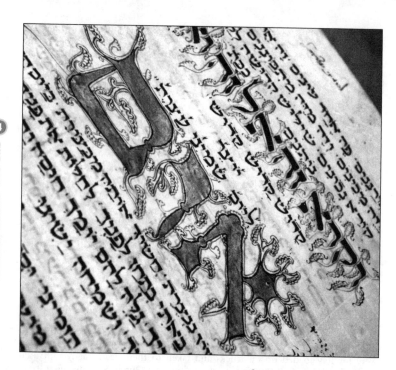

△ Scroll in the Joods Historisch Museum

Moving on, the **Nieuwe Synagoge** of 1752 contains a complementary history of the Jews in the Netherlands from 1890 until today, focusing, inevitably, on the trauma of World War II. Here you'll find the moving gouaches of the German Jew **Charlotte Salomon** (1917–43), who died in Auschwitz; Salomon painted several hundred pieces in her short life and the museum owns a large sample of them.

The third building in the complex – the Obbene Shul – holds a **Children's Museum**, and the fourth, the Dritt Shul, a **resource centre** with numerous books, periodicals and photographs, mostly chronicling the Jewish experience in the Netherlands.

For more on Amsterdam during the German occupation, visit the Dutch Resistance Museum (see p.106).

The Plantagebuurt

Laid out in the middle of the nineteenth century, the pleasant, leafy streets of the **Plantagebuurt**, falling to either side of **Plantage Middenlaan** boulevard, were developed as part of a concerted attempt to provide good-quality housing for the city's expanding middle classes. Although it was never as fashionable as the older residential parts of the Grachtengordel, the new district did contain elegant villas and spacious terraces, making it the first suburban port of call for

Starting at Centraal Station, **trams** #9 and #14 run along Plantage Middenlaan, passing by – or near – all the district's main attractions.

many upwardly mobile Jews. Nowadays, the Plantagebuurt is still one of the more prosperous parts of the city, in a modest sort of way, and boasts two especially enjoyable attractions – the **Hortus Botanicus** (Botanical Gardens) and the **Verzetsmuseum** (Dutch Resistance Museum). Close by, just over the **Plantage Muidergracht** canal, and stretching west to the River Amstel, is a small parcel of old Amsterdam, dating back to the late seventeenth century. The main attraction here is the recently opened **Hermitage Amsterdam**, which showcases temporary exhibitions of fine and applied art loaned from St Petersburg's Hermitage Museum.

The Amstelhof and Hermitage Amsterdam

During the second phase of the digging of the Grachtengordel, the three main canals that ringed the city centre were extended beyond the River Amstel up towards the Oosterdok – hence "Nieuwe" Herengracht, Keizersgracht and Prinsengracht. At first, takers for the new land were few and far between and the city had no option but to offer it to charities at discount prices. One result was the establishment of the **Amstelhof**, a large *hofje* (almshouse) built for the care of elderly women (and ultimately men too) in the 1680s on behalf of the Dutch Reformed Church. In time, the Amstelhof, a singularly stern-looking structure, grew to fill the entire chunk of land between Nieuwe Herengracht and Nieuwe Keizersgracht, becoming a fully fledged hospital in the process, but in the 1980s it became clear that its medical facilities were out of date and it went up for sale. Much municipal huffing and puffing ensued until the director of the Hermitage Museum in St Petersburg and his Dutch contacts dreamed up a real cultural wheeze; they proposed that the Amstelhof be turned into a museum for the display of items loaned from the Hermitage. It was – and is – a very ambitious scheme, with work on the Amstelhof scheduled to continue until the end of the decade. The first phase, however, has been completed, with six medium-sized galleries spread over two floors now comprising **Hermitage Amsterdam**, at Nieuwe Herengracht 14 (daily 10am–5pm; €7; ⓦ www.hermitage.nl). Exhibitions, which usually last about five months, have included "Nicholas & Alexandra" and "Collectors in St Petersburg".

Nieuwe Keizersgracht

In the nineteenth century, many better-off Jews escaped the crowded conditions of the Old Jewish Quarter to live along Nieuwe Keizersgracht and Nieuwe Prinsensgracht, but this community did not survive World War II. One painful reminder of the occupation still stands at **Nieuwe Keizersgracht 58**, across the canal behind the Amstelhof. From 1940, this house, with its luxurious Neoclassical double doorway set beneath twin caryatids, was the headquarters of the **Judenrat** (Jewish Council), through which the Germans managed the ghetto and organized the deportations. The role of the Judenrat is extremely controversial. Many have argued that they were tainted collaborators, who hoped to save their own necks by working with the Germans and duping their fellow Jews into thinking that the deportations were indeed – as Nazi propaganda insisted – about the transfer of personnel to new employment in

Germany. Just how much the council leaders knew about the gas chambers remains unclear, but after the war the surviving members of the Jewish Council successfully defended themselves against charges of collaboration, claiming that they had been a buffer against the Germans rather than their instruments.

Hortus Botanicus

From Nieuwe Keizersgracht, it's a hop, skip and a jump to the lush **Hortus Botanicus** (Mon–Fri 9am–5pm, Sat & Sun 10am–5pm; closes 4pm Dec & Jan; open till 9pm July & Aug; €6; ⓦwww.hortus-botanicus.nl), an appealing – if smallish – botanical garden whose entrance is on Plantage Middenlaan. The Hortus was founded in 1682 as **medicinal gardens** for the city's physicians and apothecaries after an especially bad outbreak of the plague. Thereafter,

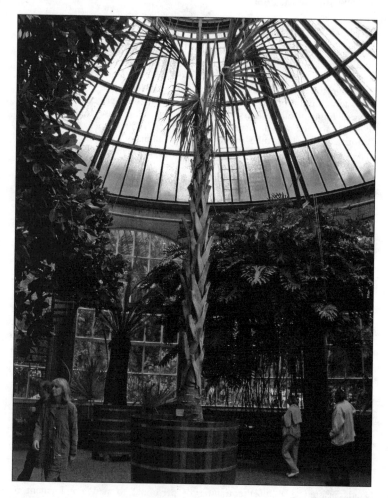

△ Hortus Botanicus

many of the city's merchants made a point of bringing back exotic species from the East, the result being the 6000-odd plant species exhibited today – both outside and in a series of hothouses. Botanical specimens also went the other way; in 1848, for instance, two oil palms left the gardens for Java, where they were used to establish the first of that island's many oil palm plantations.

The gardens are divided into several distinct sections, each clearly labelled, its location pinpointed by a map available at the entrance kiosk. Most of the outdoor sections are covered by plants, trees and shrubs from temperate and Arctic zones, with many of the more established trees dating back to a major replanting in 1895. The largest of the hothouses is the **Three-Climate Glasshouse**, partitioned into separate climate zones: subtropical, tropical and desert. The gardens also hold a **butterfly house** and a capacious **palm house** with a substantial collection of cycad palms. It's all very low-key – and none the worse for that – and the gardens make a relaxing break on any tour of central Amsterdam, especially as the **café**, in the old orangery, serves tasty lunches and a wonderful blueberry cheesecake.

Wertheimpark and De Hollandsche Schouwburg

Across the street from the botanical gardens, beside the canal, is the pocket-sized **Wertheimpark**, where the **Auschwitz monument** is a simple affair with symbolically broken mirrors and an inscription that reads *Nooit meer Auschwitz* ("Auschwitz – Never Again"). It was designed by the Dutch author and artist Jan Wolkers, who first came to prominence in the 1960s with a string of barbed novels – *Candyfloss, Oegstgeest Revisited* – railing against his Calvinist upbringing.

Proceed east down the right-hand side of Plantage Middenlaan to reach another sad relic of the war, **De Hollandsche Schouwburg**, at no. 24 (daily 10am–4pm; closed Yom Kippur; free; Ⓦ www.hollandscheschouwburg.nl). Formerly a Jewish theatre, the building became the main assembly point for Amsterdam Jews prior to their deportation. Inside, there was no daylight and families were interned in conditions that foreshadowed those of the camps they would soon be transported to. The front of the building has been refurbished, with the ground floor now holding a list of the dead and an eternal flame, and there's an excellent small **exhibition** on the plight of the city's Jews above. The exhibition, complete with lots of occupation photographs, is only labelled in Dutch, but an English translation is available at reception. By contrast, the old **auditorium** at the back of the building has been left as an empty, roofless shell. A memorial **column** of basalt on a Star of David base stands where the stage once was, an intensely mournful monument to suffering of unfathomable proportions.

Vakbondsmuseum

From De Hollandsche Schouwburg, it's a brief walk northeast to both the **Artis Zoo**, on Plantage Kerklaan (see p.249), and the **Vakbondsmuseum** (Trade Union Museum; Tues–Fri 11am–5pm, Sun 1–5pm; €2.50), at Henri Polaklaan 9. The museum building is a handsome structure, erected for the Diamond Workers' Union in 1900 to a distinctive design by **Hendrik Petrus Berlage** (1856–1934), who incorporated Romanesque features – such as the castellated balustrade and the deeply recessed main door – within an Expressionist framework. From the outside, it looks very much like a fortified mansion, hence its nickname **De**

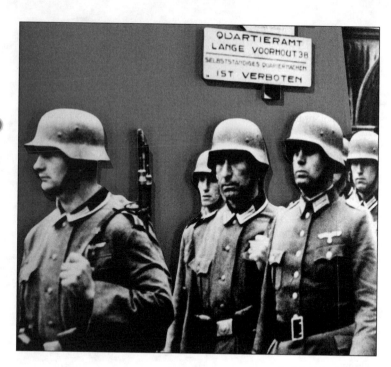

△ De Hollandsche Schouwburg

Burcht ("Stronghold"), but this design was not just about Berlage's architectural whims. Acting on behalf of the employers, the police – and sometimes armed scabs – were regularly used to break strikes, and the union believed members could, in an emergency, retreat here to hold out in relative safety.

The museum's striking, brightly coloured **interior** develops these stylistic themes with a beautiful mixture of stained-glass windows, stone arches, painted brickwork and patterned tiles. In the foyer is a bust of the remarkable **Henri Polak**, both a part-time rabbi and founder of the ANDB (Algemene Neder-landse Diamantbewerkersbond), the Diamond Workers' Association, which became the city's most powerful union. A Socialist who was committed to change via constitutional means, Polak organized the diamond workers as never before and was evangelical about members' self-improvement, arranging all manner of reading and discussion groups.

Up the stairs from the foyer, Floor 1 holds the handsome, wood-panelled **Bestuurskamer** (union boardroom), which is kitted out in classic Arts and Crafts style. The room sports three paintings on asbestos cement – one each for sleep, work and relaxation – which celebrate the introduction of the eight-hour working day in 1911, the union's most famous victory. Floor 2, the top floor, is given over to temporary exhibitions.

Verzetsmuseum

From the Vakbondsmuseum, take Henri Polaklaan eastwards and turn left at the end of the road for the excellent **Verzetsmuseum**, at Plantage Kerklaan 61

(Dutch Resistance Museum; Tues–Fri 10am–5pm, Mon, Sat & Sun noon–5pm; €5.50; Ⓦ www.verzetsmuseum.org). The museum tells the story of the **German occupation** of the Netherlands and the progress of the Resistance in World War II, from the invasion of May 1940 to the liberation of 1945. Thoughtfully presented, the display along the central gangway examines the main themes of the occupation, dealing honestly with the fine balance between cooperation and collaboration. On either side, smaller display areas are devoted to different aspects of the **Resistance**, from the brave determination of the Communist Party, who went underground as soon as the Germans arrived, to more ad hoc responses like the so-called **Melkstaking** (Milk Strike) in the spring of 1943, when hundreds of milk producers refused to deliver, in protest at the Germans' threatened deportation of 300,000 former (demobilized) Dutch soldiers to labour camps in Germany. Interestingly, the Dutch Resistance proved especially adept at forgery, forcing the Germans to make the identity cards they issued more and more complicated – but without much success.

Fascinating old **photographs** illustrate the (English and Dutch) text along with a host of original **artefacts**, from examples of illegal newsletters to signed German death warrants. Apart from their treatment of the Jews, which is detailed here, perhaps the most chilling feature of the occupation was the use of indiscriminate **reprisals** to terrify the population. For the most part this approach worked, though there was always a minority courageous enough to resist. The museum has dozens of little metal sheets providing biographical notes about and sketches of the members of the Resistance – and it's this mixture of the general and the personal that is its real strength.

The Oosterdok

Just to the north of the Plantagebuurt lies the **Oosterdok**, whose network of artificial islands was dredged out of the River IJ to increase Amsterdam's

The Dutch East India Company

Founded in 1602, the **Dutch East India Company** (the VOC – Verenigde Oostindische Compagnie) was the chief pillar of Amsterdam's wealth for nearly two hundred years. Its high-percentage profits came from importing spices into Europe, and to secure its supplies the company's ships ventured far and wide, establishing trading links with India, Sri Lanka, Indo-China, Malaya, China and Japan, though modern-day Indonesia was always the main event. Predictably, the company had a cosy relationship with the merchants who steered the Dutch government; the company was granted a trading monopoly in all the lands east of the Cape of Good Hope and could rely on the warships of the powerful Dutch Navy if they got into difficulty. Neither was their business purely mercantile; the East India Company exercised unlimited military, judicial and political powers in those trading posts it established, the first of which was Batavia in Java in 1619.

In the 1750s, the Dutch East India Company went into decline, partly because the British expelled them from most of the best trading stations, but mainly because the company had borrowed too heavily. The French army of occupation had little time for the privileges and pretensions of the VOC, abolishing its ruling council and ultimately dissolving the company in 1799.

shipping facilities in the seventeenth century. By the 1980s, this mosaic of docks, jetties and islands had become something of a post-industrial eyesore, but since then an ambitious redevelopment programme has turned things around and parts of the area are now regarded as some of the most up-and-coming in the city. The obvious sights here are the **Nederlands Scheepvaart-museum** (Netherlands Maritime Museum), though the interior is closed for a major refit until 2010, maybe later, and the **Stedelijk Museum**, which holds the city's prime collection of modern and contemporary art.

Entrepotdok

At the northern end of Plantage Kerklaan, just beyond the Verzetsmuseum (see p.106), a footbridge leads over to **Entrepotdok**, on the nearest – and most interesting – of the Oosterdok islands. Old brick **warehouses** stretch along much of the quayside, distinguished by their spout gables, multiple doorways and overhead pulleys. Built by the **Dutch East India Company** (see box p.107) in the eighteenth century, they were once part of the largest warehouse complex in continental Europe, a gigantic customs-free zone established for goods in transit. On the ground floor, above each main entrance, every warehouse sports the name of a town or island; goods for onward transportation were stored in the appropriate warehouse until there were enough to fill a boat or barge. The warehouses have been tastefully converted into offices and apartments, a fate they share with the central Dutch East India Company compound, whose two modest brick wings culminate in a chunky Neoclassical entrance at the west end of Entrepotdok on Kadijksplein.

The Nederlands Scheepvaartmuseum

The **Nederlands Scheepvaartmuseum** (Netherlands Maritime Museum; closed until further notice; ⓦ www.scheepvaartmuseum.nl) occupies the old arsenal of the Dutch Navy, a vast sandstone structure built on the Oosterdok beside Kattenburgerplein in the 1650s. It's underpinned by no less than 18,000 wooden piles driven deep into the river bed at enormous expense, a testament to the nautical ambitions of the Dutch elite. The building's four symmetrical facades are dour and imposing despite the odd stylistic flourish, principally some quaint dormer windows and Neoclassical pediments, and they surround a central, cobbled courtyard under which was kept a copious supply of fresh-water to supply the ships. It's the perfect location for a Maritime Museum and when it reopens, probably in 2010, it promises to be one of the city's key attractions.

Onward routes from the Nederlands Scheepvaartmuseum

From the Maritime Museum, there's a choice of several routes: if you're heading west, both the Canal Bus (see p.25) and the Museumboot (see p.25) will speedily return you to Centraal Station via the NEMO centre (see opposite). Alternatively, you can walk back to Centraal Station in about fifteen minutes, either along Prins Hendrikkade or rather more appealingly via the footbridge spanning the water between NEMO and the Oosterdokskade, the location of the Stedelijk Museum. Finally, diligent sightseers can either venture southeast to the De Gooyer windmill (see p.110) or northeast – from either the Stedelijk Museum or Centraal Station – to the tangle of River IJ islands that comprise Zeeburg (see pp.110–113).

ARCAM and NEMO

Strolling west from the Maritime Museum along the Prins Hendrikkade waterfront, you soon reach **ARCAM** (Tues–Sat 1–5pm; free; ⓦwww.arcam.nl), the Amsterdam Centre for Architecture, housed in a distinctive aluminium and glass structure designed by the Dutch architect **René van Zuuk**. The design was much praised, but the building does look rather disconcertingly like the head of a golf club. Inside, a small gallery area is used for an imaginative programme of temporary exhibitions on contemporary architecture.

Moored behind ARCAM are all sorts of antique **boats and barges**, which together make an informal record of the development of local shipping; the earliest boats date from the middle of the nineteenth century, and plaques, in English and Dutch, give the historical lowdown on the more important vessels. The boats lead towards the massive elevated hood that rears up above the entrance to the River IJ tunnel. A good part of this hood is now occupied by **NEMO** (Tues–Sun 10am–5pm; Mon open same hours during school holidays and in July & Aug; €11.50, under-4s free; ⓦwww.e-nemo.nl), a (pre-teenage) kids' attraction *par excellence*, with all sorts of interactive science and technological exhibits spread over six decks. For more on NEMO, see p.250.

Outside, moored at the NEMO jetty, is a full-scale replica of an East Indiaman, the 78-metre **De Amsterdam**. The ship has been temporarily relocated here whilst the Maritime Museum, which owns it, is closed. The original ship first set sail in 1748, but came to an ignominious end, getting stuck on the British coast near Hastings. Visitors can wander its decks and galleys, storerooms and gun bays at their leisure.

From NEMO, a footbridge leads over the harbour to the Stedelijk Museum (see below) or you can double back to Prins Hendrikkade for the short walk west to the Oude Schans canal (see p.61), which serves as an attractive introduction to the Old Centre.

The Stedelijk Museum

The **Stedelijk Museum** (daily 10am–6pm; €9; ⓦwww.stedelijk.nl) has long been Amsterdam's number one venue for modern and contemporary art. It was housed in a large old building on Paulus Potterstraat out near the Van Gogh Museum (see p.120) for years, but these premises are presently being gutted and won't be open again until 2008, if not later. In the meantime, two floors of the former postal building on Oosterdokskade near Centraal Station have been pressed into service as the museum's new home. It was a good move – the building is a classic 1960s tower block of industrial proportions – and one that has proved popular with Amsterdammers, so popular in fact that it has created a bit of a problem; the original plan was to return the collection to its old home after the refurbishment was complete, but now it's possible that the museum (or at least parts of it) will stay here. Meanwhile, the Oosterdokskade itself is being colonized by glass and concrete office and apartment blocks at a rate of knots.

Since moving to its new location, the museum has focused on cutting-edge, temporary exhibitions of **modern art** – from photography and video through to sculpture and collage – to such an extent that the permanent collection rarely gets much of an outing. The **permanent collection** includes drawings by Picasso, Matisse and their contemporaries, as well as paintings by Manet, Monet, Bonnard, Ensor, Cézanne and, of course, **Mondriaan** (1872–1944), from his early, muddy abstract works to the boldly coloured rectangular blocks for which he's most famous. The museum also has a good sample of the work of **Kasimir Malevich** (1878–1935), his dense attempts at Cubism leading to the dynamism and bold, primary tones of his "Suprematist" paintings – slices, blocks and bolts of colour that shift around as if about to resolve themselves into some complex computer graphic. Other highlights include several **Marc Chagall** paintings and a number of pictures by American Abstract Expressionists Mark Rothko, Ellsworth Kelly and Barnett Newman, plus the odd work by Lichtenstein, Warhol, Robert Ryman, Kooning and Jean Dubuffet.

The restaurant *11*, above the museum on the top floor of the old postal building, is one of the city's more fashionable joints, with sweeping views over the centre (for details, see p.186), whilst floors 9 and 10 are devoted to temporary exhibitions of contemporary design by some of the city's leading companies (Mon–Sat 11am–5pm, Sun noon–5pm; free).

From in front of the Stedelijk Museum, a long footbridge sticks to the edge of the harbour on its way back west to Centraal Station.

Museum Werf 't Kromhout and De Gooyer windmill

Heading east from the Nederlands Scheepvaartmuseum along Kattenburgergracht, you soon reach the footbridge spanning the Nieuwevaart canal over to Hoogte Kadijk, where, at no. 147, the **Museum Werf 't Kromhout** (Tues 10am–3pm; €5; ⓦ www.machinekamer.nl) is one of the city's few remaining **shipyards**. In their heyday, the Eastern docklands were strewn with shipyards just like this one. The first major contraction came at the end of the nineteenth century when steel and steam replaced timber; few of the existing yards were big enough to make the switch successfully. A number, including 't Kromhout, struggled on, by concentrating on the repair and construction of smaller inshore and canal boats. Even so, 't Kromhout almost went bust in 1969 and was only saved by turning into a combination of working shipyard and tourist attraction, its yard full of old boats, its museum littered with ancient engines and shipyard tools.

Continuing southeast along Hoogte Kadijk from 't Kromhout, it's about 500m to **De Gooyer windmill**, standing tall between two canals at Funenkade 5. Amsterdam was once dotted with windmills, used for pumping water and grinding corn, but most were demolished years ago and this is a rare survivor. If you have come this far, you'll be pleased to discover that the bar and mini-brewery in the old public baths adjoining the windmill – the **Brouwerij Het IJ** (Wed–Sun 3–8pm) – is a good old-fashioned place with an excellent range of beers and ales. They brew an alarmingly strong amber ale called Columbus (9%), as well as less frightening stuff, such as the creamy Natte (6.5%).

It takes about twenty minutes to walk back from the windmill to the Nederlands Scheepvaartmuseum, or take bus #22 from neighbouring Zeeburgerstraat.

Zeeburg

To the north and east of the Oosterdok, **Zeeburg** or **Oostelijk Havengebied** – basically the old docklands between the Stedelijk Museum (see p.109) and KNSM Island – has become one of the city's most up-and-coming districts.

Actually a series of artificial islands and peninsulas connected by bridges, the docks here date back to the end of the nineteenth century, but like dockland areas all over Europe they fell into disuse and disrepair during the 1970s with the advent of large container ships, which couldn't travel this far upriver. By the early 1990s, the area was virtually derelict, but it was then that the city council began a massive renovation, which has been going on for the past fifteen years or so. As a result, this is architecturally the fastest-developing part of Amsterdam, with a mixture of renovated dockside structures and new landmark buildings that give it a modern (and very watery) feel that's markedly different from the city centre – despite beginning just a fifteen-minute walk from Centraal Station. It's the general appearance of the district, rather than any specific sight, which provides its main appeal, so you're best off exploring by bike, especially as distances are, at least in Amsterdam terms, comparatively large – from the Stedelijk Museum to the east end of KNSM Island is about 4km. Alternatively, there are two useful transport connections from Centraal Station: tram #26 to Sporenburg island via Piet Heinkade and bus #42 to Java Island and KNSM Island.

To Java and KNSM islands

From the Stedelijk Museum, it takes about ten minutes to walk through to two of the Eastern docklands' prime buildings, the **Muziekgebouw** (see p.214), a brand-new, high-spec, multipurpose music auditorium overlooking the River IJ, and the neighbouring **Amsterdam Passenger Terminal**, a glass-walled behemoth, where visiting cruise ships now berth.

From the terminal building, it's a pleasant stroll east along the waterfront to the 200m-long **Jan Schaeferbrug**, which spans the IJ across to **Java Island**, a long and narrow sliver of land, where tall residential blocks, mostly five storeys high, line up along the four mini-canals that cut across it. In form and layout, these high-rises are a successful contemporary take on the seventeenth-century canal houses of the city centre; a string of quirky, wrought-iron bridges adds extra style and panache. If you're here in the evening, stop off for dinner at the sleek and slick *Voorbij het Einde* restaurant at Sumatrakade 613 (see p.199). The restaurant, literally "Beyond the End", takes its name from a squat ("The End of the World") that used to be here in the days when Java Island was a remote refuge.

The east end of Java Island merges seamlessly with **KNSM Island**, which is named after the shipping company (the Royal Dutch Steamboat Company) that was once based here. Leafy **KNSM-Laan** runs down the centre of the island, flanked by more modern blocks, of which the German-designed **Piraeus** apartment building, at the west end of the street, gives the best impression of the monumental nature of much of the architecture hereabouts. That said, waterside **Surinamekade**, on the north side of the island, is much prettier, decorated with houseboats, barges and decommissioned fishing smacks, and also has a number of decent bars and restaurants.

Sporenburg, Borneo Island and around

From beside the Piraeus building, the Verbindingsdam leads south across the water to the **Sporenburg** peninsula and the blunt modernism of the structure known as **The Whale**, a large and distinctive residential block designed by architect Frits van Dongen and completed in 1995. It takes its name from its size and shape, the sharp outlines of which apparently allow the sun to better warm the building.

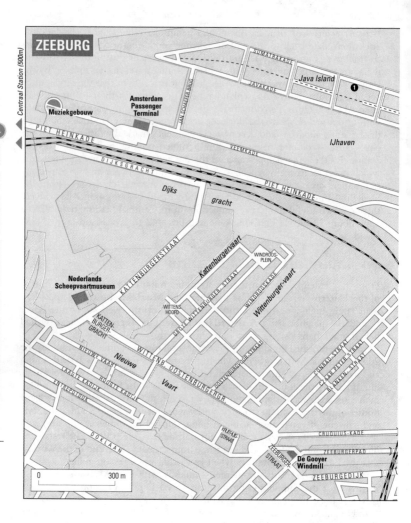

Follow Ertskade along the waterfront east from here and turn right at the end to get across Sporenburg and to reach the **Pythonbrug** footbridge, so called for its curvy, snakelike shape. On the far side of the footbridge is **Borneo Island**, where there are more modern canalside dwellings, the most striking of which fringe and frame **Scheepstimmermanstraat**. Once again, these follow their seventeenth-century predecessors in the conformity of their height and plot size, but otherwise each is utterly unique.

From the west end of Borneo Island, C van Eesterenlaan slices south across a narrow strip of water, bound for Zeeburgerkade, home to the **Nederlands Persmuseum** at no. 10 (Dutch Press Museum; Tues–Fri 10am–5pm & Sun noon–5pm; €3.50; ⓦwww.persmuseum.nl). The museum focuses on the history of the Dutch press since 1618, as revealed in newspapers, leaflets, posters and political cartoons.

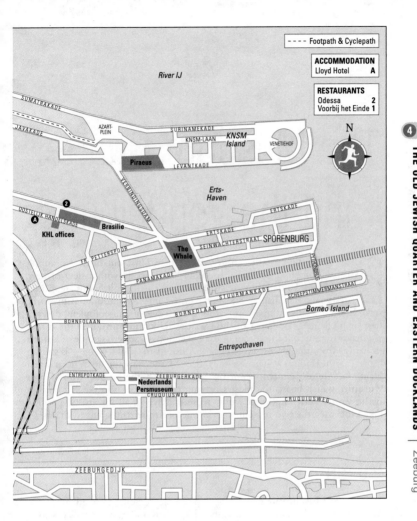

To the Lloyd Hotel

Doubling back along C van Eesterenlaan, it's about 800m to the super-slick **Lloyd Hotel** (see p.199), in an imaginatively revamped former 1920s prison at Oostelijke Handelskade 34. Close by are three minor points of interest: the **Brasilie** shopping centre, which occupies an old cocoa warehouse, the **Odessa**, a replica of a Russian merchant ship, now a restaurant, and the former offices of the **KHL shipping line** that once controlled this part of the dockland until the company went bankrupt in 1935.

To get back to Centraal Station, take tram #26 on Piet Heinkade, a couple of minutes' walk from the *Lloyd Hotel*.

5

The Museum Quarter and the Vondelpark

During the nineteenth century, Amsterdam burst out of its restraining canals, gobbling up the surrounding countryside with a slew of new, mostly residential outlying **suburbs**. These neighbourhoods are mostly described in Chapter Six, but Amsterdam's two leading **museums**, packed into a relatively small area around the edge of Museumplein, deserve their own chapter. The larger of the two, the **Rijksmuseum**, is in the throes of a major revamp, but the kernel of the collection – a superb sample of **Dutch paintings** from the seventeenth century, Amsterdam's Golden Age – is still on display in the Philips Wing, the only part of the museum to remain open during the refurbishment. Similarly impressive is the nearby **Van Gogh Museum**, which boasts the most satisfying collection of van Gogh paintings in the world, with important works representative of all his artistic periods. Taken together, the two museums form one of Amsterdam's biggest draws.

Museumplein

Pancake-flat **Museumplein** is a large open space extending south from the Rijksmuseum to Van Baerlestraat, its wide lawns and gravelled spaces used for a variety of outdoor activities, from visiting circuses to political demonstrations. Other than being the location for the sights detailed in this chapter, there's not a great deal to it, though the group of slim steel blocks about three-quarters of the way down on the left-hand side forms a **war memorial**, commemorating the women who perished in concentration camps, particularly the thousands who died at Ravensbruck.

The Rijksmuseum

Facing onto the Singelgracht, at the head of Museumplein, the **Rijksmuseum** (entrance to the Philips Wing on Jan Luijkenstraat; daily 9am–6pm, Friday until 10pm; €10; combination ticket with Van Gogh Museum, including current exhibition, €25; audio guide €4; ⓦ www.rijksmuseum.nl) is an imposing pile built by **Petrus J.H. Cuypers** (1827–1921) – also the creator of Centraal Station

THE MUSEUM QUARTER
AND VONDELPARK

△ The Rijksmuseum

– in the early 1880s. The leading Dutch architect of his day, Cuypers specialized in neo-Gothic churches, but this commission called for something more ambitious, the result being a reworking of the neo-Renaissance style then popular in the Netherlands: an intricate structure complete with towers and turrets, galleries, dormer windows and medallions. More importantly, the museum possesses an extravagant collection of **paintings** from every pre-twentieth-century period of Dutch art, together with a vast hoard of **applied art** and **sculpture**.

The museum is in the middle of an extensive (€272-million) revamp, which will last until 2009, and until this is finished, only one part of the museum – the **Philips Wing** – will remain open. The good news is that the wing's thirteen rooms are used to good effect to display the essence of the permanent collection under the title "The Masterpieces" – a splendid selection of seventeenth-century Dutch paintings from the *Gouden Eeuw* (Golden Age), as well as **delftware**, **silverware** and various other resonant items from Dutch history. There is some rotation, but you can count on seeing all the leading Rembrandts plus a healthy sample of canvases by Steen, Hals, Vermeer and their leading contemporaries.

Bear in mind that the relatively small size of the exhibition space means that **queues** can be long, especially in summer and at weekends – it's a good idea to book online first.

Rooms 1 to 5

The Philips Wing begins in style with two large galleries – Rooms 1 and 2 – which give the historical background to the **Dutch Golden Age** with features on the country's success as a trading nation and its naval prowess. Amongst the paintings on display here is the breezily self-confident *The Celebration of the Treaty of Münster*, by **Bartholomeus van der Helst** (1613–70), who became one of Amsterdam's most popular portraitists after Rembrandt abandoned the normal protocols of portraiture to adopt an introspective, religious style that did

Delftware

Named after the Dutch city of Delft, where it was manufactured, **delftware** traces its origins to fifteenth-century Mallorca, where craftsmen developed **majolica**, a type of porous pottery that was glazed with bright metallic oxides. During the Renaissance, these techniques were exported to Italy from where they spread north, first to Antwerp and then to the United Provinces (aka the Netherlands). Initially, delft pottery **designs** featured landscapes, portraits and Bible stories, whilst the top end of the market was dominated by more ornate Chinese porcelain imported by the Dutch East India Company. However, when a prolonged civil war in China broke the supply line, Delft's factories quickly took over the luxury side of the market by copying Chinese designs. By the 1670s, Delft was churning out blue-and-white tiles, plates, panels, jars and vases of all descriptions by the thousand, even exporting to China, where they undercut Chinese producers. The delft factories were themselves undercut by the British and the Germans from the 1760s on, and by the time Napoleon arrived they had all but closed down. There was a modest revival of the delft industry in the 1870s and there are several Dutch producers today, but it's mostly cheap, mass-produced stuff of little originality.

not impress the city's burghers. For the Dutch at least, the treaty was well worth celebrating; signed in 1648, it ended the Thirty Years' War and recognized the United Provinces (now the Netherlands) as an independent state, free of Habsburg control. Opposite van der Helst's painting, a smaller work, by **Gerard ter Borch**, witnesses the event itself. The Thirty Years' War had convulsed most of western Europe by pitting Catholic against Protestant. **Adriaen van de Venne** (1589–1662) was quite clear which side he was on; his curious *Fishing for Souls*, in Room 2, has the disorganized Catholics on the right river bank – and the Protestants merrily heaving in souls on the left.

Room 3 contains several antique **dolls' houses**, and several Dutch interior scenes, notably *Paternal Admonition* by Gerard ter Borch, and one of **Pieter de Hooch**'s typical interiors, showing the woman of the house changing the linen while a series of doorways reveals the canal bank in the background.

Room 4 is mostly **silverware**, and Room 5 showcases a large assortment of **delftware**, from plates and tiles through to vases, chargers and flower holders. Dating from the late sixteenth century, the earlier pieces are comparatively plain, typically decorated with rural, classical or biblical scenes, whereas the later porcelain is more elaborate and often copied from – or in imitation of – Chinese ceramics (see box above).

Rooms 6, 7 and 8

Upstairs, Room 6 holds early seventeenth-century paintings by **Thomas de Keyser**, **Gerard Honthorst** and **Hendrik Avercamp** that introduce several different genres – portraiture, still life and nature. Room 7 contains several superb canvases by **Frans Hals** (1582–1666), most notably his *Merry Drinker* and the expansive *Marriage Portrait of Isaac Massa and Beatrix Laen*. Relaxing beneath a tree, a portly Isaac glows with contentment as his new wife sits beside him in a suitably demure manner. An intimate scene, the painting also carries a detailed iconography; the ivy at Beatrix's feet symbolizes her devotion to her husband, the thistle faithfulness, the vine togetherness and in the fantasy garden behind them the peacock is a classical allusion to Juno, the guardian of marriage. In the same room, look out for the cool church interiors of **Pieter Saenredam** (1597–1665), whose *Old Town Hall of Amsterdam* is a characteristically precise work in which the tumbledown predecessor of the current building (now the Royal Palace) witnesses the comings and goings of black-hatted townsmen in the stilted manner of a Lowry.

In Room 8, examples of the work of **Salomon van Ruysdael** (1602–70) – a Haarlem artist with a penchant for soft, tonal river scenes – share space with that of **Jan Lievens**, who shared a studio with Rembrandt. Lievens' portrait of Rembrandt as a young artist is displayed here, as well as a depiction of the Golden Age statesman Constantine Huygens. There's also early work by **Rembrandt** himself – including a portrait of an old lady, perhaps his mother – and some of his better-known pupils, including **Nicholas Maes** (1632–93), whose caring *Young Woman by the Cradle* is not so much a didactic tableau as an idealization of motherhood. Another pupil, **Ferdinand Bol** (1616–80), painted *Portrait of Elizabeth Bas* in a style so close to that of his master that it was regarded as a Rembrandt until the director of the museum proved otherwise in 1911. Perhaps the most talented of Rembrandt's pupils was **Carel Fabritius**, who was killed in 1654 at the age of 32, when Delft's gunpowder magazine exploded. His *Portrait of Abraham Potter*, a restrained, skilful work of soft, delicate hues, contrasts with the same artist's earlier *The Beheading of St John the Baptist*, in which the head is served on a platter in chillingly grisly style.

Room 9

Rembrandt's *The Night Watch* is displayed in Room 12, but Room 9 has several fine examples of his work, notably the celebrated *Members of the Clothmakers Guild* and a late *Self-Portrait*, with the artist caught in mid-shrug as the Apostle Paul, a self-aware and defeated old man. Also here are the artist's touching depiction of his cowled son, *Titus*, and *The Jewish Bride*, one of his very last pictures, finished in 1667. No one knows who the couple are, nor whether they are actually married (the title came later), but the painting is one of Rembrandt's most telling, the paint dashed on freely and the hands touching lovingly – as the art historian Kenneth Clark wrote, in "a marvellous amalgam of richness, tenderness and trust". In marked contrast to these paintings are a number of landscapes by **Jan van Goyen**, **Jan Both** and **Jacob van Ruisdael**.

Room 10

Room 10 holds some examples of the small, finely realized works of **Gerard Dou** and **Gabriel Metsu**, flashes of everyday life that sit well with the work of **Johannes Vermeer** (1632–75). The latter is well represented; *The Love Letter* reveals a tension between servant and mistress – the lute on the woman's lap was a well-known sexual symbol – while *The Kitchen Maid* is an exquisitely observed domestic scene, right down to the nail – and its shadow – on the background wall. Similarly, in the precise *Young Woman Reading a Letter*, the map behind her hints at the far-flung places her loved one is writing from. What you won't get, however, is Vermeer's *Girl with a Pearl Earring* – this is on display in the Mauritshuis gallery in The Hague.

Gerard ter Borch (1617–81) also depicted apparently innocent scenes, both in subject and title, but his *Woman at a Mirror* glances in a meaningfully anxious manner at her servants, who look on with delicate irony from behind dutiful exteriors. The paintings of **Pieter de Hooch** are less symbolic – more exercises in lighting – but they're as good a visual guide to the everyday life and habits of the seventeenth-century Dutch bourgeoisie as you'll find – as evidenced by his *Woman with a Child in a Pantry*.

Room 11

From the latter half of the seventeenth century come **Gerrit Berckheyde**'s (1638–98) crisp depictions of Amsterdam and Haarlem, and the carousing

Rembrandt's progress

Born in Leiden to a family of millers, **Rembrandt Harmenszoon van Rijn** (1606–69) picked up his first artistic tips as an apprentice to Pieter Lastman in Amsterdam in the early 1620s. It was here that the artist developed a penchant for mythological and religious subjects. After his apprenticeship, in around 1625, Rembrandt went back to Leiden to establish himself as an independent master painter and, this achieved, some six years later he returned to Amsterdam, where he was to stay for the rest of his life.

In the early 1630s Rembrandt concentrated on **portrait painting**, churning out dozens of pictures of the burghers of his day, a profitable business that made him both well-to-do and well known. In 1634 he married **Saskia van Uylenburch** and five years later the couple moved into a smart house on Jodenbreestraat, now the Rembrandthuis museum (see p.96). Things seemed set fair, and certainly Rembrandt's portraits of his wife are tender and loving, but these years were marred by the death of all but one of his children in infancy, the sole survivor being his much-loved **Titus** (1641–68).

In 1642 Rembrandt produced what has become his most celebrated painting, **The Night Watch**, but thereafter his career went into decline, essentially because he forsook portraiture to focus on increasingly sombre and introspective **religious works**. Traditionally, Rembrandt's change of artistic direction has been linked to the death of Saskia in 1642, but although it is certainly true that the artist was grief-stricken, he was also facing increased competition from a new batch of portrait artists, primarily Bartholomeus van der Helst, Ferdinand Bol and Govert Flinck. Whatever the reason, there were few takers for Rembrandt's religious works and he made matters worse by refusing to adjust his spending. The crunch came in 1656, when he was formally declared insolvent, and four years later he was obliged to sell his house and goods, moving to much humbler premises in the Jordaan (see p.86). By this time, he had a new cohabitee, **Hendrickje Stoffels** (a clause in Saskia's will prevented them from ever marrying), and in the early 1660s, she and Titus took Rembrandt in hand, sorting out his finances and his work schedule. With his money problems solved, a relieved Rembrandt then produced some of his finest paintings – for example The Jewish Bride – emotionally deep and contemplative works with a rough finish, the paint often daubed with an almost trowel-like heaviness. Hendrickje died in 1663 and Titus in 1668, a year before his father.

peasants of **Jan Steen** (1625–79). Steen's *Feast of St Nicholas*, with its squabbling children, makes the festival a celebration of disorderly greed, while the drunken waywardness of his *Merry Family* and *Family Scene* verge; on the anarchic. Steen knew his bourgeois audience well; his caricatures of the proletariat blend humour with moral condemnation – or at least condescension – a mixture perfectly designed to suit their tastes. The artist was also capable of more subtle works, a famous example being his *Woman at her Toilet* (in Room 10), which is full of associations, referring to sexual pleasures just had or about to be taken; for example, the woman is shown putting on a stocking in a conspicuous manner, the point being that the Dutch word for stocking, *kous*, is also a slang word for a woman's genitalia. By contrast, **Willem van de Velde II**'s (1633–1707) preoccupations were nautical, his canvases celebrating either the might of the Dutch navy or the seaworthiness of the merchant marine, as in the churning seas of the superbly executed *Gust of Wind*, whose counterpoint is to be found in the calm waters and gunfire of *The Cannon Shot*.

Room 12

Dominating Room 12, Rembrandt's **The Night Watch** (*De Nachtwacht*) of 1642 is the most famous of all the artist's paintings. Restored after being slashed in 1975, the scene is of a **militia company** – the Kloveniersdoelen – one of the companies formed in the sixteenth century to defend the United Provinces (later the Netherlands) against Spain. As the Habsburg threat receded, so the militias became social clubs for the well-heeled, who were eager to commission their own group portraits as signs of their prestige. Rembrandt charged the princely sum of one hundred guilders for each member of the company who wanted to be in the picture; sixteen – out of a possible two hundred – stumped up the cash, including the company's moneyed captain, **Frans Banningh Cocq**, whose disapproval of Rembrandt's live-in relationship with Hendrickje Stoffels (see box, p.119) was ultimately to polish off their friendship. Curiously, *The Night Watch* is, in fact, a misnomer – the painting got the tag in the eighteenth century when the background darkness was misinterpreted. There were other misconceptions about the painting too, most notably that it was this work that led to the downward shift in Rembrandt's standing with the Amsterdam elite; in fact, there's no evidence that the militiamen weren't pleased with the picture, or that Rembrandt's commissions dwindled after it was completed.

Though not as subtle as much of the artist's later work, *The Night Watch* is an adept piece, full of movement and carefully arranged. Paintings of this kind were collections of individual portraits as much as group pictures, and for the artist their difficulty lay in doing justice to every single face while simultaneously producing a coherent group scene. Abandoning convention in vigorous style, Rembrandt opted to show the company preparing to march off: a snapshot of military activity in which banners are unfurled, muskets primed and drums rolled. There are a couple of **allegorical figures** as well, most prominently a young, spotlit woman with a bird hanging from her belt, a reference to the Kloveniersdoelen's traditional emblem of a claw. Militia portraits commonly included cameo portraits of the artist involved, but in this case it seems that Rembrandt didn't insert his likeness, though some art historians insist that the pudgy-faced figure peering out from the back between the gesticulating militiamen is indeed the great man himself.

Opposite *The Night Watch* is another Civic Guard portrait, *The Meagre Company*, started by **Frans Hals** and finished by **Pieter Codde** due to a dispute. It's a great painting, full of sensitively realized, individual portraits, but not only are the wildly differing painting styles of Hals and Rembrandt immediately apparent, but the more conservative arrangement of Hals' figures forms a massive contrast with Rembrandt's more fluid, dynamic work.

The Van Gogh Museum

Vincent van Gogh (1853–90) is arguably the most popular, most reproduced and most talked-about of all modern artists, so it's not surprising that the **Van Gogh Museum** (daily 10am–6pm, Friday until 10pm; €10, children 13–17 years €2.50, combination ticket with the Rijksmuseum, including current exhibition, €25; ⓦwww.vangoghmuseum.nl), comprising a fabulous collection of the artist's work, is one of Amsterdam's top attractions.

The museum occupies two modern buildings on the north edge of Museumplein, with the key paintings housed in an angular building designed by a leading light of the De Stijl movement, **Gerrit Rietveld**, and opened to the public in 1973. Well conceived and beautifully presented, this part of the museum provides an introduction to the man and his art based on paintings that were mostly inherited from Vincent's art-dealer brother Theo. To the rear of Rietveld's building, connected by a ground-floor escalator, is the ultramodern annexe. This aesthetically controversial structure – financed by the same Japanese insurance company that paid $35 million for one of van Gogh's *Sunflowers* canvases in 1987, and completed in 1998 – provides temporary exhibition space. Most of these **exhibitions** focus on one aspect or another of van Gogh's art and draw heavily on the **permanent collection**, which means that the paintings displayed in the older building are regularly rotated.

As you might expect, the museum can get very crowded, and the **queues** can be long, so come early to avoid the crush.

The collection

The **ground floor** of the main museum displays works by some of van Gogh's well-known friends and contemporaries, many of whom influenced his work – Gauguin, Decamps, Anton Mauve, Charles Daubigny and others. It then moves on to the works of the man himself, presented for the most part chronologically on the **first floor**. The first paintings go back to the artist's **early years** (1880–85) in Holland and Belgium: dark, sombre works in the main, ranging from an assortment of drab grey and brown still lifes to the gnarled faces and haunting, flickering light of *The Potato Eaters* – one of van Gogh's best-known paintings, and the culmination of hundreds of studies of the local peasantry.

Further along, the sobriety of these early works is easily transposed onto the urban landscape of **Paris** (1886–88), particularly in the *View of Paris*, where the city's domes and rooftops hover below Montmartre under a glowering, blustery sky. But before long, under the sway of fellow painters and – after the bleak countryside of Holland – the sheer colour of the city itself, van Gogh's approach began to change. This is most noticeable in two of his many self-portraits here and in the scenes from **Asnières**, just outside Paris, where the artist used to travel regularly to paint. In particular, look out for the surprisingly soft hues and gentle tones of his *Courting Couples*, and the disturbing yellows of *Still Life with Quinces and Lemons*.

In February 1888 van Gogh moved to **Arles**, inviting Gauguin to join him a little later (see box, p.122). With the change of scenery came a heightened interest in colour, and the predominance of **yellow** as a recurring motif; it's represented best in such paintings as *The Harvest*, and most vividly in the disconcerting juxtapositions of *The Yellow House*. Also from this period comes a striking canvas from the artist's *Sunflowers* series, justly one of his most lauded works, and intensely – almost obsessively – rendered in the deepest oranges, golds and ochres he could find. Gauguin told of van Gogh painting these flowers in a near-trance; there were usually sunflowers in jars all over their house – in fact, they can be seen in Gauguin's portrait of van Gogh from the same period, also displayed in the museum. There's also a rare **photograph** of van Gogh conversing with Emile Bernard, who also joined the two artists in Arles – testament to van Gogh's dream of establishing an artistic colony in the South.

Van Gogh's ear

In February 1888, **Vincent van Gogh** left Paris for **Arles**, a small town in the south of France. At first the move went well, with van Gogh warming to the open vistas and bright colours of the Provençal countryside. In September, he moved into the house he called the Yellow House, where he hoped to establish an artists' colony, gathering together painters of like mind. Unfortunately for van Gogh, his letters of invitation were ignored by most, and only **Gauguin**, who arrived in Arles in late October, stayed for long. Initially the two artists got on well, hunkering down together in the Yellow House and sometimes painting side by side, but the bonhomie didn't last. They argued long and hard about art, an especially tiring business for van Gogh, who complained: "Sometimes we come out of our arguments with our heads as exhausted as a used electric battery". Later, Gauguin would claim that van Gogh threatened him during several of these arguments; true or not, it is certainly the case that Gauguin had decided to return to Paris by the time the two had a ferocious quarrel on the night of December 23. The argument was so bad that Gauguin hotfooted to the local hotel, and when he returned in the morning, he was faced by the police. After Gauguin's exit, a deeply disturbed van Gogh had taken a razor to his **ear**, severing part of it before presenting the selected slice to a prostitute at the local brothel. Presumably, this was not an especially welcome gift, but in van Gogh's addled state he may well have forged some sort of connection with bullfighting, where the dead bull's ears are cut off and given as a prize to the bullfighter.

Hours after Gauguin's return, van Gogh was admitted to hospital, the first of several extended stays before, fearing for his sanity, he committed himself to the asylum of **St Rémy** in May 1889. Here, the doctor's initial assessment described him as suffering from "acute mania, with hallucinations of sight and hearing"; van Gogh attributed his parlous state to excessive drinking and smoking, though he gave up neither during his year-long stay.

In May 1890, feeling lonely and homesick, van Gogh discharged himself from St Rémy and headed north to Paris before proceeding on to the village of **Auvers-sur-Oise**. At first, van Gogh's health improved and he even began to garner critical recognition for his work. However, his twin ogres of depression and loneliness soon returned to haunt him and, in despair, van Gogh shot himself in the chest. This wasn't, however, the end; he didn't manage to kill himself outright, but took two days to die, even enduring a police visit when he refused to answer any questions, pronouncing: "I am free to do what I like with my own body".

During his time at the asylum in **St Rémy** (see box), van Gogh's approach to nature became more abstract, as evidenced by his unsettling *Wheatfield with a Reaper*, the dense, knotty *Undergrowth* and his palpable *Irises*. Van Gogh is at his most expressionistic here, the paint applied thickly, often with a palette knife, a practice he continued in his final, tortured works painted at **Auvers-sur-Oise**, where he lodged for the last three months of his life. It was at Auvers that he painted the frantic *Wheatfield with Crows*, in which the fields swirl and writhe under weird and dark skies, as well as the organized chaos of *Tree Roots* and the glowering *Landscape at Twilight*.

The second and third floors provide a backup to the lead collection. The **second floor** has a library and study area with books, catalogues and PC access to a detailed account of van Gogh's life and times, plus a number of sketches and a handful of less familiar paintings. It's here you're likely to find *A Pair of Shoes*, an idiosyncratic painting that used to hang in the house van Gogh shared with Gauguin in Arles.

The **third floor** features other paintings from the museum's permanent collection, many of which have been collected by the museum over recent years. They're mostly works by van Gogh's contemporaries, and include a seminal early painting of the Route de Versailles by **Pissarro**, views of Amsterdam and Zaandam windmills by **Monet**, and various pieces by **Toulouse-Lautrec**, **Cézanne**, **Bernard** and others.

The Concertgebouw

Across Van Baerlestraat just to the southwest of the Van Gogh Museum is the **Concertgebouw** (Concert Hall; Concertgebouwplein 2–6, ☎020/671 8345, Ⓦwww.concertgebouw.nl), home of the famed – and much recorded – Royal Concertgebouw Orchestra. When the German composer Brahms visited Amsterdam in the 1870s he was scathing about the locals' lack of culture and, in particular, their lack of an even halfway suitable venue for his music. In the face of such ridicule, a consortium of Amsterdam businessmen got together to fund the construction of a brand-new concert hall and the result was the Concertgebouw, completed in 1888. An attractive structure with a pleasingly grand Neoclassical facade, the Concertgebouw has become renowned among musicians and concertgoers for its marvellous acoustics, and after a facelift and the replacement of its crumbling foundations in the early 1990s it's looking and sounding better than ever, with a new glass gallery that contrasts nicely with the red brick and stone of the rest of the building.

The acoustics of the **Grote Zaal** (Great Hall) are still unparalleled, and the smaller **Kleine Zaal** regularly hosts chamber concerts, often by the resident Borodin Quartet. Ticket **prices** are very reasonable (€30–50), there are free Wednesday lunchtime concerts from September to May, and in July and August there's a heavily subsidized series of summer concerts.

Tours of the Concertgebouw are available on Sundays at 9.30am; these cost €4, though you have to buy a ticket for the 11am concert too (€13). The tour lasts a little over an hour and takes in the Grote Zaal and the

△ The Concertgebouw

Kleine Zaal, as well as various behind-the-scenes activities – control rooms, piano stores, artistes' dressing rooms and the like.

The Vondelpark

Amsterdam is short of green spaces, which makes the leafy expanse of the **Vondelpark**, a short stretch from both Museumplein and the Concertgebouw, doubly welcome. This is easily the largest and most popular of the city's parks, its network of footpaths used by a healthy slice of the city's population.

The park dates back to 1864, when a group of leading Amsterdammers clubbed together to transform the soggy marshland that lay beyond the old Leidsepoort gateway, on the western edge of Leidseplein, into a landscaped park. The group, who were impressed by the contemporary English fashion for natural (as distinct from formal) landscaping, gave the task of developing the new style of park to the Zocher family, big-time gardeners who set about their task with gusto, completing the project in 1865. Named after the seventeenth-century poet **Joost van den Vondel** (see p.55), the park proved an immediate success and was expanded to its present size (45 hectares) in 1877. It now possesses over a hundred tree species, a wide variety of local and imported plants, and – amongst many incidental features – a **bandstand** and an excellent **rose garden**. Neither did the Zochers forget their Dutch roots; the park is latticed with narrow waterways crossed by pretty bridges and ponds that are home to many types of **wildfowl**, including plentiful heron. There are other animals too: cows, sheep and numerous squirrels, plus – bizarrely enough – a large colony of bright-green parakeets. The Vondelpark has several children's **play areas**, and during the summer regularly hosts free **concerts** and theatrical performances, mostly in its own specially designed, **open-air theatre**, right in the centre of the park.

The Nederlands Filmmuseum and around

Housed in a grand nineteenth-century building near the northeast corner of the Vondelpark, the **Nederlands Filmmuseum** (☎020/589 1400, Ⓦwww.filmmuseum.nl) is really more an art-house **cinema** (with two screens) than a museum – a showcase for films of all kinds, most of which are shown in their original language, with subtitles in Dutch or sometimes English. There are several screenings nightly, as well as regular matinees, and the programme often follows a prescribed theme. Look out also for the free screenings of classic movies in the summer.

The Filmmuseum also possesses a large **archive** of old films and is a dab hand at celluloid restoration. In the large building next door, at Vondelstraat 69, the museum's **film library** (Tues–Fri 1–5pm) has a well-catalogued collection of books, magazines and journals (some in English), though they are for reference only and are not loaned out.

Across the street is the lugubrious, brown-brick hull and whopping spire of the **Vondelkerk**, which has had more than its share of bad luck. Work on the church, which was designed by Cuypers – the architect of Centraal Station and the Rijksmuseum – began in 1872, but finances ran out the following year and the building was not completed until the 1880s. Twenty years later, it was struck by lightning and in the ensuing fire its tower was burnt to a cinder – the present one was added much later. The church always struggled to find a decent-sized congregation, but limped on until it was finally deconsecrated in 1979, being turned into offices thereafter.

Two minutes' walk west up Vondelstraat from the church, look in on the **Hollandsche Manege** on the right (Mon, Tues, Thurs, Fri 2–11pm, Wed 9am–11pm, Sat 9am–6pm, Sun 9am–5pm), a venerable old stables, built in 1882, where you can take a peek at the riding lessons or pop upstairs for a drink in the marvellously shabby yet grand salon that overlooks the practice area – but brace yourself for the horsey smells that tend to pervade the place. See p.255 for more details on how to go for a ride at the stables.

6

The outer districts

A
msterdam is a small city, and the majority of its residential **outer districts** are easily reached from the city centre. The **south** holds most interest, made up of the **Oud Zuid** (Old South) – at the heart of which is the raucous **De Pijp** quarter, home to the Heineken Experience, sited in the company's old brewery – and the 1930s architecture of the **Nieuw Zuid** (New South), which also contains the enjoyable woodland area of the **Amsterdamse Bos**. As for the other districts, you'll find a good deal less reason to make the trek, though multicultural influences in the **east** give this part of the city some diversity, and this is also the location of the excellent **Tropenmuseum**, and, further south, the **Amsterdam ArenA**, but the **west** has nothing special at all. Finally, the **north** of the city, on the other side of the IJ, reachable by way of a short (free) ferry ride from behind Centraal Station, is again almost entirely residential, but it's pleasant enough if you're cycling through on the way to open country.

The Oud Zuid and De Pijp

Amsterdam's city centre is ringed by the Singelgracht, beyond which lies the **Oud Zuid**, and its most authentic district, **De Pijp** ("The Pipe"), Amsterdam's first real suburb. New development beyond the Singelgracht began around 1870, but after laying down the street plans, the city council left the actual house-building to private developers, who constructed the long rows of cheaply built and largely featureless five- and six-storey buildings that still dominate the area today. It is these sombre canyons of brick tenements which give the district its name (the apartments here were said to resemble pipe-drawers, since each had a tiny street frontage but extended deep into the building). De Pijp remains a largely working-class neighbourhood, which despite some gentrification remains one of the city's more closely-knit communities, and home to a large proportion of new immigrants – Surinamese, Moroccan, Turkish and Asian. To get here on public transport, tram #16 or #24, beginning at Centraal Station, will take you as far as Albert Cuypstraat, or take #25, which heads along Weteringschans, threads round Sarphatipark and continues south down De Pijp's main drag, Ferdinand Bolstraat.

The Wetering circuit

Just off Weteringschans, on the city-centre side of Singelgracht, the **Wetering circuit** roundabout has two low-key **memorials** to World War II. On the southwestern corner of the roundabout, by the canal, is a sculpture of a wounded man holding a bugle; it was here, on March 12, 1945, that thirty people were shot by the Germans in reprisal for acts of sabotage by the Dutch Resistance – given that the war was all but over, it's hard to imagine a crueller or more futile action. Across the main street, the second memorial commemorates H.M. van Randwijk, a Resistance leader. The restrained wording on the monument translates as:

When to the will of tyrants,
A nation's head is bowed,
It loses more than life and goods –
Its very light goes out.

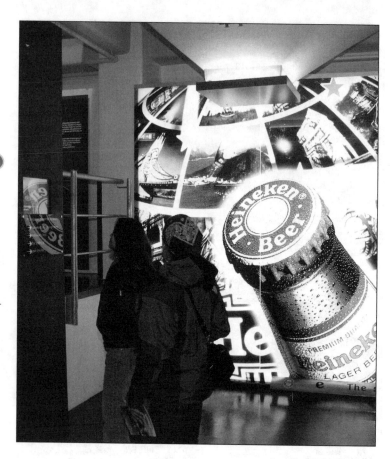

△ The Heineken Experience

The Heineken Experience

On the far side of the Singelgracht, on the northern edge of De Pijp at Stadhouderskade 78, the **Heineken Experience** (Tues–Sun 10am–6pm; €10; Ⓦ www.heinekenexperience.com; tram #16 or #24 from Centraal Station) is housed in the former Heineken brewery, a whopping building that was the company's headquarters from 1864 to 1988, at which time the firm restructured and its brewing moved to a more efficient location out of town. Since then, Heineken has developed the site as a tourist attraction, with displays on the history of beer-making in general and Heineken in particular. The old brewing hall is included on the tour, but for many the main draw is the beer itself – although the days when you could quaff unlimited quantities are long gone. Considering it's not a real brewery any more (you won't see any brewing taking place), Heineken make a decent stab at both entertaining and informing you at the same time – as well as promoting the brand, of course. There are lots of gimmicky but fun attractions. Initial displays take in postwar advertising, the idea behind the brand name's smiling "e" and a weird

Freddy Heineken

Heineken may not be the finest lager in the world, but no other brewer, Guinness apart, has thought up such catchy advertising slogans – "Heineken refreshes the parts other beers cannot reach", for one, is well-nigh impossible to beat. **Alfred ("Freddy") Heineken** (1923–2002) was the mastermind behind the company's rise to alcoholic success, but his route was far from straightforward. The company was founded in 1864 by Alfred's grandfather, Gerard, but his son and successor, Henry Pierre, sold the family's majority stake in 1942. Freddy didn't like this at all, but he bided his time, working his way up through the company ranks before skilfully amassing a majority shareholding in the 1950s. Chairman from 1979, Freddy ran the company with a beady eye for the main chance, increasing its sales dramatically both at home and abroad, whilst simultaneously developing a reputation as a playboy, or, more cordially, "bon vivant". Whatever the term, Freddy was hardly subtle; allegedly, the bedroom suite at the back of his office had a four-poster bed, a Jacuzzi and a painting of a naked woman stroking a cat entitled *The Woman with Two Pussies*.

In 1983, Freddy was **kidnapped** by three masked men and held for three weeks, before the police finally rescued him. Thereafter, he withdrew from the public eye, but maintained close relations with many of the country's richest and most powerful citizens until his death.

show on what it's like to be a bottle of Heineken, from bottling plant to delivery. You can also do a virtual-reality tour of Amsterdam by shire horse and dray, lie back and watch some Heineken TV ads, and even send a video email to a friend. You also get three drinks vouchers at bar stops that punctuate the tour, the first of which takes place after the impressive brewing hall, with its great copper drums overlooking the old (still inhabited) stables, and the last of which makes a convivial end to the proceedings (they throw in a Heineken glass as a souvenir on the way out, incidentally). All in all, not a bad way to pass an hour or two.

Albert Cuypstraat and the Sarphatipark

Ferdinand Bolstraat, running north–south, is De Pijp's main street, but the long, slim east–west thoroughfare of **Albert Cuypstraat** (pronounced "cowpstraat") is its heart. The general **market** held here – which stretches for over 1km between Ferdinand Bolstraat and Van Woustraat – is the largest in the city (in fact it claims to be the largest in Europe), with a huge array of stalls selling everything from cut-price carrots and raw herring sandwiches to saucepans and Day-Glo thongs. The market is open every day except Sunday, 10am until 5pm. Check out, too, the ethnic shops that flank the market on both sides, and the Indian and Surinamese restaurants down the side streets – they're often cheaper than their equivalents in the city centre.

A couple of blocks south of the Albert Cuypstraat market is the leafy **Sarphatipark**, a welcome splash of greenery amongst the surrounding brick and concrete. The park, complete with footpaths and a slender lake, was laid out before the construction of De Pijp got underway, and was initially intended as a place for the bourgeoisie to have a picnic. Heading east from the Sarphatipark, the main **Ceintuurbaan** artery crosses **Van Woustraat** – a long, unremarkable shopping street, though with a number of speciality ethnic food shops – before it reaches the River Amstel.

RESTAURANTS
Yamazato/Teppanyaki   A
Sazanka

ACCOMMODATION
Hotel Okura   A

0   250 m

OUD ZUID

△ De Pijp shop

The Nieuw Zuid

Southwest of De Pijp and the Oud Zuid, the **Nieuw Zuid** (New South), reachable direct from the city centre by tram #5 or #24, encompasses the whole area south of the Noorder Amstel canal to the railway tracks, as well as the old Rivierenbuurt district wedged in between the railway track, the River Amstel and the Amstel canal. By contrast with the Oud Zuid, this was the first properly planned extension to the city since the concentric canals of the seventeenth century. The Dutch architect Hendrik Petrus Berlage (1856–1934) was responsible for the relatively grand overall plan, but after his death much of the implementation passed to a pair of prominent architects of the **Amsterdam School**, Michael de Klerk (1884–1923) and Piet Kramer (1881–1961), who added a playfulness to the scheme – turrets and bulging windows, sloping roofs and frilly balustrades – that you can still see in the buildings here today. Neither was this architectural virtuosity confined to the houses of the well-to-do. In 1901 a reforming Housing Act forced the city council into a concerted effort to clear Amsterdam's slums, the principal result being several quality public housing projects designed by de Klerk and Kramer. There's one extant example in the western docklands (see p.91) and another here in the Nieuw Zuid, **De Dageraad**, though neither is as fanciful as the duo's phantasmagorical Scheepvaarthuis in the Old Centre (see p.61). Cutbacks in the city's subsidy meant that the more imaginative aspects of Berlage's original scheme for the Nieuw Zuid were toned down, but the area's wide boulevards and narrower side streets were completed as conceived. In this, Berlage wanted to reinterpret the most lauded feature of the

Amsterdamse Bos ▼▼   ▼ Amsterdamse Bos & CoBrA Museum

city's seventeenth-century canals: their combination of monumental grandeur and picturesque scale.

Nowadays the Nieuw Zuid is one of Amsterdam's most sought-after addresses. **Apollolaan**, **Stadionweg** and, a little way to the east, **Churchilllaan** are especially favoured, and are home to some of the city's most sumptuous properties – huge idiosyncratic mansions set back from the street behind trees and generous gardens. Locals pop to the shops on **Beethovenstraat**, the main drag running south right through the district from the Noorder Amstel canal. Posh residential areas are rarely much fun for the casual visitor, though, and the Nieuw Zuid is no exception; more enticing is the pleasant greenery of the **Beatrixpark**, and, slightly further southwest beyond the railway tracks, the sprawling parkland of the **Amsterdamse Bos** – both providing a pleasant interlude from the network of suburban streets.

Apollolaan and around

Apollolaan, a wide residential boulevard just south of the Noorder Amstel canal, is representative of Berlage's intended grand design, but despite its obvious gracefulness, the Nieuw Zuid was far from an instant success with the Dutch bourgeoisie. Indeed, in the late 1930s the district became something of a Jewish enclave – the family of Anne Frank, for example, lived for a time on Merwedeplein just off Churchilllaan. This embryonic community was swept away during the German occupation, their sufferings retold in Grete Weil's (Dutch-language) novel *Tramhalte Beethovenstraat*. A reminder of those terrible times is to be found at the intersection of Apollolaan and Beethovenstraat, where a **monument**, built in 1954, commemorates the shooting of 29 resistance fighters here in 1944 in retribution for the killing of a German security officer – a striking monument showing three desperate figures.

On a different note, Apollolaan is also known for the **Amsterdam Hilton** at no. 138, where John Lennon and Yoko Ono staged their famous week-long "Bed-In" for peace in 1969. Part celebrity farce, part skilful publicity stunt, the couple's anti-war proclamations were certainly heard far and wide, but in Britain the press focused on the supposed evil influence of Yoko on John, which satisfied at least three subtexts – racism, sexism and anti-Americanism.

Beatrixpark to De Dageraad

From Apollolaan, head south down **Beethovenstraat**, and, beyond the Zuider Amstel canal, take the first left, Cornelius Dopperkade, for the nearest of several entrances into the **Beatrixpark**. This appealing park, with its footpaths and attractive walled garden, is latticed by narrow waterways fed by the main Amstel canal. It's a pleasant place for a stroll and in summer you can catch free open-air concerts. The park's eastern perimeter is marked by the Boeren Wetering canal, beyond which rises the clumpy **Amsterdam RAI** exhibition centre, a trade and conference complex that was built as part of the city's plan to attract more business trade. It's of little interest in itself, but if you're at a loose end, you might want to check out one of the centre's regular trade fairs. To get there, leave the Beatrixpark at Boerenweteringpad and then follow Wielingenstraat across the canal.

A more enticing option is to take a left off Wielingenstraat up Haringvliet-straat, which leads after about 300m to the west end of **Churchilllaan**. This wide and well-heeled boulevard leads in its turn to Waalstraat, which, after crossing the Amstel canal, becomes Pieter Lodewijk Takstraat, a short, narrow street that is home to **De Dageraad** ("The Dawn") housing project, completed in 1923 and one of the most successful examples of the Amsterdam School of architecture. Architects de Klerk and Kramer used a reinforced concrete frame as an underlay to the structure, thus permitting folds, tucks and curves in the brick exterior – a technique known as "apron architecture" (*Schortjesarchitectuur*). The facades are punctuated by strong, angular doors, sloping roofs and turrets, and you'll find a corner tower at the end of every block.

From De Dageraad, you can either walk up to the Albert Cuypstraat market (see p.236), about 800m away to the northwest, or return to the Churchilllaan to catch tram #12 northwest to the Concertgebouw, and then tram #16 heading west to the Haarlemmermeer Station – for the Amsterdamse Bos.

The Amsterdamse Bos

With almost ten square kilometres of wooded parkland, the **Amsterdamse Bos** (ⓦ www.amsterdamsebos.nl) is the city's largest open space. Planted during the 1930s, the park was a laudable, large-scale attempt to provide gainful work for the city's unemployed, whose numbers had risen alarmingly following the Wall Street Crash of 1929. Originally a bleak area of flat, marshy fields, it's now a mixture of well-tended city park, leafy waterways, deep woodland and grassy meadows, intersected by footpaths and cycleways.

The main **entrance** to the Bos is in the northeast corner of the park, close to the junction of Amstelveenseweg and Van Nijenrodeweg, around 500m south of

△ The Amsterdamse Bos

The Museumtramlijn

It's a little more convoluted, but you can also get to the Amsterdamse Bos on the vintage trams of the **Museumtramlijn** (mid-April to end Oct Sun 11am–5pm, July–Aug also Wed at 1.45pm & 3.15pm; ✆0900 423 1100; €3.50 return). The trams depart from Haarlemmermeer Station, about 500m south of the western tip of the Vondelpark. The Museumtramlijn trams, imported from as far away as Vienna and Prague, clank south along the eastern edge of the Bos to the suburb of Bovenkerk on its southeast corner – a forty-minute journey in all, although you can get off earlier, at the main entrance to the park, or at other stops along the way.

the main southern ringroad and some 3km south of the west end of the Vondel-park. **Buses** #170 and #172, from Centraal Station and the Leidseplein, ply Amstelveenseweg; or you can take the #222 Schiphol Oost bus, which runs from Centraal Station via Leidseplein and Haarlemmermeer Station. Once in the park you can rent a **bike** (April–Nov daily 10am–6pm; ✆020/644 5473) just inside the entrance – much the best way of getting around. Canoes and pedaloes can be rented here too (April–Oct daily 10.30am–6pm; ✆020/645 7831). The **Bezoekerscentrum het Bosmuseum**, just inside the main entrance at Bosbaanweg 5 (daily noon–5pm; ✆020/545 6100), is a visitor information centre that provides maps and basic information on the park's facilities, and has an exhibition on its history and wildlife. Also here is the convivial **café-restaurant**, *Grand Café Bosbaan* (daily 10am till late; ✆020/404 4869), which does drinks, snacks and full meals, and whose terrace overlooks the **Bosbaan** – a dead-straight canal, over 2km long and popular for boating and swimming. There's also a first-rate pancake house located to the east of the Bosbaan at Koenenkade 56 (mid-Feb to Oct Tues–Sun 10am–7pm, Nov to mid-Feb Fri, Sat & Sun only 10am–6pm; ✆020/679 2744). Elsewhere in the park there are children's playgrounds and spaces for various sports, including ice skating, as well as a goat farm (March to mid-Nov 10am–5pm; closed Tues; ✆020/645 5034) and a reserve in the south where a small herd of Scottish Highlands cows is allowed to roam in relative solitude. Or just walk, jog or cycle your way around by way of the wide choice of clearly marked trails.

The CoBrA Museum of Modern Art

A little way east of the Amsterdamse Bos is the **CoBrA Museum of Modern Art** (Tues–Sun 11am–5pm; €7; ✆020/547 5050, ⓦwww.cobra-museum.nl), right next to Amstelveen bus station at Sandbergplein 13. To get there from the centre, take #170, #171 or #172 from Centraal Station; it's also reachable by metro to Amstelveen Centrum, or by #5 tram to its final stop Amstelveen Binnehof (it's a ten-minute walk west from the metro station, slightly less from the tram stop). This soothing white gallery, its glass walls giving a view of the canal behind, displays the works of the artists of the **CoBrA movement**, founded in 1948, which grew out of the cities of Copenhagen, Brussels and Amsterdam – hence the name. CoBrA were kind of postwar European art punks, and their first exhibition, held at Amsterdam's Stedelijk Museum, not surprisingly caused controversy; their big, colourful canvases, with bold lines and confident forms, displayed a spontaneity and inclusivity that was unusual for the art world at the time. You'll only find a scattering of their work here but there's enough to get an idea of what CoBrA were about, not least Karel Appel's weird, junky bird sculpture outside, and the brash, childlike paintings of Appel (in many ways the movement's leading light), Constant, Corneille and others in the rest of the gallery. Upstairs the museum hosts regular temporary exhibitions of works by contemporary artists. There's a good shop, too, with plenty of prints and books on the movement and the times, plus a bright café where you can gaze upon Appel's sculpture at length.

Amsterdam Oost

Next door to Amsterdam's Old South, **Amsterdam Oost** (East) is another rough-and-ready working-class quarter stretching out beyond the Singelgracht, although it's less gentrified than De Pijp. The area begins with Amsterdam's old eastern gate, the **Muiderpoort** (pronounced "mao-der-port"), overlooking the canal at the end of Plantage Middenlaan (p.102). In the 1770s the gate was revamped in pompous style, a Neoclassical refit complete with a flashy cupola and grandiosely carved pediment. Napoleon staged a triumphal entry into the city through the Muiderpoort in 1811, but his grandiose arrival was tempered by the behaviour of his half-starved troops, who were so dazzled by a city of (what was to them) amazing luxury that they could barely be restrained from looting. Despite its general lack of appeal, the Oost district does have one obvious attraction – the **Tropenmuseum**, near the Muiderpoort and located on the corner of another of the city's municipal parks, the **Oosterpark**.

The Tropenmuseum

Across the Singelgracht canal on Mauritskade rises the gabled and turreted **Royal Tropen Instituut** – formerly the Royal Colonial Institute – a sprawling complex which contains the **Tropenmuseum** (daily 10am–5pm; €7.50, 6- to 17-year-olds €4; ℡020/568 8200, ⓦwww.tropenmuseum.nl; tram #9 from Centraal Station), whose entrance is around the side at Linnaeusstraat 2. With its cavernous central hall and three floors of gallery space, this is Amsterdam's ethnographic museum, focusing on all the world's tropical and subtropical zones – and doing so incredibly well, with a spectacular collection

△ The Tropenmuseum

of art, applied art and other exhibits, displayed in an engaging, modern, yet entirely gimmick-free way. Among the many artefacts, there are Javanese stone friezes, elaborate carved wooden boats from the Pacific, a gamelan orchestra, a whole room of ancestral and death masks, and some incredible ritual poles cut from giant New Guinea mangroves. The collection is explained in English and imaginatively presented through a variety of media – slides, DVDs and sound recordings – and you can watch everything from Dutch colonials meeting the natives over a hundred years ago to nomads of the Central Asian steppes from inside a traditional tent know as a *ger*; and there are fun, creative displays devoted to such subjects as music-making and puppetry, and traditional story-telling. Perhaps best of all are the museum's studiously authentic reconstructions of contemporary life around the world – a mock-up of a Nigerian bar and residential compound, a Middle Eastern teahouse, a south American café, a Filipino jeepney bus – plus its candid expositions on the problems besetting the developing world, both urban and rural, such as the destruction of the tropical rainforests. The permanent collection is enhanced by an ambitious programme of temporary exhibitions, such as "Dealing with the Gods", a focus on Hinduism, with exhibits of textiles and precious stones. There's also a great shop, with crafts and music from and books about the developing world, and downstairs, the **Tropentheater** (see pp.208 & 218) specializes in Third World cinema, music and dance. Part of the museum is also geared towards children aged between 6 and 12, with a section known as the **Tropenmuseum Junior**, which takes a hands-on approach to the same themes as the main museum, but operates restricted opening hours and is in Dutch only (see p.250, "Kids' Amsterdam").

The Oosterpark and beyond

Behind the Royal Tropen Instituut, the manicured greenery of the **Oosterpark** is a pleasant introduction to the massed housing that extends south and east. A working-class district for the most part, particularly on the far side of Linnae-usstraat, the area also has a high immigrant presence, and the street names – Javas-traat, Balistraat, Borneostraat – recall Holland's colonial past. This is one of the city's poorer neighbourhoods, with a sea of ageing terraced houses, though whole streets have been torn down to make way for new and better public housing – and there's the inevitable creeping gentrification. If you find yourself with some time to fill after the Tropenmuseum you might consider a stroll along **Dapper-straat market** (Mon–Sat 9am–5pm), one block east of Linnaeusstraat, the eastern equivalent to the Albert Cuypstraat market (see p.236), though with slightly less atmosphere.

Amsterdam ArenA

Not strictly in Amsterdam Oost, but nonetheless on this side of town, the new home ground of Ajax, the **Amsterdam ArenA** (April–Sept daily 10am–6pm; Oct–March Mon–Sat 10am–5pm & last Sun of the month; museum and stadium tour €8.50, museum only €3.50; ☎020/311 1333, ⓦwww.amsterdamarena .nl), is well worth the fifteen-minute metro trip, both to visit the **Ajax Museum** and to take a tour of the stadium itself. Either take the metro to Strandvliet and walk around the stadium to the main entrance on the far side, or a stop further on to Bijlmer station, from which the ArenA Boulevard, lined with new shops and cafés, leads to the main entrance. Much as you would expect, the museum is a historical homage to Holland's most successful football club, Ajax, charting its origins at the turn of the twentieth century – lots of photos of men in big shorts in muddy fields – through its various stadia and the evolution of the famous red-and-white strip. There are special shrines to two of the club's most illustrious players – Cruyff and van Basten – as well as a rather mawkish short film depicting the rise to stardom of its leading players, and the centrepiece, true to the club's obvious self-image as one of the big hitters of European football (there's relatively little on the domestic league), is a display devoted to Ajax's European campaigns, with tickets, programmes, shirts and footage of the key moments from each final, from their first victory – in 1971 against Panathinaikos – to their most recent, against AC Milan in 1995. As for the stadium, hour-long walk-in tours are conducted throughout the day in Dutch and English between 11am and 4.30pm, which will impress even the most fair-weather fan, especially if you happen to time it right and get there during training (the Ajax training ground is adjacent to the stadium). Tours take in the main concourses, the press room – where you can snap yourself in front of the sponsors' logos – and the view from up in the security box, as well as allowing you onto a strip of the hallowed turf. Actually the pitch is perhaps the most remarkable thing about the Amsterdam ArenA; the stadium is built in such a way that the grass receives hardly any sunlight and no wind, which means it doesn't drain or grow very well and has to be relaid at least two or three times a year, at a cost of €100,000 a time. See p.254, "Sports and Activities", for more on seeing a game at the ArenA.

The Oud West

Of all Amsterdam's outer districts, the western stretch is probably the least interesting for the visitor, as it's primarily a residential area with only a couple of minor parks as possible attractions. That said, the **Oud West** (Old West), beyond the Singelgracht and north of the Vondelpark, does have a busy Turkish and North African street life, which is seen at its most vigorous at the daily **Katestraat market** (10am–5pm), about halfway down **Kinkerstraat** (trams #7 and #17), which is a small but vibrant market selling anything from cheese to chairs. Beyond, in districts such as Bos en Lommer, De Baarsjes and Overtoomse Veld, the best you'll do is the large but really rather ordinary **Rembrandtpark**.

Amsterdam Noord

Solidly residential, **Amsterdam Noord** (North), on the far side of the River IJ, has flourished since the construction of the IJ tunnel linked it with the city centre in the 1960s. A modern suburban sprawl, the district is short on charm, but the determined can weather the aesthetic gloom to reach the open countryside beyond. The area to head for is the **Waterland**, an expanse of peat meadows, lakes, polders and marshland to the northeast of the built-up area. Until the turn of the twentieth century, this parcel of land was a marshy fen, whose scattered population made a healthy living raising and grazing cattle to be sold in Amsterdam. The Waterland was then made much more tractable by the digging of drainage canals, prompting wealthy Amsterdammers to build their summer residences here. These myriad waterways still pattern the Waterland and are home to a wide range of **waterfowl**, as are the many lakes, the largest of which – abutting the Markermeer, formerly part of the Zuider Zee – is the **Kinselmeer**. Easily the best way to explore the Waterland is by **bike**, and the VVV sells a Waterland leaflet which outlines a circular, 38-kilometre bike tour. The recommended route begins at the **Adelaarswegveer ferry dock** (see below) on the north side of the IJ, from where you follow Meeuwenlaan to the large roundabout at the start of Nieuwendammerdijk. This long, thin lane leads east, running parallel to the river, before it meets Schellingwoudedijk and then Durger Dammerdijke, at the southern tip of the long dyke that stretches up the coast, with the polders and a scattering of tiny villages just inland.

Ferries across the IJ

GVB operates two **ferries** across the IJ from De Ruijterkade, behind Centraal Station. Neither ferry (*veer*) takes cars but both carry foot passengers, bicycles and motorbikes for free. Of the two, the **Buiksloterwegveer** (Mon–Sat 6.30am–10.54pm, till 9pm from Buiksloterweg, Sun 11.06am–6.54pm) shuttles back and forth every twelve minutes or so, running to the foot of Buiksloterweg. The smaller **Adelaarswegveer** (Mon–Sat 6.27am–11.57pm, Sun 9.12am–11.57pm) connects with the southern end of Meeuwenlaan, the starting point of the Waterland bike tour; it runs roughly every ten to fifteen minutes.

Day-trips
from the city

Amsterdammers may well try to persuade you that there's nothing remotely worth seeing outside their city, but the truth is very much the opposite – indeed, you're spoilt for choice. The fast and efficient Dutch railway network puts a whole swathe of the Netherlands within easy reach, including all of the **Randstad** (literally 'Ring City'), a sprawling conurbation that stretches south of Amsterdam to encompass the country's other big cities, primarily The Hague, Utrecht and Rotterdam. Amidst this urban pile-up, and very close to Amsterdam, is one especially appealing medium-sized town – **Haarlem**, whose attractive centre is home to the outstanding Frans Hals Museum. Haarlem is also the briefest of train rides from the wide sandy beaches of **Zandvoort**, one of Holland's most popular resorts, and but a short bus ride from the pristine coastal dunes, woods, lagoons and beaches of the **Nationaal Park Zuid-Kennemerland**, which stretches north from Zandvoort all the way up to the ugly port of IJmuiden. Further south – about 40km from Amsterdam and 15km from Haarlem – is another enticing attraction, the world–famous **Keukenhof Gardens**, the springtime showcase for the country's flower growers, the land striped by long lines of brilliant blooms.

To the north of Amsterdam, there's more countryside and less city. The most obvious targets are the old seaports bordering the freshwater **Markermeer**, comprising the southern part of the IJsselmeer, created when the Afsluitdijk dam cut the former Zuider Zee off from the North Sea in 1932 (see box p.151). No trains venture out along this coast, but it's an easy bus ride from Amsterdam to the nearest three places of interest: the former fishing village of **Marken**, the port of **Volendam** and – best of the lot – the beguiling, one-time shipbuilding centre of **Edam**. Edam is, of course, famous for its cheese, but its open-air cheese market is not a patch on that of **Alkmaar**, itself an amiable small town forty minutes by train north of Amsterdam.

Public transport to all these destinations from Amsterdam is fast, frequent and inexpensive.

DAY-TRIPS FROM THE CITY

0   20 km

N

NORTH SEA

Terschelling

Vlieland

Waddenzee

DE SLUFTER
DE MUY
Texel
De Cocksdorp
De Koog
Den Burg
Oudeschild
Den Hoorn
Noorderhaaks
Den Helder
Den Oever

Harlingen

Leeuwarden

Sneek

AFSLUITDIJK A7 E22

Stavoren

IJsselmeer

WIERINGERMEER
POLDER

NOORDOOSTPOLDER

Petten
Camperduin
SCHOORLSE DUINEN
NATIONAALPARK
Schoorl
Bergen
Bergen-aan-Zee
Egmond-aan-Zee

Medemblik

Enkhuizen

Urk

E22
Hoorn

Alkmaar

MARKERWAARDDIJK

NOORDHOLLANDS
DUINRESERVAAT

Markermeer

OOSTELIJK
FLEVOLAND

Edam
Volendam
Marken

Lelystad

Zaanse
Schans
Monnickendam
Noordzeekanaal

IJmuiden
NATIONAALPARK
ZUID-
KENNEMERLAND
Bloemendaal-
aan-Zee
Zandvoort

N 200
Zaandam

Amsterdam

ZUIDELIJK
FLEVOLAND

Haarlem

Muiden

Almere

Schiphol

Keukenhof

Lisse

Naarden
Laren

Hilversum

Leiden, The Hague & Rotterdam   Utrecht

Haarlem and around

Though only fifteen minutes from Amsterdam by train, **HAARLEM** has a very different pace and feel from its big-city neighbour, being an easy-going, medium-sized town of around 15,000 souls and benefiting from an old and

141

ACCOMMODATION
Amadeus	B
Best Western Grand Hotel Frans Hals	C
Carillon	A

HAARLEM

RESTAURANTS & BARS
Café 1900	1
Fortuyn Grand Café	2
In Den Uiver	4
Luca & Lucas	7
Proeflokaal Blauwe Druif	6
Restaurant Applause	3
Restaurant Specktakel	5

good-looking centre that's easily absorbed in a few hours or an overnight stay.

Founded on the banks of the River Spaarne in the tenth century, the town first prospered when the counts of Holland decided to levy shipping tolls here, but later it developed as a cloth-making centre. In 1572 the townsfolk sided with the Protestant rebels against the Habsburgs, a decision they must have regretted when a large Spanish army led by Frederick of Toledo besieged them later in the same year. The siege was a desperate affair that lasted for eight months, but finally the town surrendered after receiving various assurances of good treatment – assurances which Frederick promptly broke, massacring over two thousand of the Protestant garrison and all their Calvinist ministers. Recaptured in 1577 by the Protestant army of William the Silent, Haarlem went on to enjoy its greatest prosperity in the seventeenth century, becoming a centre for the arts and home to a flourishing school of painters, whose canvases are displayed at the first-rate **Frans Hals Museum**, located in the almshouse where the artist spent his last – and, for some, his most brilliant – years.

Haarlem is also within easy striking distance of the **coast**; every half hour, trains make the ten-minute trip to the clumpy modern resort of **Zandvoort-aan-Zee**, and there are frequent buses to the huddle of fast-food joints that clutter the coast at **Bloemendaal-aan-Zee** just to the north. Neither is particularly endearing in itself, but both are redeemed by the long, sandy beach that stretches along this part of the coast. Equally enticing – perhaps even more so – is the **Nationaal Park Zuid-Kennemerland**, a strip of pristine dune and lagoon that backs onto Bloemendaal-aan-Zee, crisscrossed by footpaths and cycling trails.

The Town

At the heart of Haarlem is the **Grote Markt**, a wide and attractive open space flanked by an appealing ensemble of neo-Gothic, Gothic and Renaissance architecture, including an intriguing, if exceptionally garbled, **Stadhuis**, whose turrets and towers, balconies, gables and galleries were put together in piecemeal fashion between the fourteenth and the seventeenth centuries. At the other end of the Grote Markt stands a **statue** of a certain Laurens Coster (1370–1440), who, Haarlemmers insist, is the true inventor of printing. Legend tells of Coster cutting a letter "A" from the bark of a tree, dropping it into the sand by accident, and, hey presto, he realized how to create the printed word. The statue shows him earnestly holding up the letter concerned, though actually most historians agree that it was the German Johannes Gutenberg who invented printing in the 1440s.

The Grote Kerk

The Coster statue stands in the shadow of the **Grote Kerk**, or Sint Bavokerk (Mon–Sat 10am–4pm; €2), a soaring Gothic structure supported by mighty buttresses, which dwarfs the surrounding clutter of ecclesiastical outhouses. If you've been to the Rijksmuseum in Amsterdam (see p.114) the church may seem familiar, at least from the outside, since it turns up in several paintings of Haarlem by the seventeenth-century artist Gerrit Berckheyde – only the black-coated burghers are missing. Finished in 1538, and 150 years in the making, the church is surmounted by a handsome lantern tower, which perches above the transept crossing; the tower is made of wood clad in lead, a replacement for a much grander stone tower that had to be dismantled in 1514 when its supports began to buckle.

Entry to the church is round the back, on Oude Groenmarkt, with a humble passageway leading to the southeast end of the **nave**, whose towering beauty is enhanced by the creaminess of the stone and the bright simplicity of the white-washed walls. The Protestants cleared the church of most of its decoration during the Reformation, but the splendid wrought-iron **choir screen** has survived, as have the choir's wooden stalls with their folksy misericords. In front of the screen is the conspicuous Neoclassical **tomb** of Haarlem's own Christiaan Brunings (1736–1805), a much-lauded hydraulic engineer and director of Holland's water board, who devised a strategy for controlling the waters of the lower Rhine.

Close by, next to the south transept, is the **Brewers' Chapel**, where the central pillar bears two black markers – one showing the height of a local giant, the 2.64m-tall Daniel Cajanus, who died in 1749, the other the 0.84m-high dwarf Simon Paap from Zandvoort (1789–1828). Further west still, on the

△ Haarlem Grote Markt

north side of the nave, is the pocket-sized **Dog Whippers' Chapel**, built for the men employed to keep dogs out of the church, and now separated from the nave by an iron grille.

At the west end of the church, the mighty Christian Müller **organ** was manufactured in Amsterdam in the 1730s. It is said to have been played by Handel and Mozart (the latter on his tour of the country in 1766, at the age of ten) and is one of the biggest in the world, with over five thousand pipes and lots of snazzy Baroque embellishment. Hear it at work at one of the free organ recitals held in the summer (mid-May to mid-Oct Tues 8.15pm, July & Aug also

Thurs 3pm; free). Beneath the organ, Jan Baptist Xavery's lovely group of draped marble figures represents Poetry and Music offering thanks to Haarlem, which is depicted as a patroness of the arts – in return for its generous support in the purchase of the organ.

The Hallen and the Corrie Ten Boomhuis

Back outside, just beyond the western end of the church, the rambling **Hallen** divides into two; first up is the old meat market, the **Vleeshal**, which boasts a flashy Dutch Renaissance facade and a basement given over to a modest **Archeologisch Museum** (Wed–Sun 1–5pm; free). A couple of doors along is the **Kunstcentrum De Hallen** (Tues–Sat 11am–5pm, Sun noon–5pm; €5), an art gallery where the emphasis is on temporary exhibitions of modern and contemporary art and photography.

After these modest attractions, you'll probably want to push on south to Haarlem's star turn, the Frans Hals Museum (see below), but you might consider a brief detour north from the Grote Markt to the **Corrie Ten Boomhuis**, Barteljorisstraat 19 (April–Oct Tues–Sat 10am–3.30pm; Nov–March Tues–Sat 11am–2.30pm; 1hr guided tours only; free; ⓦwww.corrietenboom.com), where a Dutch family – the Ten Booms – hid fugitives, resistance fighters and Jews alike, above their watchmaking shop during World War II. There isn't actually much to look at, but the guided tour is instructive and moving, if a tad drawn-out. The family, whose bravery sprang from their Christian faith, was betrayed to the Gestapo in 1944, and only one, Corrie Ten Boom, survived.

The Frans Hals Museum

Haarlem's biggest draw, the **Frans Hals Museum** (Tues–Sat 11am–5pm, Sun noon–5pm; €7; ⓦwww.franshalsmuseum.nl), is a five-minute stroll south of the Grote Markt at Groot Heiligland 62; to get there, take pedestrianized Warmoesstraat and keep going. The museum occupies an old almshouse complex, a much-modified, red-brick *hofje* with a central courtyard, where the aged Hals lived out his last destitute years on public funds. The collection comprises a handful of prime works by Hals along with a small but eclectic sample of Dutch paintings from the fifteenth century onwards, all immaculately presented and labelled in English and Dutch. There's also a small separate section consisting of a life-size replica of a seventeenth-century Haarlem street.

Little is known about **Frans Hals** (c.1580–1666). Born in Antwerp, the son of Flemish refugees who settled in Haarlem in the late 1580s, he has relatively few surviving works – some two hundred paintings, and nothing like the number of sketches and studies left behind by his contemporary, Rembrandt. His outstanding gift was as a portraitist, showing a sympathy with his subjects and an ability to capture fleeting expression that some say even Rembrandt lacked. Seemingly quick and careless flashes of colour characterize his work, but they are always blended into a coherent and marvellously animated whole.

The museum begins with the work of other artists; first comes a small group of early sixteenth-century paintings, the most prominent of which, displayed in Room 2, is a triptych from the School of **Hans Memling**. In the same room is a curious painting by Haarlem-born **Jan Mostaert** (1475–1555), his *West Indian Scene* depicting a band of naked, poorly armed natives trying to defend themselves against the cannon and sword of their Spanish invaders; the comparison with the Dutch Protestants was clear. Next door, Room 3 displays two works by **Jan van Scorel** (1495–1562): a polished *Adam and Eve* and *Pilgrims to Jerusalem*, one of the country's earliest group portraits.

△ The Frans Hals Museum

The adjacent Room 4 features **Cornelis Cornelisz van Haarlem**'s (1562–1638) *Wedding of Peleus and Thetis*, an appealing rendition of what was then a popular subject, though Cornelisz gives as much attention to the arrangement of his elegant nudes as to the subject. This marriage precipitated civil war amongst the gods and was used by the Dutch as an emblem of warning against discord, a call for unity during the long war with Spain. Similarly, and also in Room 4, the same artist's *Massacre of the Innocents* connects the biblical story with the Spanish siege of Haarlem in 1572. Moving on, Rooms 6 and 7 hold several paintings by the **Haarlem Mannerists**, including two tiny and precise works by **Karel van Mander** (1548–1606), leading light of the Haarlem School and mentor of many of the city's most celebrated painters, including Hals. There's more Cornelis Cornelisz van Haarlem in Room 7 too, most notably an early militia group portrait and a Mannerist biblical work entitled *Worshipping the Golden Calf*.

The **Hals paintings** begin in earnest in Room 14 with a set of five "Civic Guard" portraits – group portraits of the militia companies initially formed to defend the country from the Spanish, but which later became social clubs for the gentry. Getting a commission to paint one of these portraits was a well-paid privilege – Hals got his first in 1616 – but their composition was a tricky affair and often the end result was dull and flat. With great flair and originality, Hals made the group portrait a unified whole instead of a static collection of individual portraits, his figures carefully arranged, but so cleverly as not to appear contrived. For a time, Hals himself was a member of the Company of St George, and in his *Officers of the Militia Company of St George* he appears in the top left-hand corner – one of his few self-portraits.

Hals' **later paintings** are darker, more contemplative works, closer to Rembrandt in their lighting and increasingly sombre in their outlook. In Room 18, amongst several portraits of different groups of regents, is Hals' *Regents of St Elizabeth Gasthuis*, a serious but benign work of 1641 with a palpable sense of optimism, whereas his twin *Regents and Regentesses of the Oudemannenhuis*, currently displayed in Room 19, is deep with despair. These last two paintings were commissioned when Hals was in his eighties, a poor man despite a successful painting career, hounded for money by the town's tradesmen and by the mothers of his illegitimate children. As a result he was dependent on the charity of people like those depicted here: their cold, self-satisfied faces staring out of the gloom, the women reproachful, the men only marginally more affable. Incidentally, although the character just right of centre in the *Regents* painting looks drunk, it is inconceivable that Hals would have depicted him in this condition; it's more likely that he was suffering from some kind of facial paralysis, and his jauntily cocked hat was simply a popular fashion of the time. There are those who claim Hals had lost his touch by the time he painted these pictures, yet their sinister, almost ghostly power suggests quite the opposite. Van Gogh's remark that "Frans Hals had no fewer than 27 blacks" suddenly makes perfect sense.

Finally, just before you exit, look out for **Pieter Brueghel the Younger**'s (1564–1638) berserk *Dutch Proverbs*, illustrating a whole raft of contemporary proverbs – a detailed key next to the painting gives the lowdown.

To the River Spaarne

From the Frans Hals Museum, stroll south down Groot Heiligland and turn left at the end along the canal and you soon reach the **River Spaarne**, whose wandering curves mark the eastern periphery of the town centre. Turn left here, along riverside Turfmarkt and its continuation Spaarne, to reach the surly stone facade of the **Waag** (Weigh House) and then the country's oldest museum, the **Teylers Museum**, located in a grand Neoclassical building at Spaarne 16 (Tues–Sat 10am–5pm, Sun noon–5pm; €7; ⓦ www.teylersmuseum.nl). Founded in 1774 by a wealthy local philanthropist, one **Pieter Teyler van der Hulst**, the museum is delightfully old-fashioned, its wooden cabinets crammed with fossils and bones, crystals and rocks, medals and coins, all displayed alongside dozens of antique scientific instruments of lugubrious appearance and uncertain purpose. The finest room is the **rotunda** – De Ovale Zaal - a handsome, galleried affair with splendid wooden panelling, and there is also a room of nineteenth-century and early twentieth-century Dutch paintings, featuring the likes of Breitner, Israëls, Weissenbruch and Wijbrand Hendriks (1774–1831), who was once the keeper of the art collection here.

Teyler also bestowed his charity on the riverside **Teylers Hofje**, a little way east around the bend of the Spaarne at Koudenhorn 64. Unlike most other *hofjes*, which are decidedly cosy, this is a grandiose affair, a Neoclassical edifice dating from 1787 and featuring solid columns and cupolas. To the west, the elegant fifteenth-century tower of the **Bakenesserkerk** (no public access), on Vrouwestraat, is a flamboyant, onion-domed affair soaring high above the Haarlem skyline.

From the Bakenesserkerk, it's a five- to ten-minute walk back to the Grote Markt.

Practicalities

With fast and frequent services from Amsterdam, Haarlem's handsome **train station**, in a Dutch version of the Arts and Crafts style, is located to the north of the city centre, about ten minutes' walk from the main square, the Grote Markt. The **bus station** is in front of the train station on Stationsplein and the **VVV** is next door (April–Sept Mon 1–5.30pm, Tues–Fri 9am–5.30pm, Sat 10am–4pm; Oct–March Mon–Fri 9.30am–5pm, Sat 10am–2pm; ℡0900/61 61 600 premium line, Ⓦwww.vvvzk.nl). The VVV issues free city **maps** and brochures, sells hiking and cycling maps of the Nationaal Park Zuid-Kennemerland (see opposite), has details of a small number of **rooms in private houses**, mostly on the outskirts of town and costing in the region of €45 per double per night, and can provide **hotel** information. **Bike rental** is available at the train station. The pick of the town's **restaurants and bars** is conveniently clustered on or within easy walking distance of the Grote Markt and Oude Groenmarkt, round the back of the Grote Kerk.

Hotels

Amadeus Grote Markt 10 ℡023/532 4530, Ⓦwww.amadeus-hotel.com. Homely, medium-sized hotel with plain but perfectly comfortable en-suite rooms. The front bedrooms have pleasant views over the main square. €70

🏃 **Best Western Grand Hotel Frans Hals** Damstraat 10 ℡023/518 1818, Ⓦwww.bestwestern.com. Brand-new chain hotel, plumb in the centre of town and offering 79 smart and well-appointed modern rooms. Rack rate €150 plus, but discounts are frequently offered.

Carillon Grote Markt 27 ℡023/531 0591, Ⓦwww.hotelcarillon.com. Inexpensive place opposite the Grote Kerk with spartan modern rooms, but friendly atmosphere. €70

Eating and drinking

Café 1900 Barteljorisstraat 10. With a smashing 1930s interior, right up to its swishing ceiling fans, this has long been a popular café-bar, serving drinks and reasonably tasty light meals. Tues–Sat 9am–midnight, Sun & Mon 11am–midnight.

Fortuyn Grand Café Grote Markt 21. A popular café-bar with charming 1930s decor, including a tiled entrance and quaint glass cabinets preserved from its days as a shop.

In Den Uiver Riviervismarkt 13. Just off the Grote Markt, this lively and extremely appealing brown bar is decked out in traditional Dutch café style; it has occasional live music too.

Luca & Lucas Lange Veerstraat 51 ℡023/534 1855. Upmarket Italian restaurant with a menu that covers all the favourites and then some. Main courses from €15, pizzas from €12. Daily noon–10pm.

Proeflokaal Blauwe Druif Lange Veerstraat 7. Intimate and amenable bar – typically Dutch.

🏃 **Restaurant Applause** Grote Markt 23a ℡023/531 1425. A chic little bistro serving up Italian food with excellent main courses hovering at around e15. Wed–Sun noon–3pm & 5.30–9.30pm

Restaurant Specktakel Spekstraat 4 ℡023/532 38 41. Inventive little place that tries its hand at an international menu – everything from kangaroo through to antelope. Mostly, the main courses are very successful and cost around e17. Daily from 5pm, Sat also noon–4pm.

Hans Brinker

Given that the Dutch have spent most of their history struggling to keep the sea from flooding their land, it's hardly surprising that their folklore abounds with tales of watery salvation, either by luck or by bravery. One well-known hero is **Hans Brinker**, a young lad who supposedly saved the Haarlem area from disaster by sticking his finger into a hole in the dyke. The village of **Spaarndam**, just north of Haarlem, has a statue in his honour, but in fact the tale is entirely fictitious – invented by the American writer Mary Mapes Dodge in her 1873 children's book *The Silver Skates*. The monument to the little chap was unveiled in 1950 – more, it seems, as a tribute to the opportunistic Dutch tourist industry than anything else.

Around Haarlem: Zandvoort and the Nationaal Park Zuid–Kennemerland

The suburbs of Haarlem ramble out almost as far as **ZANDVOORT-AAN-ZEE**, a major seaside resort just 5km away to the west. As Dutch resorts go, Zandvoort is pretty standard – packed in summer, dead and gusty in winter – and its agglomeration of modern apartment blocks hardly cheers the heart, but then again its beach is wide and sandy, it musters up a casino and a car-racing circuit and it is one of the few places in the Netherlands where the rail network reaches the coast; there's a half-hourly service from Haarlem, and Zandvoort train station is just a five-minute walk (if that) from the beach.

If, however, you're after more than just a few hours sunbathing, the better option for exploring the coast is to delve into the pristine woods, dunes and lagoons of the **Nationaal Park Zuid-Kennemerland**, which stretches north from Zandvoort all the way up to the eminently missable industrial town of **IJmuiden**, at the mouth of the Nordzeekanaal; maps of the park are available from Haarlem VVV (see opposite). Hourly bus #81 from Haarlem bus station travels west to cut across the national park along the N200 before reaching the coast at the minuscule beachside settlement of **Bloemendaal-aan-Zee**; it then travels the 4km south to Zandvoort bus station, on Louis Davidsstraat, a short, signposted walk from the train station. En route, between Haarlem and Bloemendaal-aan-Zee, several bus stops give access to the clearly marked **hiking trails** that pattern the national park, but the best option is to get off at the **Koevlak** entrance – ask the driver to let you off. Three colour-coded hiking routes are posted at Koevlak; the most appealing is the nine-kilometre (3hr) jaunt west through pine woods and dunes to the seashore at the **Parnassia café** (April–Nov), where you can wet your whistle gazing out across the North Sea. From the café, it's 2km by minor road to Bloemendaal-aan-Zee, where you can catch bus #81 back to Haarlem.

The Dutch bulbfields

The pancake-flat fields extending south from Haarlem towards Leiden are the heart of the **Dutch bulbfields**, whose bulbs and blooms support a billion-euro industry and some ten thousand growers, as well as attracting tourists in their droves. Bulbs have flourished here since the late sixteenth century, when a certain **Carolus Clusius**, a Dutch botanist and one-time gardener to the Habsburg emperor, brought the first **tulip bulb** over from Vienna, where it had – in its turn – been brought from modern-day Turkey by an Austrian aristocrat. The tulip flourished in Holland's sandy soil and was so highly prized that it created a massive speculative bubble. At the height of the boom – in the mid-1630s – bulbs were commanding extraordinary prices; the artist Jan van Goyen, for instance, paid 1900 guilders and two paintings for ten rare bulbs, while another set of one hundred bulbs was swapped for a coach and pair of horses. The bubble burst in 1636, thanks to the intervention of the government, and the bulb industry returned to normal, though it left hundreds of investors ruined, much to the satisfaction of the country's Calvinist ministers, who had railed against the excesses.

Other types of bulb were introduced after the tulip, and today the **spring flowering sequence** begins in mid-March with crocuses, followed by daffodils and yellow narcissi in late March, hyacinths and tulips in mid- and late April through to May, and gladioli in August.

The Keukenhof Gardens

The **views** of the bulbfields from any of the trains heading towards Leiden from the north and northeast can often be sufficient in themselves, with the fields divided into stark geometric blocks of pure colour, but with your own transport you can take in their full beauty by way of special **routes** marked by hexagonal signposts; local VVVs (tourist offices) sell pamphlets describing the routes in detail. Alternatively, if you're after bulbs, then make a beeline for bulb growers' showcase, the **Keukenhof Gardens** (late March to late May daily 8am–7.30pm; €13, Ⓦwww.keukenhof.com), located on the edge of the little town of **LISSE**, beside the N208 about 15km north of Leiden. The largest flower gardens in the world, dating back to 1949, the Keukenhof was designed by a group of prominent bulb growers to convert people to the joys of growing flowers from bulbs in their own gardens. Literally the "kitchen garden", its site is the former estate of a fifteenth-century countess, who used to grow herbs and vegetables for her dining table. Several million flowers are on show for their full flowering period, complemented – in case of especially harsh winters – by thousands of square metres of glasshouse holding indoor displays. You could easily spend a whole day here, swooning with the sheer abundance of it all, but to get the best of it you need to come early, before the tour buses pack the place. There are several restaurants in the grounds and a network of well-marked footpaths explore every horticultural nook and cranny.

To get to the Keukenhof by **public transport** from Amsterdam, take the train from Centraal Station to Leiden Centraal (every 30min; 40min journey) and then catch **bus #54** (every 30min; 30min journey) from the main bus station next door.

The east coast: Marken, Volendam and Edam

The turbulent waters of the **Zuider Zee** were once busy with Dutch trading ships shuttling to and from the Baltic. This trade was the linchpin of Holland's prosperity in the Golden Age, revolving around the import of huge quantities of grain, the supply of which was municipally controlled to safeguard against famine. The business was immensely profitable and its proceeds built a string of

The closing of the Zuider Zee

The ports, towns and villages dotted along the east coast of the province of **Noord-Holland** (North Holland) flourished during Amsterdam's Golden Age, their economies buoyed up by shipbuilding, the Baltic sea trade and the demand for herring. They had access to the open sea via the waters of the **Zuider Zee** (Southern Sea) and, further to the north, the connecting **Waddenzee** (Mud Sea). Both seas were comparatively new, created when the North Sea broke through from the coast in the thirteenth century; the original coastline is marked by Texel and the Frisian Islands. However, the Zuider Zee was shallow and tidal, part salt and part freshwater, and accumulations of silt began to strangle its ports from the end of the seventeenth century; shortly afterwards the Baltic trade slipped into decline. As a consequence, the Zuider Zee ports were effectively marooned by the 1750s and the only maritime activity was fishing – just enough to keep a cluster of tiny hamlets ticking over, including **Volendam** and **Marken**.

The Zuider Zee may have provided a livelihood for local fishermen, but most of the country was more concerned by the flood danger it posed, as time and again storms and high tides combined to breach the east coast's defences. The first plan to seal off and reclaim the Zuider Zee, was proposed in 1667, but the rotating-turret windmills that then provided the most efficient way of drying the land were insufficient for the task, and matters were delayed until suitable technology arrived – in the form of the steam-driven pump. In 1891, a certain **Cornelis Lely** proposed a retaining dyke at the mouth of the Zuider Zee and his plans were finally put into effect after devastating floods hit the area in 1916. Work began on this dyke, the **Afsluitdijk**, in 1920, and on May 28, 1932, the last gap in the dyke was closed and the Zuider Zee simply ceased to exist, replaced by the freshwater **IJsselmeer**.

The original plan was to reclaim all the land protected by the Afsluitdijk, turning it into farmland for settlers from the country's overcrowded cities, and three large-scale land reclamation schemes were completed over the next forty years. In addition, a complementary dyke linking Enkhuizen with Lelystad was finished in 1976, thereby creating lake **Markermeer** – a necessary prelude to the draining of another vast stretch of the IJsselmeer. The engineers licked their contractual lips, but they were out of sync with the majority of the population, who were now opposed to any further draining of the lake. Partly as a result, the grand plan was abandoned and, after much governmental huffing and puffing, the Markermeer was left alone – and thus most of the former Zuider Zee remained water.

There were many **economic benefits** to be had in the closing of the Zuider Zee. The threat of flooding was removed, the country gained great chunks of new and fertile farmland, and the roads that were built along the top of the two main retaining dykes brought Noord-Holland within twenty minutes' drive of Friesland. The price to pay was the demise of the old Zuider Zee **fishing fleet**. Without access to the open sea, it was inevitable that most of the fleet would go down the pan, though some skippers wisely transferred to the north coast before the Afsluitdijk was completed. Others learnt to fish the freshwater species that soon colonized the Markermeer and IJsselmeer, but in 1970 falling stocks prompted the government to ban trawling. This was a bitter blow for many fishermen and there were several violent demonstrations before they bowed to the inevitable. Today, villages such as Marken and Volendam are shadows of their former selves, forced to rely on tourism to survive.

prosperous seaports – including **Volendam** – and nourished market towns like **Edam**, while the Zuider Zee itself supported a batch of fishing villages such as **Marken**. In the eighteenth century, the Baltic trade declined and the harbours silted up, leaving the ports economically stranded, and, with the rapid increase in the Dutch population during the nineteenth century, plans were made to reclaim the Zuider Zee and turn it into farmland. In the event, the Zuider Zee was only partly reclaimed (see box p.151), creating a pair of freshwater lakes – the **Markermeer** and the **IJsselmeer**.

These placid, steel-grey **lakes** are popular with day-tripping Amsterdammers, who come here in their droves to sail boats, observe the waterfowl, and visit a string of attractive small towns and villages. These begin on the coast just a few kilometres north of Amsterdam with the picturesque old fishing village of Marken and the former seaport of Volendam just up along the coast. From Volendam, it's a couple of kilometres further up the coast to Edam, the pick of the local bunch, a small and infinitely pretty little town of narrow canals and handsome old houses.

There are fast and frequent **buses** from Amsterdam's Centraal Station to Marken, Volendam and Edam, but more poetically, there's a seasonal **passenger ferry**, the Marken Express (see below), which skittles along the coast between Marken and Volendam, giving a taste of the pond-like Markermeer. At a bit of a push, all three places can be visited in a day.

Marken

Once an island in the Zuider Zee, **Marken** was, until its road connection to the mainland in 1957, pretty much a closed community, supported by a small fishing industry. Despite its proximity to Amsterdam, its biggest problem was the genetic defects caused by close and constant intermarrying, but now it's how to contain the tourists, whose numbers can reach alarming proportions on summer weekends. That said, there's no denying the picturesque charms of the island's one and only village – also called **MARKEN** – where the immaculately maintained houses, mostly painted in deep green with white trimmings, cluster on top of artificial mounds raised to protect them from the sea.

There are two main parts to the village: **Havenbuurt**, behind the harbour, and **Kerkbuurt** around the church (mid-May to Oct Mon–Sat 10am–5pm; free), an ugly 1904 replacement for its sea-battered predecessor. Of the two, Kerkbuurt is the less touristy, its narrow lanes lined by ancient dwellings and a row of old eel-smoking houses, now the **Marker Museum**, Kerkbuurt 44 (April–Sept Mon–Sat 10am–5pm, Sun noon–4pm; Oct Mon–Sat 11am–4pm; €2.50; Ⓦwww.markermuseum.nl), devoted to the history of the former island and its fishing industry. Over in the Havenbuurt, one or two of the houses are open to visitors, proclaiming themselves to be "typical" of Marken, and the waterfront is lined by snack bars and souvenir shops, often staffed by locals in traditional costume. It's all a tad prosaic, but now and again you do get a hint of how hard life used to be – many of the waterfront houses are raised on stilts and, although these are now panelled in, they were once open, allowing the sea to roll under the floors in bad weather, enough to terrify most people half to death.

Practicalities

Marken is accessible direct from Amsterdam by **bus** #111, departing from outside Centraal Station (every 30min); the journey takes forty minutes. The bus drops passengers beside the car park on the edge of Marken village, from where it's a five-minute walk to the lakeshore. Marken does not have a VVV. A **passenger ferry**, the Marken Express (Ⓣ029/936 3331, Ⓦwww.markenexpress .nl; April–Oct daily 11am–5pm, every 30–45min; 30min journey; €6.75 return, €4.25 single, bikes an extra €1 one-way) links Marken with Volendam (see opposite), but otherwise travelling between the two means a fiddly bus trip involving a change of buses – and bus stops – at **Monnickendam**, itself a former

Zuider Zee port, but now a busy sailing centre; the Amsterdam–Marken bus #111 stops on the southern edge of Monnickendam at the Swaensborch stop, from where it's a ten-minute walk across Monnickendam to the Bernhardbrug stop for bus #110 or #118 north to Volendam and Edam.

Volendam

Larger but not nearly as quaint as Marken, the former fishing village of **VOLENDAM**, just up along the coast from Monnickendam, has had, by comparison with its neighbours, some rip-roaring cosmopolitan times. In the early years of the twentieth century it became something of an artists' retreat, with both Picasso and Renoir spending time here, along with their assorted acolytes. The artists are, however, long gone and nowadays Volendam is crammed with day-trippers running the gauntlet of the souvenir stalls that run the length of the cobbled main street, whose perky gables line up behind the harbour. It's a pleasant enough scene, if you don't mind crowds, and you can wander around the antique-filled public rooms of the *Best Western Hotel Spaander*, on the waterfront at Haven 15 (℡029/936 3595, Ⓦwww.hotelspaander.com; from €115), with their creaking wooden floors, low ceilings, paintings and sketches – pleasant reminders of more artistic times. The hotel was opened in 1881 and its first owner, Leendert Spaander, was lucky enough to have seven daughters, quite enough to keep a whole bevy of artists in lust for a decade or two. Some of the artists paid for their lodgings by giving Spaander paintings – hence today's collection.

Practicalities

In Volendam, **buses** #110 and #118 from Amsterdam and Monnickendam drop passengers on Zeestraat, just across the street from the **VVV**, at Zeestraat 37 (mid-March to Oct Mon–Sat 10am–5pm; Nov to mid-March Mon–Sat 10am–3pm; ℡029/936 3747, Ⓦwww.vvvvolendam.nl). From the VVV, it's a five-minute walk to the waterfront, from where, in the summertime, there is a regular **passenger ferry** to Marken (see opposite).

Edam

Just 3km from Volendam, you might expect **EDAM** to be jammed with tourists, considering the international fame of the rubbery red balls of cheese that carry

The Edam mermaid

A number of **mermaid legends** have evolved around the coastal towns of northern Holland, but Edam's is the best. In 1403, two milkmaids were rowing across the lake to the north of Edam to get to their cows, when they spied a mermaid, whom they agreed must have been washed up over the sea dyke during a storm. Later, they returned to fish the mermaid out of the lake and, in the way of such things, blushes were saved all round by the layer of seaweed and moss protecting the creature's modesty. Back in town, the mermaid slipped into a dress willingly enough and soon picked up all the necessary domestic and devotional skills, learning how to spin, cook and kiss the crucifix, though some versions of the legend feature a less obliging mermaid who didn't take kindly to her chores and was forever trying to escape. The mermaid is supposed to have lived in Edam for fifteen years and one of the now-demolished town gates was decorated with a mermaid statue in her memory. More important was the municipal subtext; as the legend confirmed, the women of Edam were so kind and the town so pleasant that even a slippery siren was prepared to hole up here.

△ Edam waterfront houses

its name. In fact, Edam usually lacks the crowds of Volendam and Marken and remains a delightful, good-looking and prosperous little town of neat brick houses, high gables, swing bridges and slender canals. Founded by farmers in the twelfth century, it experienced a temporary boom in the seventeenth as a shipbuilding centre with river access to the Zuider Zee. Thereafter, it was back to the farm – and the excellent pasture land surrounding the town is still grazed by large herds of cows, though nowadays most **Edam cheese** is produced elsewhere – in Germany, among other places ("Edam" is the name of a type of cheese and not its place of origin). This does, of course, rather undermine the authenticity of Edam's open-air cheese market, held every Wednesday morning in July and August on the Kaasmarkt (see p.156), but it's still a popular attraction and the only time the town heaves with tourists.

The Edams Museum and the Stadhuis

At the heart of Edam is **Damplein**, a pint-sized main square alongside which an elongated, humpbacked bridge vaults the Voorhaven canal, which now connects the town with the Markermeer and formerly linked it to the Zuider Zee. At a stroke, the bridge stopped the canal flooding the town, which occurred with depressing regularity, but local shipbuilders hated the thing, as it restricted navigation, and on several occasions they launched night-time raids to break it down, though eventually they bowed to the will of the local council. Facing the bridge is the **Edams Museum** (late April Tues–Sun 11am–5pm; May–Oct Tues–Sat 10am–4.30pm, Sun 1–4.30pm; €3; ⓦ www.edamsmuseum.nl), which occupies an attractive old house whose crow-stepped gables date back to 1530. Inside, a series of cramped and narrow rooms holds a modest display on the history of the town as well as an assortment of local bygones, including a couple of splendid box beds. The museum's pride and joy is, however, its **floating cellar**, supposedly built by a retired sea captain who couldn't bear the thought of sleeping on dry land, but actually it was constructed to stop the house from flooding.

Across the square – over the bridge – stands Edam's eighteenth-century **Stadhuis**, a severe Louis XIV-style structure whose plain symmetries culminate in a squat little tower. The ground floor of the Stadhuis is home to the VVV (see below). Upstairs is the second part of the Edams Museum (same times & ticket), comprising a handful of old Dutch paintings; the most curious is the portrait of **Trijntje Kever** (1616–1633), a local girl who grew to over 2.5m tall – displayed in front of the portrait is a pair of her specially made shoes.

The Grote Kerk and onto Schepenmakersdijk

From Damplein, it's a short walk along Breestraat and then Grote Kerkstraat to the rambling **Grote Kerk** (April–Oct daily 2–4.30pm; free), on the edge of the fields to the north of town. This is the largest three-ridged church in Europe, a handsome, largely Gothic structure whose strong lines are disturbed by the almost comically stubby spire, which was shortened to its present height after lightning started a fire in 1602. The church interior is distinguished by its magnificent stained-glass windows – which date from the early seventeenth century and sport both heraldic designs and historical scenes – and by its whopping **organ**.

Stroll back from the church along Matthijs Tinxgracht, just to the west of Grote Kerkstraat, and you soon reach the **Kaasmarkt**, site of the summer **cheese market** (July to mid-Aug Wed 10.30am–12.30pm). It's a good deal humbler than Alkmaar's (see p.159), but follows the same format, with the cheeses laid out in rows before buyers sample them. Once a cheese has been purchased, the cheese porters, dressed in traditional white costumes and straw boaters, spring into action, carrying them off on their gondola-like trays. Overlooking the market is the **Kaaswaag** (Cheese Weighing House), whose decorative panels feature the town's coat of arms, a bull on a red field with three stars.

From the Kaasmarkt, it's a couple of hundred metres south to the fifteenth-century **Speeltoren**, an elegant, pinnacled tower that is all that remains of Edam's second most important medieval church, and roughly the same distance again – south along Lingerzijde – to the impossibly picturesque **Kwakelbrug** bridge. This leads over to Schepenmakersdijk, from where it takes about five minutes to regain Damplein.

Practicalities

Every thirty minutes or so, **buses** #110 and #118 leave from outside Amsterdam Centraal Station bound for Edam; the journey takes forty minutes. Edam's **bus station** is on the southwest edge of town, on Singelweg, a five- to ten-minute walk from Damplein, where the **VVV**, in the Stadhuis (mid-March–Nov Mon–Sat 10am–5pm, also Sun 1–4.30pm in July & Aug; Nov to mid-March Mon–Sat 10am–3pm; ☎0299/31 5125, ⓦwww.vvv-edam.nl), issues town maps and brochures. The VVV also has details of – and takes bookings for – local **boat trips**, both along the town's canals and out into the Markermeer. **Bike rental** is available at Ronald Schot, in the town centre at Grote Kerkstraat 7 (Tues–Fri 8.30am–6pm & Sat 8.30am–5pm; ☎0299/37 2155, ⓦwww.ronaldschot.nl); one-day bike rental costs €6.50.

As regards accommodation, the VVV has a small supply of **rooms in private houses** (averaging €40–50 for a double), which they will book on your behalf for no extra charge. **Hotels** are scarce in Edam, but the charming ⚓ *De Fortuna*, just round the corner from the Damplein at Spuistraat 3 (☎0299/37 1671, ⓦwww.fortuna-edam.nl; from €92), is an attractive option. Abutting a narrow canal, this three-star hotel is the epitome of cosiness, its 23 guest rooms distributed amongst two immaculately restored old houses and three cottage-like buildings round the back. The nearest **campsite**, *Camping Strandbad*, is east of town on the way to the lakeshore at Zeevangszeedijk 7A (☎0299/37 1994,

@www.campingstrandbad.nl; April–Sept) – a twenty-minute walk east along the canal from Damplein.

For food, 🍴 *De Fortuna* has a first-rate **restaurant**, a lively and eminently agreeable spot decorated in traditional style and with an imaginative, modern menu featuring local ingredients; main courses average around €20. Reservations, especially at the weekend, are essential.

Alkmaar

Forty minutes north of Amsterdam by train, the amenable little town of **ALKMAAR** has preserved much of its medieval street plan, its compact centre surrounded by what was once the town moat and laced with spindly canals. The town is also dotted with fine old buildings, but is best known for its much-touted **cheese market**, an ancient affair that these days ranks as one of the most extravagant tourist spectacles in the province of Noord-Holland. Alkmaar was founded in the tenth century in the middle of a marsh – hence its name, which is taken from the auk, a diving bird which once hung around here in numbers – as in *alkeen meer*, or auk lake. Just like Haarlem, the town was besieged by Frederick of Toledo, but heavy rain flooded its surroundings and forced the Spaniards to withdraw in 1573, an early Dutch success in their long war of independence. At the time, Alkmaar was small and comparatively unimportant, but the town prospered when the surrounding marshland was drained in the 1700s and it received a boost more recently when the northern part of the old moat was incorporated into the Noordhollandskanaal, itself part of a longer network of waterways running north from Amsterdam to the open sea.

The Town

Even if you've only come here for the cheese market, it's well worth seeing something of the rest of the town before you leave. On the main square, the **Waag** (Weighing House) was originally a chapel – hence the imposing tower – dedicated to the Holy Ghost, but was converted and given its delightful east gable shortly after the town's famous victory against the Spanish. The **gable** is an ostentatious Dutch Renaissance affair bedecked with allegorical figures and decorated with the town's militant coat of arms. The Waag holds the **VVV** (see p.160) and the **Hollands Kaasmuseum** (Cheese Museum; April–Oct Mon–Thurs & Sat 10am–4pm, Fri 9am–4pm; €2.50; @www.kaasmuseum.nl), with displays on – predictably enough – the history of cheese, cheese-making equipment and the like.

Heading south from the Waag along Mient, it's a few metres to the jetty from where **canal trips** leave for a quick zip round the town's central waterways – an enjoyable way to spend forty minutes (April–Oct daily, hourly 11am–5pm; 40min; €5); tickets are on sale at the VVV. At the south end of Mient is the open-air **Vismarkt** (Fish Market), which marks the start of the **Verdronkenoord** canal, whose attractive medley of facades and gables leads east to the spindly **Accijnstoren** (Excise Tower), part harbour master's office, part fortification built in 1622 during the long struggle with Spain. Turn left at the tower along Bierkade and you'll soon reach **Luttik Oudorp**, another attractive corner of the old centre, its slender canal jammed with antique barges, leading back to the Waag.

ALKMAAR

ACCOMMODATION
Best Western   A
Amrath   B
Te Laat

RESTAURANTS & BARS
Restaurant De Bios   1
Het Hof van Alkmaar   2
De Pilaren   4
Proeflokaal 't Apothekertje 3
Café Stapper   5

The Stadhuis and St Laurenskerk

One block south of the Waag, pedestrianized **Langestraat** is Alkmaar's main and mundane shopping street, whose only notable building is the **Stadhuis**, a florid edifice, half of which (the Langestraat side) dates from the early sixteenth century. At the west end of Langestraat lurks **St Laurenskerk** (early April to early Sept Fri 10am–5pm, June–Aug also Tues–Sun same hours; €2.50), a Gothic church of the late fifteenth century whose pride and joy is its **organ**, commissioned at the suggestion of the diplomat and political bigwig Constantijn Huygens in 1645. The case was designed by Jacob van Campen, the architect who was later to design Amsterdam's town hall (see p.47), and decorated with paintings by **Caesar van Everdingen** (1617–78). The artist's seamless brushstrokes – not to mention his willingness to kowtow to the tastes of the burgeoning middle class – were to make Everdingen a wealthy man. In the apse is the **tomb** containing the intestines of the energetic Count Floris V of Holland (1254–96), who improved the region's sea defences, succoured the poor and did much to establish the independence of the towns hereabouts, until his untimely demise at the hands of his own nobles; the rest of him ended up in Rijnsburg, near Leiden.

The Stedelijk Museum

Across from the church, Alkmaar's Cultureel Centrum holds a theatre, offices and a mildly diverting museum, the **Stedelijk Museum** (Municipal Museum; Tues–Fri 10am–5pm, Sat & Sun 1–5pm; €4.50; Ⓦ www.stedelijkmuseumalkmaar.nl), whose three floors focus on the history of the town. Well displayed, but almost entirely labelled in Dutch only, the collection begins with two floors – the ground

Alkmaar's cheese market

Cheese has been sold on Alkmaar's main square since the 1300s, and although it's no longer a serious commercial concern, the **kaasmarkt** (cheese market; Friday 10am–12.30pm, from the first Friday in April to the first Friday in Sept) continues to pull in the crowds – so get there early if you want a good view. The ceremony starts with the buyers sniffing, crumbling, and finally tasting each cheese, followed by intensive bartering. Once a deal has been concluded, the cheeses – golden discs of Gouda mainly, laid out in rows and piles on the square – are borne away on ornamental carriers by groups of four **porters** (*kaasdragers*) for weighing. The porters wear white trousers and shirt plus a black hat whose **coloured bands** – green, blue, red or yellow – represent the four companies that comprise the cheese porters' guild. Payment for the cheeses, tradition has it, takes place in the cafés around the square.

floor and the basement – devoted to Alkmaar's seventeenth-century **Golden Age**. In the basement, a large assortment of archeological finds is divided into themes – "Light and Warmth", "Blue and White Porcelain" and so forth – while the ground floor has sections on different aspects of the town, from trade, war and the militias through to replica scenes. Many of the exhibits are illustrated by **paintings**; highlights among them include a typically precise interior of Alkmaar's St Laurenskerk by Pieter Saenredam (1597–1665), a striking *Holy Family* by the Mannerist Gerard van Honthorst (1590–1656), a departure from his usual glossy portraits of high officials, and a huge canvas depicting the bloody siege of 1573 by the medievalist Jacobus Hilverdink (1809–64). The top floor explores the history of the town during the twentieth century.

Practicalities

From Alkmaar's train and bus station, it's a ten-minute walk to the centre of town; outside the station head straight along Spoorstraat, turn left at the end onto Geestersingel and then turn right over the bridge to get to Kanaalkade; keep going along here until you reach Houttil Pieterstraat. This leads straight to the main square, Waagplein, where you'll find the **VVV** (Mon–Fri 10am–5.30pm, Sat 9.30am–5pm; ☎072/511 4284, ⓦwww.vvvalkmaar.nl). They sell a useful town brochure, have details of the area's walking and cycling routes, and can give advice on bike rental. Amongst several places, **cycle rental** is available at the train station and at de Kraak, Verdronkenoord 54 (☎072/512 5840, ⓦwww.dekraak.nl).

Accommodation

Alkmaar only takes an hour or two to explore, but if you decide to stay, the VVV has plenty of **rooms in private houses** for around €40 per double per night, including breakfast, though most places are on the outskirts of town. As for hotels, there are two good options; the first is the *Best Western Amrath Hotel Alkmaar*, in a strikingly modern building just across the canal from the west end of the centre at Geestersingel 15 (☎072/51 86186, ⓦwww.bestwestern.com; from €120). Opened in 2005, the hotel has sixty rooms decorated in crisp, modern, chain-hotel style. A pleasant alternative is the *Hotel Te Laat*, whose seven bright and spacious en-suite rooms are located in an older building right in the centre at Laat 117 (☎072/512 5506, ⓦwww.telaat.com; €70).

Eating and drinking

Alkmaar has a generous scattering of **cafés and restaurants**, the pick of which is ⚘ *Het Hof van Alkmaar*, in a delightfully restored medieval nunnery just off Nieuwesloot at Hof van Sonoy 1 (daily noon–10pm; ☎072/512 1222). During the day they offer inexpensive snacks, sandwiches and pancakes, and at night they serve up tasty Dutch cuisine with main courses averaging €15–20; there's an outside terrace too. Just along the street, a good second choice is *Restaurant De Bios*, in modern premises at Gedempte Nieuwesloot 54 (Tues–Sat noon–10pm; ☎072/512 4422), whose menu has a Mediterranean slant.

Alkmaar has two main groups of **bars**, one on Waagplein, the other just a couple of minutes' walk away around the Vismarkt. Among the former, the best is *Proeflokaal 't Apothekertje*, an old-style bar open until 2am, with an antiques-cluttered interior and a laid-back atmosphere. On the Vismarkt, there's *De Pilaren*, a livelier, more youthful spot catering to a cooler crowd, some of whom take refuge in the *Café Stapper* next door if the music gets too much.

The *Golden Age*

Ever wondered about those portraits of black-hatted Dutch burghers who stare grimly at us out of the gloom? The Dutch Golden Age was an amazing phenomenon; in the first half of the seventeenth century, the Netherlands were the dominant economic force of Europe, and the Dutch people – for a brief period at least – grew richer than they could ever have imagined. This prosperity was matched by a progressive, tolerant attitude towards religion, the poor and the elderly unparalleled in the rest of Europe – and it heralded an explosion of artistic creativity that has left us with a magnificent record of the time – its values, its achievements and its people.

The history

After the death of Philip II, Spain was more or less forced to accept the **independence** of the northern part of the Netherlands, then known collectively as the United Provinces. This was consolidated with the **Peace of Westphalia** in 1648, which also enforced the closure of the Scheldt river to sea traffic – a key factor in the decline of Antwerp as a seaport and the rise of Amsterdam, to which the upturn in trade brought extraordinary wealth. This sparked a **bourgeois revolution**, a triumph of the nouveau riche, which, coinciding as it did with the rise of Protestantism, had a dramatic impact on the art and architecture of the time; Amsterdam's burghers didn't build churches and fill them with religious art, and their **architecture** was domestic, rather than monumental, in scale. Though certain families became very rich, there was little ostentation of their new-found wealth, and

Herengracht architecture

their relative humility was mirrored by the collective spirit promoted by the authorities. The city's **hofjes**, complexes for the elderly and needy, are a prime example of the city's community-minded approach – which in some ways makes seventeenth-century Holland the world's first example of a modern welfare state.

Rembrandt's *The Night Watch*

The art

Jan Steen's *The Feast of St Nicholas*

The first half of the seventeenth century in Amsterdam – like the Renaissance in Florence, or the Counter-Reformation in Rome – was a time of extraordinary **creative output**, with the arts benefiting from – and mirroring perfectly – the society that funded them. But here, works of art weren't commissioned by the church; instead, the patrons were the businesspeople who had grown rich thanks to the success of the Dutch republic, and they acquired art either to promote their own importance, or to decorate their homes. Painters no longer visited Italy to learn their craft but developed their own, distinctively Dutch, style on home turf; the leading lights of the Golden Age – Hals, Rembrandt and Vermeer – stayed in the Netherlands all their lives. With the focus off religious subjects, **portraiture** flourished, as did so-called **genre painting** – basically scenes of everyday domestic life – and **landscapes**.

The movers and shakers of seventeenth-century Holland had their **portraits** painted to dignify their roles and glorify their achievements, either in stiff, formal pose – as in **Jan Lievens'** depiction of the politician Constantijn Huygens, in Amsterdam's Rijksmuseum – or with their wives, as in **Frans Hals'** marriage portrait of a smug-looking Isaac Massa, also in the Rijksmuseum. Groups were painted together, most famously in the so-called **Civic Guard portraits** of ex-military luncheon clubs, of which **Rembrandt's** *The Night Watch* is the best-known example – although you can see plenty more in the Schuttersgalerij of the Amsterdams Historisch Museum (see p.53). It was also common for the groups that ran the country's almshouses and orphanages to have their portraits captured for posterity; Frans Hals' two late, great paintings of the regents of the Haarlem almshouse where he died are still displayed there today, in the marvellous Frans Hals Museum.

Among the genre painters, **Gerrit Dou**, an early pupil of Rembrandt, **Gerard ter Borch** and **Jan Steen** stand out – the latter for his raucous scenes of workaday Dutch life – as does **Jan Vermeer** of Delft, whose small output belies the massive popularity of his peaceful and quietly meaningful domestic scenes.

Most people would recognize the bucolic landscapes of **Jacob van Ruysdael**, even if they couldn't name the painter. He, his namesake **Salomon van Ruysdael**, and **Jan van Goyen**, among others, capture perfectly the huge skies and expanses of water that characterize the partly man-made Dutch landscape of the time – and perhaps their innate national pride in another of their country's achievements.

All of these painters are well represented in the Rijksmuseum (see pp.114–120), and to a lesser extent in the Amsterdams Historisch Museum (see pp.53–54). For more on the history, art and architecture of the Dutch Golden Age, see pp.278–290 and the *Architecture in Amsterdam* colour section.

Tulipmania

Nothing exemplifies the economic bubble of seventeenth-century Holland more than the arrival of the **tulip**. As a relatively exotic flower, a native of Turkey, it had already captured the imagination of other parts of Europe, and its arrival in Holland – coinciding as it did with an abrupt rise in personal domestic wealth – led to it becoming the bloom of choice for the discerning collector and horticulturalist. New varieties were developed voraciously and the trade in tulip bulbs boomed in the 1630s, with prices spiralling out of control and culminating in three rare bulbs changing hands for the price of a house. By this time it was less about flowers, and more about speculation, with tulips being seen as a way of getting rich quick. However, such speculation couldn't be sustained, and the bottom fell out of the tulip market in 1637, when within three months prices collapsed to around ten percent of their previous value, and thousands lost everything they had.

Tulipa Perfica non aperta — *Tulipa polyanthos præcox rosea colore mixta.* — *Tulipa Perfica aperta*

Today tulips and other blooms still define the Dutch landscape, but getting up close is easiest at the Keukenhof Gardens (see p.150), if you're here in springtime, or at Amsterdam's wonderful Bloemenmarkt (p.82).

Listings

Listings

8

Accommodation

Accommodation in Amsterdam can be difficult to find, and is often a major expense; the hotels are among the most expensive in Europe, and even hostels are pricey for what you get. At **peak times** of the year – July and August, Easter and Christmas – you'd be advised to **book well ahead** as hotel rooms and hostel beds can be swallowed up remarkably quickly, and if you arrive without a reservation at any time of the year you may be hard pushed to find somewhere decent. On the plus side, **prices** are very sensitive to demand, so special **deals and discounts** are commonplace, especially during the week, and the city's compactness means that you'll almost inevitably end up somewhere central, or at least well connected. Most of the places listed in this chapter – even the larger hostels – will accept **bookings** from abroad by fax or email, although the cheaper ones may require some guarantee of payment (such as a credit card number). Telephone bookings are not always accepted, particularly at the hostels during peak season. You can also reserve rooms in advance by contacting the **Netherlands Reservations Centre**, or NRC (℡0299/689 114, Ⓦwww.hotelres.nl); on the website you can view availability and prices before making a booking. Two other useful websites (in Dutch) are Ⓦwww.weekendcompany.nl and Ⓦwww.weekendjeweg.nl. Once you've arrived, the city's **VVVs** (tourist offices) will make hotel reservations on your behalf, either in advance or on the same day for a nominal fee, but note that during peak periods and weekends they get extremely busy with long and exhausting queues. VVVs also sell an Accommodation guide detailing most of the city's hotels; for VVV locations and opening hours, see p.36.

Where to stay

To help you choose a place to stay, the **listings** in this chapter are **divided by area**, using the same headings as in the guide chapters – "The Old Centre", "The Grachtengordel", etc. All of the hostels, hotels and B&Bs we describe are marked on the **colour maps** at the end of the book. For **gay accommodation** listings, see Chapter Twelve.

Touts

If, like most visitors, you arrive at Amsterdam's **Centraal Station**, you may well be approached outside – or even inside – by **touts** offering rooms or beds in hostels and cheap hotels. Usually they walk you to the place and claim a fee from the management. Despite the fact that most of them are genuine enough, it's best to steer clear. Although the possibility of encountering unpleasantness is small, it does exist – and anyway, there are plenty of good, cheap and reliable places within five minutes' walk of Centraal Station.

If you choose to stay in the **Old Centre**, you'll never have to search for nightlife. Cheap hotels abound in the Red Light District, as you might expect – and this is the first place to start looking if money is tight, although women travellers may find it a little intimidating. However, there's also a good selection of quiet, reasonably priced places in more agreeable locations in the Old Centre, on and near the canals and conveniently close to restaurants and shopping areas.

Grachtengordel west is only a few minutes' walk from the bustle of Dam Square, but it has a number of quiet canalside hotels, though the least expensive places are concentrated along Raadhuisstraat, one of the city's busiest streets. **Grachtengordel south** is not as appealing a district as its neighbour, but it is ideally positioned for the plethora of nightclubs, bars and restaurants on and around Leidseplein and Rembrandtplein. There are plenty of hotels for all budgets here, including a number of very appealing – and occasionally stylish – options along the surrounding canals.

Staying in the **Jordaan** puts you in among the locals, well away from the prime tourist zones. There's no shortage of bars and restaurants in this up-and-coming area either – and some of the most beautiful of the city's canals are here too – but you'll be at least fifteen minutes' walk from the bright lights. Be aware when looking for a place to stay that Marnixstraat and Rozengracht are busy traffic streets.

Very few tourists stay in the **Old Jewish Quarter**; the streets and canals off the main traffic arteries of Weesperstraat and Plantage Middenlaan are purely residential, with very few bars or restaurants. Consequently, although you're pretty much guaranteed a quiet night's sleep here, you'll be a tram ride away from any of the leading sights.

The main reason for staying out of the centre in the **Museum Quarter** is to be close to the city's two premier museums – the Van Gogh and the Rijksmuseum – although the nightlife around Leidseplein is also within easy striking distance. There are no canals in the area, and two of the main drags, Overtoom and 1e Constantijn Huygensstraat, constantly rumble with traffic, but there are plenty of quiet and comfortable hotels in the smaller side streets, as well as two of the city's best hostels on the edge of leafy Vondelpark.

There's not too much reason to venture out into the city's far-flung suburbs, but the **outer districts** do possess two noteworthy hotels (see p.174).

Many of Amsterdam's buildings have narrow, very steep **staircases**, and no lifts; indeed, in the older houses, the installing of lifts is actually illegal. If this is a consideration for you, check before you book.

Finally, note that all **directions** given in the listings, including trams, are from Centraal Station (usually abbreviated as "CS"), unless otherwise indicated.

Accommodation prices

The **hotel and guesthouse prices** in this book are given for the cheapest **double** room available during the high season, and, unless indicated otherwise, include breakfast. **Single** rooms, where available, usually cost between sixty and eighty percent of the price of a double. For **hostel accommodation**, the price per person for a dorm bed is given. Note that in the low season hotel prices can drop by as much as fifty percent and dorm beds can be up to €5 cheaper; most of the larger hotels will offer rooms at various prices.

Hotels and B&Bs

Aside from a couple of ultra-cheap places, Amsterdam's **hotels** start at around €120 for a double and can be pretty poor value for money, even though some form of **breakfast** – "Dutch" (ham, bread and jam) or "English" (eggs, ham, bread and jam) – is normally included in the price. Given this state of affairs, at the city's budget hotels, it's advisable to ask to see the room first before you slap down any money, and if you don't like it, refuse it. Note too that with some of the independently run hotels the cheapest rooms often have **shared facilities**, and en-suite rooms, if available, could be an extra €5–15. A significant number of hotels in Amsterdam have large three- or four-bed family rooms available from €180. **B&Bs** are on the increase; those listed are among the best.

Prices given below are, unless otherwise indicated, for the high (summer) season, though Amsterdam is such a popular spot that you can't assume you'll pay much less in the winter.

Old Centre

Bellevue Martelaarsgracht 10 ☏ 020/707 4500, ⓦ www.bellevuehotel.nl. **Two-minute walk from CS.** The rooms here are newly renovated in a modern style and the location couldn't be more convenient. Prices start at around €160 for a double, not including breakfast.

Botel Amstel Moored at Oosterdokskade 2 ☏ 020/626 4247, ⓦ www.amstelbotel.com. **Five-minute walk from CS.** The idea of a floating hotel may seem romantic – or at least perfect in houseboat-heaven Amsterdam – but the 175 identically decorated rooms here are poky and connected by claustrophobic corridors. Something a bit different certainly, but you might find staying here is a bit like spending your holiday on a cross-Channel ferry. The well-equipped bar has Internet access and stays open till 12.45am. Prices depend on whether you want a view of the water or not, but rooms are at least cheap, at €90–100 for a double, and around €120 for a triple (with bunk bed).

The Crown Oudezijds Voorburgwal 21 ☏ 020/626 9664, ⓦ www.hotelthecrown.com. **Five-minute walk from CS.** This is really a hotel for single people, and its pricing policy – €40–45 per person – reflects that. The rooms at the back are dark and a bit austere; the ones at the front are nicer, but prone to the noise from the busy canal outside. Very safe, and very friendly, despite the location – right in the middle of the Red Light District. "Smoker-friendly" bar open until 3am. Triples, quads and six-person rooms also available.

Doelen Nieuwe Doelenstraat 24 ☏ 020/554 0600, ⓦ www.nh-hotels.com. **Trams #4, #9, #16, #24 or #25 to Muntplein.** Famous as the hotel where Rembrandt painted *The Night Watch* (see p.119), and with a stately elegance about it that might appeal if your budget won't stretch to the *Hotel de l'Europe* along the water. It's smaller than it looks from the outside, and has a nice breakfast room overlooking the water. Doubles range from €220–300, not including breakfast – though deals abound, especially at weekends.

France Oudezijds Kolk 11 ☏ 020/535 3777, ⓦ www.francehotel.nl. **Five-minute walk fom CS.** This friendly but rather characterless hotel is gradually refurbishing to take advantage of its location on a tiny and little-trafficked canal just off the burgeoning Zeedijk; the lobby has already been treated to a re-style and the rooms themselves are slowly being done up too. Its decent-sized doubles go for €150, with bath and breakfast; wi-fi access in every room is free.

De Gerstekorrel Damstraat 22–24 ☏ 020/624 9771, ⓦ www.gerstekorrel.com. **Trams #4, #9, #16, #24 or #25 to Dam Square.** The cheapest choice in this location, but rooms are pretty basic – and, at €149 for a double, not all that cheap either. Still, much of the time you will end up paying less than this (just ask), and as there are no common areas you get to eat the inclusive breakfast in bed whether you like it or not. No lift.

Grand Oudezijds Voorburgwal 197 ☏ 020/555 3111, ⓦ www.thegrand.nl. **Trams #4, #9, #16,**

#24 or #25 to Dam Square. Originally a Royal Inn dating from 1578, and after that the Amsterdam Town Hall, this fine Classical building is one of the city's architectural high points, and now part of the Sofitel chain. The rooms are large, well appointed and boldly decorated in crisp, modern style. There are all the usual facilities you would expect from a five-star hotel, including a spa with indoor pool and Turkish bath, and a Roux brothers restaurant on site. Doubles start at €420, excluding 5 percent tax and breakfast, which is a whopping €25 extra.

Grand Hotel Krasnapolsky Dam 9 ☎ 020/554 9111, ⓦ www.nh-hotels.com. **Trams #4, #9, #16, #24 or #25 to Dam Square.** Located in a huge, striking mid-nineteenth-century building, this four-star hotel occupies virtually an entire side of Dam Square. Its rooms are attractively decorated, if unspectacular, and doubles go for €200–250 (no breakfast), though bargains are sometimes available.

Hotel de l'Europe Nieuwe Doelenstraat 2–8 ☎ 020/531 1777, ⓦ www.leurope.nl. **Trams #4, #9, #16, #24 or #25 to Muntplein.** One of the city's top hotels, and retaining a wonderful *fin-de-siècle* charm, with large, well-furnished rooms, an attractive riverside terrace – and a great central location. Standard doubles start at €365 without breakfast and tax, but this is about as luxurious as the city gets.

▽ Hotel de l'Europe

Hotel des Arts Rokin 154–156 ☎ 020/620 1558, ⓦ www.hoteldesarts.nl. **Trams #4, #9, #16, #24 or #25 to Muntplein.** This hotel's 22 rooms are

cosy and well furnished and the welcome is friendly. Prices start at around €145 including breakfast, though the larger canal-facing ones are around €170.

Le Coin Nieuwe Doelenstraat 5 ☎ 020/524 6800, ⓦ www.lecoin.nl. **Trams #4, #9, #16, #24 or #25 to Muntplein.** In a good location opposite the swanky *Hotel de l'Europe*, but a quarter of the price, with doubles starting at €130. All rooms have kitchenettes and are kitted out in contemporary style.

Misc Kloveniersburgwal 20 ☎ 020/330 6241, ⓦ www.hotelmisc.com. **Ten-minute walk from CS.** Very friendly hotel in a good location on the edge of the Red Light District with six good-sized, en-suite rooms, each with a different theme. The bright breakfast area overlooks the canal and is great for people-watching. Wi-fi connection. Rates start at €135, including an excellent breakfast – great value.

Nes Kloveniersburgwal 137–139 ☎ 020/624 4773, ⓦ www.hotelnes.nl. **Trams #4, #9, #16, #24 or #25 to Muntplein.** Pleasant and quiet hotel with helpful staff, and well positioned too – away from noise but close to shops and nightlife. The size and quality of the rooms can vary quite a bit, so don't be afraid to ask to see other rooms if you're disappointed. Prices vary too; they start at €75, but you can reckon on paying €130–150 for a double room, and triples and quads are available from €80–135.

NH City Centre Spuistraat 288 ☎ 020/420 4545, ⓦ www.nh-hotels.com. **Tram #1, #2 or #5 to Spui.** This appealing chain hotel occupies a sympathetically renovated 1920s Art Deco former textile factory, and is well situated for the cafés and bars of the Spui, and the Museum Quarter. Rooms vary in size, some have canal views, and all boast comfy beds and good showers. There are often deals available, but doubles generally go for around €150 in high season. The buffet breakfast is extra, but will set you up for the day.

Rho Nes 5 ☎ 020/620 7371, ⓦ www.rhohotel. com. **Trams #4, #9, #16, #24 or #25 to Rokin.** Built as a theatre in 1908, the lovely, high-ceilinged, *fin-de-siècle* lobby gives a slightly misleading impression; the rooms are on the small side and have been unimaginatively modernized. Still, it's pleasant enough, and in a good central location just off Dam Square. Doubles from €115 including buffet breakfast. Daily bike rental available.

Rokin Rokin 73 ☎020/626 7456, ⓦwww.rokin-hotel.com. Tram #4, #9, #16, #24 or #25 to Rokin. This three-star family hotel has recently had a facelift and undergone major expansion – although it doesn't seem to have lifted the smiles of the people behind the reception desk. There are small, modern doubles with exposed beams, some singles, and two triples also available, and a pleasant basement room where breakfast (included) is served. Lift access to three of the four floors. The private car park is a handy bonus. €115–145.

Sint Nicolaas Spuistraat 1a ☎020/626 1384, ⓦwww.hotelnicolaas.nl. Five-minute walk from CS. More characterful than many of the other budget hotels in the area, the *St Nicolaas's* cosy downstairs bar-reception gives way to around thirty recently refurbished rooms, all with baths, that start at around €120 in high season.

Victoria Damrak 1–5 ☎020/623 4255, ⓦwww.parkplaza.com. Two-minute walk from CS. This tall, elegant building opposite Centraal Station has been one of the city's best hotels for years, although its decor is beginning to look fusty compared to the crop of sleeker options that has arrived in recent years. Still, its location couldn't be more convenient, and there are often bargains to be had in its well-kitted-out rooms; amenities include a fitness centre and pool. The cheapest doubles are about €250–300, not including breakfast.

Vijaya Oudezijds Voorburgwal 44 ☎020/626 9406, ⓦwww.hotelvijaya.com. Five-minute walk from CS. Right in the heart of the Red Light District, next door but one to the Amstelkring (see p.57), this is a warren of rooms spread over a couple of old canal houses. It's rather threadbare, but not bad value at €100 for a double, and has a

friendly charm that's enhanced by the Indian restaurant downstairs. No lift.

Winston Warmoesstraat 129 ☎020/623 1380, ⓦwww.winston.nl. Ten-minute walk from CS. This self-consciously young and cool hotel has funky rooms individually decorated with eccentric art and a busy ground-floor bar that has occasional live music performances. It's a formula that works a treat; the *Winston* is popular and often full – though this is probably also due to its low prices: €80–100 for a double, with breakfast, €120–160 for triples and quads. Rooms are light and airy, some en suite, some with a communal balcony. Erotic images abound in some, so if you're travelling as a family you might want to check first to prevent any embarrassing questions. Lift and full disabled access.

Grachtengordel west

Agora Singel 462 ☎020/627 2200, ⓦwww.hotelagora.nl. Tram #1, #2 or #5 to Koningsplein. Handily located, small and amiable hotel near the flower market and close to the Spui. The guest rooms here, of which there are just sixteen, all en suite, are kitted out in simple, modern style and vary greatly in size. As well as doubles, three- and four-bed rooms are available, and there's a large breakfast room too. Rooms cost upwards of €125, €140 with a canal view; rates stay the same throughout the year.

Ambassade Herengracht 341 ☎020/555 0222, ⓦwww.ambassade-hotel.nl. Tram #1, #2 or #5 to Spui. Elegant, canalside hotel made up of ten seventeenth-century houses, with friendly staff, attractive furnished lounges, a well-stocked library and comfortable en-suite rooms. There's free Internet access too. Breakfast is €16 extra, but well worth it. Doubles from €195.

Clemens Raadhuisstraat 39 ☎020/624 6089, ⓦwww.clemenshotel.com. Tram #13 or #17 to Westermarkt. This excellent, friendly, budget hotel, close to the Anne Frank Huis, is run by a very knowledgeable owner. The individually decorated doubles, some with en-suite bathroom, have free Internet connection, and you can rent laptops for

€8. One of the better options along this busy main road. Rooms without shower start from €80.

Dylan Keizersgracht 384 ℡ 020/530 2010, ⓦ www.dylanamsterdam.com. Tram #1, #2 or #5 to Keizersgracht. This stylish hotel, housed in a seventeenth-century building, is built around a beautiful courtyard and terrace. Its 41 sumptuous rooms, designed by Anouschka Hempel, range in style from opulent reds or greens to minimalist white and oatmeal, and each has a flat-screen TV and a stereo. The restaurant combines French and African cuisine and there's a bar, open to non-guests. The ambience is hip without being pretentious, and that goes for the staff too, making it very popular – guests often return. Standard doubles from €460; luxury suites overlooking the Keizersgracht canal will set you back €1500. Breakfast €25.

▽ Dylan

Estherea Singel 303–309 ℡ 020/624 5146, ⓦ www.estherea.nl. Tram #1, #2 or #5 to Spui. This appealing hotel, comprising a pair of intelligently revamped old canal houses, has a great location and, although the rooms may lack the personal touch, all are decorated in trim, modern style; the best overlook the canal. Doubles from €255.

Hegra Herengracht 269 ℡ 020/623 7877, ⓦ www.hegrahotel.com. Tram #1, #2 or #5 to Spui. Welcoming atmosphere and relatively inexpensive for the location, on a pleasant stretch of the canal. Rooms are small but comfortable; some with en-suite bathroom. Doubles with shared facilities start from €70.

Hoksbergen Singel 301 ℡ 020/626 6043, ⓦ www.hotelhoksbergen.nl. Tram #1, #2 or #5 to Spui. Friendly, small hotel, in an old canal house and with a light, open breakfast room overlooking the water. Simple en-suite rooms, all with telephone and TV. Self-catering apartments available too. Doubles start at around €90.

't hotel Leliegracht 18 ℡ 020/422 2741, ⓦ www.thotel.nl. Tram #13 or #17 to Westermarkt. This extremely pleasant hotel located along a quiet canal is owned by the proprietors of the downstairs design shop, who believe in making people feel at home. The eight spacious rooms – three with canal views – are kitted out in appealing, contemporary style with large beds, TV, fridge and either bath or shower. Minimum three-night stay at the weekend (Thurs–Mon). Doubles from €145.

New Amsterdam Herengracht 13–19 ℡ 020/522 2345, ⓦ www.hotelnewamsterdam.nl. Ten-minute walk from CS. Small, ultra-friendly hotel in an old canal house, which has been lovingly revamped having stood vacant for years, overlooking a quiet stretch of the canal on the northern edge of the Grachtengordel. There are 25 double rooms here, each of which has been comfortably furnished in clean, modern style, with Internet connection and either a bath or shower. Buffet breakfast is provided, along with tea- and coffee-making facilities. There's also a TV lounge area with daily newspapers. Doubles from €120, from €130 with a canal view.

Pax Raadhuisstraat 37 ℡ 020/624 9735. Tram #13 or #17 to Westermarkt. Straightforward, city-centre cheapie with a mixture of fair-sized rooms sleeping one to four people;

plans are afoot to refurbish all rooms in minimalist style. As with most of the hotels along this busy stretch, ask for a room at the back. Doubles from €70.

Pulitzer Prinsengracht 315 ☎020/523 5235, ⓦwww.starwood.com. Tram #13 or #17 to Westermarkt. An entire row of seventeenth-century canal houses creatively converted into a prestigious, five-star hotel. Very popular with visiting businessfolk, but although the public areas are tastefully decorated and the breakfasts very good, the modern rooms lack character and some – considering the price – are very disappointing. Doubles from €300.

Toren Keizersgracht 164 ☎020/622 6033, ⓦwww.hoteltoren.nl. Tram #13 or #17 to Westermarkt. The *Toren's* forty bedrooms are distributed between two sympathetically revamped seventeenth-century canal houses just a few doors away from each other. One of them – no. 164 – was once the home of a Dutch prime minister and both are now popular with American visitors. The bedrooms themselves are large, modern and well appointed, and staff are friendly and efficient. Doubles from €185.

▽ Toren

Wiechmann Prinsengracht 328–332 ☎020/626 3321, ⓦwww.hotelwiechmann.nl. Tram #13 or #17 to Westermarkt. Family-run for over fifty years, this medium-sized hotel near the Anne Frank Huis occupies an attractively restored, Art Nouveau canal house, with dark wooden beams and restrained decor throughout. Large, bright rooms in first-rate (if slightly old-fashioned) condition, with TV and shower, cost €130, €20 more for a canal view; prices stay the same throughout the year.

Grachtengordel south

Amsterdam American Leidsekade 97 ☎020/556 3000, ⓦwww.amsterdamamerican.com. Tram #1, #2 or #5 to Leidseplein. This landmark Art Deco hotel, dating from 1902, was once the height of chic; the high rollers have since moved on, and the bedrooms are now standard-issue modern affairs, but they are large and comfortable, with double-glazed windows (a useful addition, since the hotel is just off Leidseplein). Doubles from as little as €130 if booked well in advance.

Dikker & Thijs Fenice Prinsengracht 444 ☎020/620 1212, ⓦwww.dtfh.nl. Tram #1, #2 or #5 to the corner of Prinsengracht and Leidse-straat. Small and stylish hotel not far from Leidseplein. The modern rooms vary in decor but all include a minibar, telephone and TV; those on the top floor offer a good view of the city. Standard doubles from €160 including breakfast.

Jolly Hotel Carlton Vijzelstraat 4 ☎020/521 6810, ⓦwww.jollyhotels.nl. Tram #4, #9, #16, #24 or #25 to the Muntplein. Next door to the flower market, this large, four-star chain hotel has over two hundred well-appointed bedrooms equipped with standard modern fittings and furnishings. Some of the "deluxe" rooms on the top floor have balconies and grand views over the city centre. The official rate is €300 and upwards for a double, but discounts are commonplace, with guests usually paying €170–190.

Marcel van Woerkom Leidsestraat 87 ☎020/622 9834, ⓦwww.marcelamsterdam. com. Tram #1, #2 or #5 to Prinsengracht.

Popular guesthouse run by an English-speaking graphic designer and artist, who attracts like-minded people to this stylishly restored house. This is a relaxing and peaceful haven from the buzz of the city, with regulars returning year after year, so you'll need to book well in advance in high season. Four en-suite doubles, including one with private patio garden, available for two, three or four people sharing. No breakfast, but there are tea- and coffee-making facilities. Rates start at €120 for a double.

De Munck Achtergracht 3 ☎020/623 6283, ⊛www.hoteldemunck.com. Tram #4 to Frederiksplein. This pleasant, family-run hotel off the beaten track, south of the centre and a stone's throw from the River Amstel, has neat, modern rooms in an old, neck-gabled house. The Sixties-style breakfast room sports a Wurlitzer jukebox with a good collection of 1960s hits. Booking recommended. En-suite doubles from €105, including breakfast.

Op de Gracht Prinsengracht 826 ☎020/626 1937, ⊛www.opdegracht.nl. Tram #4 to Prinsengracht. Amiable B&B in a good-looking old house on one of the main canals. The two rooms are tastefully decorated, and both have an en-suite bathroom. Minimum stay two nights, three at the weekend. Doubles €100–110.

Prinsenhof Prinsengracht 810 ☎020/623 1772, ⊛www.hotelprinsenhof.com/hotel/info.html. Tram #4 to Prinsengracht. One-star hotel with smartly decorated rooms, some en suite, and a bright breakfast room. This is one of the city's top budget options, usually booked up for months in advance, so reservations are essential. Doubles €69 without shower, €89 with shower.

Schiller Rembrandtplein 26–36 ☎020/554 0700, ⊛www.nh-hotels.com. Tram #4 or #9 to Rembrandtplein. Once something of a hangout for Amsterdam's intellectuals, the Schiller, named after the painter and architect, still has one of the city's better-known brasseries on its ground floor

decorated in fetching Art Deco style. The drawback is its location – on tacky Rembrandtplein – but if you're here to sample a few of the city's nightclubs, the Muziektheater or the shops along Leidsestraat, you couldn't be better situated. Rates without breakfast begin at around €200.

Seven Bridges Reguliersgracht 31 ☎020/623 1329 ⊛www.sevenbridgeshotel.nl. Tram #16, #24 or #25 to Keizersgracht. One of the city's most charming hotels – and excellent value for money too. Takes its name from its canalside location, which affords a view of no less than seven quaint little bridges. Beautifully decorated in antique style, its spotless rooms are regularly revamped, and it's small and popular, so advance reservations are pretty much essential. Breakfast is served in your room. Rates start at €110 per double, and vary with the view.

▽ Seven Bridges

The Jordaan and Western docklands

Acacia Lindengracht 251 ☎020/622 1460, ⊛www.hotelacacia.nl. Bus #18 to Willemstraat, or a 15-minute walk from CS. This small hotel, situated in the heart of the Jordaan, is on a corner, so some of the rooms have sweeping views of the canal and its adjoining streets. The pastel-pink rooms, which sleep two to four people, are rather nondescript with small beds and a shower room. Doubles from €80, including breakfast; there are also self-catering studios (€90).

Johanna's B&B Van Hogendorpplein 62
⊤062/413 3056 (mobile). Tram #10 from
Leidseplein to Van Limburg Stirumplein. A
privately run B&B, very friendly and helpful
to newcomers. It's a little difficult to get to,
situated out near the Westergasfabriek, but
is excellent value. Two double rooms only,
so be sure to call before you set out. €90.

Mark's Studio Van Beuningenstraat 80a ⊤6526
81011 (mobile), ⓦwww.marksamsterdam.com.
Bus #18, or a five-minute taxi ride from CS.
Comfortable and stylishly decorated non-
smoking studio apartment situated
northwest of the city centre in Westerpark.
Sleeps up to four people (two on a sofa
bed), with facilities such as TV and DVD
player. No breakfast is provided, but there's
a fridge and tea- and coffee-making facilities. There's a pleasant garden terrace too.
Online bookings only; minimum stay two
nights. Cash only; payment upon check-in.
Price depends on length of stay and
number of people staying, but is generally
around €45 per person.

Van Onna Bloemgracht 102 ⊤020/626 5801,
ⓦwww.vanonna.nl. Tram #13 or #17 to Westermarkt. A quiet, well-maintained place on a
tranquil canal. The building dates back over
three hundred years and still retains some of
its original fixtures, though the rooms
themselves are rather modest, with lemon-
painted walls and blankets on beds. This is
a simple setup – no TV, no smoking and
cash payment only. Booking advised.
Rooms sleeping up to four people for €45
per person, including breakfast.

The Old Jewish Quarter and Eastern docklands

Adolesce Nieuwe Keizersgracht 26
⊤020/626 3959, ⓦwww.adolesce.nl.
Tram #9 to Waterlooplein. This
popular and welcoming hotel in
an old canal house not far from
Waterlooplein has ten neat,
modern rooms and a large dining
room. Doubles €100, triples
€120. No breakfast.

Hotel Arena 's-Gravesandestraat 51
⊤020/850 2410, ⓦwww.hotelarena.

nl. Tram #7 from Leidseplein. A little way east
of the centre, in a renovated old convent on
the edge of the Oosterpark, this place has
been thoroughly revamped, transforming a
popular hostel into a hip three-star hotel
complete with split-level rooms and
minimalist decor. Despite the odd pretentious flourish, it manages to retain a relaxed
vibe, attracting both business clients and
travellers alike. Lively bar, intimate restaurant, and late-night club (Fri & Sat; see
p.209) located within the former chapel.
Doubles start at €120.

Fantasia Nieuwe Keizersgracht 16 ⊤020/623
8259, ⓦwww.fantasia-hotel.com. Tram #9 to
Waterlooplein. Appealing, family-run hotel in a
sympathetically revamped old canal house
on a broad, quiet canal just off the River
Amstel; the eighteen en-suite rooms are well
maintained and the attic rooms are
especially attractive. Doubles cost €90,
including breakfast. Triples (€125) and a
four-berth family room (€145) are also
available. Closed most of Dec, and
Jan–March.

InterContinental Amstel Professor Tulpplein 1
⊤020/622 6060, ⓦwww.amsterdam
.intercontinental.com. Metro Weesperplein. The
absolute top of the range – one of the best
and most luxurious hotels in the country,
occupying a grand, chateau-style, nineteenth-
century mansion beside the Singelgracht
canal. Favoured by visiting celebrities, the
hotel was treated to a sumptuous renovation
to the tune of €50 million in the late nineties.
If you have the means, splash out; cheapest
doubles from €450.

 Lloyd Hotel Oostelijke Handelskade 34
⊤020/561 3636, ⓦwww.lloydhotel.com.

▽ Lloyd Hotel

Tram #26 from CS. See map p.111. Situated in the Eastern docklands, this ex-prison and one-time migrant workers' hostel has been carefully renovated to become one of Amsterdam's coolest hotels. Rather pretentiously subtitled a "cultural embassy", it's an arts centre too, with regular exhibitions, readings and performances, an art library, and an appealing, bustling feel that revolves around its airy central restaurant and lobby area on the ground floor. Uniquely, it serves all kinds of travellers, with rooms ranging from one-star affairs for €100 to €300 offerings. Some rooms are great, others not so, so don't be afraid to ask to change. The location is better than you might think – just a five-minute tram ride from Centraal Station – but at these prices you still might prefer to be in the centre.

The Museum Quarter and Vondelpark

Acro Jan Luyckenstraat 44 ☏020/662 5538, ⓦ www.acro-hotel.nl. Tram #2 or #5 to **Hobbemastraat.** This hotel has small and fairly functional rooms, but a friendly welcome and a nice bar on the ground floor mean that it gets booked up a long way in advance. Doubles €100–135 with breakfast.

Bema Concertgebouwplein 19b ☏020/679 1396, ⓦ www.bemahotel.com. Tram #5 or #24 to **Van Baerlestraat.** Large, clean rooms within a huge house under the canny eye of the friendly manager-owner. The eight rooms aren't modern but they're full of funky character, and the hotel is handy for the Concertgebouw and the main museums. Minimum two-night stay at weekends. En-suite doubles €85, including breakfast delivered to your room. Triples and quads also available, and a couple of apartments too.

Bilderberg Hotel Jan Luyken Jan Luykenstraat 58 ☏020/573 0730, ⓦ www.janluyken.nl. Tram #2 or #5 to **Hobbemastraat.** Good-sized rooms, which have been nicely refurbished relatively recently, mark out this decent stab at a mini four-star, full-service hotel, with prices starting at €150 for one of the smaller standard rooms. There's a pleasant lounge and bar downstairs too.

College Roelof Hartstraat 1 ☏020/571 1511, ⓦ www.thesteingroup.com/college. Tram #5 or #24 to junction of **Roelof Hartstraat** and **Van Baerlestraat.** Converted from an old schoolhouse, the *College* is one of the most original and elegant recent additions to Amsterdam's accommodation scene. Original because it's largely run by students of the city's catering school; elegant because of the sheer class of the refurbishment. The cheapest doubles start at €235 – and are well worth it.

▽ College

Filosoof Anna van den Vondelstraat 6 ☏020/683 3013, ⓦ www.hotelfilosoof.nl. Tram #1 from CS to **Jan Pieter Heijestraat.** A lovely small hotel, delightfully overseen by the philosophical Ida, who saw fit to decorate each room according to a different philosophical theme when it opened thirty years ago. It's all beautifully kept, nothing is too much trouble, and the garden outside is a rare Amsterdam treat. Doubles cost around €130, including breakfast.

Fita Jan Luykenstraat 37 ☏020/679 0976, ⓦ www.fita.nl. Tram #2 or #5 to **Hobbemastraat.** Mid-sized, friendly, family-run hotel in a quiet spot between the Vondelpark and the museums. Comfortable en-suite doubles, all non-smoking, cost €130–160, though stays of four nights or more get a ten percent discount. Another bonus is free phone calls within Europe and to America, and free use of the hotel's wi-fi (and laptop if you need it).

Karen McCusker Zeilstraat ☎ 020/679 2753 (mornings), ⊛ www.bedandbreakfastamsterdam. net. *Tram #2 to Amstelveenseweg.* This small B&B, run by an Englishwoman who moved to Amsterdam in 1979, comprises of two cosy and clean, Laura Ashley-style (non-smoking) double rooms in her home, close to the Vondelpark. There's also a suite available, with bathroom, kitchen and private balcony, suitable for longer stays. Ring first, because the owner isn't always around and you'll also need to reserve well in advance. Doubles with shared bathroom cost around €80, €115 with en-suite bathroom – a little less if you stay for longer than three nights. They also have a couple of apartments available for short-term let (minimum one-month stay) for €750–1250 a month.

Owl Hotel Roemer Visscherstraat 1 ☎ 020/618 9484, ⊛ www.owl-hotel.nl. *Tram #1 from CS to Leidseplein.* The reasonably priced doubles at this hotel are rather blandly furnished, but its location is nice and quiet. There's a downstairs lounge opening onto a lovely garden, and the staff are a welcoming bunch – the hotel has been run by the same family for nearly forty years. Doubles from €125.

Parkzicht Roemer Visscherstraat 33 ☎ 020/618 1954, ⊛ www.parkzicht.nl. *Tram #1 from CS to Leidseplein.* This quiet, unassuming hotel, on a pretty backstreet near the Vondelpark and museums, has been going since the 1930s and has an appealingly lived-in look. Clean and characterful, some rooms have fireplaces and each is furnished with old Dutch wood furniture. Singles, doubles and triples available, with a mixture of shared and en-suite facilities; prices are €65–80 for a double, €105 for a triple.

Piet Hein Vossiusstraat 53 ☎ 020/662 7205, ⊛ www.hotelpiethein.nl. *Tram #2 or #5 from CS to Leidseplein.* Five minutes' walk from Leidseplein, this sleek three-star has large rooms with views over the entrance to the Vondelpark and slightly more expensive rooms in the modern annexe, which overlooks its peaceful back garden. There's also a comfy bar (with Internet access) that's normally open until 1am. Rates start at about €120 – good value.

Prinsen Vondelstraat 36–38 ☎ 020/616 2323, ⊛ www.prinsenhotel.nl. *Tram #1 from CS to Leidseplein.* Family-run hotel built in the nineteenth century by Dutch architect P.J.H. Cuypers (he of Centraal Station fame) on the edge of the Vondelpark. It's not especially friendly, but it is quiet and has a large, secluded back garden. En-suite doubles with all mod cons go for €125–35, triples and quads for €150–200.

Toro Koningslaan 64 ☎ 020/673 7223, ⊛ www. hoteltoro.nl. *Tram #2 from CS to Valeriusplein.* Housed in a grand old villa overlooking the Vondelpark's westerly reaches, this hotel is like a small country house, with a welcoming downstairs sitting room and tastefully furnished rooms from €150, some of which overlook the park. There's also a private garden and terrace which overlooks a lake in the Vondelpark. Run by the people who own the more central *Toren* (see p.169), it's a good choice if you don't mind being slightly out of the action.

Verdi Wanningstraat 9 ☎ 020/676 0073. *Tram #5 or #24 to Van Baerlestraat.* Small and simple hotel with large, basic but bright and comfortable rooms near the Concertge-bouw. Doubles with shower around €120, excluding tax.

Vondel Vondelstraat 18–30 ☎ 020/616 4075 ⊛ www.hotelvondel.com. *Tram #1 from CS to Leidseplein.* This newly refurbished hotel tries hard to be cool and sleek, and mostly succeeds, with black paint and light, natural wood characterizing the lovely rooms, which have flat-screen TVs. There's a pleasant bar and breakfast room and modern art decorates the common areas. Doubles from around €160.

Zandbergen Willemsparkweg 205 ☎ 020/676 9321, ⊛ www.hotel-zandbergen.com. *Tram #2 to Emmastraat.* This light, airy, family-run hotel on a busy street near the Vondelpark has eighteen non-smoking rooms that are clean, spacious and tastefully decorated, with minibar and free wi-fi connection. Doubles go for €120–155 depending on season and type of room, and triples and quads are available too for €145–205, as well as a bright and spacious penthouse apartment for €1000 a week, €3000 a month.

The outer districts

Hilton Apollolaan 138 ☏ 020/710 6000, ⓦ www. amsterdam.hilton.com. Tram #5 or #24 to Apollolaan. See map p.132. Way outside the centre in the distinctly upmarket Nieuw Zuid district, this hotel has all the facilities you could hope for, from lounge bar, café and health club through to a fine Italian restaurant. Mainly attracting business-oriented clientele, it's only really worth considering if you can afford to soak up a bit of 1960s nostalgia in its (admittedly stunning) Lennon and Ono suite, where the couple held their famous 1969 "Bed-In" for peace; one night here will set you back €1400, otherwise doubles hover around the €260 mark.
Okura Ferdinand Bolstraat 333 ☏ 020/678 7111, ⓦ www.okura.nl. Tram #25 to Cornelis Troostplein. See map p.130. Don't be fooled by its concrete, purpose-built facade: this deluxe hotel, situated close to the RAI, comes equipped with all the usual facilities you would expect, even including a shopping arcade with a Japanese food store. Its 315 rooms boast huge marble bathrooms, and in its suites, mod cons include mood lighting and controls for the curtains. Three of its four restaurants (see p.201) have Michelin stars. If you're feeling particularly flush you could book "The Suite", set over two floors with a suspended glass staircase, cinema and private butler; a night here will set you back a cool €10,000. Doubles from €295.
Van Ostade Van Ostadestraat 123 ☏ 020/679 3452, ⓦ www.bicyclehotel.com. Tram #25 to Van de Helststraat. Friendly, youthful place down a quiet residential street, not far from Albert Cuypmarkt in De Pijp. It bills itself as the "bicycle hotel", renting bikes for €5 per day and giving advice on routes and suchlike. There's also garage space for two cars (€17.50 per car; book in advance). Two-, three- and four-bed rooms, plus one with bunk beds, are basic but clean. Doubles start from €80 with shared facilities, including breakfast.
Xaviera Hollander B&B Stadionweg 17 ☏ 020/673 3934, ⓦ www.xavierahollander.com. Tram #5 or #24 to Stadionweg. See map p.132. Spending a night at the home of illustrious former madam, Xaviera Hollander, better known as the "Happy Hooker", may sound dubious but the experience is a whole lot more respectable than you'd imagine. Situated in the chichi Nieuw Zuid, this spacious, homely villa has two kitschy rooms, the larger of which has a terrace, though it suffers a little from traffic noise. Prudish it ain't, with semi-clad photos of Xaviera and friends dotted about and shelves of well-thumbed sex-help books, but memorable nonetheless. Parking available. No credit cards. Both rooms have shared facilities. Rates from €125.

Hostels

If you're on a tight budget, the least expensive central option is to take a dorm bed in a **hostel**, and there are plenty to choose from: Hostelling International places, unofficial private hostels, even Christian hostels. Most hostels will either provide (relatively) clean bed linen or charge a few euros for it – your own sleeping bag might be a better option. Many places also lock guests out for a short period each day to clean; some also set a nightly curfew, though these are usually late enough not to cause too much of a problem. Some hostels don't accept reservations from June to August.

The cheapest **dorms** you'll find are in the "Shelter" Christian-run hostels, between €16–22 per person per night; the average elsewhere is closer to €25.

A few otherwise good-value places have a policy of charging more at **weekends** than during the week – a price hike of as much as €5 that can come as an unpleasant surprise. Note that you can pay the same rate for a bed in a sixteen-person dorm as you'd pay to be in a four-person dorm elsewhere, and that any place which won't allow you to see where you'll be sleeping before you pay is worth avoiding. If you want a little extra privacy, many hostels also offer triples, doubles and singles for much less than you'd pay in a regular hotel – though the quality and size of rooms can leave a lot to be desired.

Old Centre

Bob's Youth Hostel Nieuwezijds Voorburgwal 92 ☏020/623 0063, ⓦ www.bobshostel.nl. Ten-minute walk from CS. An old favourite with backpackers, Bob's is a lively place with small, basic dorm beds for €19 per person, including breakfast in the coffeeshop on the ground floor. They also let four apartments (€70 for two people, €80 for three). However, they kick everyone out at 10.30am to clean – not ideal if you want a lie-in.

Bulldog Hotel Oudezijds Voorburgwal 220 ☏020/620 3822, ⓦ www.bulldoghotel.com. Trams #4, #9, #16 or #24 to Dam Square. Part of the *Bulldog* coffeeshop chain, and recently renovated, with a bar and DVD lounge downstairs complete with leather couches and soft lighting. Dorm beds with TV and shower cost €25–29 depending on season, including breakfast, with linen €3 extra, and there are also double rooms for €84–93, triples and quads for €110–140, as well as fully equipped apartments from €140–150 for two, around €200 for four – all with bathrooms and TVs.

Flying Pig Downtown Nieuwendijk 100 ☏020/420 6822, ⓦ www.flyingpig.nl. Five-minute walk from CS. Clean, large and well run by ex-travellers familiar with the needs of backpackers. As such, it's a relaxed and friendly place, with the free use of kitchen facilities and no curfew; there's a late-night coffeeshop next door and the hostel bar is open all night. It's justifiably popular, and a very good deal, with mixed dorm beds from about €25 depending on the size of the dorm; queen-size bunks sleeping two also available; €10 deposit for sheets and keys. During the peak season you'll need to book well in advance. See also the *Flying Pig Uptown*, p.176.

The Globe Oudezijds Voorburgwal 3 ☏020/421 7424, ⓦ www.hostel-theglobe.nl. Trams #4, #9, #16 or #24 to Dam Square. A popular hostel that's a favourite with those on all-day drinking binges, partly due to its 24hr sports-screen bar. It's not a palace by anyone's standards, but may do the trick if you're not in Amsterdam to sleep much. Spartan but clean dorm beds from €22 (weekends €28), twins for a steep €95. €5 key deposit. Breakfast is an extra €4.50.

Meeting Point Warmoesstraat 14 ☏020/627 7499, ⓦ www.hostel-meetingpoint.nl. Ten-minute walk from CS. Warm and cosy central hostel with space in twelve- to eighteen-bed dorms. Private bar and pool table for guests is open 24 hours. Cash payment only. Four-person dorms €85. Breakfast €2.50. Midweek dorms go for €16.

Shelter City Barndesteeg 21 ☏020/625 3230, ⓦ www.shelter.nl. Metro Nieuwmarkt. A non-evangelical Christian hostel smack in the middle of the Red Light District. Beds in large dorms for €16–19, including bed linen, shower and sizeable breakfast, which makes this one of the city's best deals; it's €18–21 for a bed in a smaller dorm, and €21–23 in a four-bed dorm. Dorms are single-sex; lockers require a €5 deposit and there's a midnight curfew (1am at weekends). You might get invited to a prayer meeting, but the Christian message isn't oppressive, and the sheets are clean, as is everything else. There's even a bar open until 1am. See also *The Shelter Jordan*, p.176.

Stay Okay Stadsdoelen Kloveniersburgwal 97 ☏020/624 6832, ⓦ www.stayokay.com /stadsdoelen. Metro Nieuwmarkt, or trams #4, #9, #16, #24 or #25 to Muntplein. The closest to Centraal Station of the two official hostels, with clean, semi-private dorms at around €20 for members, who get priority in high season; non-members pay €23.75 (€2 extra at weekends), and there are two-, four- and six-person rooms available for prices ranging from €22 to €36 per person, depending on the room and the season. Prices include linen, breakfast and locker, and the use of a communal kitchen. Guests get a range of discounts on activities in the city too, and you can also book Eurolines bus tickets here, with members receiving a ten percent discount. The bar overlooks the canal and serves good-value if basic food, and there's a 2am curfew (though the door opens for three 15min intervals between 2am and 7am). See also the city's other HI hostel, the *Stay Okay Vondelpark* (see below), which has a greater choice of rooms.

Grachtengordel south

Hans Brinker Budget Hotel Kerkstraat 136 ☎020/622 0687, ⊛www.hans-brinker.com. **Tram #1, #2 or #5 to Leidsestraat at Kerkstraat.** Well-established and raucously popular Amsterdam cheapie, which has over 550 beds, mostly in dorms, but singles and doubles are available too. The facilities are good: breakfast, free Internet after 10pm, disco every night, and clean if basic dorms; it's near to the buzz of Leidseplein too. A hostel to head to if you're out for a good time (and not too bothered about getting a good night's sleep), though be prepared to change dorms several times during your stay to accommodate larger groups. Dorm beds go for €21–24.

International Budget Hostel Leidsegracht 76 ☎020/624 2784, ⊛www .internationalbudgethostel.com. **Tram #1, #2 or #5 to Prinsengracht.** An excellent budget option on a peaceful little canal in the heart of the city. Small, simple rooms sleeping up to four with shared bathroom; breakfast in the café is extra. Young, friendly staff. Singles and twin rooms with private facilities (€70), dorm beds €30 per person.

The Jordaan and Western docklands

The Shelter Jordan Bloemstraat 179 ☎020/624 4717, ⊛www.shelter.nl. **Tram #13 or #17 to Marnixstraat.** The second of Amsterdam's two Christian hostels (the other is *Shelter City*, see p.175) is situated in a particularly attractive and quiet part of the Jordaan, close to the Lijnbaansgracht canal. Great-value beds start at €19.50 (down to €16 in low season) including breakfast; bed linen is €2 extra. Fri & Sat €3 supplement. Dorms sleeping 14–20 are single-sex and non-smoking; downstairs there's a decent café. Lockers require a refundable deposit.

The Museum Quarter and Vondelpark

Flying Pig Uptown Vossiusstraat 46 ☎020/400 4187, ⊛www.flyingpig.nl. **Trams #1, #2 or #5 to Leidseplein, then a short walk.** The better of the two *Flying Pig* hostels, facing the Vondelpark and close to the city's most important museums. Immaculately clean and well maintained by a staff of travellers. Free use of kitchen facilities, no curfew and good tourist information. Fourteen-bed dorms start at €23.90 per person and there are a few two-person queen-size bunks, as well as double rooms – great value.

Stay Okay Vondelpark Zandpad 5 ☎020/589 8996, ⊛www.stayokay.com/ vondelpark. **Trams #1, #2 or #5 to Leidseplein, then a five-minute walk.** Well located and, for facilities, the better of the city's two HI hostels, with a bar, restaurant, TV lounge, Internet access and bicycle shed, plus various discount deals on tours and museums. Non-member rates are €23.75 per person in the dorms (€2 extra at weekends), including use of all facilities, shower (though no towels), sheets and breakfast. Singles, doubles and rooms sleeping up to six are also available; prices range from €25–30 per person in a six-person dorm to €75–85 for a double room. Secure lockers and no curfew. To be sure of a place in high season you'll need to book at least two months ahead.

Apartments and houseboats

For groups or families, short-term **apartment** rentals can work out cheaper than staying in a hotel, with the further advantages of privacy and the convenience (or at least relative cheapness) of self-catering. Apartments sleeping four or five can often be found for the same price as a double room in a hotel. **Houseboats** tend to be significantly more luxurious and expensive. Both are often organized through local hotels. **City Mundo** (Ⓦ www.citymundo.com) is a booking service for private accommodation, including rooms, apartments and houseboats. Bookings of three to twenty-one days start from €24–29 per person per night (for up to 4 people). The website lists a hundred properties at any one time, taken from a database of a couple of hundred, and changes according to availability. Alternatively, the following are reliable city-centre options.

Acacia Lindengracht 251 ℡ 020/622 1460, Ⓦ www.hotelacacia.nl. Studios sleeping two people €90 per night; houseboats from €100.
Amsterdam House 's Gravelandseveer 7, 1011 KN Amsterdam ℡ 020/626 2577, Ⓦ www.

amsterdamhouse.com. Two-room apartments start at €115 per night; houseboats €150.
Hoksbergen Apartments Singel 301 ℡ 020/626 6043, Ⓦ www.hotelhoksbergen.nl. Apartments sleeping up to five from €120.

Camping

There are a number of **campsites** on the peripheries of Amsterdam, most of them readily accessible by car or public transport. Those listed below are two of the more established and central options.

Campsites

Vliegenbos Meeuwenlaan 138 ℡ 020/636 8855, Ⓦ www.vliegenbos.com. Bus #32 or #33 from CS; drivers take Exit S116 off the A10. A relaxed and friendly site, just a ten-minute bus ride into Amsterdam North from CS. Facilities include a general shop, bar and restaurant. Rates start at €8 per night per person with hot showers included. There are also huts with bunk beds and basic cooking facilities for €70 per night for four people; phone ahead to check availability. Car parking is €8. Under-16s need to be

accompanied by an adult; no pets. Open April to Sept.
Zeeburg Zuider IJdijk 20 ℡ 020/694 4430, Ⓦ www.campingzeeburg.nl. Tram #26 from CS to Zuiderzeeweg, then a ten-minute walk; drivers take Exit S114 off the A10. Well-equipped campsite in the Eastern docklands with a bar, restaurant, laundry, kayak and bicycle rental plus lots of green fields. Tent pitches cost €5 in addition to a €5 charge per person per night, and €4.50 for a car. Two-berth cabins cost €40, four-berth €80, and six-berth €120, including bed linen. Open all year.

Eating and drinking

Amsterdam may not be Europe's gastronomic capital, but the **food** in the average Dutch restaurant has improved by leaps and bounds in recent years, and there are any number of places serving good, often inventive, home-grown cuisine. The city also boasts a wide range of ethnic restaurants, especially Indonesian, Chinese and Thai, as well as numerous cafés and bars – often known as *eetcafés* – that serve adventurous, reasonably priced food in a relaxed and unpretentious setting. Amsterdam is also, of course, a great place for a **drink**; the Netherlands' proximity to the great beer-drinking nation of Belgium – the birthplace of modern beer – helps explain the variety on offer.

The city is filled to the gunnels with places to eat and drink, and you should have no trouble finding somewhere convenient and enjoyable to suit your budget. On Thursday, Friday and Saturday nights it's advisable to start early (between 6pm and 7pm), or make a reservation, if you want to get a table at any of the more popular **restaurants**. If you just want lunch, or a bite between sights, there are plenty of places throughout the city – **cafés and tearooms** – where you can just grab a cup of coffee and a sandwich or light lunch. **Bars** almost always serve sandwiches, and usually something more substantial as well; those that serve good-quality food are indicated in the listings.

Dutch meal times are a little idiosyncratic; breakfast tends to be later than you might expect, and other meals tend to be eaten earlier. If you choose to eat **breakfast** away from your hotel, you'll find very few cafés open before 8am or 8.30am. The standard Dutch **lunch** hour is from noon to 1pm; most restaurants are at their busiest at **dinner**, between 7pm and 8pm, and mostly stop serving by 10 or 10.30pm.

With Amsterdam's singular approach to the sale and consumption of cannabis, you might choose to enjoy a joint after your meal rather than a beer; included in this chapter is a selection of **"coffeeshops"** where you can buy and smoke grass or hash.

Bars, cafés and restaurants are listed in the index at the back of the book.

What to eat

Dutch food tends to be higher in protein content than in variety; steak, chicken and fish, along with filling soups and stews, are staples, usually served up in substantial quantities. At its best, though, it can be excellent, with many restaurants, and even bars and *eetcafés*, offering increasingly adventurous crossovers with French and Mediterranean cuisine, at reasonable prices.

Dutch cheese

Dutch **cheeses** have a somewhat unjustified reputation abroad for being bland and rubbery, but in fact they can be delicious, even if there isn't the variety you find in, say, France or Britain. Most Dutch cheeses vary little from the familiar pale yellow, semi-soft **Gouda**, within which differences in taste come from the varying stages of maturity: *jong* (young) cheese has a mild flavour, *belegen* (mature) has a fuller flavour, while *oud* (old) can be pungent and strong, with a grainy, flaky texture. Generally, the older they get, the saltier they are. Best-known among the other cheeses is **Edam**, also semi-soft in texture but slightly creamier than Gouda; it's usually shaped into balls and coated in red wax ready for export – it's not eaten much in the Netherlands. **Leidse** is simply a bland Gouda laced with cumin or caraway seeds, with most of its flavour coming from the seeds; **Maasdam** is a Dutch version of Emmental or Jarlsberg: strong, creamy and full of holes, sold under brand names such as Leerdammer and Maasdammer; you'll also come across Dutch-made Emmental and Gruyère. The Dutch like their cheese in thin slices, cut with a cheese slicer, rather than in large chunks.

Amsterdam has several specialist **cheese shops** (see p.231) and there's also a good range of cheeses on sale at the Saturday farmers' produce market on the Noordermarkt (9am–1pm). Finally, Amsterdam is within easy striking distance of two world-famous cheese markets, one at Edam (see p.156), the other at Alkmaar (see p.159).

Breakfast

In all but the cheapest and the most expensive of hotels, **breakfast** (*ontbijt*) will be included in the price of the room. Though usually nothing fancy, it's always substantial; rolls, cheese, ham, hard-boiled eggs, jam and honey or peanut butter are the principal ingredients. Many bars and cafés serve rolls and sandwiches in similar mode, although few open much before 8am or 8.30am.

Dutch **coffee** is normally good and strong, served with a little tub of *koffiemelk* (evaporated milk); ordinary milk is rarely used. If you want coffee with warm milk, ask for a *koffie verkeerd*. Tea generally comes with lemon – if anything; if you want milk you have to ask for it. Chocolate (*chocomel*) is also popular, hot or cold; for a real treat, drink it hot with a layer of fresh whipped cream (*slagroom*) on top. Some cafés also sell aniseed-flavoured warm milk (*anijsmelk*).

Snacks and sandwiches

Dutch **fast food** has its own peculiarities. Chips/fries (*friet* or *patat*) are the most common standby; *vlaamse* or "Flemish-style", sprinkled with salt and smothered with lashings of mayonnaise (*frietesaus*) are the best, or with curry, goulash, or tomato or *sateh* (peanut) sauce. If you just want salt, ask for *patat zonder*; fries with salt and mayonnaise are *patat met*. You'll also come across *kroketten* – spiced minced meat (usually either veal or beef), covered with breadcrumbs and deep-fried – and *fricandel*, a frankfurter-like sausage. All these are available over the counter at pungent fast-food places, or, for a euro or so, from coin-op heated glass compartments on the street and in train stations.

Much tastier are the **fish** specialities sold by street vendors, which are good as a snack or a light lunch; raw herring (*haring*), rollmops, smoked eel (*gerookte* *paling*), mackerel in a roll (*broodje makreel*), mussels (*mosselen*) and various kinds of deep-fried fish are all delicious. Look out, too, for "green" or *maatje* herring, eaten raw with onions in early summer; hold the fish by the tail, tip your head back and dangle it into your mouth, Dutch-style. Another snack you'll see everywhere is **shwarma** or *shoarma* – another name for a doner kebab: shavings of lamb pressed into a pitta bread – sold in numerous Middle Eastern restaurants and takeaways for about €3. Other, less common, street foods include **pancakes** (*pannenkoeken*), sweet or spicy, also widely available at restaurants; waffles (*stroopwafels*), doused with syrup; and, in November and December, *oliebollen*, greasy doughnuts sometimes filled with fruit (often apple) or custard (known as a *Berliner*) and traditionally eaten on New Year's Eve.

Bars often serve **sandwiches and rolls** (*boterham* and *broodjes*) – mostly open, and varying from a slice of tired cheese on old bread to something so embellished it's almost a complete meal – as well as more substantial dishes. A sandwich made with French bread is known as a *stokbrood*. In the winter, *erwtensoep* (or *snert*) – thick pea soup with smoked sausage, served with smoked bacon on pumpernickel – is available in many bars, and, for about €5 a bowl, makes a cheap but hearty lunch. Alternatively, there's a *uitsmijter* (a "kicker-out", derived from the practice of serving it at dawn after an all-night party to prompt guests to depart); now widely available at all times of day, it comprises one, two, or three fried eggs on buttered bread, topped with a choice of ham, cheese or roast beef; at about €5, it's another good budget lunch option.

Cakes and biscuits

Dutch **cakes and biscuits** are always good, best eaten in a *banketbakkerij* (patisserie) with a small serving area; or buy to take away and munch them on the hoof. Top of the list is the ubiquitous Dutch speciality *appelgebak* – chunky, memorably fragrant apple-and-cinnamon pie, served hot in huge wedges, often with whipped cream (*met slagroom*). Other sweet nibbles include *speculaas*, a crunchy cinnamon cookie with a gingerbread-like texture; *stroopwafels*, butter wafers sandwiched together with runny syrup; and *amandelkoek*, cakes with a crisp biscuit outside and melt-in-the-mouth almond paste inside.

Full meals

The majority of bars serve food – everything from sandwiches to a full menu – in which case they may be known as an **eetcafé**. This type of place is usually open all day, serving both lunch and evening meals. Full-blown **restaurants**, on the other hand, tend to open in the evening only, usually from around 5.30pm or 6pm until around 10pm.

If you're on a budget, stick to the **dagschotel** (dish of the day) wherever possible, for which you pay around €12 for a meat or fish dish, with a generous serving of potatoes and other vegetables or salad; note, though, that it's often only served at lunchtime or between 6 and 8pm. Otherwise, you can pay up to €20–25 for a meat or fish main course in an average restaurant. **Vegetarian** dining isn't a problem; many *eetcafés* and restaurants have at least one meat-free dish on the menu, and the city has a scattering of veggie restaurants, offering full-course set meals from about €10.

As for foreign cuisines, the Dutch are particularly partial to **Indonesian** food; *Nasi goreng* and *Bami goreng* (rice or noodles with meat) are good basic dishes, though there are normally more exciting items on the menu, some very spicy;

chicken or beef in peanut sauce (*sateh*) is always available. Or you could ask for a **rijsttafel** – a sampler meal, comprising boiled rice and/or noodles served with perhaps ten or twelve small, often spicy dishes and hot *sambal* sauce on the side. Usually ordered for two or more people, you can reckon on paying around €20–25 per person. Surinamese restaurants are much rarer, but they offer a distinctive, essentially Creole cuisine - try *roti*, flat pancake-like bread served with a spicy curry, hardboiled egg and vegetables. **Italian** food is ubiquitous, with pizzas and pasta dishes starting at a fairly uniform €10 or so in most places.

What to drink

Amsterdam's favourite tipple is **beer**, mostly Pilsener-style lager usually served in a relatively small measure (just under a half-pint, with a foaming head) – ask for *een pils*. The three leading Dutch brands – Amstel, Grolsch and Heineken – are worldwide bestsellers, but are available here in considerably more potent formats than the insipid varieties shunted out for export. Different beers come in different glasses – white beer (*witbier*), which is light, cloudy and served with lemon, has its own tumbler; and most of the speciality Belgian beers have their own distinctive glasses with stems of different shapes and sizes.

Wine and spirits

Wine is reasonably priced – expect to pay around €6 or so for an average bottle of French white or red in a supermarket, €15 in a restaurant. As for spirits, **jenever**, Dutch gin, is not unlike English gin but a bit weaker and a little oilier, made from molasses and flavoured with juniper berries. It's served in a small glass and is traditionally drunk straight, often knocked back in one gulp with much hearty back-slapping. There are a number of varieties, principally *oude* (old), which is smooth and mellow, and *jong* (young), which packs more of a punch – though neither is terribly alcoholic. The older *jenevers* (including *zeer oude*, very old) are a little more expensive but stronger and less oily. Ask for a *borreltje* (straight *jenever*), a *bitterje* (with Angostura bitters) or, if you've a sweeter tooth, try a *bessenjenever* – blackcurrant-flavoured gin. A glass of beer with a *jenever* chaser is a *kopstoot*.

Other drinks you'll come across include numerous Dutch **liqueurs**, notably *advocaat* (eggnog), and the sweet blue *curaçao*; and an assortment of lurid **fruit brandies**, which are best left for experimentation at the end of an evening. There's also the Dutch-produced **brandy**, *Vieux*, which tastes as if it's made from prunes but is in fact grape-based.

Bars

There are, in essence, two main kinds of Amsterdam bar: the traditional, old-style bar or **brown café** – a *bruin café* or *bruine kroeg* – cosy, intimate places so called because of the dingy colour of their walls, stained by years of tobacco smoke; and the slick, self-consciously modern **designer bar**, sometimes known as a "grand café", which tends to be as un-brown as possible and geared towards a largely young crowd. Bars, of either kind, **open** daily at around 10am or 5pm; those that open in the morning do not close at lunchtime, and both stay open until around

1am during the week, 2am at weekends (sometimes until 3am). Another type of drinking spot – though there are very few of them left – is the tasting house (*proeflokaalen*), originally the sampling rooms of small private distillers, now tiny, stand-up places that sell only spirits – mainly Dutch gin or *jenever* – and often close early, around 8pm. As in the rest of Europe, there's also a growing number of Irish pubs, all featuring Guinness and other stouts on tap, Gaelic music of varying quality, and English football live via satellite most weekends. The clue to their success seems to lie much more in the football than the fiddlers – all have rapidly become "locals" for the relatively large numbers of British and Irish living and working in Amsterdam, and although at quiet times the clientele might include a smattering of Amsterdammers, most of the (generally male) drinkers in these places are expats rather than locals. For listings of **gay bars** see Chapter Twelve.

Many bars – often designated **eetcafés** – offer a complete food menu, and most will make you a sandwich or a bowl of soup; at the very least you can snack on hard-boiled eggs from the counter. Those bars that specialize more in food than drink are listed in our "Restaurants" section (see pp.190–202).

Prices are fairly standard everywhere, and the only time you'll pay through the nose is when there's music, or if you're desperate enough to step into the obvious tourist traps around Leidseplein and along the Damrak. Reckon on paying roughly €1.60–1.80 for a standard-measure small draught beer, €3 or so for wheat and bottled beer, and €2.40 for a glass of wine or a shot of *jenever*.

Locations are marked on the colour **maps** at the back of this book.

The Old Centre

Absinthe Nieuwezijds Voorburgwal 171. Small, late-night basement lounge bar, slightly hidden from the street, but in a prime position close to the area's bars and clubs. Not surprisingly, it specializes in absinthe – or at least the turn-of-the-twentieth-century decadence that's associated with it. DJs at the weekend. Opens 10pm.

In 't Aepjen Zeedijk 1. This building has been a bar since the days when Zeedijk was the haunt of sailors gambling away their last few guilder and having to pay by barter rather than cash. Its name – literally "In the Monkeys" – refers to the fact that monkeys were once the stock in trade here. There are no monkeys now, but not much else has changed.

De Bekeerde Suster Kloveniersburgwal 6. Don't waste your time in the unappealing drink-eries of the Red Light District proper; this place is a few steps away and offers home-brewed beer, a good bar menu and a very convivial atmosphere, just off the top end of Nieuwmarkt.

Belgique Gravenstraat 2. Tiny and very appealing bar behind the Nieuwe Kerk that specializes in brews from Belgium. Sample them with plates of Dutch and Trappist cheese.

Blincker St Barberenstraat 7. Squeezed between the top end of Nes and Oudezijds Voorburgwal, this hi-tech theatre bar, all exposed steel and hanging plants, is very nicely done – and more comfortable than it looks. Also serves decent food.

De Buurvrouw St Pieterspoortsteeg 29. Dark, noisy bar with a wildly eclectic crowd; a great alternative place to head for in the centre.

Dante Spuistraat 320. A wannabe trendy bar-cum-art gallery right in the heart of the city's densest concentration of watering holes. There are cosier places, but to peruse the art – and the people perusing the art – it's decent enough.

Diep Nieuwezijds Voorburgwal 256. Not much more than an ordinary brown café during the day, but a hip hangout with DJs at night.

Het Doktertje Roozenboomsteeg 4. Small, dark, brown café with stained glass to keep you from being ogled by the world outside. Liqueurs fill the shelves behind the tiny bar.

De Drie Fleschjes Gravenstraat 16. Long-standing tasting house for spirits and liqueurs. No beer, and no seats either; its clients tend to be well-heeled or well-soused (often both).

De Engelbewaarder Kloveniersburgwal 59. Once the meeting place of Amsterdam's bookish types, this is still known as a literary café. It's relaxed and informal, with live jazz on Sunday afternoons.

De Engelse Reet Begijnensteeg 4. Also known as the Pilsener Club, this place is more like someone's living room than a bar – indeed, all drinks mysteriously appear from a back room. Photographs on the wall record generations of drinking – which has been going on here since 1893.

Gaeper Staalstraat 4. Convivial brown café packed during the termtime with students from the university across the canal. Tasty food – and outdoor seating makes for good people-watching.

't Gasthuis Grimburgwal 7. Another brown café popular with students. Both this place and *Gaeper* are run by brothers, and they're done up in more or less the same style. Here, some of Amsterdam's cheapest hot food is served, both at lunchtime and in the evenings.

Gollem Raamsteeg 4. Small, cosy, split-level bar with rickety furniture, wood panelling

▽ Gollem

and a comprehensive selection of Belgian beers, plus a few Dutch brews for variety – and with the correct glasses to drink them from. The genial barman will help you choose.

Harry's American Bar Spuistraat 285. Cramped but very popular, split-level cocktail bar with a jazzy soundtrack, moving into ear-shattering house as the night wears on.

Hoppe Spui 18. One of Amsterdam's longest-established and best-known bars, and a likeably scruffy joint, popular with the city's businessfolk. Summer is especially good, when the throng spills out onto the street.

Kapitein Zeppos Gebed Zonder End 5. This currently hip hangout is tucked away down a tiny street off Grimburgwal and is very easy to miss. It's a bar and a restaurant and boasts a theatricality worthy of its place at the top end of Amsterdam's small theatre district; regular live music too.

De Koningshut Spuistraat 269. In the early evening, at least, it's standing room only in this small, spit-and-sawdust bar, popular with office folk on their way home or to dinner.

Lime Zeedijk 104. Right in the middle of Chinatown, this cool yet comfy hangout is the ideal place for a post-dinner cocktail or pre-club livener. One of the best of the recent additions to the Old Centre bar scene.

Lokaal 't Loosje Nieuwmarkt 32. Quiet, old-style brown café that's been here for two hundred years and looks it, with an attractive old tiled interior. A pleasant atmosphere, and always busy.

Mercurius Prins Hendrikkade 20. This cool, spacious bar and restaurant almost opposite Centraal Station hosts live TV shows and Sunday-night jazz singers.

De Ooievaar Stolofspoort 1. Old *proeflokaal* that's a civilized escape from the nearby sleaze of the Red Light District – and handily situated for Centraal Station too. Boiled eggs at the bar go down well with the gin, and there's beer too.

Het Paleis Paleisstraat 16. This bar is a favourite with students from the adjoining university buildings. Trendily refurbished, they also serve food – focaccia sandwiches, salads and suchlike.

EATING AND DRINKING | Bars

Scheltema Nieuwezijds Voorburgwal 242.
Formerly a journalists' bar, but all the newspaper headquarters along here have since moved to the suburbs, so its faded early twentieth-century interior, with reading tables, isn't quite the hub of activity it once was. It's cosy and atmospheric, though, with an outdoor terrace in summer.

Schuim Spuistraat 189. Popular and spacious bar-café with retro furniture and a young and unpretentiously boho crowd.

The Tara Rokin 85–89. Amsterdam has quite a few Irish pubs these days, but this is one of the best, on several levels, decent food (including a great all-day breakfast), regular football and other sports on TV and live music from 10.30pm Saturdays during the winter. It's very central too.

In de Wildeman Kolksteeg 3. This lovely old-fashioned bar has a barely changed wood and tile interior that still boasts its original low bar and shelving: a very peaceful escape from the loud and tacky shops of nearby Nieuwendijk. One of the centre's most appealing watering holes.

Wynand Fockink Pijlsteeg 31. This small, intimate bar, hidden just behind the Krasnapolsky hotel off Dam Square, is one of the city's older *proeflokaalen*, and it offers a vast range of its own flavoured *jenevers* that were once distilled down the street. It's standing-room only here – you bend down at the counter and sip your *jenever* from a filled-to-the-brim glass.

Grachtengordel west

Brix Wolvenstraat 16 ☎020/639 0351, ⊛www. cafebrix.nl. Chic, basement bar-café featuring jam and jazz sessions twice weekly, plus Asian fusion cuisine with mains from as little as €8. Open daily from 5pm.

Café 't Arendsnest Herengracht 90. In a handsome old canal house, this bar boasts impressive wooden decor – from the longest of bars to the tall wood-and-glass cabinets – and specializes in Dutch beers, of which it has 130 varieties, twelve on tap. Rather surprisingly, however, it can be very quiet.

Daily from 4pm till midnight, 2am at the weekend.

Hegeraad Noordermarkt 34. Lovingly maintained, old-fashioned brown café-bar with a fiercely loyal, older clientele. The back room, furnished with paintings and red plush seats, is the perfect place to relax with a hot chocolate.

Het Molenpad Prinsengracht 653. This is one of the most appealing brown café-bars in the city – a long, dark, dusty bar that also serves very good food. Fills up with a young, professional crowd after 6pm.

▽ Het Molenpad

Het Papeneiland Prinsengracht 2. With its wood panelling, antique Delft tiles and ancient stove, this rabbit warren of a place is one of the cosiest bars in the Grachtengordel, though it does get packed late at night with a garrulous crew. Popular with locals and tourists alike.

De Pieper Prinsengracht 424. Laid-back neighbourhood brown bar, at the corner of Leidsegracht, with rickety old furniture and a mini-terrace beside the canal. Has a surprisingly large selection of liqueurs.

De Prins Prinsengracht 124. With its well-worn decor and chatty atmosphere, this popular and lively bar offers a wide range of drinks and a well-priced bar menu with food served from 10am to 9pm.

Van Puffelen Prinsengracht 375/7. Recently enlarged, this long-established and popular spot is divided into two with a brown café-bar on one side and an *eetcafe* on the other. The café-bar (daily 3pm–1/2am) is an appealing place to drink, with a good choice of international beers, while the restaurant (Mon–Fri 6–11pm, Sat & Sun noon–4pm & 6–10pm) concentrates on Dutch(ish) dishes with lots of organic frills, but the results are variable. Main courses average around €18, but the daily specials are much more economical.

Grachtengordel south

De Duivel Reguliersdwarsstraat 87. Tucked away on a street of bars and coffeeshops, this is the best hip-hop bar in Amsterdam, with continuous beats and a faithful clientele. Daily 8pm–3/4am.

Lux Marnixstraat 403. Designer bar geared up for the pre-club scene with a good line in full-volume house and regular DJs, attracting a young, alternative crowd. Mon–Sat 8pm–3am, sometimes 4am at the weekend.

Morlang Keizersgracht 451. Lively, split-level bar-cum-restaurant decorated in soft, modern style and attracting a prosperous clientele. Good bar and occasional live music too. Next door to the Walem (see below). Daily 11am–1am.

Oosterling Utrechtsestraat 140. Intimate neighbourhood bar that's been plying its trade for donkeys' years. Kitted out in attractive traditional style, it specializes in *jenever*, with dozens of brands and varieties. No mobiles.

Walem Keizersgracht 449. A chic bar-restaurant – cool, light and vehemently un-brown; eat in or chill out at the bar sipping a Mojito. The clientele is stylish, and the food a hybrid of French-Dutch-inspired dishes; the salmon and trout with crème fraîche is particularly good; mains start at €10. Breakfast in the garden during the summer is a highlight. Open daily 10am–1am.

De Zotte Proeflokaal Raamstraat 29. Down a grubby alley not far from the Leidseplein, this amenable, laid-back bar specializes in Belgian beer, of which it has dozens of varieties. Open daily 4pm–1am, bar food served 6–9.30pm.

The Jordaan and Western docklands

Chris Bloemstraat 42. Very proud of itself for being the Jordaan's (and Amsterdam's)

oldest bar, dating from 1624. Comfortable, homely atmosphere.

Dulac Haarlemmerstraat 118. Very appealing Art Deco grand café, with lots of nooks to sit in, housed in what was an old city bank – the metal doors remain but nowadays the only money changing hands is at the bar, especially at weekends when it stays open till 3am. DJs from Thursday to Sunday play a mixture of funk, disco and pop. Mon & Tues from 4pm, Wed–Sun from noon.

Finch Noordermarkt 5. This smart café-lounge bar situated near the Noorderkerk attracts a stylish, relaxed crowd, drawn by the design-school ambience, good tunes and superb location overlooking the Prinsengracht.

▽ Finch

De Kat in de Wijngaert Lindengracht 160. With the enticing name "The Cat in the Vineyard", this small bar is the epitome of the Jordaan local, and quiet enough for conversation.

Nol Westerstraat 109. Raucous but jolly Jordaan singing bar, this luridly lit dive closes late, especially at weekends, when the back-slapping joviality and drunken sing-alongs keep you rooted until the small hours. Opens 9pm.

De Reiger Nieuwe Leliestraat 34. Situated in

the thick of the Jordaan, this is one of the area's many meeting places, an old-style café-bar filled with modish Amsterdammers, and with faded portraits on the walls. Mains around €18.

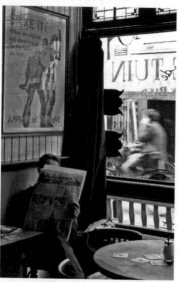 **'t Smalle Egelantiersgracht 12.** Candle-lit and comfortable café-bar, with a pontoon on the canal out front for relaxed summer afternoons.

De Tuin 2e Tuindwarsstraat 13. The Jordaan has some marvellously unpretentious bars, and this is one of the best: agreeably unkempt and always full of locals.

▽ De Tuin

Old Jewish Quarter and Eastern docklands

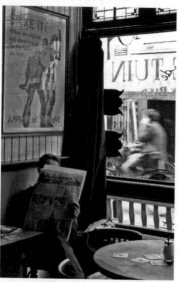 **11 Oosterdokskade 3 ☎020/625 59 99.** One of the hippest joints in town, this sprawling bar-club-restaurant has minimalist/industrial decor inherited from its previous incarnation as the top floor of the old postal building – one of the floors below now holds the modern art of the Stedelijk Museum. The views out over the city centre are second to none and the journey up in one of the enormous old postal lifts is good fun, but the food doesn't match the setting

and really the place is best used as a bar-club. Sun–Wed 11am–10pm, Thurs–Sat (club nights) 11am–4am (kitchen till 10pm).

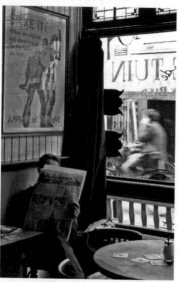 **Brouwerij Het IJ Funenkade 7.** Intimate, old-fashioned bar and mini-brewery in the old public baths adjoining the De Gooyer windmill. Serves up an excellent range of beers and ales, from the thunderously strong (9%) Columbus amber ale to the creamier, more soothing Natte (6.5%). Wed–Sun 3–8pm.

De Druif Rapenburgerplein 83. Possibly the city's oldest bar, and one of its most beguiling, this is a resolutely brown establishment with barrel-ends on one wall, old photos on another. Attracts a local crew, who give it a village pub feel. Daily from noon.

De Groene Olifant Sarphatistraat 510. Metres from the Muiderpoort, this is a characterful old wood-panelled brown *eetcafe*, with floor-to-ceiling windows and an excellent, varied menu of dishes from an international but Dutch-based menu; mains from €13. Daily from 11am, but kitchen daily noon–4pm & 6–10.30pm.

Odessa Veemkade 259 ☎020/419 3010. This bar-restaurant in a replica of an old Russian boat serves up middling Dutch and international food, good cocktails, and turns into a club after 10pm. An advantageously watery place to hang out on a summer's evening. Daily except Mon & Thurs from 4pm.

De Sluyswacht Jodenbreestraat 1. This pleasant little bar occupies an old and now solitary gabled house that stands sentry by the lock gates opposite the Rembrandthuis. A great spot to nurse a beer on a warm summer's night, with a lovely view down the canal towards the Montelbaanstoren.

The Museum Quarter and Vondelpark

Ebeling Overtoom 52. Dark and cosy lounge bar converted from an old bank. The toilets are in the vaults, and the whole thing is a pretty far cry from the traditional brown café vibe. There's Guinness on tap, decent music and a modern, comfortable environment. Open Mon–Sat from 11am (from noon on Sun) till late.

The outer districts

Bazar Albert Cuypstraat 182. This cavernous converted church is usually buzzing with activity long after the market traders have packed up. A lively place to share a bottle of wine or eat dinner; choose from the Middle Eastern- and South African-influenced menu. Mon–Fri 8am–1/2am, Sat & Sun 9am–midnight/2am.

Café Krull Sarphatipark 2. On the corner of 1e van der Helststraat, a few metres from the Albert Cuypstraat, this is an atmospheric and lively place. Drinks and snacks all day long from 11am.

Chocolate 1e Van der Helststraat 62a. Cool, disco-inspired café-bar that's open for tasty food and cocktails at any time of the day. Perch at the bar on leather stools or lounge in the cosy room out back. It's a shame, though, that the service can be somewhat lackadaisical. Daily 10am–midnight.

East of Eden Linnaeusstraat 11. A wonderfully relaxed café-bar across the road from the Tropenmuseum (see p.136), providing inexpensive food and good cocktails. There's an appealing combination of high-ceilinged splendour and gently waving palm trees – with James Dean pictures thrown in to boot. A good place to spend a sunny afternoon.

Kingfisher Ferdinand Bolstraat 24. A nice neighbourhood café that's good for lunch or just a drink if you want to continue imbibing after the Heineken Experience (see p.128) – it's right around the corner. Mon–Thurs 11am–1am, Fri & Sat 11am–3am, Sun noon–1am.

Welling J.W. Brouwersstraat 32. Situated right behind the Concertgebouw, this traditional haunt of gloomy Amsterdam intellectuals is usually packed solid with performers and visitors alike before and after evening performances.

Wildschut Roelof Hartplein 1. Just a five-minute walk from the Concertgebouw, around the corner from the *College Hotel*, this busy bar-café is famous for its congenial, spacious Art Deco interior and outdoor seating in summer. Much the nicest place to drink in the area, and with a decent menu too.

Cafés and tearooms

Amsterdam has plenty of **cafés and tearooms**, serving good coffee, sandwiches, light snacks and cakes at very affordable prices throughout the day. Some may serve alcohol but you wouldn't class them as bars, and most don't allow dope-smoking. Usual opening hours are 9am or 10am to 5pm or 6pm; some are closed on Sundays. Locations are marked on the colour **maps** at the back of this book.

Old Centre

Arnots Singel 441. Just around the corner from Heiligeweg, this basement café serves some of the best coffee in town along with wholemeal sandwiches and freshly squeezed apple juice. A great summertime spot, with people spilling out onto the pavement. Mon–Fri 11.30am–5.30pm.

Café Beurs van Berlage Beursplein 1. The best chance to glimpse the interior of the Beurs, and an elegantly furnished place for coffee or lunch. There are tables outside too. Tues–Sun 10am–6pm.

Café Esprit Spui 10. Attached to the euro-chain clothes shop, this is a swish, modern café, with wonderful sandwiches and rolls and superb salads. Mon–Sat 10am–6pm, Thurs till 10pm, Sun noon–6pm.

De Jaren Nieuwe Doelenstraat 20. One of the grandest of the grand cafés, overlooking the Amstel next to the university, with three floors, two terraces and a cool, light feel. A great place to read the Sunday paper – unusually you'll find English ones here. Reasonably priced food too, and a great salad bar. There are sandwiches and snacks downstairs and a full restaurant upstairs. Daily 10am–midnight.

▽ De Jaren

Latei Zeedijk 143. Homely shop and café that sells bric-a-brac as well as serving good coffee and decent lunches. Quite a find if you fancy something different from the Chinese restaurants that dominate this end of Zeedijk. Mon–Wed 8am–6pm, Thurs & Fri 8am–10pm, Sat 9am–10pm, Sun 11am–6pm.

Luxembourg Spui 22. The prime watering hole of Amsterdam's advertising and media brigade, this is a long, deep café-bar with a pleasant pavement terrace and an elegant, if faded, area at the back overlooking the Singel. Competent, reasonably priced bar food – and possibly the best hamburgers in town. Very popular. Daily 9am–11pm.

't Nieuwe Kafé Eggerstraat 8. Adjoining the Nieuwe Kerk, this bistro-style café is popular with shoppers and tourists, serving good, reasonably priced breakfasts, lunches, light meals and great pancakes too, plus mountainous sundaes and ice creams. Daily 9am–6pm.

Puccini Staalstraat 21. This lovely café serves great salads, sandwiches, cakes and pastries, a few doors down from its sister chocolate shop (see p.230). Mon–Fri 8.30am–6pm, Sat & Sun 10am–6pm.

Restaurant 1e Class Platform 2b, Centraal Station. Though more of a fully fledged restaurant than a café, and with the huge menu to prove it, *1e Class'* location in Centraal Station means that you're more likely to choose to enjoy its sumptuous turn-of-the-twentieth-century interior and solid menu of omelettes, sandwiches or more substantial meat and fish offerings at lunchtime. And it's certainly the best option in the station's immediate vicinity. Daily 8.30am–11pm.

Tisfris St Antoniesbreestraat 142. Colourful, split-level café and bar metres from the Rembrandthuis – and minutes from Water-looplein. Youthful and popular, with hot rolls, sandwiches, salads and so forth. Daily 9am–6.30pm.

Villa Zeezicht Torensteeg 7. Small and central, this pastel-coloured café serves excellent rolls and sandwiches, plus some of the freshest apple cake in the city. Daily 8am–9pm.

Vlaamse Friethuis Voetboogstraat 33. This hole-in-the-wall takeaway has a long-estab-lished and pretty much undisputed reputation for serving the best *frites* in town.

Grachtengordel west

Buffet van Odette & Yvette Herengracht 309.
Neat little place decorated in attractive,
modern style and serving tasty snacks and
light meals, from homemade quiches, soups
and pastas through to fruit tarts; cheese
omelettes are the house speciality. Open
Mon–Fri 8.30am–5.30pm, Sat 10am–
5.30pm & Sun noon–5.30pm.
Greenwood's Singel 103. Amenable, pocket-
sized café serving up a tasty line in salads,
omelettes and cakes. Look out for the daily
specials and order an English-style pot of
tea. Daily 9.30am–6pm.
Lunchcafé Winkel Noordermarkt 43. Packed to
the gunnels on market days, this popular
café on the corner of Westerstraat may be
plainly decorated, but the food is tasty and
wholesome; the salads are good, but the
doorstep apple pie is better. Daily
8am–10pm.
Pompadour Patisserie Huidenstraat 12.
This patisserie sells fifty different sorts
of bonbon as well as a mouthwatering
selection of cakes and candied fruits –
either take out or eat in, with a drink. Mon–
Fri 9am–6pm, Sat 9am–5pm.
Spanjer & van Twist Leliegracht 60. Hip café-
bar with an arty air and brisk modern
fittings. Tasty snacks and light meals plus an
outdoor terrace right on the canal. Lunch
served daily 10am–4pm, evening meals
from 6pm.

Grachtengordel south

Bagels & Beans Keizersgracht 504. Bagel
specialists, with all sorts of imaginative
fillings and attracting a young clientele; their
version of strawberries and cream cheese is
a big favourite in the summer. The "Beans"
part of the name refers to the coffee you
can have to accompany your bagel. There
are also several other branches, including
one in De Pijp (see p.190). This one is open
Mon–Fri 9am–5.30pm, Sat & Sun
10am–6pm.
Café Americain American Hotel, Leidseplein 28.
There was a time when this café was the
trendiest spot in the city, attracting – at one

time or another – artists, poets and TV folk.
Nowadays, things are much more routine,
even canteen-like, but the fanciful Art
Nouveau decor, coordinated down to the
doorknobs, has survived intact and makes a
visit worthwhile(ish). Daily 7am–10pm.
Metz Leidsestraat 34. Pleasantly appointed café
on the top floor of the Metz department store,
offering panoramic views over the city centre.
The food, however, is really rather routine.
Mon–Sat 10am–5pm & Sun noon–5pm.
Panini Vijzelgracht 3. Formica may be a thing
of the past almost everywhere else, but not
here, which gives this split-level, Italian café-
cum-restaurant a vaguely beatnik air. Great
coffee, sandwiches, pastas and snacks
during the day; reasonably priced meat, fish
and pasta dishes at night. Daily
9.30am–10pm.

The Jordaan and Western docklands

Arnold Cornelis Elandsgracht 78. Long-established confectioner and patisserie with a
mouthwatering display of pastries and
cakes. Take away or eat in the snug
tearoom out back. Mon–Sat 9.30am–5pm.
Festina Lente Looiersgracht 40b. Relaxed,
neighbourhood café-bar with mismatched
furniture and armchairs to laze in. The
outside tables overlooking the canal are a
suntrap in the summer when the locals
come out to relax with friends for the
afternoon; inside is cosy in the winter, and
has a good selection of board games. As
for the cons: service at the weekend can be
slow. Mon 2pm–1am, Tues–Fri 10am–
1/3am, Sat 11am–3am, Sun noon–1am.

The Old Jewish Quarter and Eastern docklands

De Hortus Plantage Middenlaan 2a. The
amenable café in the orangery of the Hortus
Botanicus (see p.104) serves a good range
of tasty sandwiches and rolls – plus the best
blueberry cheesecake in the Western world.
Unfortunately, you do have to pay to get into
the gardens to get to the café. Mon–Fri
9am–4.30pm, Sat & Sun 10am–4.30pm;
Dec & Jan till 3.30pm; July & Aug till 8.30pm.

't Blauwe Theehuis Vondelpark 5. These days this is a slightly shabby tearoom/café/bar in the middle of the Vondelpark, but its building dates from the De Stijl period. Downstairs it's a regular self-service park café; upstairs it's a pleasant, circular bar that hosts DJs on Friday and Saturday nights. Daily 10am–10pm.

Cobra Hobbemastraat 18. This stand-alone asymmetric structure behind the Rijksmuseum mainly caters for tourists looking for a convenient place for a drink or a quick bite between exhibitions. It's also a popular late-night hangout, open from 10am until 3am at weekends, otherwise until 9pm.

Keyser Van Baerlestraat 96. In operation since 1905, and right next to the Concertgebouw, this café-restaurant exudes a *fin-de-siècle* charm, with ferns, gliding bow-tied waiters and a dark, carved-wood interior. It's open all day, and you can come here for dinner, but these days it's best as a venue for lunch or coffee. Mon–Sat 10am–11pm, Sun 11am–11pm.

KinderKookKafé Vondelpark 6. A café run entirely by children aged from six to twelve years of age; the food is simple but tasty. See "Kids' Amsterdam", p.250.

De Roos PC Hooftstraat 183. The downstairs café at this New Age centre on the edge of the Vondelpark is one of the most peaceful spots in the city, selling a range of drinks and organic snacks and meals. There's also an upstairs bookshop, and any number of courses in yoga and meditation. Mon–Fri 8.30am–9.30pm, Sat & Sun 8.30am–5.30pm.

Toussaint Café Bosboom Toussaintstraat 26. This cosy, very friendly café not far from the Vondelpark is a pleasant spot for lunch – excellent sandwiches, toasties and *uitsmijters,* as well as a tapas-type menu, although service can be slow. Daily 10am–midnight, Fri & Sat until 1am.

Vertigo Vondelpark 3. Attached to the Filmmuseum, this is a pleasant place to while away a summer afternoon at the tables outside, overlooking the park, or take refuge in winter in the intimate basement interior. Good food, too, at all times of day. Daily 10am–1am.

The outer districts

Bagels & Beans Ferdinand Bolstraat 70. Large southern branch of this popular coffee and bagel joint, just opposite the Albert Cuypmarkt, with outside tables. Snacks include tuna melts, soups and club sandwiches. The whimsical opening hours are Mon–Fri 8.28am–5.31pm. Sat 9.31am–6.01pm, Sun 9.29am–6.01pm.

Granny 1e van der Helststraat 45. Just off the Albert Cuypmarkt, with faded, stuck-in-the-past Dutch appeal and terrific *appelgebak* and *pana montata.*

Restaurants

Traditionally at least, **Dutch cuisine** lacks a certain finesse, with its origins firmly rooted in the meat, potato and cabbage school of cooking. That said, things have improved markedly in the last few years with a slew of restaurants now offering tasty renditions of Dutch dishes, plus a healthy selection of vegetarian and seafood places. Nonetheless, it's the city's non-Dutch restaurants that usually steal the gastronomic limelight – especially the abundance of outstanding Indonesian restaurants.

Intense competition keeps **prices** down to manageable proportions, and in all but the ritziest of joints you can expect to pay no more than €20–25 for a main course, usually less. As for **opening hours**, the Dutch eat out early, with most restaurants opening at 5.30pm or 6pm and closing their doors around 10pm, though you'll still be served if you're already seated. At all but the least expensive places, it's a good idea to call ahead and **reserve** a table, especially on Thursday, Friday and Saturday nights. Almost all of the larger or smarter restaurants take **credit cards**, but don't assume this to be the case at smaller or cheaper places. A fifteen percent service charge is included in the bill, but nonetheless a **tip** of

Restaurants on the web

Among the many websites providing information on Amsterdam's restaurant scene, one of the most useful is ⓦ**www.iens.nl**, an independent index of all the major restaurants in Amsterdam and several other Dutch cities. The reviews are of mixed quality, but the opening hours and telephone numbers are regularly updated and there is an easy-to-follow grading system for the quality of the food and service.

between ten and fifteen percent is pretty much expected; the custom is generally to hand some change directly to your server rather than adding it to the bill.

We've listed the restaurants below by **type of cuisine**, but there's an alphabetical list in the index at the back of the book; locations are marked on the colour **maps**, also at the back of this book.

The Old Centre

Chinese

Golden Chopsticks Oude Doelenstraat 1 ⓣ**020/620 7040**. Cheap and cheerful canteen-style Chinese food on the edge of the Red Light District. Very central, and, despite the spartan interior, among the best Chinese food you'll find in Amsterdam. No credit cards. Daily 11.30am–1pm.

Hoi Tin Zeedijk 122 ⓣ**020/625 6451**. You can always trust a restaurant where you have to walk through the kitchen to get to your table, and this one is no exception: a constantly busy Chinatown favourite with an enormous menu (in English too). Dim sum at lunchtime. Daily noon–midnight.

▽ Hoi Tin

Wing Kee Zeedijk 76 ⓣ**020/623 5683**. Simple Chinese restaurant that's popular with the local Chinatown community. Good food, and very cheap, too, although the service isn't great. Daily noon–10pm.

Dutch and Modern European

Blauwe Aan De Waal Oudezijds Achterburgwal 99 ⓣ**020/330 2257**. Quite a haven, situated down an alley in the heart of the Red Light District, with tremendous French-Dutch food and a wonderfully soothing environment after the mayhem outside. Mon–Sat 6–11pm.

Brasserie Harkema Nes 67 ⓣ**020/428 2222**. Very sleek, very stylish converted warehouse restaurant, whose moderately priced food – mains €10–15 – is sometimes good, and sometimes more variable than you might expect. The menu is appealing enough, but service sometimes leaves something to be desired, delivered by fresh-faced youths who tend not to have a clue. Daily 11am–11pm.

Hemelse Modder Oude Waal 9 ⓣ**020/624 3203**. Sleek, modern restaurant serving a tasty menu of Dutch and vaguely European food in an informal atmosphere. Service is very attentive and – despite the trendy environment – not at all precious, and the food is excellent and reasonably priced. Deservedly popular, and now much larger having expanded next door. Main courses around €16, and three-course menus for €27.50. Daily 6–11pm.

In de Waag Nieuwmarkt ☎ 020/422 7772.
Comfortable café-restaurant housed in a
historic building bang in the centre of the
Nieuwmarkt. The building has been well
converted, there's outside seating, and the
food is reasonable, if not great. Sandwiches,
burgers and salads are served at lunchtime,
more substantial fare in the evening – or
there's a menu of tapas, oysters and various
other nibbles if all you want is a snack with
a drink. Daily 10am–midnight.

Keuken Van 1870 Spuistraat 4 ☎ 020/620 4018.
This large, light room has been serving
hearty Dutch food to cheapskates for years
and continues – justifiably – to thrive. Its
three-course €7.50 menu is one of the
city's best bargains. Mon–Sat 4–10.30pm.

De Roode Leeuw Damrak 93 ☎ 020/555 0666.
Fusty old Dutch restaurant that's good for
both a quick bite at lunchtimes at the front –
pea soup, herrings, *uitsmijters* – or a full
evening meal in the more formal main
restaurant just behind. A good place if you
want to sample a traditional Dutch feed.
Main courses go for €15–20. Daily 7–10am
& noon–10pm.

De Silveren Spiegel Kattengat 4 ☎ 020/624
6589. There's been a restaurant in this
location since 1614, and "The Silver Mirror"
is one of the best in the city, with a
delicately balanced menu of Dutch cuisine.
The proprietor lives on the coast and brings
in the fish himself. Spectacular food, with a
cellar of 350 wines. Four-course dinner for
two at a table set with silver is a cool €100,
though you can get away with a main
course for €30. Mon–Sat 5.30–10.30pm.

Supper Club Jonge Roelensteeg 21 ☎ 020/344
6400. A five-course set menu is served at
8pm to customers lounging on mattresses,
smoking joints and listening to a DJ on a
raised stage. The fusion food is of a very
high standard, though some may find the
whole concept pretentious or downright
disconcerting – it's not the most comfortable way to eat dinner. Diners have free
entry to the members-only club downstairs.
It's expensive, since there's no à la carte
and you have to have the set dinner at €65
a pop; booking essential. You can also try

Supperclub Cruise, which leaves from pier
4, behind Centraal Station, on Friday and
Saturday nights (☎ 020/344 6403). Daily
8pm–1am.

Van Beeren Koningsstraat 54 ☎ 020/622 2329.
This *eetcafé* serves a satisfying mixture of
Dutch staples and modern European fare in
relaxed surroundings. The food is good, and
the setting cosy – and it remains a moderately priced choice. Daily 5.30–10.15pm.

Van Kerkwijk Nes 41 ☎ 020/620 3316. It
looks like a bar but is more of a
restaurant these days, serving steaks, fish
and so on, from an ever-changing menu
that isn't written down but is heroically
memorized by the attentive waiting staff.
Good food, and cheap too – mains from
€10. Daily noon–10pm.

D' Vijff Vlieghen Spuistraat 294 ☎ 020/530
4060, ⊛ www.thefiveflies.com. One of the
city's best restaurants, "The Five Flies"
occupies immaculate ground-floor premises
kitted out in a smart version of traditional
Dutch style, from the tile- and wood-
panelled walls to the beamed ceiling and
antique embossed leather hangings.
Intimate and very cosy, its enterprising
menu features imaginative renditions of
traditional dishes, with herrings and suckling
pig being two favourites. Superb service
too. Main courses €20–30. Daily 6–10pm.

Fish

Kopke Adega Koggestraat 1 ☎ 020/622 4587.
Mediterranean-style fish restaurant that
does a great *bouillabaise*, as well as some
tasty, mainly Iberian fish and shellfish dishes
– and you can sample them in the restaurant itself or in the more informal tapas bar.
Decent prices too – you'll spend no more
than about €25 for three-course à la carte.
Daily 6–10.30pm.

Lucius Spuistraat 247 ☎ 020/624 1831. This
long-established restaurant has been
uneven over the years, but when it gets it
right – as it usually does – it's one of the
best fish restaurants in town; not a large
place, and reasonably informal. Try the
seafood platters, which can be superb.
Daily 5pm–midnight.

French, Belgian and Swiss

Café Bern Nieuwmarkt 9 ☎020/622 0034. This place is really more of a bar, but it's well-known for its food, which is excellent, and alcoholic cheese fondue. They do steaks too, for around €10–15 a head. It's very cosy and usually extremely crowded, so it's best to book. If not, just get plastered at the bar while you wait for a table. Daily 6–11pm.

De Brakke Grond Nes 43 ☎020/626 0044. Modern, high-ceilinged *eetcafé* specializing in Belgian beer and food, often full of people discussing the performance they've just seen at the adjacent Flemish Cultural Centre. Daily noon–10pm.

De Compagnon Guldenhandsteeg 17 ☎020/620 4225. This traditional restaurant serves decent French food to a self-consciously discerning clientele in an old-fashioned atmosphere. There's a great, if not especially cheap, wine list, too. It's expensive – reckon on €20-plus for a main course – and tends to be fully booked well in advance, but you might get in for lunch. Daily except Sun noon–2pm & 6–10pm; evenings only on Sat.

Luden Spuistraat 304 ☎020/622 8979. Excellent French restaurant (part of a Dutch chain) that does good-value *prix fixe* menus, for which you can expect to pay around €30 for three courses, as well as a more moderately priced à la carte menu and brasserie. Daily noon–midnight.

Palmers Zeedijk 4 ☎020/427 0551. This French fusion restaurant (set up, according to the menu, by an ex-aviator who crashed over Greenland and married an Eskimo), serves an interesting variety of dishes that includes burgers, swordfish sashimi, grilled tuna and chicken *sateh*. Main courses €10–15. Daily 5.30–10pm.

Indonesian

Kantjil en de Tijger Spuistraat 291 ☎020/620 0994. High-quality Indonesian food averaging around €30 per person, served in a stylish wood-panelled grand café. Mon–Fri 4.30–11pm, Sat & Sun noon–11pm.

Sie Joe Gravenstraat 24 ☎020/624 1830.

Small café-restaurant whose great value-for-money menu is far from extensive but comprises well-prepared, simple dishes such as *gado gado*, *sateh* and *rendang*. Mon–Sat 11am–7pm, Thurs till 8pm.

Italian

La Piccola Trattoria Nieuwezijds Voorburgwal 346 ☎020/627 1305. A small, family-run Italian café-restaurant serving good, cheap Italian staples – authentically prepared. Cash only. Daily except Mon 5.30–10.30pm.

Mappa Nes 59 ☎020/528 9170. Classic Italian food with some inventive twists, incorporating good homemade pasta dishes and excellent service in an unpretentious and modern environment. Daily noon–10.30pm.

Vasso Roozenboomsteeg 12 ☎020/626 0158. Genuine, creative restaurant off a corner of the Spui, housed in three curvy, sixteenth-century buildings. Polite and attentive service and moderate prices – around €20 for a main course. Daily 5–10.30pm.

Japanese

Kobe House Nieuwezijds Voorburgwal 77 ☎020/622 6458. Not a lot of atmosphere, partly because it's a big restaurant that rarely seems to get full. But if you're craving sushi or other Japanese treats, this is the place. Daily 5pm–midnight.

Pancakes

Pannekoekhuis Upstairs Grimburgwal 2 ☎020/626 5603. Minuscule place in a tumbledown house opposite the university buildings, with sweet and savoury pancakes at low prices. Student discounts. Mon–Fri noon–6.30pm, Sat noon–5.30pm, Sun noon–4.30pm.

Spanish and Portuguese

Centra Lange Niezel 29 ☎020/622 3050. This authentic Spanish *cantina* is a long-standing Red Light District favourite, with a wonderful selection of Spanish food, masterfully cooked and genially served. Daily 1–11pm. Cash only.

De Portugees Zeedijk 39 ☎020/427 2005. Truly a little piece of Portugal on the Zeedijk, with chaotic service and authentically hearty and filling (rather than gourmet) food – tasty fish stews, garlicky sausages, salt cod and eggs. Daily 6–10.30pm.

Thai

Bird Zeedijk 77 ☎ 020/420 6289. This Thai canteen is always packed, and rightly so, drawing people from far and wide for its cheap and authentic Thai fare. Its big brother across the road serves much the same food in slightly more upscale surroundings. Daily 2–10pm.

De Klaes Compaen Raamgracht 9 ☎ 020/623 8708. Good Thai food at affordable prices. Daily except Mon 5–10pm.

Krua Thai Staalstraat 22 ☎ 020/622 9533. High-quality Thai restaurant that has replaced *Tom Yam*, which used to be here, and is much better on the whole. Excellent fish and seafood dishes, and moderate prices, with most main dishes going for around €15. Daily except Mon 5–10.30pm.

Vegetarian

Green Planet Spuistraat 122 ☎ 020/625 8280. Cute mezzanine café with lots of tofu dishes and a varied international menu. Main courses start at around €15. Cash only. Tues–Sat 5.30–10.30pm.

Grachtengordel west

Dutch and Modern European

Bar-restaurant 5 Prinsenstraat 10 ☎ 020/428 2455. Stylish, split-level bar-cum-restaurant with high ceilings and oodles of antiques plus an imaginative menu featuring the likes of calf with onion compote and a red mustard *jus*. Main courses average a very reasonable €17–20. Daily 6–11pm.

Belhamel Brouwersgracht 60 ☎ 020/622 1095. Smashing restaurant where the Art Nouveau decor makes a delightful setting and the menu is short but extremely well chosen, mixing Dutch with French dishes. Main courses at around €20–25. Daily 6–10pm.

Damsteeg Reestraat 28 ☎ 020/627 8794. Superb French-inspired cuisine with more than the occasional Dutch gastro-

nomic flourish. Candlelit tables in a charmingly renovated old canal house. Main courses hover around €25. Mon–Sat 2pm–midnight.

▽ Damsteeg

Dylan Keizersgracht 384 ☎ 020/530 2010. Lauded fusion restaurant decorated in crisp, modern style and located inside the city's first – and arguably smartest (or most contrived) – boutique hotel, *The Dylan* (see p.168). The food is a fusion of Japanese, Thai and European styles and main courses start at €25, though you can pay a lot more. Reservations essential; Mon–Sat noon–2.30pm and from 6.30pm; brunch on Sunday.

De Luwte Leliegracht 26 ☎ 020/625 8548. Pleasant, low-key restaurant with yellow tables and pastel walls that serves a good line in Dutch/Mediterranean cuisine – the salads are especially tasty. Mains €16. Daily 6–10pm.

't Zwaantje Berenstraat 12 ☎ 020/623 2373. Traditional Dutch restaurant, down to the mini-rugs on the tables, that serves up well-cooked, reasonably priced food with main courses from €17. Well known for its liver and onions. Daily 4.30–11pm.

French and Belgian

Chez Georges Herenstraat 3 ☏ 020/626 3332. Smart, split-level restaurant offering highly rated, upmarket Belgian cuisine with an emphasis on meat dishes; mains €20–25. Open from 6pm, but closed Wed & Sun.

D'Theeboom Singel 210 ☏ 020/623 8420. Traditional French restaurant in an old, attractive canal house a short walk from Dam Square. Relaxed atmosphere; attentive service. Mains from around €20. Daily 6–10pm.

Greek

De Twee Grieken Prinsenstraat 20 ☏ 020/625 5317. In a tastefully and creatively renovated old shop, this very appealing Greek restaurant, with its wood panelling and attractive outside terrace, offers all the favourites in an intimate, informal setting. Main courses average €13–18. Daily 5–11pm.

Indian

Purna Hartenstraat 29 ☏ 020/623 6772. With its traditional Indian décor, this well-established restaurant serves up all the standards and does a particularly good line in spicy tandoori. Main courses €12–15. Open daily except Tues from 5pm till late.

Indonesian

Cilubang Runstraat 10 ☏ 020/626 9755. Small and cosy restaurant, serving well-presented, spicy dishes at affordable prices – the *rijsttafel* costs around €20. Tues–Sun from 6pm.

Italian

Prego Herenstraat 25 ☏ 020/638 0148. Informal Italian restaurant with sharp modern decor offering an exceptionally inventive menu including such delights as stuffed guinea fowl and chicory cooked every which way. Mains €20 and up. Daily 6–10pm.

Pancakes

Pancake Bakery Prinsengracht 191 ☏ 020/625 1333. Located in the basement of an old canal house, this long-established restaurant offers a mind-boggling range of fillings for its pancakes. Very popular with tourists; pancakes from €8. Daily noon–9.30pm.

Thai

Top Thai Herenstraat 28 ☏ 020/623 4633. Popular restaurant serving up some of the best, spiciest and most authentic Thai food in the city – no mean feat given the quality of the opposition. Main courses average around €12. Daily from 4pm.

Vegetarian

Bolhoed Prinsengracht 60 ☏ 020/626 1803. Something of an Amsterdam institution, this popular vegan and vegetarian restaurant features New Age decor and a daily changing menu, plus organic beer to wash it all down with. Main courses average €12–20. Daily noon–10pm.

▽ Bolhoed

Grachtengordel south

African

Axum Utrechtsedwarsstraat 85 ☏ 020/622 8389. Small and inexpensive Ethiopian café-restaurant offering a wide choice of authentic dishes. Daily except Mon from 5–11pm.

Pygma-Lion Nieuwe Spiegelstraat 5a ☏ 020/420 7022. Appealing restaurant serving up South African dishes, including crocodile steaks, along with a tempting selection of authentic Afrikaner desserts. Main courses around €15–20. Tues–Sun 5.30–11pm.

Dutch

Piet de Leeuw Noorderstraat 11 ☏020/623 7181. Arguably Amsterdam's best steakhouse, an old-fashioned, darkly lit, wood-panelled affair dating back to the 1940s. Doubles as a local bar – hence the smoky atmosphere – but the steaks, served in several different ways and costing around €16, are excellent. Mon–Fri noon–11pm, Sat & Sun 5–11pm.

Fish

Le Pêcheur Reguliersdwarsstraat 32 ☏020/624 3121. Smart, pastel-painted seafood restaurant with a lovely garden terrace in the summer. The fish arrives daily from the port of IJmuiden and defines both the menu and the daily specials. Prompt and efficient service. Main courses average around €25. Mon–Fri noon–3pm & Mon–Sat 5.30–11pm.

French and Belgian

Bonjour Keizersgracht 770 ☏020/626 6040. Bistro-style French restaurant in a cosy basement setting; particularly good charcoal-grilled dishes. Mains around €18. Wed–Sun 5–11pm.

Le Zinc… et les autres Prinsengracht 999 ☏020/622 9044. Wonderfully atmospheric little place decorated in rustic style and featuring imaginatively prepared French "peasant" food. Main courses in the region of €20, plus a particularly good wine list. Mon–Sat 5.30–11pm.

Quartier Latin Utrechtsestraat 49 ☏020/622 7419. Split-level, intimate, bistro-style restaurant serving up a (broadly) French menu – for example, tournedos with Roquefort sauce. Main courses €17–20. Tues–Sun 5.30–11pm.

Van de Kaart Prinsengracht 512 ☏020/625 9232. Excellent French/Mediterranean basement restaurant decorated in minimalist style and featuring an inventive menu, with stand-out dishes including lobster carpaccio, home-cured bacon and pumpkin-stuffed ravioli. Main courses around €25. There's a good cellar too. Mon–Sat 6.30–10.30pm.

Indian

Shiva Reguliersdwarsstraat 72 ☏020/624 8713. One of the city's best Indian restaurants in terms of quality and price, with a good selection of dishes, all expertly prepared. Vegetarians are well catered for too. Main courses from as little as €10. Daily 5–11pm.

Indonesian

Bojo Leidsedwarsstraat 51 ☏020/622 7434. One of the best-value Indonesian places in town. Recommended for its young, lively atmosphere and late opening hours, though the food itself is very much a hit-and-miss affair, and you may have to wait a long time both for a table and service. Main courses average €9–13. Sun–Thurs 4pm–2am, Fri 4pm–3am, Sat noon–3am.

Puri Mas Lange Leidsedwarsstraat 37 ☏020/627 7627. Exceptionally good-value Indonesian restaurant near the Leidseplein. Friendly and informed service preludes spectacular *rijsttafels*, both meat and vegetarian. Main courses from €15. Daily 5–11pm.

Tempo Doeloe Utrechtsestraat 75 ☏020/625 6718. Reliable, cosy, top-quality place close to Rembrandtplein. As in all Indonesian restaurants, be guided by the waiter when choosing – some of the dishes are very hot indeed. Main courses from €18. Daily 6–11.30pm.

Tujuh Maret Utrechtsestraat 73 ☏020/427 9865. Impressive Indonesian food, notable for its rich combinations which don't compromise on authentic taste. Mains from €15–25. Daily noon–10pm.

Italian

D'Antica Reguliersdwarsstraat 80 ☏020/623 3862. Long-established restaurant serving authentic Italian cuisine in plain but pleasant premises; no pizza, and dreadful chips, but otherwise perfectly fine. Main courses average €18. Open Tues–Sat 5–11pm.

Japanese

Japan-Inn Leidsekruisstraat 4 ☏020/620 4989. Warm and welcoming restaurant in the midst of the Leidseplein buzz. Sushi and sashimi popular with Japanese tourists and

Dutch businessfolk alike. Main courses range from €15 to €35. Daily 5pm–midnight.

Tomo Sushi Reguliersdwarsstraat 131 ⓣ020/528 5208. Quality, hip Japanese grill and sushi place, popular with a young, professional crowd. Mains begin at €15. Daily 5.30–10.30pm.

Pancakes

Le Soleil Nieuwe Spiegelstraat 56 ⓣ020/622 7147. Pretty, downbeat restaurant painted in cheerful pastel colours (and once visited by the Queen), which makes a delicious range of pancakes – arguably the best in town – from as little as €6. No credit cards. Daily 10am–6pm.

Thai

Dynasty Reguliersdwarsstraat 30 ⓣ020/626 8400. Lavishly appointed restaurant – all orchids and murals – offering a first-rate choice of Indochinese food, with both Vietnamese and Thai options. Main courses from €20. Daily except Tues 5.30–11pm.

Vegetarian and organic

Golden Temple Utrechtsestraat 126 ⓣ020/626 8560. Laid-back place with a little more soul than the average Amsterdam veggie joint. Inexpensive, well-prepared, lacto-vegetarian food and pleasant, attentive service. No alcohol and non-smoking throughout. Daily 5–9.30pm.

The Jordaan and Western docklands

African

Semhar Marnixstraat 259 ⓣ020/638 1634. This small and popular restaurant's simple but authentic Ethiopian menu features meat, fish or vegetable dishes, such as lamb, catfish or chickpeas, soaked up with a large, flat, spongy bread. The vegetarian dish of lentils, spinach and pumpkin is delicious. Try also the local African beer served in a *calabash*. Mains from €10.50. Daily 1–11pm.

Dutch and Modern European

Claes Claesz Egelantiersstraat 24 ⓣ020/625 5306. Exceptionally friendly Jordaan restau-

rant that attracts a mixed crowd and serves excellent Dutch food. Fridays and Saturdays feature various Dutch theatrical and musical acts between courses. Choose between two- and four-course menus (€25–30). Wed–Sun 6–11pm.

▽ Claes Claesz

De Eettuin 2e Tuindwarsstraat 10 ⓣ020/623 7706. Hefty, eminently affordable portions of Dutch food, with salad from a serve-yourself bar. Non-meat-eaters can content themselves with a choice of tasty vegetarian dishes, and all mains (from €13) come with a choice of rice or potatoes. Daily 5.30–11.30pm.

Jur Egelantiersgracht 72 ⓣ020/423 4287. Friendly restaurant and bar serving a varied menu, including fish, steaks and cheese fondue. Lunch menu also available. Main courses €15–18. Tues–Fri from 4pm till late, Sat & Sun from noon.

Fish

Albatros Westerstraat 264 ⓣ020/627 9932. Nautically themed, family-run restaurant, with a cosy conservatory out front, serving some mouthwateringly imaginative fish dishes. A great place to splash out and linger over a meal; mains from €20;

three-course menu €30. Daily except Tues & Wed 6–11pm.

French and Belgian

Bordewijk Noordermarkt 7 ☏ 020/624 3899. A chic, well-lit and roomy restaurant decorated in relaxed, minimalist style and serving delicious French cuisine with Italian gastronomic influences. Mains start at €25. Daily from 6.30pm, except Mon.

De Gouden Reael Zandhoek 14 ☏ 020/623 3883. Fine French food in an attractive waterside setting in the Westerdok. Its bar, as described in the novel of the same name by Jan Mens, has a long history of association with dockworkers. Main courses hover around €15–20. Daily 11am–midnight.

Indian

Himalaya Haarlemmerstraat 11 ☏ 020/622 3776. Cosy and welcoming atmosphere, with a good selection of dishes to choose from. Curries from €12.50, with rice and dhal. Set three-course menus from €17.50. Take-away service available too. Daily from 7pm till late.

Italian

Burgers Patio 2e Tuindwarsstraat 12 ☏ 020/623 6854. Despite the name (the site used to be occupied by a butcher's), there isn't a burger in sight in this long-established and convivial restaurant, which has managed to retain its informal atmosphere without compromising on service and taste. The food is wonderfully presented, with Italian-inspired dishes and a good choice of daily specials as well as vegetarian options. Mains from €15. Daily from 6pm till late.

Capri Lindengracht 61 ☏ 020/624 4940. Large café-restaurant serving pizza and pasta at reasonable prices from €7. Saturdays are usually busy, with much of the joyful atmosphere of the neighbouring market, while evenings are popular with local families. Daily 5–10pm.

Cinema Paradiso Westerstraat 186 ☏ 020/623 7344. Fast-moving restaurant covering all the Italian classics with vim and gusto. It's in a former cinema, complete with chandeliers, and is very popular, so you may have to

shout to be heard. Dress to kill/thrill. Main courses kick off at around €15. Tues–Sun 6–11pm.

Da Noi Haarlemmerdijk 128 ☏ 020/620 1409. A friendly open-kitchen restaurant where two chefs prepare three- or five-course dinners from an à la carte menu. A place to settle down for the evening and enjoy Italian food beyond pasta and pizza. Fixed-price menus begin at €27. Daily from 6pm.

Yam Yam Frederik Hendrikstraat 90 ☏ 020/681 5097. Top pizzeria and trattoria in a simple, tradional-style dining room with an open kitchen. It attracts the couples and hip young parents of the neighbourhood with its excellent pizza toppings, including fresh *rucola* and truffle sauce. Pizzas €10–12. Booking strongly advised. Tues–Sun 6–10pm.

Spanish

Duende Lindengracht 62 ☏ 020 420 6692. Wonderful and busy tapas bar (€3–5), with a tiled interior, mismatched wood furniture, and a warm and inviting feel. Also includes a small venue out back for live dance and music performances, including regular flamenco every Saturday from 11pm. Mon–Fri 5–11pm, Sat & Sun 4–11pm.

Thai

Rakang Thai Elandsgracht 29 ☏ 020/627 5012. Richly decorated restaurant with striking paintings and glassware. The Thai food is fresh and delicious and not too highly spiced. The adjacent takeaway is of similarly good quality. Main courses average around €16. Daily from 6pm.

Turkish

Divan Elandgracht 14 ☏ 020 626 8239. A wonderful, uncomplicated restaurant, with attentive and knowledgeable staff, serving tasty Turkish food – good meze – along with a selection of fish dishes. Starters around €5, mains €16. Small terrace out front. Daily 5–11pm.

Vegetarian and organic

De Vliegende Schotel Nieuwe Leliestraat 162 ☏ 020/625 2041. Perhaps the pick of the city's cheap and wholesome vegetarian restaurants, "The Flying Saucer" serves delicious food in large portions. Lots of space and a peaceful ambience. Mains around €10. Daily 4–10.30pm.

The Old Jewish Quarter and Eastern docklands

African

Kilimanjaro Rapenburgerplein 6 ⊤020/622 3485. Bright African restaurant in a largely forgotten part of town, serving such delicacies as West African antelope goulash, Moroccan *tajine* and crocodile steak. Vegetarian options available too. Small, moderately priced, simple and super-friendly. Tues–Sun 5–10pm.

Dutch and Modern European

🏃 **Greetje** Peperstraat 23 ⊤020/77 97 450. New kid on the gastronomic block, *Greetje* is a cosy, busy restaurant and bar that serves up Dutch staples with a modern twist. A changing menu reflects the seasons and the favourite dishes of the owners' mother – a native of the southern Netherlands. Great home cooking in a convivial atmosphere. Tues–Sun 5.30–10pm, Sat till 11pm.

Koffiehuis van de Volksbond Kadijksplein 4 ⊤020/622 1209. Formerly a Communist Party café and the place where the local dockworkers used to receive their wages, this is now an Oosterdok neighbourhood restaurant with a varied and filling menu ranging from grilled steak to Thai green curry with mussels. Homely decor and inexpensive food with mains from as little as €10. Daily 6–10pm. No credit cards.

Lloyd Hotel Oostelijke Handelskade 34 ⊤020/561 3636, ⓦ www.lloydhotel.com. Situated in the Eastern docklands, just five minutes by tram #26 from Centraal Station, this is one of Amsterdam's most unusual hotels (see p.171). It comes complete with an airy, canteen-like, café-restaurant on the ground floor, where they serve a wide range of European dishes made with local ingredients. Mains cost €10–15, sandwiches €5–7. Daily 7am–1am.

Voorbij Het Einde Sumatrakade 613 ⊤020/419 1143. See map p.111. Literally "Beyond the End", this restaurant's name refers to a nearby but now defunct squat called "The End of the World". It's still a little tricky to get to – take bus #42 from Centraal Station – but this bar-restaurant couldn't be further from the days when this part of town was the haunt of squatters; it's a modern eatery housed in a glass cube, where the emphasis is on style and quality. The food is good, inventive – and not too expensive either. Reckon on €20 or so for a main course. Daily 6.30–11pm.

Fish

éénvistwéévis Schippersgracht 6 ⊤020/623 2894. An uncomplicated fish restaurant serving an interesting selection of seafood, such as oyster and mussel soup for starters and sea bass with rosemary and thyme as a main course. No menu – the waiters will tell you what's cooking. Mains at around €20. Tues–Sun 6–10pm.

Italian

🏃 **Rosario** Peperstraat 10 ⊤020/627 0280. Very attractive, canalside restaurant serving top-quality Italian food in a slightly out-of-the-way corner of the city. The smart, modern decor features an open kitchen. The ravioli goes down a storm. Mains from €21. Open 6–11pm, but closed Sun & Mon.

Jewish

King Solomon Kosher Restaurant Waterlooplein 239 ⊤020/625 5860. Approved by the Rabbi of Amsterdam, this downbeat restaurant has a straightforward and inexpensive kosher menu. Sun–Thurs noon–10pm; limited opening on Fri & Sat before/after Shabbat; closed Yom Kippur.

The Museum Quarter and Vondelpark

African

Lalibela 1e Helmersstraat 249 ⊤020/683 8332. First-rate Ethiopian restaurant, with a well-balanced menu and attentive service. Mains from €8. Take tram #1 or #6 along Overtoom to Jan Pieter Heijstraat. Daily 5–11pm.

Dutch and Modern European

Bosboom Bosboom Toussaintstraat 29 ☎020/683 6854. Owned by the same people who own the *Toussaint Café* across the road, this bright, welcoming restaurant serves food with a Mediterranean slant, and is especially strong on fish dishes. Three-course menus are €25. Wed–Sun 5.30–10.30pm.

Loetje Johannes Vermeerstraat 52 ☎020/662 8173. Excellent steaks, fries and salads are the order of the day at this *eetcafé*. The service can be touch and go, but the food is great, and fairly inexpensive. The pleasant outdoor terrace in the summer is a bonus. Mon–Fri 11am–10pm, Sat evening only.

French and Belgian

Brasserie de Joffers Willemsparkweg 163 ☎020/673 0360. This small, café-like brasserie is a short walk from the park, with a terrace out front, serving soups, salads and sandwiches from around €13. Mon–Fri 8am–8pm, Sat & Sun 8am–6pm.

Gent aan de Schinkel Theophile de Bockstraat 1 ☎020/388 2851. Situated just outside the top end of the Vondelpark, a five-minute walk across the pedestrian bridge, this lovely corner restaurant overlooking the Sloterkade canal serves mainly Belgian food, and there's a huge range of bottled Belgian beers to enjoy on their summer terrace. Daily 6–10pm.

Le Garage Ruysdaelstraat 54 ☎020/679 7176. This elegant restaurant, with an eclectic French and Italian menu, is popular with a media crowd, since it's run by the well-known Dutch TV cook Joop Brakhaekke. Call to reserve at least a week ahead and dress to impress. Prices are moderate to high, with two-course menus for around €40, three courses for €50. If you just want a snack, try the next-door cocktail bar instead. Noon–2pm and 6–11pm; Sat & Sun dinner only.

Greek

Dionysos Overtoom 176 ☎020/689 4441. Inexpensive Greek restaurant just west of the Vondelpark, with the distinct advantage of serving until 1am. Live music every first Sunday of the month. Mains from around €12. Daily 5pm–1am.

Indian

Dosa Overtoom 146 ☎020/616 4838. Halfway along the Vondelpark, this brightly lit corner restaurant concentrates on Southern Indian dishes at moderate prices – mains begin at around €15. Daily 5–11pm.

Indonesian

Orient Van Baerlestraat 21 ☎020/673 4958. This moderately priced Indonesian restaurant serves up a wide range of excellently prepared dishes, and vegetarians are very well taken care of. Expect to pay around €22 for a *rijsttafel*. Daily 5–10pm.

Sama Sebo P.C. Hooftstraat 27 ☎020/662 8146, ⊛www.samasebo.com. Amsterdam's best-known Indonesian restaurant, especially for its *rijsttafel* (€27.50), although, if this seems a little pricey, it's easy to eat more economically by choosing à la carte dishes, and there's a reasonable set lunch for €15 a head too. The food is usually pretty good, though the waiters can be extravagantly rude. Mon–Sat noon–3pm & 6–10pm.

Thai

Khorat Top Thai 2e Const. Huygensstraat 64 ☎020/683 1297. Small, simple restaurant serving generous helpings of inexpensive Thai food. Service is efficient, though not always with a smile. Mains from just €11. Daily 4–10pm.

The outer districts

Central American

Il Cantinero Marie Heinekenplein 4 ☎020/618 1844. Right behind the Heineken Experience (see p.128), this fair-sized restaurant has a wide choice of good-value Mexican, Caribbean and Surinamese dishes. Tapas average €4.50 and main dishes €16. Worth a visit for its live salsa evenings from 6pm; at 10pm there's a DJ playing salsa and South American rumba tunes. Daily 4pm–1am (Fri & Sat till 3am).

Dutch

Tolhuis Buiksloterweg 7 ☎020/636 0270. **Off map.** Large Amsterdam Noord restaurant that's two minutes from the Buiksloterweg ferry terminal across the River IJ from Centraal Station. A heart-warming and inexpensive place for a late breakfast, lunch or an early dinner. Mon–Sat 9.30am–7.30pm.

Italian and Modern European

L'Angoletto Hemonystraat 18 ☎020/676 4182. This small, traditional trattoria in the De Pijp neighbourhood has a reputation for simple, hearty food. It's inexpensive and always packed, with long wooden tables and benches that create a very sociable atmosphere. Not everything they serve is on the menu so keep an eye on the glass showcase in front of the kitchen for any specials. No bookings, so just turn up and hope for the best. Daily except Sat 6–11.30pm; closed Aug.

Palma Johannes Verhulststraat 104 ☎020/379 5900. **See map p.132.** Within comfortable walking distance of the Concertgebouw, this excellent southern European and Mediterranean mezzanine restaurant, with tables out front during the day, offers a good choice of steak, fish and pasta. Portions are large and the atmosphere is relaxed. Three-course menu €34.50, mains €17–22. Daily noon–11pm.

Japanese

Yamazato and Teppanyaki Sazanka Ferdinand Bolstraat 333 ☎020/678 7111. Situated in the swanky *Okura Hotel* (see p.174), and dating back over thirty years, this was the first place to serve Japanese haute cuisine food in the Netherlands. Today three of the hotel's four restaurants (including the French *Ciel Bleu*, on the 23rd floor) have Michelin stars, and this is one of the best places to eat Japanese food in the city; *Yamazato* is a very traditional sushi restaurant with over fifty specialities, and an

▽ Yamazato

à la carte menu featuring expertly prepared tempura, sashimi and sukiyaki. Reckon on paying €50–65 per person. *Teppanyaki Sazanka* is the renowned grill restaurant, where the chef prepares fish, steaks and vegetables at the table; set menus €65.50. To get there, take tram #25 from CS to Cornelis Troostplein. Advance bookings essential. Daily 6.30–10pm.

Middle Eastern

Artist 2e Jan Steenstraat 1 ☎020/671 4264. A small Lebanese restaurant just off Albert Cuypstraat. Inexpensive, though not a place for a drawn-out meal. Set menus €12.50, smaller dishes around €5. Daily 2–11pm.

Eufraat 1e van der Helststraat 72 ☎020/672 0579. Basic *eetcafé*, with a small menu, in the midst of the cosmopolitan De Pijp district, run by Assyrian Christians. Grills from €13, meze for two €11.50. Tues–Sun 11am–midnight.

Zagros Albert Cuypstraat 50 ☎020/670 0461. Popular, no-frills Kurdish restaurant run by four brothers, serving inexpensive traditional dishes from around €3 for starters and €11 for marinated lamb and chicken mains. Fish and vegetarian options available too. Daily 4–11pm.

Spanish

Más Tapas Saenredamstraat 37 ☎020/664 0066. Small, Moorish-style restaurant with mosaic tiles everywhere, serving inexpensive tapas (€3.50) and an interesting variety of main dishes (€7.50–9.50). There's outside seating, too, on a leafy, happening intersection. Daily 4pm–midnight.

Surinamese

Warung Swietie 1e Sweelinckstraat 1 ☎020/671 5833. Cheap and cheerful Surinamese-Javanese *eetcafé*, with only a few seats. Budget prices: nothing over €10. Daily 11am–9pm, Sun from 2pm.

Turkish

Saray Gerard Doustraat 33 ☎020/671 9216. Excellent Turkish eatery in the De Pijp neighbourhood. It's cheap too, with an intimate living-room ambience and main courses for €10–13.50; meze from €6.50 per person. Daily 5–11pm.

Vegetarian and organic

De Waaghals Frans Halsstraat 29 ☎020/679 9609. Well-prepared organic dishes in this cooperative-run restaurant near the Albert Cuypmarkt. This place gets busy early so book ahead to be sure of a table. The menu changes twice a month, and though food takes a while to prepare, the results are generous and delicious. Mains around €13. No credit cards. Tues–Sun 5–9.30pm.

De Witte Uyl Frans Halsstraat 26 ☎020/670 0458. Good restaurant serving free-range poultry and meat and organic vegetables; dishes include a smoked halibut starter and a main course of rabbit sausages. Two-course menus €39. Tues–Sat 6–11pm.

Coffeeshops

This is the one Western country where the purchase of **cannabis** has been decriminalized (see "Basics" p.30), the most conspicuous result of which has been the rise of the licensed **coffeeshop**, selling bags of dope in much the same way as bars sell glasses of beer. When you first walk into a coffeeshop, however, it isn't immediately apparent how to buy the stuff – it's illegal to advertise cannabis in any way, which includes calling attention to the fact that it's available at all. What you have to do is ask to see the **menu**, which is normally kept behind the counter. This will list all the different hashes and grasses on offer, along with (if it's a reputable place) exactly how many grammes you get for your money. The in-house dealer will be able to help you out with queries. The seedier coffeeshops are concentrated in and around the Red Light District; the more congenial in the Grachtengordel. Current **prices** per gramme of hash and marijuana range from €10 for low-grade stuff up to €25 for top-quality hash, and as high as €40 for really strong grass; most coffeeshops open around 10am or 11am and close around midnight.

The **hash** on sale originates in various countries and is pretty self-explanatory, apart from Pollem, which is compressed resin and stronger than normal. **Marijuana** is a different story, and the old days of imported Colombian, Thai and sensimilia are fading away; taking their place are limitless varieties of *Nederwiet* – Dutch-grown under UV lights and more potent than anything you're likely to have come across. Skunk, Haze and Northern Lights are all popular types of Dutch weed, and should be treated with caution – a smoker of low-grade British draw will be laid low (or high) for hours by a single spliff of Skunk. You would be equally well advised to take care with **space-cakes** (cakes or biscuits baked with hash), which are widely available: you can never be sure exactly what's in them and they tend to have a delayed reaction (up to two hours before you notice anything strange – don't get impatient and gobble down another one!). Once they kick in, they can bring on an extremely intense, bewildering high – 10–12 hours is common. You may also come across cannabis seeds for growing your own; while locals are permitted to grow a small amount of marijuana for personal use, the import of cannabis seeds is illegal in any country, so don't even think about trying to take some home.

Away from the coffeeshops, don't assume you can smoke – if in doubt ask, as the worst you'll get will be a "no" – and don't buy drugs of any sort on the street; if you do, you're simply asking for trouble. The ⓦwww.coffeeshop.freeuk. com website gives potted descriptions of all the city's main coffeeshops. The locations of those listed below are marked on the colour **maps** at the back of this book.

Old Centre

Abraxas Jonge Roelensteeg 12. Quirky, mezzanine coffeeshop with spiral staircases that can prove challenging after a spliff. The hot chocolate with added hash is not for the susceptible. Daily 10am–1am.
The Bulldog Oudezijds Voorburgwal 132. The biggest and most famous of the coffeeshop chains with three Oudezijds Voorburgwal outlets – at nos. 90, 132 and 218. This one is open daily 10am–1am.
Dampkring Handboogstraat 29. Colourful coffeeshop with loud music and laid-back atmosphere, known for its good-quality hash. Sun–Thurs 10am–1am, Fri & Sat 10am–2am.
Extase Oude Hoogstraat 2. Part of a chain run by the founder of the Hash Museum (see p.58). Considerably less chichi than the better-known coffeeshops, but a handy Red Light District standby. Daily 9am–1am.
Grasshopper Oudebrugsteeg 16. This multi-level coffeeshop, with bar, sports screen and restaurant, has tried to steal some of *The Bulldog*'s thunder over recent years, and is one of the city's more welcoming places for visitors, although its proximity to Centraal Station means that at times it can be overwhelmed by tourists. There's another location – the original – at Nieuwezijds Voorburgwal 57. Sun–Thurs 8am–1am, Fri & Sat 7am–3am.
Homegrown Fantasy Nieuwezijds Voorburgwal 87a. Attached to the Dutch Passion Seed Company, this sells the widest selection of marijuana in Amsterdam, most of it local, hence the name. Daily noon–11pm, until midnight at weekends.

Kadinsky Rosmarijnsteeg 9. Fairly small, but still the largest of the three branches of this small chain. Strictly accurate deals weighed out to a background of jazz dance. The chocolate chip cookies are to die for. Daily 10am–1am, until 2am at weekends.

▽ Kadinsky

Rusland Rusland 16. One of the first Amsterdam coffeeshops, a cramped but vibrant place that's a favourite with both dope fans and tea addicts (it has 43 different kinds). A cut above the rest. Daily 10am–1am.
De Tweede Kamer Heisteeg 6. A friendly and cosy coffeeshop, in a tiny alley off the Spui, with experienced staff and an enormous variety. Daily 10am–1pm.

Grachtengordel west

Amnesia Herengracht 133. Bright and cheerful coffeeshop with a canalside terrace.

La Tertulia Prinsengracht 312. Tiny corner coffeeshop, complete with indoor rockery and tinkling fountain. Much better outside, though, as it's on a particularly fine stretch of canal. Tues–Sat 11am–7pm.

Siberië Brouwersgracht 11. Bright, modern coffeeshop set up by the former staff of *Rusland* (see p.203) and notable for the way it's avoided the overcommercialization of the larger chains. Very relaxed, very friendly, and worth a visit whether you want to smoke or not; has a good selection of magazines as well as a chessboard. Sun–Thurs 11am–11pm, Fri & Sat 11am–midnight.

Grachtengordel south

The Bulldog Leidseplein 15, ⊛ www.bulldog.nl. The biggest and most famous of the coffee-shop chains, and a long way from its pokey Red Light District origins, *The Bulldog*'s main branch is here on the Leidseplein, housed in a former police station. It has a large cocktail bar, coffeeshop, juice bar and souvenir shop, all with separate entrances. It's big and brash, not at all the place for a quiet smoke, though the dope they sell (packaged up in neat little brand-labelled bags) is reliably good. Daily 9am–1am.

Global Chillage Kerkstraat 51. Celebrated slice of Amsterdam dope culture, always comfortably filled with stoners propped up against the walls; many sentences go unfinished. Daily 1pm–1am.

Mellow Yellow Vijzelgracht 33. Spartan but bright coffeeshop with a small but good-quality dope list. It's a little out of the way, but makes up for it in friendliness. Mon–Thurs 9am–midnight, Fri–Sun 8am–1am.

The Otherside Reguliersdwarsstraat 6. Popular with (but not exclusively occupied by) gay smokers, this is a crowded and fun coffee-shop near the Muntplein. In Dutch, "the other side" is a euphemism for gay.

Stix Utrechtsestraat 21. The quietest branch of an Amsterdam institution in dope-smoking. You can get it all here: a coffee, a newspaper and a smoke. Daily 11am–1am.

The Jordaan and Western docklands

Barney's Breakfast Bar Haarlemmerstraat 102. Something of an Amsterdam institution, this extremely popular café-cum-coffeeshop is simply the most civilized place in town to enjoy a big joint with a fine breakfast – at any time of the day. A few doors down, at no. 98, *Barney's Brasserie* is a nice sunny spot in the morning and serves alcohol. Daily 7am–10pm.

▽ Barney's Breakfast Bar

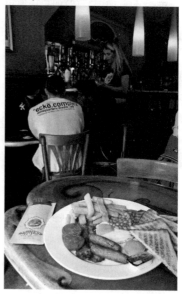

Bronx Marnixstraat 92. Smart-looking, multi-level place equipped with a large coma-inducing fish tank and Internet access up on the mezzanine floor. Daily 10am–midnight.

Paradox 1e Bloemdwarsstraat 2. If you're fed up with the usual coffeeshop food offerings, *Paradox* satisfies the munchies with outstanding natural food, including spectac-ular fresh fruit smoothies and veggie burgers. Daily 10am–8pm.

Old Jewish Quarter and Eastern docklands

Pollinator Company Nieuwe Herengracht 25, **www.pollinator.nl.** Not strictly a coffeeshop, this place is for those serious about growing their own marijuana. The owner can tell you everything you need to know, and stocks the products you need to do it, from seeds to compost, as well as various peripherals such as pipes, cannabis lollies and hemp rock. The small chill-out area offers free tea and coffee and has a large collection of back issues of *High Times*. Mon–Fri 11am–7pm, Sat noon–7pm.

The outer districts

Greenhouse Tolstraat 91. Consistently sweeps the board at the annual Cannabis Cup (see p.261), with medals for its dope as well as for "Best Coffeeshop". Staff are extremely knowledgeable in their "grassy" field; if you're only buying once, buy here. Tolstraat is south of the centre – take tram #4 or #25 from Centraal Station; there are also branches at Waterlooplein 345 and OZ Voorburgwal 191. Daily 9am–1am.

Yo-Yo 2e Jan van der Heijdenstraat 79. About as local as it's possible to get, down in De Pijp, to the east of the Sarphatipark, this is a small, airy little place to seek out smoking solitude. A little gallery at the back exhibits works by local artists. Daily except Sun noon–7pm.

Entertainment and nightlife

A lthough Amsterdam is not generally considered one of the world's major cultural centres, both the quality and quantity of **music, dance and film** on offer in the city are high – largely thanks to the government's long-term subsidy to the arts. With its youthful population, the city is at the cutting edge in many ways, and its frequent arty **festivals** and fringe events (see pp.259–262) provide plenty of offbeat entertainment. The city is crammed with places offering a wide range of affordable entertainment; lovers of the **performing arts** are particularly well catered for, with venues such as the brand new Muziekgebouw (see p.214) and the prestigious Concertgebouw (see p.213) top of the list for culture vultures, plus a host of concert halls, theatres and churches hosting all manner of cultural happenings, from modern dance to stand-up comedy. Something of a Mecca for **clubbers**, the city comes into its own after dark, with numerous venues clustered around Leidseplein and its environs buzzing into the small hours.

Information and tickets

For information about **what's on**, a good place to start is the **Amsterdam Uitburo**, or **AUB** (Mon–Sat 10am–7.30pm, Sun noon–7.30pm), the city council's cultural office, housed in a corner of the Stadsschouwburg theatre on Leidseplein. You can get advice on anything remotely cultural here, as well as tickets and copies of listings magazines.

Of the **listings magazines**, the AUB's own monthly *Uitkrant* is comprehensive and free, but in Dutch; or you could settle for the VVV's bland, English-language *Day By Day* (also free). *Amsterdam Weekly* is a free cultural newspaper in English, which comes out every Wednesday and has information on film, music and the arts. Any cinema can provide the fold-out *Film Agenda*, which gives details of all films showing in the city that week (Thursday to Wednesday). Bars and restaurants often stock similar fortnightly or monthly listings leaflets.

Tickets for most concerts and events can be bought from the Uitburo and VVV offices, or reserved by phone through the **AUB Uitlijn** (☏0900/0191 9am–8pm; €0.40 per min); in all cases a booking fee applies, usually 1–2 percent. You can also buy tickets for any live music event in the country at the GWK bureau de change offices at the Leidseplein, at Centraal Station and at the post office at Singel 250, for a fee of around €3–4. If you're under 26 and plan to take in a few events, you might want to invest in a **Cultureel Jongeren Passport** (**CJP**), which costs €15 and gets you reductions on entry to theatres, concerts and *filmhuizen*, and is available from the AUB. Aside from CJP cardholders, the only people generally eligible for **discounts** at cultural events and venues are students and over-65s (though most places will only accept Dutch ID).

Rock, pop and folk

As far as **live music** goes, Amsterdam is a regular tour stop for many major artists – it's worth keeping an eye on the listings. Until a few years ago, **Dutch rock and pop** was almost uniformly dire, but mercifully times have changed, and Dutch groups nowadays can lay claim to both quality and originality. Look out for the celebrated Zuco 103, Junky XL and other members of the dance/hip-hop scene, or try to catch rock bands such as Bløf, Kane or Spinvis. Anouk is also a popular draw whenever she comes back home to play.

In the southeastern suburbs, the superb 50,000-seater Amsterdam ArenA doubles as the city's music **stadium** for rock bands or artists suitably legendary to fill it. The Heineken Music Hall, a simple but acoustically impressive black box close to the ArenA, hosts smaller acts, while the two dedicated **music venues** in Amsterdam city centre – the Paradiso and the Melkweg – are on a much smaller scale, and supply a daily programme of music to suit all tastes (and budgets). Alongside the main venues, the city's clubs, bars and multimedia centres host occasional performances by live bands. As far as **prices** go, for big names you'll pay anything between €20 and €50 a ticket; ordinary gigs cost €8–15, although some places charge a membership fee (*lidmaatschap*) on top.

The Dutch **folk music** tradition is virtually extinct in Amsterdam, except for occasional performances by the duo Acda and de Munnik. There are still one or two touring folk singers who perform traditional *smartlappen* ("torchsongs") at the Carré Theatre and a few other sympathetic venues, but the best place to catch these traditional songs – a brash and sentimental adaptation of French chanson – is the café *Nol* (see p.185), in the heart of the Jordaan, where they made their name.

More accessible is **world music**, for which there are several good venues, including the Akhnaton, the Tropentheater and the Melkweg, the latter two being venues for the **Amsterdam Roots Festival** held in June (see p.260). Amsterdam doesn't have many **outdoor music festivals**, but the few events that do take place are usually well attended. Aside from the summer concerts held in the Vondelpark (see p.124), the Oosterpark hosts the free Roots Open Air Festival, a huge one-day event that attracts over 60,000 people and kicks off the aforementioned Roots Festival. Of the music and dance festivals outside the city, the most famous is the Pinkpop Festival (@www.pinkpop.nl) in May/June, down in the south in Landgraaf, near Maastricht. Others include A Campingflight to Lowlands (@www.lowlands.nl), held over one weekend in August in Flevoland, and Parkpop (@www.parkpop.nl), Europe's largest free festival, in June at The Hague's Zuiderpark. Dates vary, so check websites before making plans.

Major venues	The home soccer stadium for Ajax also plays host to world-class music acts such as the Rolling Stones and Madonna.
Amsterdam ArenA ArenA Boulevard (Amsterdam Oost; metro or train to Bijlmer station) ☎020/311 1333, @www.amsterdamarena.nl.	**Heineken Music Hall** ArenA Boulevard (Amsterdam Oost; metro or train to Bijlmer

station) ☎0900/68742 4255, ⊛www.heineken-music-hall.nl. A hi-tech music venue attracting international bands ranging from Pink to Franz Ferdinand.

🏃 **Melkweg** Lijnbaansgracht 234a (Grachtengordel south) ☎020/531 8181, ⊛www.melkweg.nl. The Melkweg ("Milky Way") is probably Amsterdam's most famous entertainment venue – often featuring on the itinerary of international bands on tour – and also ranks as one of the city's prime multimedia arts centres, with a young, hip clientele. A former dairy (hence the name) just round the corner from Leidseplein, it has two separate halls for live music, giving space to a broad range of bands covering everything from reggae to rock. Excellent DJ sessions go on till late at the weekend, with Que Pasa providing a Latino flavour to Friday nights, and anything from dancehall to indie pop being thrown down on Saturdays. There's also a monthly film programme, as well as a theatre, gallery and café-restaurant (Marnixstraat entrance; Wed–Sun noon–9pm).

🏃 **Paradiso** Weteringschans 6–8 (Grachtengordel south) ☎020/626 4521, ⊛www.paradiso.nl. This converted church near the Leidseplein, revered by many for its atmosphere and excellent programme, features local and international bands, ranging from the newly signed to the more established. Also holds popular club nights (see p.210), and has been known to host classical concerts, as well as debates and multimedia events (often in conjunction with the nearby Balie centre).

Smaller venues

Akhnaton Nieuwezijds Kolk 25 (Old Centre) ☎020/624 3396, ⊛www.akhnaton.nl. A "Centre for World Culture", hosting a wide-ranging programme of events, from salsa nights to Turkish dance parties. On a good night, the place heaves with revellers.

De Buurvrouw St Pieterspoortsteeg 29 (Old Centre) ☎020/625 9654. Eclectic, alternative bar, occasionally featuring loud local bands. Opens 9.30pm.

Cruise Inn Zuiderzeeweg 29 (Old Jewish Quarter and Eastern docklands) ⊛www.cruise-inn.com. This volunteer-run clubhouse was set up over twenty years ago by a group of rockabillys. Open Saturdays only from 9pm and located somewhat off the beaten track in Zeeburg (tram #26 from CS), to the

northeast of the Oosterdok, but worth the trek, with jam sessions and great live band nights with music from the 1950s and 1960s.

De Heeren van Aemstel Thorbeckeplein 5 (Grachtengordel south) ☎020/620 2173, ⊛www.deheerenvanaemstel.nl. Warm, atmospheric café with swinging soul, jazz and funk gigs Wed–Sun.

Maloe Melo Lijnbaansgracht 163 (Jordaan and Western docklands) ☎020/420 4592, ⊛www.maloemelo.nl. Dark, low-ceilinged bar, with a small back room featuring lively, local blues acts every day of the week. Jam sessions daily except Wed. Free before 11pm, €5 thereafter.

Meander Café Voetboogstraat 5 (Old Centre) ☎020/625 8430, ⊛www.cafemeander.nl. Live music of the soul, funk and blues variety, as well as DJs playing funk and hip-hop, in a relaxed, convivial atmosphere. Mon, Thurs–Sun from 10pm.

Mulligan's Amstel 100 (Grachtengordel south) ☎020/622 1330, ⊛www.mulligans.nl. Irish bar that's head and shoulders above the rest for atmosphere and authenticity, with Gaelic musicians and storytellers most nights for free.

OCCII Amstelveenseweg 134 (Museum Quarter and Vondelpark) ☎020/671 7778, ⊛www.occii.org. Former squat bar opposite the western entrance of the Vondelpark, with live alternative music, from indie pop to electro-punk.

The Waterhole Korte Leidsedwarsstraat 49 (Grachtengordel south) ☎020/620 8904, ⊛www.thewaterhole.nl. Late-night bar with live music every night, ranging from punk and rock to jazz and blues. Popular for its regular Monday jam sessions, which attract a raucous but friendly crowd, and for its pool table and cheap beer. Sunday night is ladies' night, with half-price drinks.

Tropentheater Linnaeusstraat 2 (Amsterdam Oost) ☎020/568 8500, ⊛www.tropentheater.nl. Part of the Royal Tropen Instituut, east of Artis Zoo (Tram #9 from CS, or #10 from Leidseplein), this formal theatre specializes in non-Western drama, dance, film and music. A great place to take in acts that you wouldn't normally get to see.

Winston International Warmoesstraat 123 (Old Centre) ☎020/623 1380, ⊛www.winston.nl. Part of the arty *Winston Hotel* (see p.167), this adventurous small venue attracts an eclectic crowd and offers a mix of live bands, electro, drum 'n' bass and cheesy pop nights.

Clubbing

Clubbing in Amsterdam used to be a relatively low-key affair, but in recent years the city has established itself as more of a clubbers' destination, with an array of decent venues, from large, commercial places to intimate bars, which are just as style-conscious as those in other European capitals. Many regularly feature big-name DJs at the weekend, playing variations on house, trance, garage and techno.

The best place to find out what's on is the free weekly **listings** magazine *nl20*, available in restaurants, hotels and bars, or pick up the printed "flyer-newspaper" *guestlist.nu* (ⓦ www.guestlist.nu), which carries information on upcoming events. Also check for flyers at Midtown Records, Nieuwendijk 104 (Old Centre), which also runs a ticket service for most dance events.

Most clubs charge for entry, with **ticket prices** hovering between €8 and €12.50 at weekends and dropping to around €5 during the week. A singular feature of Amsterdam clubbing, however, is that you're expected to tip the bouncer if you want to get back into the same place next week; €1 or €2 in the palm of his hand will do very nicely. **Drinks** prices are just slightly more expensive than in cafés at around €3–4, though you'll usually pay more for spirits, but not excessively hiked up. **Dress** up if you want to get into some of the smaller, hipper clubs where space is limited and door staff have carte blanche about who they let in. As far as **drugs** go, smoking joints is generally fine – though if you can't see or smell the stuff, ask the barman if it's OK. Should you need reminding, ecstasy, acid, speed and cocaine are all completely illegal, and you can expect less than favourable treatment from the bouncers (and the law) if you're spotted with anything.

Although all the places listed below **open** at either 10pm or 11pm, there's not much point turning up anywhere before midnight; unless stated otherwise, everywhere stays open until 5am on Friday and Saturday nights, 4am on other nights.

For gay and lesbian clubs see Chapter Twelve.

Clubs and venues

Arena Part of a large, hip hotel (see p.171), this club, situated in a former chapel, opens Friday and Saturday only. Occasionally hosts popular international acts, such as Hed Kandi.

Bitterzoet Spuistraat 2 (Old Centre) ☎020/521 3001, ⓦ www.bitterzoet.com. Spacious but cosy two-floored bar and theatre hosting a mixed bag of events: DJs playing acid jazz, R&B, funk and disco, film screenings and occasional urban poetry nights.

't Blauwe Theehuis Vondelpark 5 (Museum Quarter and Vondelpark) ☎020/662 0254, ⓦ www.blauwetheehuis.nl. Free open-air dancing with DJs playing throughout the summer in the Vondelpark; usually weekends but check website for programme.

Dansen bij Jansen Handboogstraat 11 (Old Centre) ☎020/620 1779, ⓦ www .dansenbijjansen.nl. Founded by – and for –

students, these popular dance nights have an emphasis on disco, club classics and R&B – and, as you would expect, cheap beer. Open nightly from 10pm; officially you need student ID to get in.

Escape Rembrandtplein 11 (Grachtengordel south) ☎020/622 1111, ⓦ www.escape.nl. The days of the "super-club" may be over, but this vast venue with room for two thousand people still manages to pull in crowds of mainstream punters. Saturday night's Framebusters is their most popular club night. Impressive sound system and visuals. Thurs–Sun from 11pm.

Heineken Music Hall See p.207. Hosts dance events featuring well-known Dutch DJs, including the renowned Tiesto.

Jimmy Woo Korte Leidsedwarsstraat 18 (Grachtengordel south) ☎0202/626 3150, ⓦ www.jimmywoo.nl. Intimate and stylish club spread over two floors. Upstairs, the black lacquered walls, Japanese lamps and cosy booths with leather couches ooze sexy chic, while downstairs a packed dance floor throbs under the oscillating light from hundreds of light bulbs studded into the ceiling. Popular with young, well-dressed locals, so look smart if you want to join in. Thurs–Sun from 11pm.

Loveboat Steiger 14, behind Centraal Station (Old Centre), Ⓦ www.loveboat2.nl. This famous DJ partyship puts on regular dress-coded club nights. Sets sail 1am. Buy tickets (around €25) in advance.

▽ Jimmy Woo

🏃 **Melkweg** See p.208. After the bands have finished, excellent offbeat disco sessions go on well into the small hours, sometimes featuring the best DJs in town. Also plays host to some of the most enjoyable theme nights around, ranging from African dance to experimental jazz-trance.

▽ Odeon

Nachttheater Sugar Factory Lijnbaansgracht 238 (Grachtengordel south) ☎ 020/627 0008, Ⓦ www.sugarfactory.nl. Busy Leidseplein's latest addition is this "theatrical nightclub", which hosts a stimulating programme of cabaret, live music, poetry and theatre – up to two events a night, plus a late-night club that kicks off after the last show. Pulls in a young, trendy crowd. Closed Tues.

Odeon Singel 460 (Grachtengordel west) ☎ 020/521 8555, Ⓦ www.odeontheater.nl. Originally a brewery, this beautifully restored seventeenth-century canal house has since been a theatre, a cinema and a concert hall, until it was gutted in a fire in 1990. Rescued by the owners of the *Arena* hotel (see p.171), it's now a stylish nightclub (Thurs–Sat) with a splendid bar overlooking the canal. There's also a restaurant (Thurs–Sat) and a café (daily).

🏃 **Panama** Oostelijke Handelskade 4 (Old Jewish Quarter and Eastern docklands) ☎ 020/311 8686, Ⓦ www.panama.nl. One of Amsterdam's coolest clubs, Panama overlooks the IJ and plays host to top-name international DJs Wed–Sun; Friday night's RUSH is very popular. Dress to impress. There's also a restaurant, which is open daily from noon.

🏃 **Paradiso** See p.208. One of the principal venues in the city, this converted church just round the corner from the Leidseplein is popular with an alternative crowd. Friday's Paradisoul continues to draw in the crowds, and look out too for DJ sets featuring live performances on Saturdays. Also hosts one-off club nights.

The Powerzone Spaklerweg ☎ 020/681 8866, Ⓦ www.thepowerzone.nl. Situated near Amstel

station, southeast of the
centre (metro Spaklerweg),
this is a Saturday-night party
zone, with good trance and
techno DJs – both Dutch and
international – and a capacity
of five thousand.

**Sinners Wagenstraat 3
(Grachtengordel south)**
☎020/620 1375, ⓦwww.sinners.
nl. Located near the
Rembrandtplein, this plush,
intimate club has a small
dance floor that gets packed
early and plays a mix of
house, R&B and club classics
to a well-dressed and affluent
crowd. Choosy door staff.
Open Thurs–Sat.

**Winston Kingdom Warmoesstraat 131 (Old
Centre)** ☎020/623 1380, ⓦwww.winston.nl.
This small venue adjacent to the *Winston
Hotel* (see p.167) offers eclectic club nights
and performances.

▽ Panama

Zebra Lounge Korte Leidsedwarsstraat 14
☎020/612 6153, ⓦwww.the-zebra.nl. This
small, stylish bar set over two floors attracts
a lively, younger crowd than the neighbouring Jimmy Woo – possibly owing to its
less picky door staff. Open Fri & Sat only.

Jazz and Latin

For **jazz** fans, Amsterdam can be a treat. Ever since the 1940s and 1950s, when
American jazz musicians began moving to Europe to escape discrimination
back home, the city has had a soft spot for jazz. Paris stole much of the limelight,
but Chet Baker lived and died in Amsterdam, and he and any number of
legendary jazzbos could once be found jamming into the small hours at
Casablanca on Zeedijk. Venues have changed a lot since then, varying from tiny
bars staging everything from Dixieland to avant-garde, to the large, modern
Bimhuis – the city's major jazz venue – which plays host to both international
names and homegrown talent. Pianist Michiel Borstlap, cellist Ernst Reijseger
and sought-after percussionist Han Bennink – member of the acclaimed
contemporary jazz collective, ICP – are among the **Dutch musicians** you
might come across, and they're well worth catching if you get the chance.

The jazz season runs from September to July, with concerts and festivals being
held all over the country. The Netherlands boast one of the best jazz festivals in
the world, the **North Sea Jazz Festival**, held during July, which has recently
moved from The Hague to the Ahoy in Rotterdam. Comprising three days and
nights of continuous jazz on fourteen stages, the festival involves around 1200
musicians, among them world-class performers, from Oscar Peterson to Guru's
Jazzmatazz. **Tickets** cost from about €60 a day, with supplements for the big
names. Information on the event is available from ☎015/214 8393, ⓦwww.
northseajazz.nl.

The Dutch connection with **Surinam** – a former colony tucked in between
Venezuela and Brazil – means that there's a sizeable **Latin American**
community in the city, and plenty of authentic salsa and other Latin sounds to
be discovered; the best venue for this type of music is Akhnaton, while the
Melkweg and Paradiso put on occasional salsa nights.

Akhnaton See p.208. This crowded, lively venue is your best bet for Latin music.

Bimhuis Piet Heinkade 3 (Old Jewish Quarter and Eastern docklands) ℡020/788 2150, ⓦwww.bimhuis.nl. In 2004 the city's premier jazz and improvised music venue moved to its spanking new building overlooking the IJ, east of Centraal Station and next to the Muziekgebouw (see p.214). It hosts Dutch and international artists throughout the week, as well as jam sessions and workshops; Tuesday features a free improv workshop (not July & Aug). There's also a bar and restaurant with fantastic views over the water.

Bourbon Street Leidsekruisstraat 6 (Grachtengordel south) ℡020/623 3440, ⓦwww.bourbonstreet.nl. Friendly bar with a relaxed atmosphere and quality blues and jazz nightly, until 4am Mon–Thurs & Sun, until 5am Fri & Sat. Free entry before 11pm.

Café Alto Korte Leidsedwarsstraat 115 (Grachtengordel south) ℡020/626 3249, ⓦwww.jazz-cafe-alto.nl. It's worth hunting out this legendary little jazz bar just off Leidseplein for the quality modern jazz every night from 9pm until 3am (and often much later). Though slightly cramped, it's big on atmosphere, entry is free, and you don't have to buy a beer to hang out and watch the band.

Casablanca Zeedijk 26 (Old Centre) ℡020/625 5685, ⓦwww.casablanca-amsterdam.nl. Though a shadow of its former self, Casablanca still hosts live jazz most nights of the week, when it's not putting on variety and cabaret shows. Check website for programme details.

De Engelbewaarder Kloveniersburgwal 59 (Old Centre) ℡020/625 3772. Comfy old bar with excellent live jazz sessions Sunday afternoons 4–7pm.

't Geveltje Bloemgracht 170 (Jordaan and Western docklands) ℡020/623 9983. This jazz café offers workshops on Tuesdays and Thursdays, and professional and beginners' jam sessions on Fridays and Mondays respectively. Open till 3am weekdays; till 4am Sat & Sun.

Le Maxim Leidsekruisstraat 35 (Grachtengordel south) ℡020/624 1920. Spirited piano bar that's been going since the Sixties, with live music nightly.

Classical and opera

There's no shortage of **classical music** concerts in Amsterdam, with two major orchestras based in the city, plus regular visits by other Dutch ensembles. The **Royal Concertgebouw Orchestra** remains one of the most dynamic in the world, and occupies one of the finest concert halls to boot. The other resident orchestra is the **Netherlands Philharmonic**, based at the Beurs van Berlage concert hall, which has a wide symphonic repertoire and also performs with the Netherlands Opera at the Muziektheater. Among visiting orchestras, the Rotterdam Philharmonic and the Utrecht Symphony have world-class reputations, as does the Radio Philharmonic Orchestra, based in Hilversum outside Amsterdam.

As far as **smaller classical ensembles** go, Dutch musicians pioneered the use of **period instruments** in the 1970s, of which Ton Koopman's Amsterdam Baroque Orchestra and Frans Brüggen's Orchestra of the 18th Century are two internationally renowned exponents. Koopman's Amsterdam Baroque Choir and the Amsterdam Bach Soloists are also pre-eminent.

As well as the main concert halls, a number of Amsterdam's churches (and former churches) host regular performances of classical and chamber music – both types of venue are listed here. Others, including the huge Nieuwe Kerk on Dam Square, the Westerkerk, the Noorderkerk, the Mozes en Aaronkerk on Waterlooplein, and the tiny Amstelkerk on Kerkstraat, as well as numerous small churches out in the residential south and west, occasionally put on one-off concerts, often at very reasonable prices (check with venues for programme details).

The most prestigious venue for **opera** is the Muziektheater (otherwise known as the Stopera) on Waterlooplein, which is home to the Netherlands Opera company – going from strength to strength under the guidance of Pierre Audi – as well as the Dutch National Ballet. Visiting companies sometimes perform here, but more often at the Stadsschouwburg or the Carré Theatre.

Tickets are excellent value and aren't as exclusively priced as some European cities, starting from as little as €7.50 for matinee concerts, and rising to €70 for big-name performers.

As far as **contemporary classical music** goes, the recently opened Muziekgebouw, overlooking the IJ, has taken over as the city's leading showcase for musicians from all over the world. Local talent is headed by the Asko and Schoenberg ensembles, as well as the Nieuw Ensemble and the Volharding Orchestra. Look out also for Willem Breuker and Maarten Altena, two popular musicians who successfully combine improvised jazz with composed, contemporary classical music.

By far the most prestigious multi-venue Dutch festival for contemporary classical music is the annual **Holland Festival** (W www.hollandfestival.nl) in June, which attracts the best of the country's mainstream and fringe performers in all areas of the arts, as well as an exciting international line-up. Otherwise, one of the more interesting music-oriented events is the popular **Grachtenfestival**, held at the end of August, a week-long classical music festival (W www.grachtenfestival.nl), which concludes with a piano recital on a floating stage outside the *Pulitzer Hotel* on the Prinsengracht – with the whole area floodlit and filled with small boats, and every available spot on the banks and bridges taken up, this can be a wonderfully atmospheric evening. Also around this time – and from two ends of the musical spectrum – Utrecht plays host to the internationally renowned **Early Music Festival** (W www.oudemuziek.nl), while in early September, Amsterdam holds the **International Gaudeamus Music Week** (W www.gaudeamus.nl), a forum for debate and premiere performances of cutting-edge contemporary music.

Venues

Beurs van Berlage Damrak 277 (Old Centre) ☏020/521 7575, W www.berlage.com. The splendid interior of the former stock exchange (see p.43) is the setting for regular exhibitions and concerts, though nowadays it's used more as a hall-for-hire for conferences. The resident Netherlands Philharmonic rehearse in the huge Amvest Zaal, the former Corn Exchange Hall, a glassed-in pavilion, while the glass-roofed Yakult Zaal (Main Hall) was the location for the royal wedding of Prince Willem-Alexander and Princess Máxima in 2002.

Carré Theater Amstel 115–125 (Grachtengordel south) ☏020/524 9452, W www.theatercarre.nl. This splendid late nineteenth-century structure (originally built for a circus) represents the ultimate venue for Dutch folk artists, and hosts all kinds of international performances: anything from Antony and the Johnsons to *Carmen*, with reputable touring orchestras and opera companies squeezed in between.

Concertgebouw Concertgebouwplein 2–6 (Museum Quarter and Vondelpark) ☏020/671 8345, W www.concertgebouw.nl. A concert at the Concertgebouw, one of the most impressive looking – and sounding – venues in the city, is a wonderful experience, especially when the Netherlands Philharmonic Orchestra put on one of their regular performances. The acoustics of the Grote Zaal (Great Hall) are unparalleled, while the smaller Kleine Zaal regularly hosts chamber concerts. Though both halls boast a star-studded international programme, prices are very reasonable, ranging from €15 to €50 (€14 for the sponsored Sunday-morning events, June–Sept). Free Wednesday lunchtime concerts are held from Sept to May (doors open 12.15pm; arrive early), and in July and Aug there's a heavily subsidized series of summer concerts. Look out also for occasional world music and swing/jazz nights.

Engelse Kerk Begijnhof 48 (Old Centre)
☎020/624 9665. The church with the biggest programme: three to four performances a week, usually Fri, Sat & Sun (performances at 3.15pm or 8.15pm). Tickets are available from the church thirty minutes before the start of performance or in advance from the Uitburo (see p.206).

Marionetten Theater Nieuwe Jonkerstraat 8 (Old Centre) ☎020/620 8027, ⓦ www .marionettentheater.nl. Maintains an old European tradition with its performances of operas by Mozart and Offenbach. Although they're touring the Netherlands and the rest of Europe for most of the year, the wooden marionettes return to Amsterdam around May, October and Christmas. Call for details of performances, and to find out about their opera dinners.

Muziekgebouw Piet Heinkade 1 (Old Jewish Quarter and Eastern docklands) ☎020/788 2000, ⓦ www.muziekgebouw.nl. East of Centraal Station, Amsterdam's newest concert hall for over a hundred years, with two new medium-sized concert halls, a café, bar and state-of-the-art acoustics, has given new impetus to the redevelopment going on along the IJ. Its top-quality programme of opera and orchestral music draws a highbrow crowd to this part of town. Worth a visit just for the building alone; the café offers great views over the water. The same development also includes the relocated Bimhuis.

Muziektheater Waterlooplein 22 (Old Jewish Quarter and Eastern docklands) ☎020/625 5455, ⓦ www.hetmuziektheater.nl. Part of the €150 million complex that includes the city hall. The theatre's resident company,

Netherlands Opera, offers the fullest, and most reasonably priced, programme of opera in Amsterdam; not surprisingly, tickets go very quickly. Look out for free Tuesday lunchtime concerts (Sept–May).

Oude Kerk Oudekerksplein 23 (Old Centre) ☎020/625 8284. Hosts organ and carillon recitals, as well as occasional choral events.

Stadsschouwburg Leidseplein 26 (Grachtengordel south) ☎020/624 2311, ⓦ www.ssba.nl. Somewhat overshadowed by the Muziektheater these days, but still staging significant opera, theatre and dance, as well as occasionally hosting visiting English-language theatre companies.

Waalse Kerk Oudezijds Achterburgwal 159 (Old Centre) ☎020/623 2074. Weekend afternoon and evening concerts of early classical music and chamber music.

▽ Muziekgebouw

Theatre, cabaret and comedy

Surprisingly for a city that functions so much in English, there is next to no **English-language drama** to be seen in Amsterdam, though a handful of amateur companies put on two or three English productions during the summer and there are also occasional performances by touring groups at the theatres listed below and at other venues dotted around town.

English-language **comedy** and **cabaret**, on the other hand, has gained some ground in Amsterdam, spearheaded by the resident and extremely successful "Boom Chicago" comedy company. During the summer in particular, a number of small venues host mini-seasons of English-language stand-up comedy and cabaret, featuring touring British performers, and material that's generally targeted at visitors to the city.

Most of Amsterdam's **larger theatre companies** concentrate either on foreign works in translation or Dutch-language theatre, neither of which is likely to be terribly interesting for the non–Dutch speaker. However, there are plenty of **avant-garde** theatre groups in the city, much of whose work relies on visual rather than verbal impact, as well as one or two companies devoted to **mime**. Look out also for performances at the Amsterdam Marionetten Theater (see p.214). The Amsterdamse Bos Theatre (www.bostheater.nl) puts on summertime open-air performances of Shakespeare plays (in Dutch). It's an atmospheric evening, with audiences picnicking before the show.

The main event to watch out for, apart from the mainstream Holland Festival (see p.213), is the summer-long **Over Het IJ Festival** (info ☎020/624 6380, www.overhetij.nl), a showcase for all kinds of performance arts at large, often outdoor locations in Amsterdam Noord (thus "over the IJ"). The participation of many interesting small companies pushes the standard of the average production well above that of the usual fringe festival fare. In June, the **International Theatre School Festival** (www.itsfestival.nl) sees the four theatres on Nes, a tiny alley running from Dam square parallel to Rokin, host productions by local and international theatre schools.

Major venues

De Balie Kleine-Gartmanplantsoen 10 (Grachtengordel south) ☎020/553 5100, www.debalie. nl. A multimedia centre for culture and the arts, located off the Leidseplein, which often plays host to drama, debates, international symposia and the like, sometimes in conjunction with the Paradiso next door. Also has a lovely, roomy, mezzanine bar.

Boom Chicago Leidseplein 12 (Grachtengordel south) ☎020/423 0101, www.boomchicago.nl. Something of a phenomenon in Amsterdam, this rapid-fire improv comedy troupe hailing from America performs at the Leidseplein Theater nightly to crowds of both tourists and locals, and receives rave reviews. With inexpensive food, cocktails and beer served in pitchers, the comedy need not be funny – but it is.

Carré Theater See p.213. A chunky old building on the eastern bank of the Amstel which, aside from its folk associations, hosts all kinds of top international acts, with an emphasis on hit musicals.

Comedy Café Max Euweplein 43 (Grachtengordel south) ☎020/638 3971, www.comedycafe.nl. Small stand-up theatre with a bar and restaurant that sometimes hosts English-language acts; look out for Sunday night's "In Your Face", an improv show in English.

De Kleine Komedie Amstel 56 (Grachtengordel south) ☎020/624 0534, www.dekleine-komedie.nl. One of Amsterdam's oldest theatres, established in 1786, which occasionally hosts English-language shows,

as well as performances by the odd pop megastar.

Melkweg See p.210. At the centre of the city's cultural scene, this is often the first-choice venue for foreign touring companies.

Stadsschouwburg See opposite. Occasionally hosts productions on tour from London or New York.

Avant-garde and mime

De Brakke Grond Nes 45 (Old Centre) ☎020/622 9014, www.brakkegrond.nl. See also www.nestheaters.nl. Mainly Flemish productions.

DasArts Mauritskade 56 (Old Jewish Quarter and Eastern docklands) ☎020/586 9636, www.dasarts.nl. Situated east of the centre, beyond Artis Zoo, this is less of a venue than a global clubhouse for theatre-makers, a think-tank and postgraduate institute, with international workshops and performances.

Felix Meritis Keizersgracht 324 (Grachtengordel south) ☎020/626 2321, www.felix.meritis.nl. Unique, restored eighteenth-century centre for arts and sciences. Hosts theatre, debate, music and visual arts events, and features a wonderful foyer bar and café that's open 9am–7pm during the week and at weekends if there's an event.

De Nieuw Amsterdam Grote Bickersstraat 2 (Jordaan and Western docklands) ☎020/627 8672, www.denieuwamsterdam.nl. Theatre company with a multicultural background and a focus on non-Western productions.

Dance

Of the major **dance companies** based in Amsterdam, the largest and most prestigious is the Muziektheater's **Dutch National Ballet**, under Ted Brandsen. Also working regularly in Amsterdam are the noted Dutch choreographers Toer van Schayk and Rudi van Dantzig, while for fans of **folk dancing**, the excellent Internationaal Danstheater is based in the city. Dance in the Netherlands has long been a draw for non-Dutch choreographers and dancers; the work of William Forsyth, Lloyd Newson, Saburo Teshigawara and others is regularly on show.

Among the most innovative of the other leading **Dutch dance companies**, which can be seen on tour in Amsterdam – or in nearby Rotterdam and The Hague – is The Hague's Netherlands Dance Theatre, with a repertoire of ballet and modern dance featuring inspired choreography by Jirí Kylian and artistic director Anders Hellström. The oldest company in the country, the Scapino Ballet (based in Rotterdam), has spruced up its image under artistic director Ed Wubbe and is gathering a new generation of admirers.

Though on a smaller scale, Amsterdam is particularly receptive to the latest trends in **modern dance**, and has many experimental dance groups, which often incorporate other media into their productions; small productions staged by dance students also abound. Look out for performances by the Dans Werkplaats Amsterdam and the extraordinary Cloud Chamber company, as well as mime specialists Griftheater and Shusaku Takeuchi's vast, open-air, water-based extravaganzas. Modern dance and movement theatre companies from outside Amsterdam which often perform in the city include the Rotterdamse Dansgroep, who mainly focus on New York modern dance, and Introdans, similar in style to the Netherlands Dance Theatre.

Dance **festivals** are a little thin on the ground: **Julidans** (Ⓦwww.julidans. com), held in theatres around the Leidseplein area every July, is the leading event in the city; beyond, there's **Dansweek** (Ⓦwww.dansweek.nl), an event held throughout the Netherlands in October. The Hague – just a 45-minute train ride from Centraal Station – hosts two dance festivals: the **Holland Dance Festival** (Ⓦwww.hollanddancefestival.com), which takes place every two years (October 2007 and 2009) and attracts many leading international companies; and the biennial **CaDance** (Ⓦwww.cadance.nl; next festival is in Oct/Nov 2008), which premieres contemporary dance works.

Venues

Dans Werkplaats Amsterdam Arie Biemond-straat 107b (Jordaan and Western docklands) Ⓣ020/689 1789, Ⓦwww.danswerkplaats.nl. A dance company staging occasional productions at studio Het Veem (located west of the city, on the River IJ) and other locations around the city.

Internationaal Danstheater Kloveniersburgwal 87 (Old Centre) Ⓣ020/623 9112, Ⓦwww .intdanstheater.nl. Original folk dancing from around the world, with international choreographers brought in to work with the dancers.

Melkweg See p.210. Upstairs in this pop and world music venue, there's a little theatre which puts on modern and funky productions.

Muziektheater See p.214. Home of the National Ballet, but with a third of its dance schedule given over to international companies.

Stadsschouwburg See p.214. This theatre is the principal host to the Julidans dance festival in July, as well as staging regular productions.

Film

Most of Amsterdam's commercial **cinemas** are huge multiplex affairs showing a selection of general releases. There's also a scattering of film houses (*filmhuizen*) showing **revival and art-house films** and occasional retrospectives. Two Amsterdam cinemas worth a visit no matter what's showing are the extravagant, Art Deco Tuschinski and the atmospheric The Movies (see p.218).

Pick up a copy of the weekly *Film Agenda* from any cinema for details of all films showing in the city, or check ⑩www.filmladder.nl. Weekly programmes change on Thursdays. All foreign movies playing in Amsterdam (almost no Dutch movies are screened, anyway) are shown in their **original language** and subtitled in Dutch – which is fine for British or American fare, but a little difficult if you fancy Tarkovsky or Pasolini. If you're interested in seeing a non-English-language movie, check with the venue whether it's been **subtitled** in English (*Engels Ondertiteld*) before you go. Films are almost never dubbed into Dutch; if they are, *Nederlands Gesproken* will be printed in the listings. **Tickets** cost between €4.50 and €8.50, depending on the day and time you go. For details of gay and lesbian film programmes see Chapter Twelve.

Aside from occasional film festivals held by the likes of Amnesty International, Amsterdam's only regular event is the excellent **International Documentary Film Festival** in November/December (⑩www.idfa.nl), when up to three hundred documentaries from all over the world are shown over ten days. The event has established itself as the biggest international documentary festival in the world. Simultaneously, there's the **Shadowfestival** (⑩www.shadowfestival.nl), which showcases alternative documentaries and is held at three locations: Melkweg, de Uitkijk and the Filmmuseum. While the **Netherlands Film Festival** (⑩www.filmfestival.nl), held each September in Utrecht, features only home-grown productions, January's **Rotterdam Film Festival** (⑩www.filmfestivalrotterdam.com) is truly international, with screenings of well over a hundred art-house movies from all parts of the world, as well as the usual accompanying lectures and seminars.

Cinemas

De Balie See p.215. Cultural centre for theatre, politics, film and new media, showing movies at noon on Sundays and selected evenings during the week, often with English subtitles.

Cavia Van Hallstraat 52 ☎020/681 1419, ⑩www.filmhuiscavia.nl. Incongruously sited above a martial arts centre west of the centre, this is one of the best of the small *filmhuizen*, with an eclectic and non-commercial programme of international and art-house movies.

Cinecenter Lijnbaansgracht 236 (Grachtengordel south) ☎020/623 6615, ⑩www.cinecenter.nl. Opposite the Melkweg, this cinema shows independent and quality commercial films, the majority originating from non-English-speaking countries, shown with an interval.

City Kleine Gartmanplantsoen 10 (Grachtengordel south) ☎0900/9363, ⑩www.city-

bioscoop.nl. Cinema with seven screens, located just off Leidseplein, showing mainstream films along with the occasional local or Bollywood offering.

Filmmuseum Vondelpark 3 (Museum Quarter and Vondelpark) ☎020/589 1400, ⑩www.filmmuseum.nl. Subsidized by the government since the 1940s, the Filmmuseum has a library of tens of thousands of films. Dutch films show regularly, along with all kinds of movies from all corners of the globe, sometimes with a themed run, such as retrospectives of directors' work. Silent movies often have live piano accompaniment, and on summer weekend evenings there are free open-air screenings on the terrace. Matinees are often cheap. Most films have English subtitles.

Kriterion Roeterstraat 170 (Old Jewish Quarter and Eastern docklands) ☎020/623 1708, ⑩www.kriterion.nl. Stylish duplex cinema close to Weesperplein metro (tram #7 or

#10). Shows art-house and quality commercial films, with late-night cult favourites. Friendly bar attached.

Melkweg See p.215. As well as music, art and dance, the Melkweg manages to maintain a consistently good monthly film programme, ranging from mainstream fodder through to more obscure imports.

The Movies Haarlemmerdijk 161 (Jordaan and Western docklands) ☎ 020/638 6016, ⓦ www.themovies.nl. A beautiful Art Deco cinema, and a charming setting for independent films. Worth visiting for the bar and restaurant alone, fully restored to their original sumptuousness. "Filmdinner" nights (Mon–Thurs) include a three-course meal and film from €29. There are late showings (11.45pm) of classic or cult films at weekends.

De Munt Vijzelstraat 15 (Grachtengordel south) ☎ 0900/1438, ⓦ www.pathe.nl/ demunt. Huge multi-screen cinema with up to six showings a day of mainstream films, as well as a few home-grown productions.

Rialto Ceintuurbaan 338 (De Pijp) ☎ 020/676 8700, ⓦ www.rialtofilm.nl. The only fully authentic art-house cinema in Amsterdam, showing an enormously varied programme of European and World movies supplemented by themed series and classics. The cinema boasts a large café open to the public, and, thanks to the staff of volunteers, the place has a friendly, welcoming atmosphere.

Smart Cinema 1e Const. Huygensstraat 10 (Museum Quarter and Vondelpark) ☎ 020/427 5951, ⓦ www.smartprojectspace.net. Small cinema near the Filmmuseum (tram #3 or #12 to Overtoom) showing the best non-mainstream offerings, with short experimental films, sometimes video art, before the film begins.

Tropentheater See p.208. Attached to the Tropenmuseum, this theatre concentrates mostly on music and dance, but puts on ad hoc themed film events focusing on cultures from around the world. No screenings June & July.

▽ Tuschinski Theater

Tuschinski Theater Reguliersbreestraat 26 (Grachtengordel south), ⓦ www.tuschinski.nl. Fabulous Art Deco theatre, famous for its hand-woven carpet and painted wallpaper, this film house shows the artier offerings from the mainstream list.

De Uitkijk Prinsengracht 452 (Grachtengordel south) ☎ 020/623 7460 ⓦ www.uitkijk.nl. Pronounced "out-kike", the oldest cinema in the Netherlands is a converted canal house with no bar, no ice cream and no popcorn – but low prices. Shows popular movies for months on end.

Shopping

Variety is the essence of Amsterdam **shopping**. Whereas in other capital cities you can spend days trudging around in search of something interesting, here you'll find every kind of store packed into a relatively small area. Throw in a handful of great **street markets**, and Amsterdam's shopping possibilities look even more inviting. There are, of course, the obligatory generic malls and pedestrianized shopping streets, where you can find exactly the same stuff you'd see at home, but where Amsterdam scores is in its excellent, unusual **speciality shops** – dedicated to rubber stamps, Indonesian arts or condoms, to name but three, almost always owned by a family or individual.

Shopping in Amsterdam can be divided roughly by **area**, with similar shops often huddled together in neighbouring streets. Broadly speaking, the **Nieuwendijk/Kalverstraat** strip running just west of Dam Square in the Old Centre is home to high-street fashion and mainstream department stores – crowded Saturday afternoons here can be a grim experience – while nearby **Koningsplein** and **Leidsestraat** offer a good selection of affordable designer clothes and shoe stores. In the **Grachtengordel** and the **Jordaan**, further to the south and west, many local artists ply their wares; you can find individual items of genuine interest here, as well as more specialized and offbeat clothes shops and some affordable antiques. Bear in mind, however, that the major canals of the Grachtengordel (Herengracht, Keizersgracht and Prinsengracht) are mostly given over to homes and offices, and it's along the small radial streets that connect them that you'll find the more interesting and quirky shops, many of which are listed on the website Ⓦ www.theninestreets.com; the **nine streets** concerned extend south from Reestraat/Hartenstraat to Runstraat/Huidenstraat in Grachtengordel west.

Elsewhere, pricier antiques – the cream of Amsterdam's renowned trade – can be found in the Spiegelkwartier, centred on **Nieuwe Spiegelstraat**, while to the south of the centre, **P.C. Hooftstraat**, **Van Baerlestraat** and, further south still, **Beethovenstraat** play host to designer clothes shops, upmarket ceramics stores, confectioners and delicatessens.

As regards **opening hours**, many shops take Monday morning off, not opening until noon or 1pm and closing again at 6pm. On Tuesday, Wednesday and Friday, hours are mostly a standard 9am to 6pm, although the larger shops in the centre have shifted towards a 7pm closing time. Thursday is late-opening night (*koopavond*), with most places staying open from 9am until 9pm. Saturday hours are normally 8.30 or 9am to 5 or 5.30pm, and most shops stay closed on Sundays, though this is changing fast, with noon to 5pm the common formula.

△ Shopping on the nine streets

A few "night shops" are open between roughly 4pm and 1am – see the box on p.229.

Finally, note that many small and medium-sized shops won't accept **credit cards** – ask if in doubt; traveller's cheques are accepted hardly anywhere.

Shops

Antiques

By necessity, this is only a sample of what's on offer – you'll find **antiques** shops in every corner of Amsterdam – but there is a top-end-of-the-market concentration in the **Spiegelkwartier** along Nieuwe Spiegelstraat and Spiegelgracht.

Affaire D'Eau Haarlemmerdijk 150 (Jordaan and Western docklands) ☎020/422 0411. Antique bathtubs, taps, sinks and toilets, as well as lamps, mirrors and soaps. Mon–Fri 10.30am–6pm, Sat 10.30am–5pm.

Jan Beekhuizen Nieuwe Spiegelstraat 49 (Grachtengordel south) ☎020/626 3912, ⊛www.janbeekhuizen.nl. European pewter from the fifteenth century onwards. Tues–Sun 10.30am–6pm.

Amsterdam's commercial art galleries

Amsterdam has a small but thriving **commercial art scene** and some great private galleries, and these are well worth visiting either to view specific exhibitions or – if you're in the mood and have the means – for buying some art.

Arti et Amicitae Rokin 112 (Old Centre) ☎020/623 3508, ⊛www.arti.nl. This centrally situated gallery, part of a private art academy, is one of the city's most prestigious exhibition spaces, with a gallery at the top of a Berlage-designed staircase usually given over to exhibitions of modern art in a variety of media. Tues–Sun 1–8pm.

Binnen Galerie Keizersgracht 82 (Grachtengordel west) ☎020/625 9603. A gallery of interior design, with regular exhibitions of furniture and a small permanent collection too. At Prinsenstraat. Wed–Sat noon–6pm.

Chiellerie Raamgracht 58 (Old Centre) ☎020/320 9448, ⊛www.chiellerie.nl. Cutting-edge gallery off Kloveniersburgwal that focuses on photography and has regular temporary exhibitions. Wed–Sun 2–6pm, Fri until 10pm.

FOAM Keizersgracht 609 (Grachtengordel south) ☎020/551 6500, ⊛www.foam.nl. One of the city's major exhibition spaces for photography, with regular large exhibits and a small collection of material that's always on view. Entrance €7. Daily 10am–5pm, Thurs & Fri until 9pm.

Huis Marseille Keizersgracht 401 (Grachtengordel west) ☎020/539 8181, ⊛www. huismarseille.nl. The city's prime photo exhibition space, housed in a fabulous location in a restored, mid-seventeenth-century canal house that was once the home of a French merchant – hence the name. It hosts quarterly exhibitions, to which admission is usually around €3. At Runstraat. Tues–Sun 11am–5pm.

Mokum OZ Voorburgwal 334 (Old Centre), ☎020/624 3958, ⊛www.galeriemokum. com. This historic Amsterdam gallery, named after the Jewish word for the city and a famous magical realist novel, still exhibits both fantastical and realist modern works. Wed–Sat noon–5pm, and first Sun of each month 1–5pm.

Galerie Paul Andriesse Prinsengracht 116 (Grachtengordel west) ☎020/623 6237, ⊛www.galeries.nl/andriesse. This long-running space shows modern art with an emphasis on homegrown works by more established artists. At Leliegracht. Tues–Fri 11am–6pm, Sat 2–6pm and first Sun of each month 2–5pm.

Reflex Modern Art Gallery Weteringschans 79a (Grachtengordel south) ☎020/627 2832, ⊛www.reflex-art.nl. You'll always find something interesting in this gallery, which represents some big international names, most notably some of the artists of the CoBrA school – Appel, Corneille and others. At Spiegelgracht. Tues–Sat 11am–6pm.

Torch Lauriergracht 94 (Jordaan and Western docklands) ☎020/626 0284, ⊛www. torchgallery.com. One of the city's most challenging contemporary galleries.

W139 Warmoesstraat 139 (Old Centre) ☎020/622 9434, ⊛www.w139.nl. Long-established gallery in the heart of the city that can always be relied upon to take a chance on new and up-and-coming artists. Also has an exhibition space in the basement of the Post CS building, near Centraal Station, where you'll also find the Stedelijk Museum (see p.109). Sun–Thurs 11am–8pm, Fri & Sat 11am–10pm.

Jan Best Keizersgracht 357 (Grachtengordel west) ☏020/623 2736. Famed antique lamp shop, with some wonderfully kitsch examples. Offbeat new lamps and lights too. Corner Huidenstraat. Mon–Fri 10.30am–6pm & Sat 10am–5pm.

Blitz Nieuwe Spiegelstraat 37a (Grachtengordel south) ☏020/623 2663. Specializes in antique ceramics from China. Tues–Sun 10.30am–6pm.

Gallery de Munt Munttoren, Muntplein 12 (Old Centre) ☏020/623 2271. One of the best outlets for gifts of antique delftware, pottery, hand-painted tiles and the like. Mon–Sat 10am–6pm.

Harrie van Gennip Govert Flinckstraat 402 (De Pijp, Outer districts) ☏020/679 3025, ⓦwww.harrievangennip.nl. A huge collection of old and antique stoves from all parts of Europe, lovingly restored and all in working order. Thurs 1–6pm & Sat 11am–4pm.

Eduard Kramer Nieuwe Spiegelstraat 64 (Grachtengordel south) ☏020/623 0832, ⓦwww.antique-tileshop.nl. Holds a wonderful selection of Dutch tiles from the fifteenth century onwards. Operates an online ordering service too. Tues–Sun 10.30am–6pm.

Thom & Lenny Nelis Keizersgracht 541 (Grachtengordel south) ☏020/623 1546. Medical antiques and spectacles. Just off Spiegelstraat. Thurs–Sat 11am–5pm.

Tóth Ikonen Nieuwe Spiegelstraat 68 (Grachtengordel south) ☏020/420 7359, ⓦwww.tothikonen.com. Antique Russian icons from the sixteenth to the nineteenth century. Tues–Sun 11am–5.30pm.

Van Dreven Nieuwe Spiegelstraat 38 (Grachtengordel south) ☏020/428 8442, ⓦwww.antique-horology.org/vandreven. Antique clocks, barometers and music boxes. Tues–Sun 10.30am–6pm.

Van Hier tot Tokio Prinsengracht 262 (Grachtengordel west) ☏020/428 2682, ⓦwww.vanhier-tottokio.com. This split-level store just south of Reestraat has a good variety of modern and antique Japanese furniture, crafts, kimonos and the like. Tues–Fri noon–6pm, Sat 11am–6pm & Sun noon–7pm.

Art supplies, postcards and posters

Art Unlimited Keizersgracht 510 (Grachtengordel south) ☏020/624 8419, ⓦwww.artunlimited.com. Sprawling postcard, card and poster shop, with excellent stock. All kinds of images: good for communiqués home that avoid windmills and clogs. Near the corner of Leidsestraat. Mon–Sat 10am–6pm (Thurs till 9pm) & Sun noon–5pm.

De Lach 1e Bloemdwarsstraat 14 (Jordaan and Western docklands) ☏020/626 6625, ⓦwww.moviepostersdelach.com. Movie poster shop that also stocks Hollywood classics and some international films. An original *Barbarella* poster will set you back no less than €250. Tues–Sat 11am–6pm.

Van Beek Stadhouderskade 62–65 (De Pijp, Outer districts) ☏020/662 1670. Long-established outlet for art materials of all kinds. Mon 1–6pm, Tues–Fri 9am–6pm, Sat 10am–5pm.

Van Ginkel Bilderdijkstraat 99 (Oud West, Outer districts) ☏020/618 9827. Supplier of art materials, with an emphasis on print-making. Mon–Fri 10am–5.30pm, Sat 10am–4pm.

Bikes

Bikes can be rented from a veritable raft of outlets all over town (you'll need to show ID and pay a €50 or €100 deposit, or leave a credit card); see "Basics" for further details. If you're buying a bike, don't be tempted by anything you're offered on the street or in a bar – more often than not you'll end up with a stolen edition. Try instead the shops listed below, which rent, sell and repair bikes of all qualities. If you find that no one in the shop speaks English, check out the glossary of basic bike terms on p.301.

Bike City Bloemgracht 70 (Jordaan and Western docklands) ☏020/626 3721, ⓦwww.bikecity.nl. The best of the rental places for service and quality – try here first. Daily rate €8.50. Daily 9am–6pm.

Damstraat Rent-a-Bike Damstraat 20–22 (Old Centre) ☏020/625 5029, ⓦwww.bikes.nl. Bike repair and rental near Dam Square from €3.50

an hour, €7 a day, €31 a week. Traditional Dutch bikes for sale, too, both used and new. **Freewheel** Akoleienstraat 7 (Jordaan and Western docklands) ☏020/627 7252. Women-run bike repairs and sales. Tues–Fri 10am–6pm, Sat 10am–5pm.

MacBike Centraal Station (Eastpoint), Station-splein; Mr Visserplein 2; and Weteringschans 2, on the edge of Leidseplein ☏020/620 0985, ⓦwww.macbike.nl. Three locations (but one central phone number) for this well-established and very popular bike rental, repair and sales firm, though the circular MacBike disks sported by every one of their bikes do look distinctly un-cool. They also organize city tours. Rental from €6 for three hours, €8.50 a day and €30 a week. Daily 9am–5.45pm.

Books and comics

Virtually all of Amsterdam's many **bookshops** stock at least a small selection of English-language books, though prices are always inflated (sometimes dramatically). A particular speciality is the city's range of **second-hand and antiquarian** bookshops, several of which are listed below, but for a comprehensive list pick up the free *Antiquarian & Secondhand Bookshops of Amsterdam* leaflet at any of them. For gay and lesbian bookstores see Chapter Twelve.

General bookstores

American Book Center Spui 12 (Old Centre) ☏020/625 5537. This recently relocated store has a vast stock of books in English, as well as lots of imported US magazines and books. Mon–Wed, Fri & Sat 10am–8pm, Thurs 10am–9pm, Sun 11am–6.30pm.

Athenaeum Spui 14–16 (Old Centre) ☏020/514 1460. Perhaps the city's most appealing bookshop, and although it's relatively short on stuff in English, its array of books about Amsterdam is always current, and its selection of international newspapers and magazines is one of the best in the city. Mon 11am–6pm, Tues & Wed, Fri & Sat 9.30am–6pm, Thurs 9.30am–9pm, Sun noon–5.30pm.

The English Bookshop Lauriergracht 71 (Jordaan and Western docklands) ☏020/626 4230, ⓦwww.englishbookshop.nl. A small, quirky collection of titles on a wide range of subjects, in particular literature, but also cookery, travel and children's books. Tues–Sat 11am–6pm.

Martyrium Van Baerlestraat 170–172 (Museum Quarter and Vondelpark) ☏020/673 2092. Good general bookshop with lots of material in English. Mon–Fri 9am–6pm, Sat 9am–5pm, Sun noon–5pm.

Scheltema Koningsplein 20 (Grachten-gordel south) ☏020/523 1411, ⓦwww.scheltema.nl. Amsterdam's biggest and arguably best bookshop. Six floors of absolutely everything (mostly in Dutch). Daily 10am–6pm (Thurs till 9pm).

De Slegte Kalverstraat 48–52 (Old Centre) ☏020/622 5933. The Amsterdam branch of a nationwide chain specializing in new and used books at a discount. Mon 11am–6pm, Tues–Sat 9.30am–6pm (Thurs till 9pm), Sun noon–5pm.

Waterstone's Kalverstraat 152 (Old Centre) ☏020/638 3821. Amsterdam branch of the UK high-street chain, with four floors of books and magazines. A predictable selection, but prices are sometimes cheaper here than elsewhere. Sun & Mon 11am–6pm, Tues & Wed 9am–6pm, Thurs 9am–9pm, Fri 9am–7pm, Sat 10am–7pm.

Secondhand and antiquarian

Boekenmarkt Spui (Old Centre). Open-air book market every Friday 10am–6pm.

The Book Exchange Kloveniersburgwal 58 (Old Centre) ☏020/626 6266. Large and rambling old shop with a friendly American proprietor, and a great selection of English secondhand books. Mon–Fri 11am–6pm, Sat 11am–5.30pm, Sun 11.30am–4pm.

Book Traffic Leliegracht 50 (Grachtengordel west) ☏020/620 4690. An excellent and well-organized selection of mostly secondhand books. Mon–Fri 11am–6pm, Sat 11am–6pm & Sun noon–5pm.

Brinkman Singel 319 (Grachtengordel west) ☏020/623 8353, ⓦwww.antiquariaatbrinkman.nl. A stalwart of the Amsterdam antiquarian book trade, *Brinkman* has occupied the same premises for forty years. Lots of good local stuff. Corner Ramsteeg. Mon–Fri 10am–5pm & Sat 11am–5pm.

Egidius Haarlemmerstraat 87 (Jordaan and Western docklands) ☏020/624 3255. A good selection of literature, art and poetry, plus a gallery selling lithographs. Mon–Fri 11am–6pm, Sat 11am–5pm.

Fenix Frans Halsstraat 88 (De Pijp, Outer Districts) ☏020/673 9459, ⓦwww.xs4all.nl. General secondhand bookstore, with piles of stuff stacked up on the floor. A good range of books in English, with the emphasis on Celtic literature, history and culture. Mon–Sat noon–6pm.

De Kloof Kloveniersburgwal 44 (Old Centre) ☏020/622 3828, ⓦwww.kloof.nl. Enormous, higgledy-piggledy used bookshop on four floors – great for a rummage. Lots of titles in English, especially on law, history, science and philosophy. Thurs–Sat 1.15–5.30pm.

A. Kok Oude Hoogstraat 14 (Old Centre) ☏020/623 1191. Vintage and secondhand bookstore, especially strong on prints and maps.

Magic Galaxies Oude Schans 140 (Old Centre) ☏020/627 6261. Run from home by a couple whose spare time is spent collecting science fiction, fantasy and other esoteric books, many of which are in English. Call first.

Oudemanhuispoort Book Market Mon–Fri 11am–4pm. See p.62.

Art and architecture

Architectura & Natura Leliegracht 22 (Grachtengordel west) ☏020/623 6186, ⓦwww .architectura.nl. Books on architecture and interior design. An eclectic collection with many English titles. Mon noon–6pm & Tues–Sat 9am–6pm.

Boekie Woekie Berenstraat 16 (Grachtengordel west) ☏020/639 0507. Books on – and by – leading Dutch artists and graphic designers. Entertaining postcards too. Tues–Fri noon–6pm & Sat noon–5pm.

Mendo Berenstraat 11 (Grachtengordel west) ☏020/612 1216. Stylish, à la mode bookshop specializing in architecture, art, interior design, photography and graphic design. Wed–Fri noon–6pm, Sat noon–5pm, Sun 1–5pm.

Nijhoff en Lee Staalstraat 13a (Old Centre) ☏020/620 39 80. This small corner store specializes in art, architecture and design titles, and is especially good on the art of printing, typography and lithography. Mon noon–6pm, Tues–Fri 9am–6pm, Sat 10–6pm. There's a remainders shop opposite, too, at no.26 – open Mon–Sat 11am–6pm, Sun 11am–5pm.

Robert Premsela Van Baerlestraat 78 (Museum Quarter and Vondelpark) ☏020/662 4266. Great art and architecture book specialist, with lots of stuff in English. Mon–Fri 10am–6pm, Sat 10am–5.30pm.

Comics

Gojoker Zeedijk 31a (Old Centre) ☏020/620 5078. Classic and contemporary comic store. Tues–Sat 11am–7pm, Thurs until 9pm.

Lambiek Kerkstraat 132 (Grachtengordel south) ☏020/626 75 43, ⓦwww.lambiek. nl. The city's largest, oldest and best comic bookshop and gallery, with an international stock. Their website features the biggest comiclopedia in the world. Mon–Fri 11am–6pm & Sat 11am–5pm.

Stripwinkel Kapitein Rob 2e Egelantiersdwarsstraat 7 (Jordaan and Western docklands) ☏020/622 3869. Alternative Dutch comics old and new – and not a superhero in sight. Mon–Fri noon–6.30pm (Thurs till 8pm), Sat 11am–5pm.

Vandal Com-x Rozengracht 31 (Jordaan and Western docklands) ☏020/420 21 44, ⓦwww. vandalcomx.com. US comic imports, as well as related toy figures, games and masks. Mon 1–5.30pm, Tues–Thurs 11am–5.30pm, Fri 11am–6pm, Sat 11am–5pm, Sun noon–5pm.

Language

Intertaal Van Baerlestraat 76 (Museum Quarter and Vondelpark) ☏020/575 6756. Teach-yourself books and dictionaries in every language you can think of, and then some. Tues–Fri 10am–6pm, Sat 10am–5pm.

Scheltema See p.223. Amsterdam's biggest and best bookshop has an excellent range of language books and all sorts of stuff on the Dutch and their habits.

Politics and society

Fort van Sjakoo Jodenbreestraat 24 (Jewish Quarter and Eastern docklands) ℡020/625 8979, ⓦwww.sjakoo.nl. Anarchist bookshop stocking a wide selection of radical political publications. Mon–Fri 11am–6pm, Sat 11am–5pm.

Religion and occult

Au Bout du Monde Singel 313 (Grachtengordel west) ℡020/625 1397, ⓦwww.auboutdumonde. nl. Astrology, philosophy, psychology and mysticism, with classical music playing while you browse. Near Raamsteeg. Mon 1–6pm & Tues–Sat 10am–6pm.

Theatre and film

Cine-Qua-Non Staalstraat 14 (Old Centre) ℡020/625 5588, ⓦwww.cinequanon.nl. Film and cinema history books, posters and other film paraphernalia.

Travel

A la Carte Utrechtsestraat 110 (Grachtengordel south) ℡020/625 0679. Large and friendly travel bookshop. Prinsengracht cross-street. Mon 1–6pm, Tues–Fri 10am–6pm, Sat 10am–5pm.

Evenaar Singel 348 (Grachtengordel west) ℡020/624 6289. Concentrates less on guide-books and more on travel literature, of which it has an exemplary selection in both English and Dutch. Near Raamsteeg. Mon–Fri 12.15–6pm, Sat 11am–5pm.

Pied-à-Terre Overtoom 135 (Museum Quarter and Vondelpark) ℡020/627 4455, ⓦwww. piedaterre.nl. Hiking maps for Holland and beyond, mostly in English. Also adventure holiday guides. Mon–Fri 10am–6pm, Sat 10am–5pm.

Jacob van Wijngaarden Overtoom 97 (Museum Quarter and Vondelpark) ℡020/612 1901, ⓦwww.jvw.nl. The city's best travel bookshop, with knowledgeable staff and a huge selection of books and maps. Also sells inflatable and illuminated globes. Mon 1–6pm,

Tues–Fri 10am–6pm (Thurs till 9pm), Sat 10am–5pm.

Women's

Xantippe Unlimited Prinsengracht 290 (Grachtengordel west) ℡020/623 5854, ⓦwww. xantippe.nl. Amsterdam's foremost women's bookshop, with a wide selection of new feminist titles in English, plus guidebooks and postcards too. At Berenstraat. Mon 1–7pm, Tues–Fri 10am–7pm, Sat 10am–6pm, Sun noon–5pm.

Clothes and accessories

In many ways, Amsterdam is an ideal place for **clothes shopping**; prices aren't too high and the city is sufficiently compact to save lots of shoe leather. On the other hand, don't expect the huge choice of, say, London or New York. There are good-value, if somewhat predictable, mainstream styles along **Kalverstraat** and **Nieuwendijk**, with better-quality wares along **Rokin** and **Leidsestraat**; the really fancy goods are to be found down in the south of the city on **P.C. Hooftstraat**, **Van Baerlestraat** and, further south still, on **Beethovenstraat**.

There's a fair range of one-off **secondhand clothing shops** dotted around the Jordaan, on **Oude and Nieuwe Hoogstraat**, and along the narrow streets that connect the major canals in **Grachtengordel west**. The

▽ Jacob van Wijngaarden

Waterlooplein flea market (see p.237) is also a great hunting ground for vintage bargains. For children's clothes, see "Kids' Amsterdam", p.251.

High-street and designer clothes

Agnès B Rokin 126 (Old Centre) ☎020/627 1465. Amsterdam city-centre shop of the chic French designer, Agnès Troublé.

Antonia Gasthuismolensteeg 18–20 (Grachtengordel west) ☎020/320 9443, ⓦwww.antoniabyyvette.nl. High-fashion shoes, slippers and handbags spread over two smallish shops. Tues–Fri 10am–7pm (Thurs till 8pm), Sat 10am–6pm, Sun 1–5pm.

Diversi 1e Leliedwarsstraat 6 (Jordaan and Western docklands) ☎020/625 0773. Small but inspired collection of reasonably priced, Dutch and Italian classically designed clothes for women. Good selection of sunglasses and belts too. Mon–Fri 11am–6pm (closed Tues), Sat 11am–5.30pm.

Hemp Works Nieuwendijk 13 (Old Centre) ☎020/421 1762. Not all hemp is like sackcloth – check out the silky hemp shirts, fleeces and jeans in this clothing store that sells nothing but clothes made from the stuff. Mon–Wed 11am–7pm, Thurs–Sat 11am–9pm, Sun 11am–7pm.

Cora Kemperman Leidsestraat 72 (Grachtengordel south) ☎020/625 1284, ⓦwww.corakemperman.nl. Well-made, elegant, relaxed designer womenswear that won't break the bank. Mon noon–6pm, Tues–Sat 10am–6pm (Thurs till 9pm), Sun noon–6pm.

Laundry Industry Spui 1 (Old Centre) ☎020/420 2554. On the corner of the Rokin, this Dutch clothing brand does cool, chic, youthful clothes for women and men. There's another branch in Magna Plaza (Old Centre) and a third at Van Baerlestraat 76 (Museum Quarter and Vondelpark). Mon 11am–6.30pm, Tues–Fri 10am–6.30pm (Thurs till 9pm), Sat 10am–6pm, Sun noon–6pm.

Linhard Van Baerlestraat 50 (Museum Quarter and Vondelpark) ☎020/679 0755. Cheerful, well-priced separates. Mon 1–6pm, Tues–Fri 9.30am–6pm (Thurs till 9pm), Sat 9.30am–5.30pm, Sun noon–5pm.

Local Service Keizersgracht 400 (Grachtengordel west) ☎020/626 6840. Men's and women's fashions. Ultra-trendy in an alternative, funky kind of way – but expensive. At Runstraat. Mon–Fri 10am–6pm, Sat 10am–5pm, Sun 1–5.30pm.

Margriet Nannings Prinsenstraat 8 (Grachtengordel west) ☎020/620 7672. Pricey designer clothes for women, mostly casual chic. Classy handbags and jewellery too. There's also a menswear shop just along the street at Prinsenstraat 15 (☎020/420 20 97). Mon 1–6pm, Tues–Sat 10.30am–6pm, Sun 10.30am–8pm.

Robin's Bodywear Nieuwe Hoogstraat 20 (Old Centre) ☎020/620 11522. Great lingerie and swimwear shop, with all the designer names and good, personal service. Mon noon–6pm, Tues–Sat 11am–6pm.

Rodolfo's Magna Plaza mall (Old Centre) ☎020/623 1214. Huge collection of skates and skateboards, plus the latest matching fashions. Mon 11am–7pm, Tues–Sat 10am–6pm (Thurs till 9pm), Sun noon–7pm.

Sissy Boy Leidsestraat 15 (Grachtengordel south) ☎020/623 8949. Simply designed but classy and affordably priced clothes for men and women. A number of designer labels are featured here. Also at Kalverstraat 199 (☎020/626 0088; Old Centre) and Van Baerlestraat 12 (☎020/672 0247; Museum Quarter and Vondelpark). Mon noon–6pm, Tues–Sat 9.30am–6pm (Thurs till 9pm), Sun noon–5pm.

Solid Haarlemmerdijk 20 (Jordaan and Western docklands) ☎020/627 4114. Interesting and hip womenswear from designers such as Moschino, Kenzo and Chlöe. Mon 1–6pm, Tues–Sat 10am–6pm (Thurs till 7pm).

Secondhand clothes

Daffodil Jacob Obrechtstraat 41 (Museum Quarter and Vondelpark) ☎020/679 5634. Right behind the Concertgebouw, this store sells secondhand designer labels only. Tues–Fri noon–6pm, Sat noon–5pm.

Jojo Huidenstraat 23 ☎020/623 3476 (Grachtengordel west). If you're hankering after a natty suit with a certain vintage cut, this charmingly antiquated gentlemen's outfitters has plenty. There are also shirts and ties in a myriad of colours plus some rather nifty accessories. Mon noon–6pm, Tues–Sat 11am–6pm, Sun 2–6pm.

🏃 **Lady Day** Hartenstraat 9 (Grachtengordel west) ☎020/623 5820, ⓦwww.ladyday-vintage.com. A wide-ranging selection of secondhand and vintage fashion in this spacious store, where the wares aren't too crammed in. *Lady Day* also has a good military section, with old sailors' wide-leg pants and military dress jackets, plus the usual 50s-to-80s array of men's and women's fashion. Mon–Sat 11am–6pm (Thurs till 9pm), Sun 1–6pm.

🏃 **Laura Dols** Wolvenstraat 6 & 7 (Grachten-gordel west) ☎020/624 9066, ⓦwww.lauradols.nl. Top dog on the vintage fashion scene, *Laura Dols* is split into two shops opposite each other on Wolvenstraat. One has rails groaning under the weight of countless dresses all sorted according to colour to make things easier for the seasoned buyer. There is a multitude of vintage pieces for both women and men here, including some excellent swimwear ranging from the 40s to the 80s, stunningly printed fabrics from the 50s and 60s, and piles of vintage pillowcases, tablecloths and even tea towels. There's also a superb selection of children's and baby clothes where tiny sailor suits and delicious 1940s baby smocks share space with fancy-dress outfits and accessories. But the quality vintage pieces are across the road in the rather stylish sister store, where pages of high-end fashion magazines featuring *Laura Dols'* clothes adorn the walls. Prices are high, but not unaffordable for 20s flapper dresses, 30s hats and 50s skirts. Mon–Sat 11am–6pm (Thurs till 9pm), Sun 1–6pm.

Second Best Wolvenstraat 18 (Grachtengordel west) ☎020/422 0274. Most things here are from the last fifteen years, so don't expect to dig out a 50s prom dress from the racks of classy cast-offs. There is, however, some great modern(ish) stuff to be found if you're prepared to rummage – and pay a little over the odds. Mon 1–6pm, Tues–Sat 11am–6pm.

🏃 **Zipper** Huidenstraat 7 (Grachtengordel west) ☎020/623 7302. *Zipper* has

mainly cheap and cheerful stuff from the 60s, 70s and 80s, and is great for jeans. Pay attention though, as they stock new clothes alongside the vintage ones and that 60s-style shift dress may not be all that it seems. They also have a good selection of accessories, both vintage and modern. Mon–Sat 11am–6pm (Thurs till 9pm), Sun 1–5pm. Also in the Old Centre at Nieuwe Hoogstraat 8 (same hours; ☎020/627 0353).

Shoes, bags and other accessories

Body Sox Leidsestraat 35 (Grachtengordel south) ☎020/422 3544. Socks, tights and stockings in every conceivable colour and design. Mon–Sat 10am–6pm, Sun noon–5pm.

Dr Adam's P.C. Hooftstraat 90 (Museum Quarter and Vondelpark) ☎020/662 38 35. One of the city's widest selections of fashionable shoes. Also at Leidsestraat 25 (☎020/626 44 60; Grachtengordel south). Sun & Mon noon–6pm, Tues–Sat 10am–6pm (Thurs till 9pm).

The English Hatter Heiligeweg 40 (Old Centre) ☎020/623 4781, ⓦwww.english-hatter.nl. Ties, hats and various other accessories, alongside classic menswear, from shirts to cricket sweaters. Mon noon–5.30pm,

Tues–Fri 9am–5.30pm (Thurs till 9pm), Sat 9am–5pm, Sun noon–5pm.

Fred de la Bretonière St Luciensteeg 20 ☎020/623 4152; Utrechtsetstraat 77 ☎020/626 9627 (both Grachtengordel south). Designer famous for his high-quality handbags and shoes, all sold at reasonable – or at least affordable – prices. Both shops Mon 1–6pm, Tues–Fri 10am–6pm (Thurs till 7pm), Sat 10am–5pm; St Luciensteeg store also Sun noon–5pm.

De Grote Tas Oude Hoogstraat 6 (Old Centre) ☎020/623 0110. Family-run store now in the third generation, selling a wide selection of serious bags, briefcases and suitcases. Tues–Fri 9am–6pm, Sat 9am–5pm.

Hoeden M/V Herengracht 422 (Grachtengordel west) ☎020/626 3038, ⊛www.hoeden-mv.com. Pricey designer hats galore, from felt Borsalinos to straw Panamas. Gloves and umbrellas too. At Leidsestraat. Tues–Fri 11am–6pm (Thurs till 9pm), Sat 11am–5pm.

Jan Jansen Rokin 42 (Old Centre) ☎020/625 1350, ⊛www.janjansenshoes.com. This famous Dutch designer sells handmade shoes with frivolous designs. Tues–Sat 11am–5pm.

🏃 **Shoebaloo PC Hoofstraat 80 (Museum Quarter and Vondelpark)** ☎020/671 2210. Perhaps the city's coolest shoe shop for both men and women, with other branches at Koningsplein 7 (men's; Grachtengordel south) and Leidsestraat 10 (women's & children's; Grachtengordel south). All stores Mon noon–6pm, Tues–Sat 10am–6pm (Thurs till 9pm), Sun 1–6pm.

Department stores and shopping malls

On the whole, Amsterdam's **department stores** are really rather insipid, and the same applies to most of the city's **shopping malls**, the bulk of which are consigned to the suburbs. An exception is **Magna Plaza**, a shopping mall imaginatively sited in the old, neo-Gothic post office building behind Dam Square at NieuwezijdsVoorburgwal 182, though even here the shops themselves – comprising the usual big-brand stuff – don't match the setting.

De Bijenkorf Dam 1 (Old Centre) ☎020/552 1700. Dominating the northern corner of Dam Square, this is the city's top department store with an interesting history (see p.45), a huge bustling place whose name means "beehive". It's good for clothes, accessories and kids' stuff. Mon 11am–7pm, Tues & Wed 9.30am–7pm, Thurs & Fri 9.30am–9pm, Sat 9.30am–6pm, Sun noon–6pm.

HEMA Nieuwendijk 174 (Old Centre) ☎020/623 4176. A cross between Woolworths and Marks & Spencer, great for stocking up on all the important things you need – underwear, toiletries and other essentials, plus occasional designer delights. Surprises include wine and salami at the back of the shop, and a good bakery and cheese counter; great sweets too. Plus, their Fotoservice is convenient and promises same-day delivery. There's another branch at Kalverstraat 212 (Old Centre; ☎020/422 8988). Mon 11am–6pm, Tues–Sat 9.30am–6pm (Thurs until 9pm), Sun noon–6pm.

Maison de Bonneterie Rokin 140 (Old Centre) ☎020/626 2162. A venerable old department store that has somewhat reinvented itself as a hub of mainstream designer fashion. The building is attractive too, rising through balustraded balconies to a high central dome. There's also a small lunch café. Mon 11am–5.30pm, Tues–Sat 10am–6.30pm (Thurs until 9pm), Sun noon–5pm.

🏃 **Metz & Co Leidsestraat 34 (Grachtengordel south)** ☎020/520 7020. Large department store with floor upon floor of clothing, furniture and household appliances. The rooftop café offers a particularly enjoyable view over the city centre. Mon 11am–6pm, Tues–Sat 9.30am–6pm (Thurs till 9pm), Sun noon–5pm.

Peek & Cloppenberg Dam 20 (Old Centre) ☎020/623 2837. Less a department store than a multistorey clothes shop with some painfully middle-of-the-road styles. Nonetheless, this remains an Amsterdam institution. Mon 1–6pm, Tues–Sat 9.30am–6pm (Thurs till 9pm), Sun noon–6pm.

Vroom & Dreesmann Kalverstraat 203 (entrance also from Rokin; Old Centre) ☎020/622 0171.

The main Amsterdam branch of a middle-range nationwide chain, near Muntplein. It's pretty unadventurous, but take comfort from the fact that the restaurant is quite outstanding (for a department store), and they bake fresh bread on the premises as well. Check out also the listening stands in the CD section on the top floor – the best place for a free Mozart recital with a canal view. Mon–Sat 11am–6.30pm, Tues–Sat 10am–6.30pm (Wed until 9pm), Sun noon–6pm.

Food and drink

While the city centre's supermarkets may not impress, there's also a whole host of **speciality food stores** where you can buy anything from local fish to imported Heinz baked beans. The **wine and spirits shops** below have been chosen for their location, their specialities – or simply because they're good value.

Supermarkets

Supermarkets are thin on the ground in central Amsterdam and most – apart from Albert Heijn's flagship store (see below) – are crowded and cramped. If you're buying **fruit and vegetables**, note you'll usually need to weigh and price them yourself (unless a price is given per item, *per stuk*); put them on the scale, press the little picture, then press BON to get a sticky barcode. If you're buying beer, juice or water in **bottles** (glass or plastic); a deposit of €0.10–0.50 will be added on at the checkout; you get it back when you return the empties – to a different store if you like.

Albert Heijn NZ Voorburgwal 226 (Old Centre) ☏020/421 8344. Located just behind Dam Square, this is the biggest of the city's forty-odd Albert Heijn supermarkets. None of them takes credit cards. There are other central branches at Koningsplein 4 (Grachtengordel south); Vijzelstraat 113 (Grachtengordel south); Westerstraat 79 (Jordaan and Western docklands); Haarlemmerdijk 1 (Jordaan and Western docklands); Overtoom 454 (Museum Quarter and Vondelpark). Mon–Sat 8am–10pm, Sun 11–7pm.

Dirk van den Broek Marie Heinekenplein 25 (De Pijp, outer districts) ☏020/611 0812. Beats Albert Heijn hands down in everything except image. Cheaper across the board; bigger too. Trams #16, #24 or #25; more branches dotted around the suburbs. Mon–Fri usually 9am–9pm, Sat 9am–8pm.

De Natuurwinkel Weteringschans 133 (Grachtengordel south) ☏020/638 4083,

Night shops

Most **night shops** (*avondwinkels*) open when other stores are starting to think about closing up, and they stay open until well into the night – which sounds great, but you have to pay for the privilege: essentials can cost a barefaced three times the regular price. There are one or two exceptions, but most are located a fair walk from the city centre and may take time to seek out. For a complete list, see the Gouden Gids (Yellow Pages) under "*avondverkoop*". Bear in mind also that Albert Heijn supermarkets (see above) are mostly open until 10pm Monday to Saturday.

Dolf's Willemsstraat 79 (Jordaan and Western docklands) ☏020/625 9503. One of the better night shops; it is expensive, but reasonably central, tucked away in a corner of the Jordaan. Mon–Sat 3pm–1am, Sun 10am–1am.

Sterk De Clercqstraat 1–9 (Jordaan and Western docklands) ☏020/618 1727. Less a night shop than a city-centre institution, with all kinds of breads and pastries baked on the premises, a large fresh produce section, a deli and friendly staff. Beats the pants off most regular supermarkets. On the far side of the Jordaan from the Old Centre via Rozengracht. Daily 9am–1am.

www.denatuurwinkel.com. Main branch of a chain selling only organic food. Much better-tasting fruit and vegetables than anywhere else; also grains, pulses, Bon Bon Jeanette chocolates and superb bread. Also at Haarlemmerdijk 174 (Jordaan and Western docklands) and smaller branches around town. Mon–Sat 8am–8pm, Sun 11am–7pm.

Beer, wine, spirits and water

The **legal age** at which you can be sold beer is 16; for wines and spirits you need to be 18. The Dutch word for an off-licence (liquor store) is *slijterij*.

De Bierkoning Paleisstraat 125 (Old Centre) ☏020/625 2336. The "Beer King" is aptly named: 950 different beers, with the appropriate glasses to drink them from – just in case you thought beer-drinking could be taken lightly. Mon 1–7pm, Tues–Fri 11am–7pm (Thurs until 9pm), Sat 11am–6pm, Sun 1–6pm.

Le Cellier Spuistraat 116 (Old Centre) ☏020/638 6573. The largest wine, beer and spirits shop in the centre of the city, with a huge selection. Tues–Fri 9.30am–6pm, Sat 9.30am–5.30pm.

Chabrol Haarlemmerstraat 7 (Jordaan and Western docklands) ☏020/622 2781, **www.chabrolwines.com**. Excellent selection of wines (over 1500) and champagne, plus extremely knowledgeable staff. Mon–Sat 9.30am–7.30pm, Sun noon–6pm.

Gall & Gall Nieuwezijds Voorburgwal 226 (Old Centre) ☏020/421 8370. The most central branch of the largest chain of wine merchants in Amsterdam, with a good choice of wines and regular tastings. Good range of *jenevers* (Dutch gins) too. Amongst others, there are also outlets at Joden-breestraat 23 (☏020/428 70 60; Jewish Quarter and Eastern docklands); and Rozengracht 72 (☏020/624 46 66; Jordaan & Western docklands). Mon–Sat 9am–6pm, Sun noon–5pm.

Vintner Otterman Keizersgracht 300 (Grachtengordel west) ☏020/625 5088. Medium-sized, notably unpretentious store selling a first-rate selection of French wines. At Beren-straat. Mon 1–6pm, Tues–Fri 10.30am–6pm, Sat 10.30am–5.30pm.

Waterwinkel Roelof Hartstraat 10 (Oud Zuid, Outer districts) ☏020/675 5923, **www.springwater.nl**. Every type of mineral water imaginable. Mon noon–6pm, Tues–Fri 10am–6pm, Sat 10am–5pm.

Bread, pastries and chocolates

Amsterdam has a bevy of **bread and pastry shops**: a *warme bakkerij* sells bread and rolls baked on the premises, a *banketbakkerij* pastries and cream cakes. Specialist **chocolatiers** are much less common, but several of them are quite simply outstanding.

Bakkerij Paul Année Runstraat 25 (Grachtengordel west) ☏020/623 5322. The best wholegrain and sourdough breads in town, bar none – all made from organic grains. Mon–Fri 9am–6pm, Sat 9am–5pm.

J.G. Beune Haarlemmerdijk 156 (Jordaan and Western docklands) ☏020/624 8356. Long-established chocolatier with enticing window displays. Mon–Fri 8.30am–6pm, Sat 8.30am–5pm.

Crumbs Haarlemmerstraat 108 (Jordaan and Western docklands) ☏020/528 6430. Contemporary bakers and supplier to many of the city's restaurants. Wide assortment of breads baked on the premises, plus a smart café at the back. Mon 1–6pm, Tues–Fri 8.30am–6.30pm, Sat 9am–5pm.

Lanskroon Singel 385 (Grachtengordel west) ☏020/623 7743. Famously good pastry shop, with a small area for on-the-spot consumption. Near the south end of Spuistraat. Mon–Fri 8am–5.30pm, Sat 9am–5.30pm, Sun 10am–5pm.

Pompadour Chocolaterie Huidenstraat 12 (Grachtengordel west) ☏020/623 9554. Delicious chocolates and lots of homemade pastries (usually smothered in or filled with chocolate). Mon–Fri 9am–6pm, Sat 8.30am–5pm.

Puccini Singel 184 (Grachtengordel west) ☏020/427 8341, **www.puccinibomboni.com**. Arguably the best chocolatier in town, selling a wonderfully creative range of chocs in all shapes and sizes. This mini-chain has also abandoned the tweeness of the traditional chocolatier for brisk, modern decor. At the junction of Oude Leliestraat. Sun & Mon noon–5pm, Tues–Sat 11am–6pm. Also at Staalstraat 17 (Old Centre), ☎020/626 5474; Mon noon–6pm, Tues–Sat 9am–6pm, Sun noon–5pm.

▽ Puccini

Cheese

Arxhoek Damstraat 19 (Old Centre) ☎020/622 9118. Centrally situated general cheese shop. Mon–Fri 9am–6pm, Sat 9am–5pm, Sun noon–4pm.

De Kaaskamer Runstraat 7 (Grachtengordel west) ☎020/623 3483. Friendly shop with a comprehensive selection of Dutch cheeses, plus international wines, cheeses and olives. Mon noon–6pm, Tues–Fri 9am–6pm, Sat 9am–5pm, Sun noon–5pm.

Kaasland Haarlemmerdijk 1 (Jordaan and Western docklands) ☎020/625 7945. As the name suggests, this shop offers a huge selection of cheeses, plus breads and sandwiches. Mon–Fri 8am–6.30pm (Thurs till 8pm), Sat 8am–5pm, Sun 10am–7pm.

Coffee and tea

Geels & Co Warmoesstraat 67 (Old Centre) ☎020/624 0683. Oddly situated among Warmeosstraat's loud bars and porn shops, this is one of the city's oldest and best-equipped coffee and tea specialists, with low prices on beans and utensils – and fantastically stocked with coffees and teas. It also has a small museum of coffee upstairs. Mon–Sat 9.30am–6pm.

Levelt Prinsengracht 180 (Grachtengordel west) ☎020/624 0823. This specialist tea and coffee company has occupied the same premises for over 150 years and, although there are now Levelts dotted across the city, this is the best. Friendly service too. At Westermarkt. Mon noon–6pm, Tues–Fri 10am–6pm, Sat 10am–5pm.

Delis and imported foods

Eichholtz Leidsestraat 48 (Grachtengordel south) ☎020/622 0305. Old-fashioned store specializing in imported foods from Britain and the US – the only place to find Oreo cookies, Pop Tarts and Heinz beans. Mon 9am–6pm, Tues–Sat 9am–6.30pm (Thurs till 9pm), Sun noon–6pm.

Olivaria Hazenstraat 2a (Jordaan and Western docklands) ☎020/638 3552. Olive oil – and nothing but. Incredible range of oils, all self-imported from small- and medium-sized concerns around the world. Expert advice and a well-stocked tasting table. Mon 1.30–6pm, Tues–Sat 11am–6pm.

Oriental Commodities Nieuwmarkt 27 (Old Centre) ☎020/626 2797. Large and warren-like Chinese supermarket. All sorts of stuff is squirrelled away in corners – seaweed, water chestnuts, spicy prawn crackers. Get there early for the handmade tofu. Mon–Sat 9am–6pm, Sun 9am–5pm.

Fish and seafood

Although there are lots of fresh herring and **seafood stalls** dotted around the city at strategic locations, including one or two excellent ones in the Albert Cuypmarkt (see p.236), perhaps the best is the award-winning **Bloemberg** on Van Baerlestraat, just along from the Van Gogh Museum. Others worth trying are on the corner of Singel and Haarlemmerstraat, Singel and Raadhuisstraat, and Utrechtsestraat and Keizersgracht.

Organic and natural food

De Aanzet Frans Halsstraat 27 (De Pijp, Outer districts) ☎020/673 3415. Small, organic co-operative supermarket in De Pijp. Mon–Fri 9am–6pm, Sat 9am–5pm.

De Belly Nieuwe Leliestraat 174 (Jordaan and Western docklands) ☎020/330 94 83. Small and friendly shop stocking all things organic, including beer. Mon–Fri 9am–6pm, Sat 9am–5pm.

Boerenmarkt See p.237. Weekly organic farmers' market.

De Groene Weg Huidenstraat 11 (Grachtengordel west) ☎020/627 91 32. Organic butcher. Mon–Fri 9am–6pm, Sat 9am–5pm.

De Natuurwinkel See p.229. The city's widest selection of organic and natural food.

De Weegschaal Jodenbreestraat 20 (Old Jewish Quarter and Eastern docklands) ☎020/624 1765. Small, friendly natural food shop near the Waterlooplein flea market. Mon–Fri 9am–6pm, Sat 9am–5pm.

Music

The price of **CDs** in Amsterdam is higher than in Britain – and outrageous compared to the US. Where the city scores points, however, is in its variety: there are lots of small, low-key independent shops specializing in one type of music or another and it's here you can uncover vintage items unavailable elsewhere. If it's **vinyl** you're after, on the other hand, you've come to the wrong city. Some places still sell records, but it's very much taken for granted that music comes on CD. The main exception is the **Waterlooplein flea market** (see p.237), which has stacks of old records – and CDs – on offer.

Back Beat Records Egelantiersstraat 19 (Jordaan and Western docklands) ☎020/627 1657, ⓦwww.backbeat.nl. Small specialist in

soul, blues, jazz, funk, etc, with a helpful and enthusiastic owner. Mon–Sat 11am–6pm.

Blue Note Gravenstraat 12 (Old Centre) ☎020/428 1029. A great selection of jazz records and CDs. Tues–Sat 11am–7pm, Sun noon–5pm.

Boudisque Haringpakkersteeg 10–18, off Niuewendijk (Old Centre) ☎020/623 2603. One of the city's best record stores, with a good selection of metal, reggae, world music and dance – and reasonable rock and pop too. Sun & Mon noon–6pm, Tues–Sat 10am–6pm (Thurs till 9pm).

Broekmans & Van Poppel Van Baerlestraat 92–94 (Museum Quarter and Vondelpark) ☎020/675 6979, ⓦwww.broekmans.com. Specialists in classical and opera CDs and sheet music, of which they have perhaps the best selection in the city. Mon 10am–6pm, Tues–Fri 9am–6pm, Sat 9am–5pm.

Brutus Molensteeg 8 (Old Centre) ☎020/420 1605. A good selection of CDs and even some good old vinyl in this small funky store just off Spuistraat.

Concerto Utrechtsestraat 54 (Grachtengordel south) ☎020/623 5228, ⓦwww.concertomania.nl. New and used records and CDs in all categories; equally good on baroque as on grunge. One of the best all-round selections in the city, with the option to listen before you buy. Mon–Sat 10am–6pm (Thurs till 9pm), Sun noon–6pm.

Distortion Records Westerstraat 244 (Jordaan and Western docklands) ☎020/627 0004, ⓦwww.distortion.nl. Secondhand independent shop with vinyl everywhere. Tues–Fri 11am–6pm (Thurs till 9pm), Sat 10am–6pm.

Fame Kalverstraat 2 (Old Centre) ☎020/638 2525. The only large music warehouse in town; predictable selection of CDs and tapes. Books and computer games too. Mon–Sat 10am–7pm (Thurs till 9pm).

Free Record Shop Kalverstraat 32 & 230 (Old Centre) ☎020/626 5808. One of the better pop/rock chains. No vinyl. Also at Leidsestraat 24 (Grachtengordel south), Centraal Station and Nieuwendijk 229 (both Old Centre).

Smart shops

Riding on the coat-tails of Amsterdam's liberal policy towards cannabis are a number of what have become known as **"smart shops"**. Ostensibly established as outlets for "smart" drugs (memory enhancers, concentration aids, and so on), they do most of their business selling natural alternatives to hard drugs such as LSD, speed or ecstasy – as well as a variety of natural aphrodisiacs. These substitutes often have many or all of the effects of the real thing, but with greatly reduced health risks – and the added bonus of legality. A consistently popular alternative to LSD are psychotropic or **"magic" mushrooms**, which grow wild all over northern Europe, but when processed or dried are classified as hard drugs and are thus illegal. **Conscious Dreams** (see below) was forced to fight a court case over its sale of magic mushrooms, but by reclassifying its business as a greengrocery it was permitted to continue its sale of fresh magic mushrooms (dried ones remain illegal). It also retains its role at the centre of a knowledgeable Amsterdam underground devoted to exploring altered states of consciousness.

Conscious Dreams Kokopelli Warmoestraat 12 (Old Centre) ☎020/421 7000, ⓦwww.consciousdreams.nl. Magic mushrooms, aphrodisiacs, herbal remedies and psychedelic experiences at this city-centre smart shop. Daily 11am–10pm.

Dreamlounge Kerkstraat 113 (Grachtengordel south) ☎020/626 6907, ⓦwww.consciousdreams.nl. A small smart shop, sister of Conscious Dreams, and with Internet facilities. Sun & Mon noon–6pm, Tues–Sat 11am–9pm.

The Magic Mushroom Gallery Spuistraat 249 (Old Centre) ☎020/427 5765, ⓦwww.magicmushroom.com. One of the city's oldest smart shops, with the usual array of sexual stimulants, hallucinogens, pipes and basic drug accessories – and of course mushrooms.

When Nature Calls Keizersgracht 508 (Grachtengordel south) ☎020/330 0700, ⓦwww.whennaturecalls.nl. Another shop selling cannabis products such as hemp chocolate and beer, plus seeds and mushrooms. At the corner of Leidsestraat. Mon–Sat 10am–1pm, Sun 11am–10pm.

Get Records Utrechtsestraat 105 (Grachtengordel south) ☎020/622 3441, ⓦwww.getrecords.nl. Sizeable selection of independent and alternative CDs, plus some vinyl. Check out also the deceptively small R&B section in the back of the shop. Sun & Mon noon–6pm, Tues–Sat 10am–6pm.

Killa Cutz Nieuwe Nieuwstraat 19 (Old Centre) ☎020/428 4040. Specializes in all the latest techno and electronic music. Mon 1–6pm, Tues–Sat 11am–6pm, Sun 3–6pm.

Kuijper Klassiek Ferdinand Bolstraat 6 (De Pijp, Outer districts) ☎020/679 4634, ⓦwww.kuijperklassiek.nl. Classical music and Royal Concertgebouw recordings on CD and DVD. Mon 1–6pm, Tues–Fri 10am–6pm, Sat 10am–5pm.

Phantasio 2e Tuindwarssatraat 53 (Jordaan and Western docklands) ☎020/421 7110. Large

shop with a good collection of mainstream alternative music – CDs only – and a "listening table" equipped with headphones. Good for flyers. Mon–Fri 11am–7pm (Thurs & Fri till 8pm), Sat 10am–7pm, Sun noon–6pm.

South Miami Plaza Albert Cuypstraat 116 (De Pijp, Outer districts) ☎020/662 2817. Large hall specializing in Portuguese and Surinamese music, but plenty of other styles too, along with CDs, posters and DVDs. Mon–Sat 9am–6pm.

Speciality shops

Perhaps more than any other city in Europe, Amsterdam is a great source of idiosyncratic little shops devoted to one particular product or special interest. What follows is a selection of the city's more distinctive offerings.

3-D Holograms Grimburgwal 2 (Old Centre)
⊤020/624 7225. All kinds of holographic art, big and small – and erotic too. Tues–Fri noon–6pm, Sat noon–5.30pm, Sun & Mon 1–5.30pm.

Absolute Danny OZ Achterburgwal 78 (Old Centre)
⊤020/421 0915. A so-called "erotic lifestyle store", specializing in rubberwear, bondage gear, basques, etc.

Ajax Fan Shop Arena Boulevard 1–3 (Outer Districts)
⊤020/311 1688. Official club shop selling the current strips and sportsgear, as well the usual hats and duvet covers. There's also an unofficial outlet at Kalverstraat 86 (Grachtengordel west) if you can't be bothered to schlep all the way out to the stadium. Mon–Sat 9.30am–5pm, last Sun of the month 10am–5pm, match days 10am until five minutes before kick-off.

Akkerman Kalverstraat 149 (Old Centre)
⊤020/623 1649. The city's poshest pen shop, with an excellent selection of writing accessories. Mon–Fri 10am–5.45pm (Thurs until 9pm), Sat 10am–5pm, Sun 11am–5pm.

Appenzeller Grimburgwal 3 (Old Centre)
⊤020/616 6865. State-of-the-art designer jewellery, watches and spectacles. Tues–Sat 11am–5.30pm.

Baobab Elandsgracht 105 (Jordaan and Western docklands)
⊤020/626 8398, ⓦ www.baobab-aziatica.nl. Textiles and ceramics from Indonesia and the Far East, plus a huge selection of well-priced silver jewellery. Tues–Sun 11am–6pm.

Bloembollenwinkel Prinsengracht 112 (Grachtengordel west)
⊤020/421 0095, ⓦ www.amsterdamtulipmuseum.com. Charming little shop selling packets of tulip bulbs in season, as well as cards and gifts such as tulip-patterned pillows and pottery. Downstairs is a small museum that charts the tulip's history from the gardens of the Ottoman Empire to its role as Amsterdam's most iconic flower. Tues–Sun 10am–6pm.

Condomerie Het Gulden Vlies Warmoesstraat 141 (Old Centre)
⊤020/627 4174. This shop sells condoms of every shape, size and flavour imaginable (and unimaginable) – all in the best possible taste. Mon–Sat 11am–6pm.

Coppenhagen Rozengracht 54 (Jordaan and Western docklands)
⊤020/624 3681. The only thing you'll find here is beads and beady accessories – including everything you need to make your own jewellery. Mon 1–6pm, Tues–Fri 10am–6pm, Sat 10am–5pm.

Delftshop Rokin 44 (Old Centre)
⊤020/620 0000, ⓦ www.delftshop.com. If you're after that elusive present and don't want to settle for tourist tat, this is the place – a great selection of delftware, from small ashtrays and trinkets for €2 to more elaborate designs such as the €7500 replica of a tulip vase held in the Rijksmuseum. Other branches at Spiegelgracht 13 (Grachtengordel south) and Prinsengracht 440 (Grachtengordel west). Mon–Sat 9.30–6pm, Sun 11am–6pm.

Demmenie Sports Marnixstraat 2 (Jordaan and Western docklands)
⊤020/624 3652, ⓦ www.demmeniesport.nl. Large sports shop spread over two floors, selling everything you could need for hiking, camping and wilderness survival. Mon 1–6pm, Tues–Fri 10am–6pm (Thurs till 7pm), Sat 10am–5pm.

Peter Doeswijk Vijzelgracht 11 (Grachtengordel south)
⊤020/420 3133, ⓦ www.peterdoeswijk.nl. Idiosyncratic, brightly coloured, street-art style miscellany, from phones and toilet seats to painted wooden canal houses in wobbly mirror shapes – much, much better than the usual tourist stuff. Opening times vary – ring ahead to check.

Droog Design Staalstraat 7 (Old Centre)
⊤020/523 5050, ⓦ www.droogdesign.nl. Founded in 1993, Droog Design has made a serious contribution to the international reinvention of design. Some of their products, such as their milk bottle chandelier, have ended up in museum collections; this is their gallery and shop. Tues–Sat noon–6pm.

Fair Trade Shop Heiligeweg 45 (Old Centre)
⊤020/625 2245, ⓦ www.fairtrade.nl. Fair trade goods of all kinds – food, household items, books and cards. Mon 1–6pm, Tues–Fri 10am–6pm (Thurs till 9pm), Sat 10am–5.30pm, Sun noon–5pm.

Frozen Fountain Prinsengracht 629 (Grachtengordel south) ⓣ020/622 9375, ⓦwww.frozenfountain.nl. Contemporary furniture and interior design with the emphasis on all things Dutch. At Leidsegracht. Mon 1–6pm, Tues–Fri 10am–6pm, Sat 10am–5pm.

Gamekeeper Hartenstraat 14 (Grachtengordel west) ⓣ020/638 1579, ⓦwww.gamekeeper.nl. The place to go if you're into games. All kinds of "fantasy" games, mainly for adults, from Games Workshop to role-play games, collectible cards, backgammon, magic accessories, etc. Sun & Mon noon–6pm, Tues–Fri 11am–7pm, Sat 10am–6pm.

Gerda's Runstraat 16 (Grachtengordel west) ⓣ020/624 2912, ⓦwww .gerdasflowers.com. Amsterdam is full of flower shops, but this one is the most imaginative and sensual. Bouquets to melt the hardest of hearts. Mon–Fri 9am–6pm, Sat 9am–5pm.

P.G.C. Hajenius Rokin 92 (Old Centre) ⓣ020/623 7494. Long-established tobacconist selling its own and other brands of cigars, tobacco, smoking accessories, and every make of cigarette you can think of. There's also a room at the back where you can sit and smoke and have a coffee as you view the amazing range of cigars, pipes and smoking accessories, and even leaf through a magazine or book from its library. Mon noon–6pm, Tues–Sat 9.30am–6pm (Thurs till 9pm), Sun noon–5pm.

The Head Shop Kloveniersburgwal 39 (Old Centre) ⓣ020/624 9061. Every dope-smoking accessory you could possibly need, along with assorted marijuana memorabilia. Mon–Sat 11am–6pm.

Hera Candles Overtoom 402 (Museum Quarter and Vondelpark) ⓣ020/616 2886. A wonderful little all-wood shop selling nothing but handmade candles of all shapes, sizes and scents. Tues–Fri 11am–6pm, Sat 11am–5pm, Sun noon–5pm.

Himalaya Warmoesstraat 56 (Old Centre) ⓣ020/626 0899. Something of an oasis of calm in the Red Light District, this cosy shop has a wide selection of books and magazines from around the world, with New Age music, tarot cards and bric-a-brac, as well as readings, a changing photo/art exhibition, and a café with a terrace and canal view out back. Mon noon–6pm, Tues–Sat 10am–6pm (Thurs till 10pm), Sun noon–5.30pm.

Jacob Hooij Kloveniersburgwal 10–12 (Old Centre) ⓣ020/624 3041. Homeopathic chemist with any amount of herbs and natural cosmetics, as well as a huge stock of *drop* (Dutch liquorice). In business at this address since 1778 – and the shop and its stock seem as if they are the same now as then. Mon 1–6pm, Tues–Fri 10am–6pm, Sat 10am–5pm.

Joe's Vliegerwinkel Nieuwe Hoogstraat 19 (Old Centre) ⓣ020/625 0139. Kites, frisbees, boomerangs, diabolos, yo-yos, juggling balls and clubs. Mon 1–6pm, Tue–Fri 11am–6pm, Sat 11am–5pm.

Kitsch Kitchen Rozengracht 8 (Jordaan and Western docklands) ⓣ020/622 8261, ⓦwww. kitschkitchen.nl. Crammed full of chunky furniture, bowls and kitsch home stuff, plus bags, aprons, umbrellas and diaries, all in bright primary colours. Mon–Sat 10am–6pm.

't Klompenhuisje Nieuwe Hoogstraat 9a (Old Centre) ⓣ020/622 8100. Amsterdam's best and brightest array of clogs and kids' shoes. Mon–Sat 10am–6pm.

Kramer and Pontifex Reestraat 20 (Grachtengordel west) ⓣ020/626 5274. On one side of the shop, Mr Kramer repairs old broken dolls and teddies; on the other, Pontifex sells all kinds of candles, oils and incense. Mon–Fri 10am–6pm, Sat 10am–6pm.

Kruiderij De Munt Vijzelstraat 1 (Grachtengordel south) ⓣ020/624 4533. A very wide range of herbal remedies, essential oils, teas and dietary supplements. Mon 1–6pm, Tues–Fri 11am–6pm, Sat 11am–5.30pm.

Posthumus Sint Luciensteeg 23 (Old Centre) ⓣ020/625 5812. Upmarket stationery, cards and, best of all, hundreds of rubber stamps. Mon noon–5pm, Tues–Fri 9am–5pm, Sat 11am–4pm.

De Roos PC Hooftstraat 183 (Museum Quarter and Vondelpark) ⓣ020/689 0081, ⓦwww.roos. nl. New Age bookshop with a wide selection of esoteric books, crystals and remedies. Part of a larger centre with a café (see p.190) and lots of training/learning courses.

 Santa Jet Prinsenstraat 7 (Grachtengordel west) ☎020/427 2070. Handmade Latin American items, from collectables to humorous knick-knacks to religious icons – and a selection of hand-painted skulls. Mon–Fri 11am–6pm, Sat 10am–5pm, Sun noon–5pm.

Tibet Winkel Spuistraat 185a (Old Centre) ☎020/420 4538, ⓦwww.tibetwinkel.nl. Books, music, jewellery and more, all made by Tibetan refugees in Nepal and India. The Tibet Support Group (☎020/623 7699) can give travel advice, information on Tibetan restaurants in Holland, and on anything else concerned with Tibet. Mon 1–6pm, Tues–Sat 10am–6pm, Sun noon–5pm.

Tikal Hartenstraat 2a (Grachtengordel west) ☎020/623 2147. Colourful textiles and jewellery from Mexico and Guatemala. Mon 1–6pm, Tues–Fri 11am–6pm, Sat 11am–5.30pm

't Winkeltje Prinsengracht 228 (Grachtengordel south) ☎020/625 1352. Jumble of bargain-basement glassware and crockery, candlesticks, antique tin toys, kitsch souvenirs, old apothecaries' jars and flasks. Perfect for browsing. At Reestraat. Mon 1–5.30pm, Tues–Fri 10am–5.30pm, Sat 10am–5pm.

 Witte Tandenwinkel Runstraat 5 (Grachtengordel west) ☎020/623 3443. The "White Teeth Shop" sells wacky toothbrushes and just about every dental hygiene accoutrement you could ever need – and then some. Mon 1–6pm, Tues–Fri 10am–6pm, Sat 10am–5pm.

 Wonderwood Rusland 3 (Old Centre) ☎020/625 3738, ⓦwww.wonderwood.nl. Claims to be a cross between a shop and a gallery, and it certainly is a good place to browse, packed as it is with vintage furniture designs in wood from the 1940s to the 1960s – as well as its own creations based on the classics. Wed–Sat noon–6pm.

Markets

 Albert Cuypmarkt Albert Cuypstraat (De Pijp, Outer districts). The city's principal

▽ Albert Cuypmarkt

general goods and food market, with some great bargains to be had – including slick fashionwear and shoes. Mon–Sat 9am–5pm.

Amstelveld Prinsengracht, near Utrechtsestraat (Grachtengordel south). This market sells flowers and plants, but with much less of a scrum than the Bloemenmarkt. Mon 10am–3pm.

Artplein Spui (Old Centre). Low-key but high-quality art market, with much lower prices than you'll find in the galleries; prints and occasional books as well. March–Oct Sun 10am–6pm.

Bloemenmarkt Singel, between Koningsplein and Muntplein (Grachtengordel south). Flowers and plants, ostensibly for tourists, but regularly frequented by locals. Bulbs for export (with health certificate). Some stalls open on Sunday as well. Mon–Sat 8.30am–5pm.

Boerenmarkt Noordermarkt, next to the Noorderkerk (Jordaan and Western docklands). Organic farmers' market selling all kinds of produce, plus amazing fresh breads, exotic fungi, fresh herbs and homemade mustards. Sat 9am–4pm.

Kunstmarkt Thorbeckeplein, south of Rembrandtplein (Grachtengordel south). Quality art market with more reasonable prices than you'll find in the galleries; vintage books too. Mar–Oct Sun 10am–6pm.

Lindengracht Lindengracht, south of Brouwersgracht (Jordaan and Western docklands). Rowdy and raucous general household supplies market, a complete switch from the gentility of the neighbouring Boerenmarkt (see above). Sat 8am–4pm.

Noordermarkt Noordermarkt, next to the Noorderkerk (Jordaan and Western docklands). Junk-lover's goldmine, full of all kinds of bargains, tucked away beneath piles of useless rubbish. Get there early. Mon 9am–1pm.

Waterlooplein Waterlooplein, behind the Stadhuis (Old Jewish Quarter and Eastern docklands). A real Amsterdam institution, and the city's best flea market by far. Sprawling and chaotic, it's the final resting place for many a pair of yellow corduroy flares; but there are more wearable clothes to be found too, and some wonderful antique/junk stalls to root through. Secondhand vinyl too. Mon–Sat 9am–5pm.

Westermarkt Westerstraat, from the Noorderkerk onwards (Jordaan and Western docklands). Another general goods market, though the emphasis here is on fabrics and textiles, roll after roll of the stuff. Very popular with the Jordaan locals. Mon 8am–1pm.

Gay and lesbian Amsterdam

I n keeping with the Dutch reputation for tolerance, no other city in Europe accepts **gay people** as readily as Amsterdam, a liberalism that is displayed publicly at any of the gay events and festivals organized throughout the year; Amsterdam Pride is a huge occasion on the gay calendar, as are Queen's Day and the many memorial days that take place around the **Homomonument**. And, with the Dutch willingness to speak English, French and just about any other language, Amsterdam has become a magnet for the international gay scene – a city with a good network of advice centres, bars, clubs and cinemas. The **COC** (pronounced "say-oh-say"), the national gay and lesbian pressure group, celebrated its sixtieth birthday in 2006 – one of the longest-lived, and largest, groups of its kind in the world, and there are a number of smaller organizations representing the city's ethnic groups which also run regular workshops and events.

Homosexuality was decriminalized in the Netherlands way back in 1811; a century later – still sixty years ahead of the UK – the gay **age of consent** was reduced to 21, and in 1971 it was brought into line with that of heterosexuals at 16. In 2001 the Netherlands were again at the vanguard of gay and lesbian liberties, when the country legalized **same-sex marriages** and introduced non-discriminatory adoption rights.

Gay couples have full legal rights, and it is maybe a mark of the level of acceptance of gay lifestyles in mainstream Dutch society that every year there is a party in Amsterdam for Holland's gay and lesbian civil servants. It also says much for the strength of the gay community that the arrival of **AIDS** was not accompanied by the homophobia seen in many other places. Rather than close down clubs and saunas, the city council has funded education programmes, encouraged the use of condoms, and has generally displayed a non-judgmental attitude towards the issue of HIV and homosexuality.

Gay men in Amsterdam are much better catered for than **lesbians,** however. Although there is a sizeable lesbian community, the city lacks strictly women-only establishments, and the lesbian scene is largely limited to a few women-only nights held in otherwise male or mixed clubs.

The city has four recognized gay areas: **Reguliersdwarsstraat**, with its trendy bars and clubs, is the best known, attracting a young, lively and international crowd, while quieter **Kerkstraat** is populated as much by locals as visitors, and includes a smattering of straight venues. The streets just north of **Rembrandtplein** and along the Amstel are a camp focus, as well as being home to a number of traditional Dutch pubs and rent-boy bars, while **Warmoesstraat**, in the heart of the Red Light District, is cruisey and mainly leather-oriented.

Same-sex couples holding hands and kissing in the streets are no more worthy of comment than straight couples. **Cruising** is generally tolerated in places where it's not likely to cause offence, such as in known gay areas, and most bars and clubs have **darkrooms**, which are legally obliged to provide safe sex information and condoms.

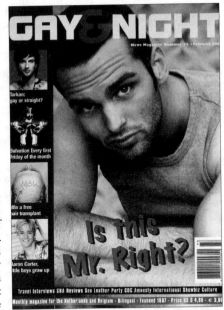

△ *Gay and Night* magazine

If you want more information, get hold of a copy of the free **Amsterdam Gay Map** for visitors, published by the producers of the monthly magazine **Gay News** (€3), both of which can be picked up from the COC (see p.240) or from most of the bars and shops listed in this chapter. Their website ⓦ www.gayamsterdam.com is also a good resource for bar and club listings. Another free map is the **Friends Gaymap Amsterdam**, available online at ⓦ www.gaymap. info. You could also purchase a copy of *The Bent Guide To Gay & Lesbian Amsterdam* (€9.95), a practical and witty **guidebook** written in English by the volunteers of Pink Point (see p.240) and available from the booth at Westermarkt or from bookshops listed on p.245. Among the many local gay **newspapers and magazines**, *Gay & Night* (ⓦ www.gay-night.nl), which appears monthly and costs €3.60 in newsagents (or free in a number of bars and shops), features interviews, news and film reviews. The fortnightly *Gay Krant* (€2.95; ⓦ www.gaykrant.nl) has all the details you could conceivably need, including up-to-the-minute listings, though it is in Dutch only. Flyers and brochures for parties and gay-oriented shops can be found in most gay bars and businesses.

Resources and contacts

In addition to the organizations and centres listed below, two important sources of information on the gay and lesbian scene are the **Gay and Lesbian Switchboard** (☎020/623 6565; ⓦ www.switchboard.nl; Mon–Fri noon–10pm, Sat & Sun 4–8pm), an English-speaking service which provides help and advice on all manner of things including where to go out in Amsterdam, and **MVS Radio** (Ⓦ www.mvs.nl), Amsterdam's gay and lesbian radio station, which broadcasts Monday to Saturday from 7pm to 8pm on 106.8FM (or 88.1 via cable), with the English-language talk show *Alien* on Sunday from 6pm to 8pm.

COC Rozenstraat 14 (Jordaan and Western docklands) ☎ 020/626 3087, Ⓦ www .cocamsterdam.nl. Amsterdam branch of the national gay and lesbian organization, offering advice and contacts. Mon–Fri 10am–4pm.

Gala ☎ 020/676 2317, Ⓦ www.gala-amsterdam. nl. Organization responsible for Pink Point and the various Homomonument Festivals, including those on Queen's Day, Roze Wester and Amsterdam Pride, and the popular twice-monthly parties at *The Eagle* (see p.242).

Homodok (The Documentation Centre for Lesbian and Gay Studies) Nieuwpoortkade 2a (Jordaan and Western docklands) ☎ 020/606 0712, Ⓦ www.ihlia.nl. A major archive of all forms of literature, as well as videos and photographs, relating to lesbian and gay studies, contemporary and historical. Prospective visitors should write several weeks ahead detailing areas of interest. Tues, Thurs & Fri by appointment only.

Pink Point Near the Homomonument, Wester-markt (Jordaan and Western docklands) Ⓦ www. pinkpoint.org. This free advice and informa-tion point run by a team of knowledgeable volunteers offers practical information about where to go and what to do in the city, and is stocked with flyers and brochures, as well as a range of souvenirs and T-shirts. Also publishes the excellent *Bent Guide*. Daily 11am–6pm.

Schorer Sarphatistraat 35 (Grachtengordel south) ☎ 020/573 9444, Ⓦ www.schorer.nl. Gay and lesbian counselling centre offering professional and politically conscious advice on identity, sexuality and lifestyle (Mon–Fri 10am–4pm; July & Aug noon–4pm). Its clinic, held at the Municipal Health Depart-ment, provides STD examinations and treatment.

Stichting Tijgertje ☎ 06/1024 9026, Ⓦ www. tijgertje.nl. Information on gay and lesbian sports clubs throughout Amsterdam.

Wild Side Rozenstraat 14 (Jordaan and Western docklands) Ⓦ www.wildside.dds.nl. An informed lesbian S&M group which holds regular open meetings, workshops and parties, and provides support and education for women who wish to find out more about S&M.

Accommodation

The city's **gay-friendly hotels** are reviewed below and are marked on the colour maps at the back of the book. Prices are for the cheapest double in high season (see also p.164). While there are no women-only hotels, two unofficial, privately run bed-and-breakfasts – *Johanna's* (p.171) and *Liliane's Home* (p.241) – cater for gay women, though all the places listed below are lesbian-friendly. Note that it's illegal for any hotel to refuse entry to anyone on the grounds of sexual orientation.

Old Centre

Anco Oudezijds Voorburgwal 55 ☎ 020/624 1126, Ⓦ www.ancohotel.nl; 10min walk from CS. Small and friendly hotel in the Red Light District, with a private bar catering exclu-sively to leather-wearing gay men. There are three- and four-person dorms (€43 per person) with shared facilities and a studio with private bathroom and kitchenette. Booking advised. Doubles with shared facili-ties €90.

Centre Apartments Heintje Hoekssteeg 27 ☎ 020/627 2503, Ⓦ www .gayapartmentsamsterdam.com; 5min walk from CS. Private self-catering studios and

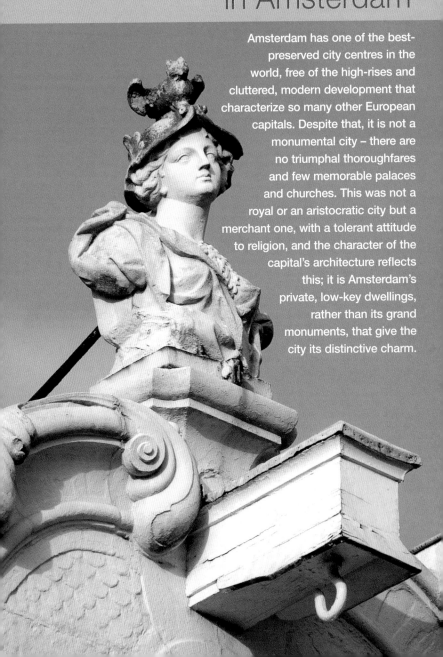

Architecture
in Amsterdam

Amsterdam has one of the best-preserved city centres in the world, free of the high-rises and cluttered, modern development that characterize so many other European capitals. Despite that, it is not a monumental city – there are no triumphal thoroughfares and few memorable palaces and churches. This was not a royal or an aristocratic city but a merchant one, with a tolerant attitude to religion, and the character of the capital's architecture reflects this; it is Amsterdam's private, low-key dwellings, rather than its grand monuments, that give the city its distinctive charm.

Beginnings

Amsterdam was a great site for a trading city, bang on the confluence of two rivers. But in other respects it was a terrible choice – like many Dutch towns, a flat and waterlogged plain, in which buildings needed to be supported by thousands of wooden piles bashed into the sandy soil. There aren't many houses left from the medieval city, but one or two landmarks survive. Just across from Centraal Station, the wooden house at **Zeedijk 1** – now home to the *In 't Aepjen* bar – is one of very few timber buildings still left, dating back to around 1550, while not far from here, one of Amsterdam's oldest surviving buildings is the **Oude Kerk**, dating from the 1300s. Deeper into the city centre, the **Houten Huys** in the **Begijnhof** dates from 1477, and still boasts its original Gothic timber frontage.

The Golden Age

Brick became the building material of choice from the late sixteenth century onwards, and buildings began to acquire the distinctive **gables** that adorn houses all over the city. The earliest type was the step-gable; the house at **Oudezijds Voorburgwal 14** is a good example of this early Renaissance style, with its stone embellishments on red brick. The gable soon developed – most notably under the greatest Dutch architect of the period, **Hendrick de Keyser** (1565–1621) – into a more distinctively "Amsterdam" form, in which the previously plain step-gables were decorated with stonework and sculpture. One of the most lavish examples is the double-step-gabled residence at **Singel 140–142** – where Captain Banning Cocq (the principal figure in Rembrandt's *The Night Watch*) lived – built in 1600 by de Keyser himself.

The seventeenth century saw a dramatic surge in the city's population, partly due to its prosperity, and partly to the refugees who arrived here from other parts of the crumbling Spanish empire – and the city required a major **expansion** if it was successfully to absorb its newcomers. This was an exercise in city planning which was way ahead of its time, using as it did the expansion to create the

Herengracht

graceful sweep of canals you see today. It was also the heyday of Dutch architecture, and Hendrick de Keyser, among others, left their mark with a series of trailblazing works, such as the **Huis Bartolotti** at Herengracht 170–172, with its heavily ornate step-gables, as well as two of the city's most characteristic seventeenth-century churches: the **Westerkerk**, on the Prinsengracht canal, and the **Zuiderkerk**, just off the Kloveniersburgwal canal.

De Keyser's distinctive Westerkerk tower was finished by his successor as the leading city architect, **Jacob van Campen** (1595–1657), who brought overseas – particularly Italian – influences to his work. He is best known for building Amsterdam's new town hall in 1665, now the **Royal Palace** – a more restrained building than its predecessors, exhibiting the Palladian proportions that the architect had absorbed in Italy.

Van Campen's contemporary, **Philip Vingboons** (1607–78), was responsible for a good number of the private houses on the by now burgeoning city extension, many of them sporting the fashionable neck-gable – basically a slimmed-down version of the step-gable; some particularly appealing examples can be seen at **Herengracht 168** and the Cromhouthuizen at **Herengracht 364–370**.

Zuiderkerk

The nineteenth century

The eighteenth century was a relatively uneventful time in Amsterdam, but in the nineteenth century the city developed a distinctive new style, partially spearheaded by

Centraal Station

Petrus J.H. Cuypers (1827–1921), famed for his neo-Gothic creations. Cuypers not only built the deliberately monumental **Centraal Station** on what was then the edge of the Old Centre, but also contributed a series of buildings in the outskirts – not least the **Rijksmuseum**, which was purpose-built as the country's national museum, and shouts from its gabled rooftops the importance of tradition and the legacy of Dutch art.

The turn of the century ushered in further changes with the international, modern style of **Hendrik Petrus Berlage** (1856–1934), exemplified in his **Beurs**, on the Damrak, exhibiting all the attributes of a restrained yet highly decorative vision. Berlage's work inspired the **Amsterdam School**, a group of architects working in the city in the early twentieth century, led by **Piet Kramer** (1881–1961) and **Michael de Klerk** (1884–1923). The movement's keynote building was de Klerk's **Het Schip** housing complex of 1920, on the western edge of the centre – bolder and more expressive than the work of Berlage.

Contemporary Amsterdam

Modern Amsterdam is changing fast, with new developments constantly adding to the city's architectural variety. The largest and perhaps most influential of these are the **docklands** schemes to the west and east of the city centre, where some of the city's long-neglected waterways are being transformed into a modern-day version of the seventeenth-century master plan. The docklands to the east, and **Zeeburg** in particular, are home to some of the city's most exciting new architecture – a mixture of renovated warehouses and assertive new structures, most notable among which is the avant-garde **Muziekgebouw**, which opened in 2005. There are also some clever, contemporary takes on the traditional Dutch waterfront on **Java Island**, whose modern terraces and curvy bridges evoke the canal houses of the city centre – and as such bring the city's architectural story full circle.

The Eastern docklands

Muziekgebouw

apartments for rent in the middle of the Old Centre. No reception. Minimum three nights stay. From €125 for a studio, apartments from €140.

Stablemaster Warmoesstraat 23 ①020/625 0148, ⓦ www.stablemaster.nl; 5min walk from CS. Small, exclusively male, gay hotel above a bar in the heart of the Red Light action known for its wild "jack off" parties (see p.242). English-speaking staff. Spacious apartment with fridge, TV and coffeemaker €150. Single and a triple also available. Double €95.

Grachtengordel west

Waterfront Singel 458 ①020/421 6621, ⓦ www. waterfront.demon.nl. Tram #1, #2 or #5 to Koningsplein. Smart, value-for-money hotel with ten decent rooms on a major canal (you'll pay more for a canal view) close to the Flower Market, shopping and nightlife. Triples also available. €120

Grachtengordel south

Amistad Kerkstraat 42 ①020/624 8074, ⓦ www. amistad.nl. Tram #1, #2 or #5 to Koningsplein. Stylish and cosy gay hotel, conveniently located for the Kerkstraat area. Each room is equipped with soft lighting, snug duvets, TV, fridge, minibar and safe. Standard rooms come without shower; deluxe room (€145) has a bathtub and stereo. Breakfast is served in a convivial communal room 9am–1pm, which later becomes a public Internet lounge. From €89.

Golden Bear Kerkstraat 37 ①020/624 4785, ⓦ www.goldenbear.nl. Tram #1, #2 or #5 to Prinsengracht. Solid, well-managed budget option, with a good range of clean, comfortable rooms, some en suite; all with hand basin, safe and DVD player. Booking essential. From €74.

Orfeo Leidsekruisstraat 14 ①020/623 1347, ⓦ www.hotelorfeo.com. Tram #1, #2 or #5 to Prinsengracht. Very pleasant gay and lesbian hotel linked to an Italian restaurant round the back of Leidseplein, with decent breakfasts served until 11am. You can opt for a cheaper room sharing a shower, but en-suite rooms are also available, as are some triples and quads. €75

The Old Jewish Quarter and Eastern docklands

Liliane's Home Sarphatistraat 119 ①020/627 4006. Metro Weesperplein. This privately run B&B, owned by the aforementioned Liliane, has only two double rooms (both en suite) so you'll need to call first. €120

The Museum Quarter and the Vondelpark

Sander Jacob Obrechtstraat 69 ①020/662 7574, ⓦ www.hotel-sander.nl. Tram #16 to Jacob Obrechtstraat. Right behind the Concertgebouw, this spacious, pleasant hotel has twenty en-suite rooms; welcoming to gay men and women, and everyone else too. Triples and quads also available. Small bar open to guests only. €100

Nightlife and entertainment

The main nightlife areas in the Old Centre and the Grachtengordel are dotted with numerous **gay bars and clubs**. Some venues have both gay-only and mixed gay/straight nights, as noted. Pink Point (see opposite), near the Homomonument, has flyers and can provide good, reliable advice on where to go in the city, as can the website ⓦ www.nighttours.nl (in English), which features a guide to events, clubs and bars, as well as more general information on Amsterdam's gay scene. There are currently no clubs exclusively for lesbians, though lesbian-only nights are on the increase and the gay bars and clubs which welcome women are indicated below. Further information for women on where to go in Amsterdam can be obtained from the Gay and Lesbian Switchboard (see p.239) or from the nighttours website above. All bars are marked on the colour maps at the back of the book.

The only **cinema** that shows **gay films** on a regular basis is the Filmhuis Cavia (see p.217) which, in conjunction with De Balie (see p.215), hosts an annual event in December called **De Roze Filmdagen** ("Pink Film Days"; Ⓦ www.rozefilmdagen.nl), a mini-season of gay and lesbian movies. Call the Gay and Lesbian Switchboard (see p.239) for details of gay movies showing around town, or take a look at the AUB's *Uitlijst* (see p.206).

Bars

Old Centre

Anco Oudezijds Voorburgwal 55. Hotel leather bar with a large darkroom. Daily 9am–10pm.

Argos Warmoesstraat 95. Europe's oldest leather bar, with two bars and a cellar darkroom. Not for the faint-hearted. Mon–Thurs & Sun 10pm–3am, Fri & Sat 10pm–4am.

Casa Maria Warmoesstraat 60. Mixed gay bar in the heart of the Warmoesstraat scene. Over-25s only. Mon–Thurs & Sun noon–1am, Fri & Sat noon–2am.

Cuckoo's Nest Nieuwezijds Kolk 6. An ever-popular cruisey leather bar, this is described as "the best place in town for chance encounters". Vast and infamous darkroom. Mon–Thurs & Sun 1pm–1am, Fri & Sat 1pm–3am.

The Eagle Warmoesstraat 90. Long-established, if somewhat surly, leather bar popular with men of all ages. Hosts Gala-organized parties every second and last Sunday of the month from 4–8pm. Gets very busy after 1am. Darkroom in basement. Mon–Thurs & Sun 10pm–4am, Fri & Sat 10pm–5am.

Stablemaster Warmoesstraat 23. Small and very cruisey bar that attracts an older crowd. Well known for its regular "jack off" parties (nightly from 9pm); also has a hotel attached (see p.241). Mon, Thurs & Sun 9am–1am, Fri & Sat 9am–2am.

The Web St Jacobsstraat 6. Strict but friendly leather and bear bar and club that attracts an older crowd. Dance floor, darkrooms and a pool table. Mon–Thurs & Sun 1pm–2am, Fri & Sat 1pm–3am.

Why Not Nieuwezijds Voorburgwal 28 Ⓦ **www. whynot.nl.** Long-standing, intimate bar which puts on live shows (Fri & Sat 9–10pm), with a porn cinema and "boys'

club" above. Terrace open in summer. Mon–Thurs & Sun noon–1am, Fri & Sat noon–2am.

Grachtengordel south

April Reguliersdwarsstraat 37. On the itinerary of almost every gay visitor to Amsterdam. Lively and cosmopolitan bar, with a good selection of foreign newspapers, cakes and coffee, and a small dance floor at the back. Women welcome. Happy hour Mon–Sat 6–7pm and 11pm–1am and special 2-for-1 deals Sun 6–8pm. Open 2pm–1am (Fri & Sat till 3am).

Arc Reguliersdwarsstraat 44. Trendy, mixed, neon-lit club, with comfy couches, friendly bar staff and late-night dancing. Small fusion menu. Happy hour 5–7pm. Mon–Thurs & Sun 4pm–1am, Fri & Sat 4pm–3am.

Downtown Reguliersdwarsstraat 31. Popular café that's a favourite with visitors as well as locals. Relaxed and friendly, with inexpensive meals. Daily 10am–8pm.

Entre Nous Halvemaansteeg 14. Camp and often outrageous small bar. Can be packed at peak times, when everyone joins in the sing-alongs to cheesy Eighties music. Women welcome. Mon–Thurs & Sun 8pm–3am, Fri & Sat 8pm–4am.

Krokodil Amstelstraat 34. Amiable, noisy bar close to the discos and clubs around Rembrandtplein. Daily 4pm–1am (Fri & Sat till 3am).

Lellebel Utrechtsestraat 4. Small and popular drag-show bar, with a lively and cheerful atmosphere. Mon–Thurs 9pm–3am, Fri & Sat 8pm–4am, Sun 8pm–3am.

Mankind Weteringstraat 60. Quiet, non-scene, traditional Dutch bar away from the usual gay hangouts, with its own terrace beside the canal attracting locals and visitors alike. Inexpensive meals. Lovely in summer. Daily noon–midnight.

Mix Café **Amstel 50**. *Gezellig* Dutch bar, playing Top 40 and Europop. Mon–Thurs & Sun 8pm–3am, Fri & Sat 8pm–4am.

Montmartre de Paris **Halvemaansteeg 17**. A convivial brown café that's usually packed, with the emphasis on music and entertainment (courtesy of Whitney and Madonna); voted best gay bar by the readers of the *Gay Krant*. Happy hour 6–8pm. Open Mon–Thurs & Sun 5pm–1am, Fri & Sat 5pm–3am.

Rouge **Amstel 60**. Welcoming bar, popular with both tourists and locals. Mon, Thurs & Sun 4pm–1am, Fri & Sat 4pm–3am.

Sappho **Vijzelstraat 103**. Friendly café that not only attempts to fill the city's void of women-only venues, but manages to do it well. There's a small stage and the owner hosts a range of weekly and monthly nights. Tuesday is open mic night for singer/songwriters; Friday is women-only night; and every first Saturday of the month there's a mixed gay and lesbian club night. Small and cosy, the place fills up very quickly. Simple menu available until 10pm. Tues–Thurs & Sun 11am–1am, Fri & Sat 11am–3am.

De Spijker **Kerkstraat 4**. Friendly leather and denim bar showing porn movies, and with upstairs darkroom. Happy hour 5–7pm. Women welcome. Bingo every Sat from 6pm plus monthly leather parties (Sun from 7pm). Open Mon–Thurs 3pm–1am, Fri & Sat 1pm–3am, Sun 1pm–1am.

Vivelavie **Amstelstraat 7**. Small, campy bar patronized mostly, but not exclusively, by women, but gay men are very welcome. Quiet during the week, it gets packed at the weekend. Open noon–1am (Fri & Sat till 2am).

The Jordaan and Western docklands

Saarein **Elandsstraat 119**. Amsterdam's first women-only bar, *Saarein* finally opened its doors to men in 1999, though its clientele remains mostly female. Some of the former glory of this split-level café may be gone, but it's still a warm, relaxing place, with a cheerful atmosphere. Also a useful source of contacts and information. Open 5pm–1am (Fri & Sat till 2am). Closed Mon.

Clubs

Cockring **Warmoesstraat 96 (Old Centre)** ☏020/623 9604, ⊛www.clubcockring.com. One of Amsterdam's most popular – and cruisey – gay men's clubs with a small dance floor and bars on three floors. Expect lots of shirtless men dancing to techno. Strip shows Thurs, Sat & Sun from 1am. Get there early at the weekend to avoid queuing. 11pm–4am (Fri & Sat till 5am); entry €3.50–5.

Exit **Reguliersdwarsstraat 42 (Grachtengordel south)** ☏020/625 8788. A classic gay club ideally situated for the fall-out from the surrounding area's bars and cafés, with four bars each playing different music, from R&B to house, to an upbeat, cruisey crowd. Predominantly male, though women are admitted. Thurs 11pm–4am, Fri & Sat midnight–5am.

Getto **Warmoesstraat 51 (Old Centre)** ☏020/421 5151, ⊛www.getto.nl. Relaxed, local club-bar situated in the heart of the Red Light District, serving food and cocktails. Happy hour 5–7pm. Tarot readings every Sun from 8pm. Tues–Thurs 4pm–1am, Fri & Sat 4pm–2am, Sun 4pm–midnight.

Habibi Ana **Lange Leidsedwarsstraat 4 (Grachtengordel south)** ☏020/779 8420, ⊛www.habibiana.nl. Claiming to be the "first and only Arab gay bar in the world", this club has a small dance floor, with Arabian music and regular belly dance shows. Women welcome. Mon–Thurs & Sun 7pm–1am, Fri & Sat 7pm–3am.

De Trut **Bilderdijkstraat 165 (Jordaan and Western docklands)**. Housed in a former factory building, this popular squat venue holds a Sunday-night gay/lesbian-only dance party; there's a large dance floor, cheap drinks and a varied mix of music. Very popular with both men and women – the doors are closed at midnight and if you arrive after 11pm you may not get in. Its basement location means it can get very hot. 11pm–4am; €1.50.

Vrankrijk **Spuistraat 216 (Old Centre)** ⊛www.vrankrijk.org. Every Monday is "Blue Monday Queernight" in Amsterdam's most famous squat bar, which plays live alternative music from 9pm–1am.

You II Amstel 178 (Grachtengordel south) ☎ 020/620 4754, ⓦ www.youii.nl. Amsterdam's first – and long-awaited – lesbian, and members-only, dance club. Men are in fact welcome, as long as they're under female supervision. Fri & Sat 10pm–5am; entry Sat €5.

Events

The two leading events in Amsterdam's gay calendar are **Remembrance Day** (May 4) and **Liberation Day** (May 5), both of which prompt ceremonies and happenings around the Homomonument, symbolic focus of the city's gay community (see p.70). A few days before, there's **Queen's Day** (April 30),

△ Amsterdam Pride

when the whole town has a knees-up, with gay parties and drag acts hosted throughout the city, and the Roze Wester festival, commencing the evening of April 29 with the Drag Queen Olympics at the Homomonument, and ending on Liberation Day. Other events include **Leather Pride** (ⓦ www.leatherpride. nl), held in October and November, the infamous organized fetish parties, Trash (ⓦ www.clubtrash.com) and Wasteland (ⓦ www.wasteland.nl), held regularly throughout the year; look out for flyers in bars and shops.

The first **Amsterdam Pride** (ⓦ www.amsterdamgaypride.nl) took place in 1996 with street parties and performances, and is now one of the busiest annual events, with a "Canal Pride" flotilla of boats cruising down the Prinsengracht to musical accompaniment. If you're in the city the first weekend in August, keep an eye out for the parties in bars and clubs which take place over the weekend.

Finally, the old Amsterdam tradition of **Hartjesdag** ("Day of Hearts"; ⓦ www.hartjesdagen.nl), which ceased to be observed just before World War II, was rediscovered and then popularized by a researcher in Gay and Lesbian Studies at the University of Amsterdam. During the third weekend in August, it was once common for Amsterdammers to dress up in the clothes of the opposite sex, and, although the majority of the population have hardly flocked to the cross-dressing banner, nightclubs and bars around the Zeedijk and Nieuwmarkt often host a themed drag event during this weekend, including a drag parade on the Sunday from 4pm.

For more information on the above events or other special parties held throughout the year, see ⓦ www.nighttours.nl.

Shops and services

Bookshops

American Book Center Kalverstraat 185 (Old Centre) ☎ 020/625 5537, ⓦ www.abc.nl. Large general bookstore, with a fine gay and lesbian section. Mon–Sat 10am–8pm (Thurs till 9pm), Sun 11am–6.30pm.

Intermale Spuistraat 251 (Old Centre) ☎ 020/625 0009, ⓦ www.intermale.nl. Well-stocked gay bookshop, with a wide selection of English, French, German and Dutch literature, as well as cards, newspapers, magazines and DVDs. They have a worldwide mail order service. Mon 11am–6pm, Tues–Sat 10am–6pm (Thurs till 9pm), Sun noon–5pm.

Vrolijk Paleisstraat 135 (Old Centre) ☎ 020/623 5142, ⓦ www.vrolijk.nu. "The largest gay and lesbian bookstore on the continent", with a vast stock of new and secondhand books and magazines, as well as music and DVDs. Mon 11am–6pm, Tues–Fri 10am–6pm (Thurs till 7pm), Sat 10am–5pm, Sun 1–5pm.

Xantippe Unlimited Prinsengracht 290 (Grachtengordel west) ☎ 020/623 5854, ⓦ www. xantippe.nl. Small, general bookstore with an impressive range of books and resources by, for and about women, including a large lesbian section. Mon 1–7pm, Tues–Fri 10am–7pm, Sat 10am–6pm, Sun noon–5pm.

Sex shops and cinemas

Adonis Warmoesstraat 92 (Old Centre) ☎ 020/627 2959, ⓦ www.adonis-4men.info. This long-standing gay cinema (entry €7.50) also stocks toys, books and videos. Mon–Thurs & Sun 10am–1am, Fri & Sat 10am–3am.

Black Body Lijnbaansgracht 292 (Grachtengordel south) ☎ 020/626 2553, ⓦ www. blackbody.nl. Huge selection of rubber and leather, plus toys and much more. Online ordering service available. Mon–Fri 10am–6.30pm, Sat 11am–6pm.

Bronx Kerkstraat 53–55 (Grachtengordel south) ☎020/623 1548, 🌐www.bronx.nl. Strictly porn books, magazines and videos for men. Daily noon–midnight.

Christine le Duc Spui 6 (Old Centre) ☎020/624 8265, 🌐www.christineleduc.com. One of the least sleazy sex shops in Amsterdam, selling quality underwear and sex toys, with a good selection of DVDs for men and women. Mon–Fri 10am–9pm, Sat & Sun 10am–6pm.

Demask Zeedijk 64 (Old Centre) ☎020/620 5603, 🌐www.demask.com. Expensive rubber and leather fetish store for men and women. Mon–Fri 10am–7pm (Thurs till 9pm), Sun noon–5pm.

Drake's Damrak 61 (Old Centre) ☎020/627 9544. Gay porn cinema above a souvenir and sex shop. Entry €10, under-25s half price, free to under-20s. Daily 9am–midnight.

Female and Partners Spuistraat 100 (Old Centre) ☎020/620 9152, 🌐www.femaleandpartners.nl. Staffed by women and with an emphasis on products for women, this shop has a good selection of lingerie, plus an array of sex toys, with one of the best selections of vibrators in the city. Mon & Sun 1–6pm, Tues–Sat 11am–6pm (Thurs till 9pm).

Mantalk Reguliersdwarsstraat 39 (Grachtengordel south) ☎020/627 2525. Small shop with an enormous choice of quality underwear and T-shirts, which owing to its location is very popular with gay men. Mon 1–6pm, Tues–Sat 10am–6pm (Thurs till 9pm).

Mister B Warmoesstraat 89 (Old Centre) ☎020/422 0003, 🌐www.mrb.nl. Multi-level store selling rubber and leather clothing and sex toys. Piercing and tattoos by appointment. Mon–Fri 10am–6.30pm (Thurs till 9pm), Sat 11am–6pm, Sun 1–6pm.

RoB Amsterdam Weteringschans 253 (Grachtengordel south) ☎020/627 3220, 🌐www.rob.nl. Top-quality made-to-measure leather wear, with a worldwide mail order service. Mon–Sat 11am–7pm. A smaller branch – **RoB Accessories** (Mon–Fri noon–7pm, Sat noon–6pm, Sun 1–6pm) – is at **Warmoesstraat 32 (Old Centre)** ☎020/620 7719.

Robin and Rik Runstraat 30 (Grachtengordel west) ☎020/627 8924. Handmade, quality leather clothes and accessories. Mon 2–6pm, Tues–Sat 11am–6.30pm.

Stout Berenstraat 9 (Grachtengordel west) ☎020/620 1676, 🌐www.stoutinternational.com. A wide range of designer underwear and erotica for women in a smart environment and with helpful (female) staff. Mon–Fri noon–7pm, Sat 11am–6pm, Sun 11am–5pm.

Saunas

Sauna Damrak Damrak 54 (Old Centre) ☎020/622 6012. Centrally located gay men's sauna; €13.50, including towels. You can also get a private sauna for two for €33 per hour; towels extra. Mon–Fri 10am–11pm, Sat & Sun noon–8pm.

Thermos Day Sauna Raamstraat 33 (Jordaan and Western docklands) ☎020/623 9158, 🌐www.thermos.nl. Modern gay men's sauna, with steam room, swimming pool, sun beds, cinema, café and bar spread over five floors. Mon–Fri noon–11pm, Sat noon–10pm, Sun 11am–10pm; day pass €18, under-23s €13.50. There's also a beauty salon, offering facials, waxing, body treatments and massage (daily noon–8pm).

Thermos Night Sauna Kerkstraat 58–60 (Grachtengordel south) ☎020/623 4936, 🌐www.thermos.nl. Much the same facilities as the day sauna, with the exception of a pool and café. Cruisey atmosphere. Nightly 11pm–8am; night pass €18, under-23s €13.50.

13

Kids' Amsterdam

W
ith its canals, narrow cobbled alleys and – especially – trams, the novelty value of Amsterdam can prove entertaining enough for some kids. There's also a whole host of **attractions** specifically aimed at children, ranging from circuses and puppet theatres to urban farms and one of the best zoos in Europe, with a planetarium attached. There are also plenty of opportunities for play – practically all of the city's **parks** and most patches of greenery have some form of playground, and the recreation area in the Vondelpark is heaven for kids and parents alike.

You'll find most places pretty child-friendly; the majority of restaurants have highchairs and special children's menus, and bars don't seem to mind accompanied kids, as long as they're well-behaved. In short, having a small child in your care is unlikely to close doors to you in Amsterdam.

Though not all hotels welcome young children, this will be made clear to you when you book. If you require a **babysitting** service, contact Oppascentrale Kriterion (☏020/624 5848, daily 4.30–8pm, Mon also 9–11am; Ⓦwww.kriterionoppas.org), a long-established agency with a good reputation.

Activities

For older children, a good introduction to Amsterdam might be one of the **canal trips** that start from Centraal Station or Damrak. Much more fun, though, is a ride on a **canal bike**. This can get tiring, but jetties where these pedalo-style bikes can be picked up and dropped off are numerous, and it's quite safe; see p.25 for details. If your kids enjoy being on the water, you could also take them on a free **ferry ride** to Amsterdam Noord (only 5–10min away). The *Buiksloterwegveer* is a small, tug-like ferry, which leaves every twelve minutes or so (Mon–Sat 6.30am–11pm, Sun 11am–7pm) from behind Centraal Station

One area where Amsterdammers definitely need to try harder is in keeping **dog mess** off the streets and parks; the stuff is a major hazard, especially for kids. Although there are teams of street-cleaners armed with high-power hoses to regularly blast it off the pavement, wait another hour or two and there'll be more to replace it. Any patch of green space is obviously susceptible too, and unless an area is marked as being dog-free, you'd do well to keep one eye on your offspring and the other on your next step.

and travels back and forth to the north side of the River IJ. Cars aren't allowed, but you can take on bikes and motorbikes. For more details on the city's **canal cruises and bike tours**, see p.37.

For panoramic **views** of the city, try climbing the **tower** of the Westerkerk (summer only; see p.68). Alternatively, see Amsterdam on two wheels; it's possible to take the kids along when you're **cycling** around the city, by renting either a bike with a child seat attached, or a tandem, depending on the size of the child. Bike City at Bloemgracht 70 (℡020/626 3721) rents both types and gives friendly advice too.

In the winter, there's **ice skating** at the Jaap Eden IJsbanen (see p.256), which has indoor and outdoor rinks. If the canals are frozen over and you don't have any skates, just teeter along on the ice with everybody else; see p.255 for safety points before venturing out. Another option is **bowling**; the centre near the RAI complex has eighteen lanes and a café (see p.254).

The best **swimming pool** for kids is the indoor, tropical-style Mirandabad, De Mirandalaan 9 (℡020/546 4444; tram #25), which has all sorts of gimmicks such as wave machines, slides and whirlpools; there's also a separate toddlers' pool, and every Sunday (9am–4pm) is family day. In summer, the most popular outdoor pool is in the Flevopark; for details of this and other outdoor pools, see p.258.

Finally, **TunFun** (Mr Visserplein 7 ℡020/689 4300, ⓦwww.tunfun.nl; tram #9 from CS or #14 to Mr Visserplein), near the Portuguese Synagogue, is a large underground playground with slides, trampolines and climbing apparatus, for children aged 1 to 12. Activities include gymnastics, bowling and indoor football, as well as organized events such as discos and birthday parties, and there's plenty of equipment to clamber into, under and over. It's open daily from 10am to 6pm, and costs €7.50 for 1–12-year-olds (free for adults and under-1s). Children must be accompanied by an adult, but there's a café you can escape to if you feel you've seen one ball park too many.

Parks and farms

The city's most central park, the leafy and lawned **Vondelpark** (ⓦwww.vondelpark.nl; see p.124), has an excellent playground, as well as sandpits, paddling pools and a couple of cafés where you can take a break. *De Vondeltuin*, a café on the Amstelveen side of the park, rents out skates in the summer and is perfectly situated opposite the playground. Also in summertime, the open-air theatre, Openluchttheater (see p.124), usually puts on some free entertainment for kids – mime, puppets, acrobats and the like.

Most other city parks offer something to keep children entertained, the best being the **Gaasperpark**, located about 8km southeast of the centre (metro stop Gaasperplas), which has a play area and paddling pools. In the **Amsterdamse Bos** (ⓦwww.amsterdamsebos.nl; see p.134) you'll find playgrounds, lakes, cycle paths and a nature reserve with bison and sheep, and you can also rent canoes and pedaloes to explore the waterways, or visit the **Geitenhouderij Ridammerhoeve** (℡020/645 5034, ⓦwww.geitenhouderij.nl; March–Oct daily 10am–5pm, except Tues; Nov–Feb also closed Mon), an enjoyable mini-farm with a herd of goats and their kids. The visitors' information centre near the Bosbaan entrance has a kids' area and exhibitions about the park.

There are also plenty of **urban farms** dotted around the city – look in the phone book under *Kinderboerderij* for a full list. One of the best is the **Artis Zoo Children's Farm**, which can easily be visited as part of an Artis day out; see below for details of the zoo itself.

Theatres, circuses and funfairs

A number of **theatres** put on inexpensive (around €3–4) entertainment for children most afternoons. Furthermore, a fair proportion offer **mime**- or **puppet**-based shows, suitable for English-speakers: check the children's section ("Jeugdagenda") of the monthly *Uitkrant* (see p.206), and look for the words *mimegroep* and *poppentheater*. Public holidays and the summer season bring touring **circuses** and the occasional travelling **funfair** (*kermis*) to the city, usually setting up on Dam Square or in one of the city's many parks. Lastly, check out the **festivals** listings in Chapter Fifteen; many of them, such as the Queen's Birthday celebrations, are enjoyable for kids too.

Circustheater Elleboog Passeerdersgracht 32 (Jordaan and Western docklands) ☎020/623 5326, ⓦwww.elleboog.nl. This club runs regular courses for children aged 4 to 12 on how to juggle, walk the tightrope, unicycle and do conjuring tricks. Workshops also available for around €10 during school holidays. Students put on occasional shows at various venues around the city. Phone or email for full details of times and prices.
Deridas Hobbemakade 68 (Museum Quarter and Vondelpark) ☎020/662 1588. This excellent puppet theatre is great for under-6s. Shows are every Saturday at 3pm (4- to 12-year-olds) and Sunday at 11am & noon (2- to 6-

year-olds). Also the first Friday of the month 10.30am (2- to 6-year-olds) & 1.30pm (4- to 12-year-olds). Shows from €3. Booking essential.
De Krakeling Nieuwe Passeerdersstraat 1 (Jordaan and Western docklands) ☎020/624 5123, ⓦwww.krakeling.nl. Permanent children's theatre, with shows for youngsters up to the age of 18, often with an emphasis on full-scale audience participation. Performances are mostly in Dutch, though the theatre also puts on a number of dance performances which non-Dutch speakers will appreciate.

The zoo and museums

A trip to **Artis Zoo** is one of the best days out for kids in the city. The ticket price includes entry to the zoo and its botanical gardens, the Zoological Museum, the Geological Museum, the Aquarium and the Planetarium. You can also combine an Artis day out with a canal cruise; the Artis Express runs daily 10am–2pm every thirty minutes from Centraal Station to the zoo, including a detour through the city on the return journey (departs zoo hourly 2.15–5.15pm). A return ticket costs €20, or €16.75 for 3–9-year-olds, and includes entry to the zoo. Further information on ☎020/530 1090.

Artis Zoo Plantage Kerklaan 38–40 (Old Jewish Quarter and Eastern docklands) ☎020/523 3400, ⓦwww.artis.nl; metro Waterlooplein, tram #9, #10 or #14. Opened in 1838, this is the oldest zoo in the country, and it's now one of

the city's top tourist attractions, though thankfully its layout and refreshing lack of bars and cages mean that it never feels overcrowded. Highlights include an African savanna environment, huge aquariums and an aviary. In addition to the usual lions, monkeys and creepy-crawlies, there's also a children's farm where kids come nose-to-nose with sheep, calves, goats, etc. Feeding times always draw a crowd and take place at: 11am birds of prey; 11.30am and 3.45pm seals and sea lions; 2pm pelicans; 2.30pm crocodiles (Sun only); 3pm lions and tigers (not Fri); 3.30pm penguins. The on-site Planetarium has five or six shows daily, all in Dutch, though you can pick up a leaflet with an English translation from the desk. An English guidebook for the whole complex costs €2.50. No dogs allowed. Daily: April to mid-Oct 9am–6pm; mid-Oct to March 9am–5pm. Adults €17.50, 3- to 9-year-olds €14.

▽ Artis Zoo

Madame Tussaud's Dam 20 (Old Centre) ☏020/523 0623, ⓦwww.madametussauds.nl. Large waxworks collection with the usual smattering of famous people and rock stars, as well as Dutch celebrities and the royal family, plus a few Amsterdam peasants and merchants thrown in for local colour. Hardly

the high point of anyone's trip to the city, but some parts might be of interest to teenagers, such as Karaoke Corner, the "Models" zone…and the odd actor jumping out at you at unexpected moments. Daily 10am–5.30pm. Adults €19.95; 5- to 15-year-olds €14.95; family tickets available.

NEMO Oosterdok 2 (Old Jewish Quarter and Eastern docklands) ☏020/531 3233, ⓦwww.e-nemo.nl; bus #22 to Kadijksplein, 10min walk from CS. The whopping great green building that marks the entrance to the IJ tunnel is home to NEMO, a large, six-floor science and technology centre, whose interactive exhibits are geared towards children. Themed displays explore such topics as Why the World Works, Journey Through the Mind, Code Name DNA and Water Worlds. Interaction is encouraged and the whole experience is very hands-on. Labelling is in Dutch and English. Tues–Sun 10am–5pm, plus Mon during school holidays in July & Aug. €11.50, under-4s free.

Tropenmuseum Junior Inside the Tropenmu-seum, Linnaeusstraat 2 (Amsterdam Oost) ☏020/568 8233, ⓦwww.tropenmuseumjunior.nl; tram #9 from CS. Designed especially for children between the ages of 6 and 12, the museum's aim is to promote international understanding through exhibitions, tours and performances on other cultures. It's nowhere near as dry as it sounds, and although the show is in Dutch only, this is more than compensated for by the lively exhibits, which are expertly presented, and supported by music and dance perfor-mances, all designed to fascinate children, with lots of things for kids to get their hands on. Shows Sat, Sun & school holidays 12.30–2pm & 3–4.30pm, plus Wed 2.30–4pm; call to reserve. Adults €7.50, 6- to 17-year-olds €4, under-5s free.

Cafés and pancake houses

KinderKookKafé Vondelpark 6b/Overtoom 325 (Museum Quarter and Vondelpark) ☏020/625 3257, ⓦwww.kinderkookkafe.nl. A café run entirely by children aged 6 to 12 years old, who cook, wait tables and wash dishes (though there are adult staff on hand). The

food is fairly simple – pizzas, sandwiches, cakes – but the whole experience is worth it just for the novelty factor. During the week (9am–5pm) the café is open to all, unless closed for a party. Children are expected to bring two guests each, one of which must

▽ KinderKookKafé

be an adult. Booking essential at weekends (Sat 3.30pm, 8yrs +; Sun 12.30pm, 6yrs +).

Adults €10, 6- to 12-year-olds €5 (€10 if cooking), under-6s €2.50. **The Pancake Bakery Prinsengracht 191 (Grachtengordel west)** ☎020/625 1333. Busy, well-known pancake and omelette house that caters especially well for children. The pancakes are delicious, and kids are kept entertained at the table with pens, paper and novelty toys. Children's pancakes start at around €5.15 with toy; adults' pancakes start from €5 – but no toy. Mon–Fri noon–9.30pm.

Shops

Azzurro Kids P.C. Hooftstraat 122 (Museum Quarter and Vondelpark) ☎020/673 0457, Ⓦwww.azzurrokids.nl. Perhaps the city's chicest kids' clothes store, stocking labels such as Diesel, Replay, Armani and Baby Dior. Mon 1–6pm, Tues–Sat 10am–6pm (Thurs till 9pm), Sun noon–5pm.
De Beestenwinkel Staalstraat 11 (Old Centre) ☎020/623 1805, Ⓦwww.beestenwinkel.nl. Well-made stuffed toy animals, in all shapes and sizes. Mon noon–6pm, Tues–Fri 10am–6pm, Sat 10am–5.30pm, Sun noon–5.30pm.
De Bijenkorf Dam 1 (Old Centre) ☎020/552 1700. This department store has one of the best (and most reasonably priced) toy sections in town. Mon 11am–7pm, Tues & Wed 9.30am–7pm, Thurs & Fri 9.30am–9pm, Sat 9.30am–6pm, Sun noon–6pm.
Broer & Zus Rozengracht 104 (Jordaan and Western docklands) ☎020/422 9002, Ⓦwww.broerenzus.nl. Cool, urban streetwear and gifts with a funky twist for babies and children up to age eight, from T-shirts with logos to wooden toys and cute bags. The range includes the store's own clothing label plus a few mid-range Dutch children's designers. Mon noon–6pm, Tues–Fri 10.30am–6pm, Sat 10am–6pm.
De Geboortewinkel Bosboom Toussaintstraat 22 (Museum Quarter and Vondelpark) ☎020/683 1806, Ⓦwww.degeboortewinkel.nl. Specialists

in all kinds of stuff for new or expectant parents, from quality clothes and bedding to prams and furniture. Mon 1–6pm, Tues–Fri 10am–6pm, Sat 10am–5pm.
Intertoys Heiligeweg 26 (Old Centre) ☎020/638 3356, Ⓦwww.intertoys.nl. Amsterdam's largest toy shop, with branches throughout the city. Mon 11am–6pm, Tues–Fri 9.30am–6pm (Thurs till 9pm) Sat 9.30am–5.30pm, Sun noon–5pm.
De Kinderbrillenwinkel Nieuwezijds Voorburgwal 129–131 (Old Centre) ☎020/626 4091, Ⓦwww.kinderbrillenwinkel.com. Shop specializing in spectacles for children of all ages, with a selection of very stylish frames for all ages available next door at Marcel Barlag Visuals. Wed–Sat 11am–6pm (till 5pm Sat).
Kleine Nicolaas Cornelis Schuytstraat 19 (Oud Zuid) ☎020/676 9661. Good selection of handmade dolls and wooden toys. Mon–Sat 10am–6pm (till 5pm Sat).
Oilily P.C. Hooftstraat 131–133 (Museum Quarter and Vondelpark) ☎020/672 3361. This marvellous children's clothing chain has been dressing the luckiest Dutch kids in colourful, funky – and, let's face it, pretty expensive – outfits since the 1960s, and is still going strong here in its flagship Amsterdam location. Mon 1–6pm, Tues–Sat 10am–6pm (Thurs till 9pm).
Teuntje Haarlemmerdijk 132 (Jordaan and Western docklands) ☎020/625 3432, Ⓦwww.

teuntje.nu. Large shop stocking a wide range of prams and strollers, including models by Bugaboo and Easywalker, as well as carriers and highchairs. The store also sells toys, clothing (0–8yrs) and shoes. Mon 1–6pm, Tues–Fri 10am–6pm, Sat 10am–5pm.

Tinkerbell Spiegelgracht 10 (Grachtengordel south) ⓣ 020/625 8830, ⓦ www.tinkerbelltoys.nl. A wonderful shop full of old-fashioned toys, mobiles, models and kids' books, with all purchases beautifully gift-wrapped. Mon 1–6pm, Tues–Sat 10am–6pm.

Sports and activities

ost visitors to Amsterdam tend to confine their exercise to walking around the major sights, but if you do get the urge to stretch your muscles, there's a wide range of sports to enjoy. In winter – if it's cold enough – **skating** on the frozen waterways is the most popular and enjoyable activity; other winter sports are mostly played in private health or sports clubs, to which you can usually get a day pass, though many are well outside the city centre.

The chief spectator sport is **football**. Amsterdam is home to the legendary Ajax (pronounced "eye-axe") who play in the impressive ArenA stadium situated in the eastern suburbs. Less mainstream offerings include Holland's own *korfbal* and *carambole*. For up-to-the-minute details on all sporting activities in the city, call the city's sport and recreation information service on ☏020/552 2490 (Mon–Fri 9am–5pm), or go to ⓦwww.sport.amsterdam.nl, though this website is in Dutch only.

Baseball (Honkbal)

Local team the **Amsterdam Pirates** are in the top baseball division. They are based at Sportpark Ookmeer in Osdorp (☏020/616 2151; tram #17 then bus #19 or #192), 4km west of the centre. Matches take place on either Saturday or Sunday afternoons (2pm) in the summer, and most games are free.

Beaches

The Netherlands have some great sandy **beaches**, although it has to be admitted that the weather is notoriously unreliable. Temperatures can be bracing and the North Sea is pretty murky and often teeming with jellyfish. For swimming and sunbathing, the nearest resort is **Zandvoort** (see p.149), a couple of short train rides from Amsterdam (via Haarlem), but there are nicer, quieter stretches of coast nearby, most notably amidst the wild expanse of dune and beach that makes up the **National Park Zuid-Kennemerland** (see p.149); the park is easily reached by bus from Haarlem bus station.

Bowling

The closest bowling alley to the city centre is Knijn Bowling Centre, Schelde-plein 3, opposite the RAI complex (☎020/664 2211; Mon–Thurs 2–11pm, Fri 10am–midnight, Sat noon–12.30am, Sun 2–10pm; tram #4 or #25 from CS), with eighteen lanes and a café. Lanes cost between €18.50 and €26.50 per hour, with a maximum of six people per lane. Reservations recommended. Friday and Saturday evenings have "twilight bowling" (€11), accompanied by a DJ.

Football

It's a mark of the dominance of Amsterdam's **Ajax**, Eindhoven's **PSV** and Rotterdam's **Feyenoord** that most foreigners would be hard pushed to name any other Dutch football teams. More generally familiar perhaps is the Dutch style of play – based on secure passing with sudden, decisive breaks – which has made Dutch players highly sought-after all over Europe. Nevertheless, getting hold of tickets to watch Ajax play at their extravagant all-seater ArenA stadium in the suburbs of Amsterdam takes a little time and effort. You can't buy a ticket without a Clubcard, and although these only cost €6 for two years, you must apply in advance (☎020/3111 6666) and wait up to five weeks for your application to be processed. Having done all that, you can then buy your ticket (€15–47). Much easier for visitors from abroad is to book a package through Ajax Travel & Events (☎020/311 1940), which costs €35–50 and includes a guided tour of the grounds and entry to a match, though you'll still need to book your trip in advance.

Buying tickets for Feyenoord and PSV, whose grounds are both within easy striking distance of Amsterdam by public transport, is similarly awkward; most games require a club card, and limited numbers of tickets are available for visitors from abroad, purchased only by prior application. The football season runs from September to May, and matches are generally on Sundays at 2.30pm, with occasional games at 8pm on Wednesdays. Your best bet is to catch a game on screen in a bar. Try the *Globe* at Oudezijds Voorburgwal 3.

Ajax Amsterdam Amsterdam ArenA, Bijlmer ☎020/3111 4444, ⓦwww.ajax.nl. Metro Bijlmer.

Feyenoord Rotterdam Olympiaweg 50, Rotterdam ☎010/292 3888, ⓦwww.feyenoord.nl. Trains from Amsterdam stop near the ground.

PSV Eindhoven Frederan 10a, Eindhoviklaen ☎040/250 5505, ⓦwww.psv.nl. Matches are played at the Philips Stadium, a ten-minute walk from Eindhoven train station.

Dance and gyms

Dancestreet 1e Rozendwarsstraat 10 (Jordaan and Western docklands) ☎020/489 7676, ⓦwww.dancestreet.net. Dance and yoga centre offering a wide range of classes, from belly-dancing to flamenco, and various forms of yoga, as well as Pilates. Dance classes €10–12, yoga €12. Massage available. A café (11am–3pm & 5–11pm) overlooks the main studio.

Garden Gym Jodenbreestrat 158 (Old Jewish Quarter and Eastern docklands) ☎020/320 3666. This health club offers mainly classes (yoga, t'ai chi, Pilates and aerobics among others), as well as saunas, solarium and massage. Classes €9.50; sauna €11; class & sauna €13. Mon, Wed & Fri 9am–

10.30pm, Tues & Thurs noon–10.30pm, Sat & Sun 9am–5.30pm.
Splash Looiersgracht 26 (Jordaan and Western docklands) ☏ 020/624 8404. Very popular hi-tech fitness centre with sauna, tanning

salon, Turkish bath and a range of daily aerobic classes from €10 for non-members. Day pass €20; week pass also available. Mon–Fri 7am–midnight, Sat & Sun 7am–9pm.

Horse riding

Amsterdamse Manege Nieuwe Kalfjeslaan, Amstelveen (Nieuw Zuid) ☏ 020/643 1342, ⓦ www.amsterdamse-manege.com. The place for a ride in the Amsterdamse Bos – but only with supervision. You'll need your own boots and riding hat, and you must reserve ahead. An hour's lesson costs €18.50 for adults and €15 for under-18s. Mon–Thurs 8.30am–11pm, Fri 8.30am–10pm, Sat 8.30am–6pm, Sun 8.30am–5pm.

Hollandsche Manege Vondelstraat 140 (Museum Quarter and Vondelpark) ☏ 020/618 0942. Stables built in 1882 in neo-Renaissance style on the edge of the Vondelpark. Again, your own boots are required, though hats can be rented. A one-hour lesson costs €18.50 for adults, €15.50 for 11- to 17-year-olds, and €13.50 for under-11s. Group lessons also available.

Ice skating

Whenever the city's canals and waterways freeze over, local **skaters** are spoiled for choice, with almost every stretch of water utilized, providing an exhilarating way to whizz round the city – much more fun than a rink. Surprisingly, canal cruises continue even when the waterways are frozen over, with the boats crunching their way up and down the Prinsengracht, but they leave the Keizersgracht well alone, to be occupied by bundled-up Amsterdammers, who take to the ice in droves. Most locals have their own skates, and buying a pair from a department store will set you back over €100. Your best option is to visit one of Amsterdam's ice rinks (see p.256), which rent out their own skates.

Before you venture out onto the ice, however, take note of a few **safety points**:

• If no one's on the ice, don't try skating – locals have a better idea of its thickness.
• To gain confidence, start off on the smaller ponds in the Vondelpark.
• Be careful under bridges, where the ice takes longest to freeze.
• If the ice gives way and you find yourself underneath, head for the darkest spot you can see in the ice above – that's the hole.

Probably the easiest and safest option is to head for **Jaap Eden IJsbanen**, Radioweg 64 (Oct to mid-March: outdoor rink Mon–Fri 9.20am–4pm & 9–11pm (Wed night closed), Sat 2–4pm, Sun 11.40am–4pm; indoor rink daily 1–3.45pm & Sat also 8.40–11.30pm (disco skating), ☏ 020/694 9652; tram #9 from CS; €5.40), a large ice-skating complex to the east of the city centre, with an indoor and an outdoor rink. You can rent skates for €5 from Waterman Sport next door (☏ 020/694 9884), but only if you use them at Jaap Eden, and you're required to leave your passport or driving licence as a deposit.

One of the great events in Holland's sporting calendar is the annual **Elfstedentocht**, a race across eleven towns and 200km of frozen waterways in

Friesland, in the north of the Netherlands. If you're around in January and the ice is good, you'll hear talk of little else.

In-line skating

If you're equipped with skates or a skateboard, head for the free public **ramp** at the northeastern edge of the Museumplein (see p.114). For the more experienced skater there's also the free Friday Night Skate (Ⓦwww.fridaynightskate. nl), a fifteen-kilometre tour around Amsterdam, which takes place – weather permitting – every week at 8.30pm, departing from the Filmmuseum in the Vondelpark. You can **rent** skates, gear and boards at *De Vondeltuin* at the Amstelveen entrance of the Vondelpark (summer only; ☎020/664 5091); alter-

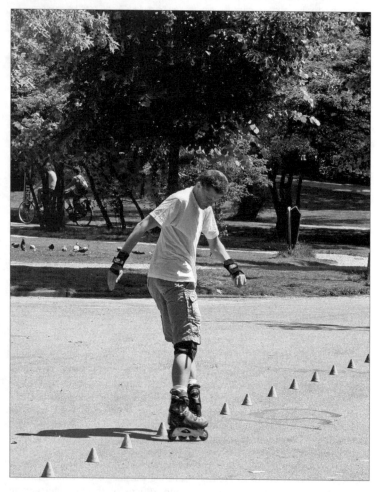

△ Skating in the Vondelpark

natively, buy your own pair at Rodolfo's skate shop (Sarphatistraat 59 ☎020/622 5488; also at Magna Plaza mall, ☎020/623 1214). If you're renting to skate around town, take care not to get stuck in the tram-tracks.

Korfbal

This is a home-grown sport, cobbled together from netball, basketball and volleyball, and played with mixed teams and a high basket. **Blauw Wit** (Ⓦ www. blauwwitamsterdam.nl) play at the Sportpark Sloten, off Sloterweg, southwest of the city (☎020/388 2374; tram #2 from CS), with matches usually held on Sundays from September to June.

Pool and carambole

A number of bars and cafés across the city have **pool** tables, although you may have to go to a hall to play snooker. A popular local variation on billiards (*biljart*) is **carambole**, played on a table without pockets. You score by *caroming* (rebounding) off the cue ball and the opponent's ball; the skill of some of the locals, often spinning the ball through impossible angles, is unbelievable in a misspent sort of way. You'll find tables dotted around the city in cafés, and you'll get plenty of advice on how to play if you so much as look at a ball.

Snooker and Pool Centre Van Ostadestraat 97 **(Oud Zuid). Tram #12 or from CS #25.** The first, third and fourth floors comprise the pool centre (Mon–Thurs 2pm–1am, Fri, Sat & Sun 2pm–2am; ☎020/676 7903), with 26 tables costing a flat rate of €8 per hour. The second floor is the snooker centre (same hours; ☎020/676 4059), which has seven tables at €8 per hour. There's also one

carambole table, charged at €8.50 per hour.
Snooker Centre de Keizer Keizersgracht 256 (Grachtengordel west) ☎020/623 1586. Nine high-quality snooker tables and two pool tables in a seventeenth-century canal house. Both games cost €8 per hour. Mon–Thurs noon–1am, Fri & Sat noon–2am, Sun 1pm–1am.

Saunas and flotation

Hammam Zaanstraat 88 (Jordaan and Western docklands) ☎020/681 4818, Ⓦ www .hammamamsterdam.nl. Situated north of the Westerpark (walk through the underpass near the northeast entrance, and turn left), this Turkish bath is a wonderful social institution for women only. Comprises hot and cold rooms and top-to-toe cleansing; other treatments such as full body scrub and massage also available. Entry costs €15. Tues–Fri noon–10pm, Sat & Sun noon–8pm.
Koan Float Herengracht 321 (Grachtengordel west) ☎020/555 0333, Ⓦ www.koan-float.com.

The place to come in Amsterdam to float in a large bath of warm water. Magnesium and sodium salt are added to aid muscular relaxation and provide buoyancy, and because the water is the same temperature as your body, the sensation is of floating freely. There are three soundproof individual floating cabins, each with its own shower; once you're inside, lights, music and clothing are optional. Advance reservations are essential. Prices start from €30 for 45min or €37.50 for an hour. The centre also offers massage. Towels and bathrobes are provided. Daily 9.30am–11pm.

Sauna Damrak **Damrak 54 (Old Centre)**
☎020/622 6012. Centrally located gay sauna, though women are also welcome at weekends. See p.246.

Sauna Deco **Herengracht 115 (Grachtengordel west)** ☎020/623 8215, ⊛www.saunadeco.nl.

Built in 1920, this is possibly Amsterdam's most stylish sauna and steam bath, with a magnificent Art Deco interior. Massage available. Entry costs €18 (€15 Mon, Wed–Fri noon–3pm); towels and bathrobes extra. No credit cards. Mon, Wed–Sat noon–11pm, Tues 3–11pm, Sun 3–7pm.

Swimming pools

It's a good idea to call before setting out to any of the pools (*zwembaden*) listed below, since certain times are set aside for small children, family groups or classes.

Flevoparkbad **Insulindeweg 1002 (Amsterdam Oost)** ☎020/692 5030. Tram #7 from Leidseplein or #14 from Dam Square. The best outdoor pool in the city; gets very busy on sunny days. May to early Sept daily 10am–5.30pm, until 7pm on warm days. Admission €2.55.

Mirandabad **De Mirandalaan 9 (Nieuw Zuid)** ☎020/546 4444. Superbly equipped swimming centre (outdoor and indoor

pools), with wave machine, whirlpools and slides. Admission €3.40.

Zuiderbad **Hobbemastraat 26 (Museum Quarter and Vondelpark)** ☎020/678 1390. Lovely old pool dating from the nineteenth century and refreshingly gimmick-free, though they do have a naturist hour on Sunday from 4.30 to 5.30pm. Pool opens 7am weekdays, Sat 8am, Sun 10am; phone for details, as hours vary according to age. Admission €3.

Tennis and squash

Most outdoor **tennis** courts are for members only, and those that aren't need to be reserved well in advance. Your best chance of getting a game at short notice is either at the open-air tennis courts in the Vondelpark, or at one of the following.

Frans Otten Stadion **IJsbaanpad 43 (Nieuw Zuid)** ☎020/662 8767, ⊛www.fransottenstadion.nl. Tram #6 from Leidseplein, #16 or #24 from CS. This complex has eight indoor and fifteen outdoor tennis courts, as well as 21 squash courts. Tennis courts €17.50–25 per hour; squash courts €16–21 per hour. Racket rental €2.50. Call ahead to reserve a court in the evening. Mon–Fri 9am–1am, Sat & Sun 9am–9pm.

Gold Star Tennis **Gustav Mahlerlaan 20 (Nieuw Zuid)** ☎020/644 5483, ⊛www.goldstar.nl. Near Vrije Universiteit, next to Station Zuid, tram #5

or #16. Twelve indoor and 24 outdoor tennis courts, for €21–25 per hour. Racket rental €2.50. Indoor courts daily 7am–11pm. Outdoor courts 9am till dark.

Squash City **Ketelmakerstraat 6 (Jordaan and Western docklands)** ☎020/626 7883, ⊛www.squashcity.nl. Situated west of Centraal Station, with thirteen squash courts at €7–9 per member for 45min; membership costs €25 and also includes use of the sauna. Racket rental €2.50. Call ahead to reserve courts. Mon–Thurs 7am–11pm, Fri 7am–1.30pm, Sat & Sun 8.45am–7.15pm.

Festivals and events

M ost of Amsterdam's festivals are music and arts events, supplemented by a sprinkling of religious celebrations, and, as you might expect, the majority take place in the summer. The Queen's Birthday (also referred to as **Queen's Day**) at the end of April is the city's most touted and exciting annual event, with a large portion of the city given over to an impromptu flea market and lots of street-partying. On a more cultural level, the **Holland Festival** art extravaganza, held throughout June, attracts a handful of big names. Check with the VVV (see p.36) for further details, and remember that many other interesting events, such as the Easter performance of Bach's *St Matthew Passion* in the Grote Kerk at Naarden and the North Sea Jazz Festival in Rotterdam (W www.northseajazz.nl), are only a short train ride away. See p.35 for a list of **public holidays**.

January

Chinese New Year Late Jan/early Feb depending on lunar calendar. Dragon dance and fireworks, held at Nieuwmarkt and along the Zeedijk.

February

Februaristaking (Commemoration of the February Strike) February 25 W www.februaris-taking.nl. Speeches and wreath-laying at the Dockworker Statue on J.D. Meijerplein (see p.101).

March

Stille Omgang (Silent Procession) Sunday closest to March 15 W www.stille-omgang.nl. Procession by local Catholics commemo-rating the Miracle of Amsterdam (see p.56), starting and finishing at Spui and passing through the Red Light District.

April

Nationaal Museumweekend Second weekend W www.museumweekend.nl. Free or discounted entrance to most of the museums in the Netherlands. Contact VVV for more information.

Koninginnedag (the Queen's Birthday) April 30. This is one of the most popular dates in the Dutch diary, a street event *par excellence*, which seems to grow annually and is almost worth planning a visit around, despite some claiming it has become too commercialized in recent years. Celebrations in honour of Queen Beatrix take place throughout the Netherlands, though festivities in Amsterdam tend to be somewhat wilder and larger in scale. Special club nights and parties are held both the night before and the night after; however, to gain entry you'll need to book in advance either at the club itself or at record stores. The next day sees the city's streets and canals lined with people, most of whom are dressed in ridiculous costumes (not surprisingly, Queen's Day is one of the most flamboyant events on the gay calendar as well). Anything goes, especially if it's orange – the Dutch national colour. A fair is held in Dam Square, and music blasts continuously from huge sound systems set

▽ Queen's Day

up across most of the major squares. This is also the one day of the year when goods can be bought and sold tax-free to anyone on the streets, and numerous stalls are set up in front of people's houses.

May

Herdenkingsdag (Remembrance Day) May 4. There's a wreath-laying ceremony and a two-minute silence at the National Monument in Dam Square, commemorating the Dutch dead of World War II, as well as a smaller event at the Homomonument in Westermarkt in honour of the country's gay soldiers who died in the conflict.

Bevrijdingsdag (Liberation Day) May 5. The country celebrates the 1945 liberation from Nazi occupation with bands, speeches and impromptu markets around the city.

National Windmill Day Second Saturday. On this day over half the country's remaining windmills and watermills, indicated by a blue flag, are opened to the public free of charge. Contact Vereniging De Hollandsche (☏020/623 8703, ✉dhm@molens.nl) or the VVV (see p.36) for further details.

KunstRAI Second week ⓦ www.kunstrai.nl. The city's annual mainstream contemporary arts fair, held in the RAI conference centre (Metro Rai or tram #4), south of the centre, featuring works from over 120 galleries. Entry costs

€15. A less commercial alternative is the Kunstvlaai (ⓦwww.kunstvlaai.nl) at the Westergasfabriek (see p.91), always held the week before or after KunstRAI.

June

Open Garden Days Third weekend ⓦwww. opentuinendagen.nl. Three-day event which sees some thirty private gardens – usually arranged around a particular theme – open their gates to the public. Gardens are open 10am–5pm and there's a canal boat to take you around. Tickets €12.

Amsterdam Roots Festival Third Sunday ⓦwww.amsterdamroots.nl. Free open-air concert in Oosterpark (Tram #3, #7 or #9 from CS) with stalls, workshops and a parade that opens a week-long world music and film festival, with over sixty acts performing in the Concertgebouw, Melkweg, Paradiso and Tropentheater.

Holland Festival Throughout June ⓦwww .hollandfestival.nl. The largest music, dance and drama event in the Netherlands, aimed at making the dramatic arts more accessible. Showcasing around forty productions, from theatre and dance to music and opera, at various venues around the city, it features a mix of established and new talent.

International Theatre School Festival Third or last week ⓦwww.itsfestival.nl. Ten-day programme of events showcasing aspiring actors, dancers, musicians and opera singers in theatres on Nes, off Dam Square, culminating in an award night with the prize presented to the most promising director.

July

Kwakoe Festival Weekends only throughout July and August ⓦwww.kwakoe.nl. A Surinamese and Antillian festival held in Bijlmerpark (Metro Bijlmer), close to the Amsterdam ArenA in the southeastern suburbs, featuring lots of music, workshops, dance acts and stand-up comedy. In the middle of the festival there's a football competition between several teams. Caribbean delicacies such as *roti* and the Surinamese *bakabana*, baked banana with peanut sauce, are widely available from stalls around the festival site.

Vondelpark Open Air Theatre June–Aug ⓦ www. openluchttheater.nl. Free theatre, dance and music performances throughout the summer, Wed–Sun only, with anything from jazz and classical concerts through to stand-up comedy.

August

De Parade First two weeks ⓦ www.deparade.nl. An excellent sixteen-day travelling theatrical fair, which puts on a host of short, independent performances, ranging from cabaret to theatre, given in or in front of artists' tents. Held in the Martin Luther King park, next to the River Amstel (tram #25 from CS), with special kid-friendly performances in the afternoon.

Amsterdam Pride First or second weekend ⓦ www.amsterdampride.nl. The city's gay community celebrates, with street parties and performances held along the Amstel, Warmoesstraat and Reguliersdwarsstraat. The Canal Parade takes place on the Saturday between 2–6pm: a flotilla of up to 75 boats cruising along the Prinsengracht watched by over 200,000 people.

Grachtenfestival Starts second or third weekend ⓦ www.grachtenfestival.nl. For nine days international musicians perform over ninety classical music events at historical locations around the three main canals, as well as the River IJ. Includes the Prinsengracht Concert, one of the world's most prestigious free open-air concerts, held opposite the *Pulitzer Hotel*.

Uitmarkt Last weekend ⓦ www.uitmarkt.nl. Every cultural organization in the city, from opera to dance, advertises its forthcoming programme of events during this weekend, with free preview performances held over three days around Dam Square, Waterlooplein and Nieuwmarkt.

September

Bloemencorso (Flower Parade) First weekend ⓦ www.bloemencorsoaalsmeer.nl. The three-day Aalsmeer–Amsterdam flower pageant in the city centre, celebrating every kind of flower except tulips, which are out of season. Each year has a different theme

with each of the floats playing a different genre of music, from chanson to reggae. Vijzelstraat is the best place to see things, since the events in Dam Square are normally packed solid.

Open Monument Day Second weekend ⓦ www. openmonumentendag.nl. For two days monuments throughout the Netherlands that are normally closed or have restricted opening times throw open their doors to the public for free.

Jordaan Festival Second or third weekend. A three-day street festival in the Jordaan. There's a commercial fair on Palmgracht, talent contests on Elandsgracht, a few street parties and a culinary fair on the Sunday afternoon at the Noordermarkt.

October

Amsterdam City Marathon Usually third Sunday ⓦ www.amsterdammarathon.nl. A 42-kilometre course around Amsterdam starting at and finishing inside the Olympic Stadium, passing through the old city centre along the way.

November

Museum Night First Saturday ⓦ www.n8.nl. Around forty museums open their doors to the public from 7pm to 2am, with various events put on, accompanied by DJs and music. Tickets €14.

Parade of Sint Nicolaas Second or third Sunday. The traditional parade of *Sinterklaas* (Santa Claus) through the city on his white horse, starting from behind Centraal Station where he arrives by steam boat, before proceeding down the Damrak towards Rembrandtplein accompanied by his helpers the *Zwarte Pieten* ("Black Peters") – so called because of their blackened faces – who hand out sweets and little presents. It all finishes in Leidseplein on the balcony of the Stadsschouwburg.

Cannabis Cup Late November ⓦ www. hightimes.com. Five-day "harvest festival" organized by *High Times* magazine with seminars, tours and music events held at the Nachttheater Sugar Factory (see p.210) and the Melkweg (see p.210), which also

▽ Cannabis Cup

hosts a competition to find the best culti-
vated seed. Judging is open to the general
public, but the entrance fee is pricey.

December

Pakjesavond (Present Evening) Dec 5. Though
it tends to be a private affair, Pakjesavond,
rather than Christmas Day, is when Dutch
kids receive their Christmas presents. If
you're in the city on that day and have
Dutch friends, it's worth knowing that it's
traditional to give a present together with an
amusing poem you have written caricaturing
the recipient.

New Year's Eve Dec 31. New Year's Eve is big
in Amsterdam, with fireworks and celebrations everywhere. Most bars and discos stay
open until morning – make sure you get
tickets in advance. This might just qualify as
the wildest and most reckless street partying
in Europe, but a word of warning: Amsterdammers seem to love the idea of throwing
lit fireworks around and won't hesitate to
send one careering into the crowd.

Contexts

Contexts

A brief history of Amsterdam

To a large degree, a **history of Amsterdam** is a history of the whole of the Netherlands (including the province of Holland), which in turn was an integral part of the **Low Countries** – today's Belgium, Luxembourg and the Netherlands – until the late sixteenth century. It was then that the Dutch broke with their Spanish Habsburg masters and, ever since, Amsterdam has been at the centre of Dutch events. The city was the country's most glorious cultural and trading centre throughout its seventeenth-century heyday, the so-called **Golden Age**, and, after a brief downturn in the eighteenth century, picked itself up to emerge as a major metropolis in the nineteenth. In the 1960s Amsterdam was galvanized by its youth, who took to **hippy culture** with gusto; their legacy is a social progressiveness – most conspicuously over drugs and prostitution – that still underpins the city's international reputation, good and bad, today.

Medieval foundations

Amsterdam's earliest history is as murky as the marshes from which it arose. Legend asserts that two Frisian fishermen were the first inhabitants and, true or not, it is indeed likely that the city began as a fishing village at the mouth of the **River Amstel**. Previously, this area had been a stretch of peat bog and marsh, but a modest fall in the sea level permitted settlement on the high ground along the riverside. The village was first given some significance when the local lord built a castle here around 1204, and then, some sixty years later, the Amstel was dammed – hence Amstelredam – and it received its municipal **charter** from a new feudal overlord, Count Floris V, in 1275. Designating the village a toll port for beer imported from Hamburg, the charter led to Amsterdam's flourishing as a trading centre from around 1300, when it also became an important transit port for Baltic grain, destined for the burgeoning cities of the Low Countries (modern-day Belgium and the Netherlands).

As Amsterdam grew, its **trade** diversified. In particular, it made a handsome profit from English **wool**, which was imported into the city, barged onto Leiden and Haarlem – where it was turned into cloth – and then much of it returned to Amsterdam to be exported. The cloth trade drew workers into the town to work along Warmoesstraat and the Amstel, and ships were able to sail right up to Dam Square to pick up the finished work and drop off imported wood, fish, salt and spices.

Though the city's **population** rose steadily in the early sixteenth century, to around 12,000 souls, Amsterdam was still small compared to Antwerp or London; building on the waterlogged soil was difficult and slow, requiring timber piles to be driven into the firmer sand below. And with the extensive use of timber and thatch, **fires** were a frequent occurrence. A particularly disastrous blaze in 1452 resulted in such destruction that the city council made building with slate, brick and stone obligatory; one of the few wooden houses that survived the fire still stands today in the Begijnhof (see p.52). In the mid-sixteenth century the city

△ Map of Amsterdam in 1662

underwent its first major **expansion**, as burgeoning trade with the Hanseatic towns of the Baltic made the city second only to Antwerp as a marketplace and warehouse for northern and western Europe. The trade in cloth, grain and wine brought craftspeople to the city, and its merchant fleet grew; by the 1550s three-quarters of all grain cargo out of the Baltic was carried in Amsterdam vessels. The foundations were being laid for the wealth of the Golden Age.

The rise of Protestantism

At the beginning of the sixteenth century the corruption and elaborate ritual of the established (Catholic) **Church** found itself under attack throughout northern Europe. First, Erasmus of Rotterdam promoted ideas of reformation, and then, in 1517, **Martin Luther** (1483-1546) went one step – or rather, leap – further, producing his 95 theses against the Church practice of indulgences, a prelude to his more comprehensive assault on the entire institution. Furthermore, when Luther's works were disseminated his ideas gained a European following amongst a range of reforming groups branded as **Lutheran** by the Church, whilst other reformers were drawn to the doctrines of **John Calvin** (1509–64). Luther asserted that the Church's political power was subservient to that of the state; Calvin emphasized the importance of individual conscience and the need for redemption through the grace of Christ rather than the confessional. Luther's writings and Bible translations were printed in the Netherlands, but the doctrines of Calvin proved more popular in Amsterdam, setting the seal on the city's religious transformation. Calvin was insistent on the separation of Church and State, but the lines were easily fudged in Amsterdam by the Church's ruling council of ministers and annually elected elders, who soon came to exercise considerable political clout. The council also had little time for other (more egalitarian) Protestant sects, and matters came to a head when, in 1535, one of the radical splinter groups, the **Anabaptists**, occupied Amsterdam's town hall, calling on passers-by to repent. Previously the town council had tolerated the Anabaptists, but, prompted by the Calvinists, it acted swiftly when civic rule was challenged; the town hall was besieged and, after its capture, the leaders of the Anabaptists were executed on the Dam.

The revolt of the Netherlands

In 1555, the fanatically Catholic **Philip II** succeeded to the Spanish throne. Through a series of marriages the Spanish monarchy – and **Habsburg** family – had come to rule over the Low Countries, and Philip was determined to rid his empire of its heretics, regardless of whether they were Calvinists or Anabaptists. Philip promptly garrisoned the towns of the Low Countries with Spanish mercenaries, imported the **Inquisition** and passed a series of anti-Protestant edicts. However, other pressures on the Habsburg Empire forced him into a tactical withdrawal and he transferred control of the Low Countries to his sister **Margaret of Parma** in 1559. Based in Brussels, the equally resolute Margaret implemented the policies of her brother with gusto. In 1561 she reorganized the Church and created fourteen new bishoprics, a move that was construed as a wresting of power from civil authority, and an attempt to destroy the local aristocracy's powers of religious patronage. Right across the Low Countries, **Protestantism** – and Protestant sympathies – spread to the nobility, who now formed the "League of the Nobility" to counter Habsburg policy. The League petitioned Margaret for moderation but were dismissed out of hand by one of her (French-speaking) advisers, who called them "ces geux" (those beggars), an epithet that was to be.enthusiastically adopted by the rebels. In 1565 a harvest failure caused a winter famine among the urban workers of the region and, after years of repression, they struck back. In 1566, a Protestant sermon in the tiny Flemish textile town of Steenvoorde incited the congregation to purge the local church of its "papist" idolatry. The crowd smashed up the church's reliquaries and shrines, broke the stained-glass windows and terrorized the priests, thereby igniting what is commonly called the **Iconoclastic Fury**. The rioting spread like wildfire and within ten days churches had been ransacked from one end of the Low Countries to the other, nowhere more so than in Amsterdam – hence the plain, whitewashed interiors of many of the city's churches today.

The ferocity of this outbreak shocked the upper classes into renewed support for Spain, and Margaret regained the allegiance of most nobles – with the principal exception of the country's greatest landowner, Prince William of Orange-Nassau, known as **William the Silent**, who prudently slipped away to his estates in Germany. Meanwhile, Philip II was keen to capitalize on the increase in support for Margaret and, in 1567, he dispatched the **Duke of Albe**, with an army of ten thousand men, to the Low Countries to suppress his religious opponents absolutely. One of Albe's first acts was to set up the Commission of Civil Unrest, which was soon nicknamed the "**Council of Blood**", after its habit of executing those it examined. No fewer than 12,000 citizens were polished off, mostly for taking part in the Fury. Initially the repression worked;

in 1568, when William attempted an invasion from Germany, the towns, including Amsterdam, offered no support. William withdrew and conceived other means of defeating Albe, sponsoring the Protestant privateers, the so-called **Waterguezen** or sea-beggars, who took their name from the epithet provided by Margaret's advisor. In April 1572, the Waterguezen entered Brielle on the Maas and captured it from the Spanish in the first of several commando-style attacks. At first, the Waterguezen were obliged to operate from England, but it was soon possible for them to secure bases in the Netherlands, whose citizens had grown to loathe the autocratic Albe and his Spanish army.

After the success at Brielle, the revolt spread rapidly. By June the rebels controlled all of the province of Holland except for Amsterdam, which steadfastly refused to come off the fence. Albe and his son Frederick fought back, but William's superior naval power frustrated him and a mightily irritated Philip replaced Albe with **Luis de Resquesens**. Initially, Resquesens had some success in the south, where the Catholic majority were more willing to compromise with Spanish rule than their northern neighbours, but the tide of war was against him – most pointedly in William's triumphant relief of Leiden in 1574. Two years later, Resquesens died and the (unpaid) Habsburg garrison in Antwerp mutinied and attacked the town, slaughtering some eight thousand of its people in what was known as the **Spanish Fury**. Though the Habsburgs still held several towns, the massacre alienated the south and pushed its peoples – including the doubting Thomases of Amsterdam – into the arms of William, whose troops now swept into Brussels, the heart of imperial power. Momentarily, it seemed possible for the whole region to unite behind William and all signed the **Union of Brussels**, which demanded the departure of foreign troops as a condition for accepting a diluted Habsburg sovereignty.

Philip was, however, not inclined to compromise, especially when he realized that William's Calvinist sympathies were giving his newly found Walloon and Flemish allies (of modern-day Belgium) the jitters. The king bided his time until 1578, when, with his enemies arguing amongst themselves, he sent another army from Spain to the Low Countries under the command of Alessandro Farnese, the **Duke of Parma**. Events played into Parma's hands. In 1579, tiring of all the wrangling, seven northern provinces agreed to sign the **Union of Utrecht**, an alliance against Spain that was to be the first unification of the Netherlands as an identifiable country – the **United Provinces**. It was then that Amsterdam formally declared for the rebels and switched from Catholicism to Calvinism in what became known as the "**Alteratie**" of 1578. The rebels had conceded freedom of religious belief, but in Amsterdam, as elsewhere, this did not extend to freedom of worship. Nonetheless, a pragmatic compromise was reached in which a blind eye was turned to the celebration of Mass if it was done privately and inconspicuously. It was this ad hoc arrangement that gave rise to "clandestine" Catholic churches (*schuilkerken*) like that of the Amstelkring on Oudezijds Voorburgwal (see p.57).

The assembly of these United Provinces was known as the **States General**, and it met at Den Haag (The Hague); it had no domestic legislative authority, and could only carry out foreign policy by unanimous decision, a formula designed to reassure the independent-minded merchants of every Dutch city. The role of **Stadholder** was the most important in each province, roughly equivalent to that of governor, though the same person could occupy this position in any number of provinces. Meanwhile, in the south – and also in 1579 – representatives of the southern provinces signed the **Union of Arras**, a Catholic-led agreement that declared loyalty to Philip II and counterbalanced the Union of Utrecht in the north. Thus, the Low Countries were, de facto, divided into two

– the Spanish Netherlands and the United Provinces – beginning a separation that would lead, after many changes, to the creation of Belgium, Luxembourg and the Netherlands. With the return of more settled times, Amsterdam was now free to carry on with what it did best – trading and making money.

The Golden Age

The brilliance of Amsterdam's explosion onto the European scene is as difficult to underestimate as it is to detail. The size of its **merchant fleet** carrying Baltic grain into Europe had long been considerable. Even the Spaniards had been unable to undermine Dutch **maritime superiority**, and, with the commercial demise of Antwerp, Amsterdam became the emporium for the products of northern and southern Europe as well as the East and West Indies. The city didn't prosper from its market alone, though, as Amsterdam ships also carried produce, a cargo trade that greatly increased the city's wealth. Dutch **banking and investment** brought further prosperity, and by the middle of the seventeenth century Amsterdam's wealth was spectacular. The Calvinist bourgeoisie indulged themselves in fine canal houses, and commissioned images of themselves in group portraits. Civic pride knew no bounds as great monuments to self-aggrandizement, such as the new **town hall** (now the Koninklijk Paleis, see p.47), were hastily erected, and, if some went hungry, few starved, as the poor were cared for in municipal almshouses.

The arts flourished and **religious tolerance** was extended even to the traditional scapegoats, the Jews, and in particular the Sephardic Jews, who had been hounded from Spain by the Inquisition but were guaranteed freedom from religious persecution under the terms of the Union of Utrecht. By the end of the eighteenth century, Jews accounted for ten percent of the city's population. Guilds and craft associations thrived, and in the first half of the seventeenth century Amsterdam's population quadrupled; the relatively high wages paid by the city's industries attracted agricultural workers from every part of the country and Protestant refugees arrived from every corner of Catholic Europe.

To accommodate its growing populace, Amsterdam **expanded** several times during the seventeenth century. The grandest and most elaborate plan to enlarge the city was begun in 1613, with the digging of the western stretches of the Herengracht, Keizersgracht and Prinsengracht, the three great canals of the **Grachtengordel** (literally "girdle of canals") that epitomized the wealth and self-confidence of the Golden Age. In 1663 this sweeping crescent was extended beyond the River Amstel, but by this time the population had begun to stabilize, and the stretch that would have completed the ring of canals around the city was left only partially developed – an area that would in time become the Jewish Quarter (see Chapter Four).

One organization that kept the city's coffers brimming throughout the Golden Age was the **East India Company** (Verenigde Oost Indische, VOC). Formed in 1602, this Amsterdam-controlled enterprise sent ships to Asia, Indonesia and China to bring back spices, wood and other assorted plunder. Given a trading monopoly in all lands east of the Cape of Good Hope, it also exercised unlimited military powers over the lands it controlled, and was effectively the occupying government in Malaya, Ceylon and Malacca. The speed of the VOC's vessels amazed the company's competitors and may well have given rise to the legend of the **Flying Dutchman**. One story has it that the fastest VOC captain of them all, a certain Bernard Fokke, only achieved the sailing times he did with the help of the devil - and his reward is to sail the seven seas forever; another has the VOC's Captain Hendrik van der Decken sailing round the Cape of Good Hope for eternity after blaspheming against the wind and the waves.

Twenty years after the founding of the VOC, the **West Indies Company** (Westindische Compagnie, WIC) was inaugurated to protect new Dutch interests in the Americas and Africa. It never achieved the success of the East India Company, expending its energies in waging war on Spanish and Portuguese colonies from a base in Surinam, but it did make handsome profits until the 1660s. The company was dismantled in 1674, ten years after its small colony of New Amsterdam had been ceded to the British – and renamed **New York**. Elsewhere, the Dutch held on to their colonies for as long as possible – Indonesia, its principal possession, only secured its independence in 1949.

Decline – 1660 to 1795

Although the economics of the Golden Age were dazzling, the **politics** were dismal. The United Provinces were dogged by interminable wrangling between those who hankered for a central, unified government under the pre-eminent **House of Orange-Nassau** and those who championed provincial autonomy. Frederick Henry, the powerful head of the House of Orange-Nassau, died in 1647 and his successor, William II, lasted just three years before his death from smallpox. A week after William's death, his wife bore the son who would become William III of England, but in the meantime the leaders of the province of Holland, with the full support of Amsterdam, seized their opportunity. They forced measures through the States General abolishing the position of Stadholder, thereby reducing the powers of the Orangists and increasing those of the provinces, chiefly Holland itself. Holland's foremost figure in these years was **Johan de Witt**, Council Pensionary (chief minister) to the States General. He guided the country through wars with England and Sweden, concluding a triple alliance between the two countries and the United Provinces in 1668. This was a striking reversal of policy; the economic rivalry between the United Provinces and England had already precipitated two **Anglo-Dutch wars** (1652–54 and 1665–67) and there was much bitterness in Anglo–Dutch relations – a popular English pamphlet of the time was titled "*A Relation Shewing How They [the Dutch] Were First Bred and Descended from a Horse-Turd Which Was Enclosed in a Butter-Box*". Much of the ill feeling came from an embarrassing defeat in the second Anglo–Dutch war, when **Admiral Michiel de Ruyter** had sailed up the Thames and caught the English fleet napping. This infuriated England's Charles II, who was quite willing to break with his new-found allies and join a French attack on the Provinces in 1672. The republic was now in deep trouble – previous victories had been at sea, and the army, weak and disorganized, could not withstand the onslaught. In panic, the country turned to **William III** of Orange for leadership and Johan de Witt was brutally murdered by a mob of Orangist sympathizers in Den Haag. By 1678 William had defeated the French and made peace with the English – and was rewarded (along with his wife Mary, the daughter of Charles I of England) with the English crown ten years later.

Though King William had defeated the French, **Louis XIV** retained designs on the United Provinces and the military pot was kept boiling in a long series of dynastic wars that ranged across northern Europe. In 1700, Charles II of Spain, the last of the Spanish Habsburgs, died childless, bequeathing the Spanish throne and control of the Spanish Netherlands (now Belgium) to Philip of Anjou, Louis' grandson. Louis promptly forced Philip to cede the latter to France, which was, with every justification, construed as a threat to the balance of power by France's neighbours. The **War of the Spanish Succession** ensued, with the United Provinces, England and Austria forming the **Triple Alliance** to thwart the French king. The war itself was a haphazard, long-winded affair distinguished by the spectacular victories of the Duke of Marlborough at Blenheim, Ramillies and Malplaquet. It dragged on until the **Treaty of Utrecht** of 1713 in which France finally abandoned its claim to the Spanish Netherlands, which reverted to the Austrian Habsburgs (as the Austrian Netherlands).

However, the fighting had drained the United Provinces' reserves and a slow economic decline began, accelerated by a reactive trend towards conservatism. This in turn reflected the development of an increasingly socially static society, with power and wealth concentrated within a small, self-regarding elite. Furthermore, with the threat of foreign conquest effectively removed, the Dutch ruling class divided into two main camps – the Orangists and the pro-French "Patriots" – whose interminable squabbling soon brought political life to a virtual standstill. The situation deteriorated even further in the latter half of the century, and the last few years of the United Provinces present a sorry state of affairs.

French occupation

In 1795 the **French**, aided by the Patriots, invaded, setting up the **Batavian Republic** and dissolving the United Provinces – along with many of the privileges of the richer Dutch merchants. Now part of the Napoleonic empire, the Netherlands were obliged to wage unenthusiastic war with England, and in 1806 Napoleon appointed his brother **Louis** as their king in an attempt to unite the rival Dutch groups under one (notionally independent) ruler. **Louis** was installed in Amsterdam's town hall, giving it its title of Koninklijk Paleis (Royal Palace; see p.47). Louis, however, wasn't willing to allow the Netherlands to become a simple satellite of France; he ignored Napoleon's directives and after just four years of rule was forced to abdicate. The country was then formally incorporated into the French Empire, and for three gloomy years suffered occupation and heavy taxation to finance French military adventures.

Following Napoleon's disastrous retreat from Moscow, the **Orangist faction** surfaced to exploit weakening French control. In 1813, Frederick William, son of the exiled William V, returned to the country and eight months later, under the terms of the **Congress of Vienna**, was crowned King William I of the **United Kingdom of the Netherlands**, incorporating both the old United Provinces and the Austrian Netherlands. A strong-willed man, he spent much of the later part of his life trying to control his disparate kingdom, but he failed primarily because of the Protestant north's attempt – or perceived attempt – to dominate the Catholic south. The southern provinces revolted against his rule and in 1830 the separate Kingdom of **Belgium** was proclaimed. During the years of the United Kingdom, Amsterdam's status was dramatically reduced. Previously, the self-governing city, made bold by its wealth, could (and frequently did) act in its own self-interest, at the expense of the nation. From 1815, however, it was integrated within the country, with no more rights than any other city. The seat of government (and the centre for all decision-making) was Den Haag (The Hague), and so it remained after the southern provinces broke away.

The nineteenth century

In the first decades of the nineteenth century, the erosion of Amsterdam's pre-eminent position among Dutch cities was largely camouflaged by its profitable colonial trade with the East Indies (Indonesia). This trade was however hampered by the character of the **Zuider Zee**, whose shallows and sand-banks presented all sorts of navigational problems given the increasing size of merchant ships. The **Noordhollandskanaal** (North Holland Canal), completed in 1824 and running north from Amsterdam to bypass the Zuider Zee, made little difference, and it was Rotterdam, strategically placed on the Rhine inlets between the industries of the Ruhr and Britain, that prospered at Amsterdam's expense. Even the 1876 opening of the **Nordzeekanaal** (North Sea Canal), which provided a direct link west from Amsterdam to the North Sea, failed to push Amsterdam's trade ahead of rival Rotterdam's, though the city did hold on to much of the country's **shipbuilding industry**, remnants of which can still be seen at the 't Kromhout shipyard (see p.110). The city council was also slow to catch on to the possibilities of rail, but finally, in 1889, the opening of **Centraal Station** put the city back on the main transport routes. Nonetheless, Amsterdam was far from being a backwater; in the second half of the nineteenth century, its industries boomed, attracting a new wave of migrants, who were settled outside of the centre in the vast tenements of De Pijp and the Oud Zuid (Old South). These same workers were soon to radicalize the city, supporting a veritable raft of Socialist and Communist politicians. One marker was a reforming **Housing Act** of 1901 that pushed the city council into a concerted effort to clear the city's slums. Even better, the new municipal housing was frequently designed to the highest specifications, no more so than under the guidance of the two leading architects of the (broadly Expressionist) **Amsterdam School**, Michael de Klerk (1884–1923) and Piet Kramer (1881–1961). The duo were responsible for the layout of much of the Nieuw Zuid (New South; see pp.131–135).

Nationally, **Jan Rudolph Thorbecke** (1798-1872), the outstanding political figure of the times, formed three ruling cabinets (1849–53, 1862–66 and 1872) and steered the Netherlands through a profound attitudinal change. The political parties of the late eighteenth century had wished to resurrect the power and prestige of the seventeenth-century Netherlands; Thorbecke and his liberal allies resigned themselves to the country's reduced status as a small power and eulogized its advantages. For the first time, from about 1850, liberty was seen as a luxury made possible by the country's very lack of power, and the malaise that had long disturbed public life gave way to a positive appreciation of the very narrowness of its national existence. One of the results of Thorbecke's liberalism was a gradual extension of the franchise, culminating in the **Act of Universal Suffrage** in 1917.

The war years

The Netherlands remained neutral during **World War I**, and although it suffered privations from the Allied blockade of German war materials, this was offset by the profits many Dutch merchants made by trading with both sides. Similar attempts to remain neutral in **World War II**, however, failed; the **Germans invaded** on May 10, 1940, and the Netherlands was quickly overrun.

Queen Wilhelmina fled to London to set up a government-in-exile, and members of the **NSB**, the Dutch fascist party which welcomed the invaders, were rewarded with positions of authority. Nevertheless, in the early months of the occupation, life for ordinary Amsterdammers went on pretty much as usual. Even when the first roundups of the **Jews** began in late 1940, many managed to turn a blind eye, though in February 1941 Amsterdam's newly outlawed Communist Party did organize a widely supported strike, spearheaded by the city's transport and refuse workers, shipbuilders and dockers. It was a gesture rather than a move to undermine German control, but an important one all the same. Interviewed after the war, one of the leaders summarized it thus: "If just one of Amsterdam's Jews did not feel forgotten and abandoned as he was packed off in a train, then the strike was well worth it."

As the war progressed, so the German grip got tighter and the Dutch **Resistance** stronger, its activities – primarily industrial and transportation sabotage as well as the forgery of identity papers, a real Dutch speciality – trumpeted by underground newspapers such as *Het Parool* (The Password), which survives in good form today. The Resistance paid a heavy price with some 23,000 of its fighters and sympathizers losing their lives, but the city's Jews (see box p.99) took the worst punishment. In 1940, the city's Jewish population, swollen by refugees from Hitler's Germany, was around 140,000, but when the Allies liberated the city in May 1945 only a few thousand were left. The Old Jewish Quarter (see Chapter Four) lay deserted, a rare crumb of comfort being the survival of the diary of a young Jewish girl – **Anne Frank**.

Reconstruction – 1945 to 1960

The **postwar years** were spent patching up the damage of occupation, though at first progress was hindered by a desperate shortage of food, fuel and building materials. Indeed, things were in such short supply – and the winter of 1945–6 so cold – that hundreds of Amsterdammers died of hunger and/or hypothermia, their black cardboard coffins being trundled to mass graves. Neither did it help that the retreating Germans had blown up all the dykes and sluices on the North Sea coast at IJmuiden, at the mouth of the Nordzeekanaal. Nevertheless, Amsterdam had not received an aerial pounding of the likes dished out to Rotterdam and Arnhem, and the reconstruction soon built up a head of steam. One feature was the creation of giant suburbs like **Bijlmermeer**, to the southeast of the city, the last word in early 1960s large-scale residential planning, with low-cost modern housing, play areas and foot and cycle paths.

Two events were, however, to mar Dutch reconstruction in the late 1940s and early 1950s. The former **Dutch colonies** of Java and Sumatra, taken by the Japanese at the outbreak of the war, were now ruled by a nationalist republican government that refused to recognize Dutch sovereignty. Following the failure of talks between Den Haag and the islanders in 1947, the Dutch sent the troops in: a colonial enterprise that soon became a bloody debacle. International opposition was intense and, after much condemnation and pressure, the Dutch reluctantly surrendered their most important Asian colonies, which were ultimately incorporated as **Indonesia** in 1950. Back at home, tragedy struck on February 1, 1953 when an unusually high tide was pushed over Zeeland's sea defences by a westerly gale, flooding 160 square kilometres of land and drowning over 1800 people. The response was the **Delta Project**, which closed off the western part of the Scheldt and Maas estuaries with massive sea dykes, thereby ensuring the safety of cities to the south of Amsterdam, though Amsterdam itself had already been secured by the completion of the **Afsluitdijk** in 1932. This dyke closed off the Zuider Zee, turning it into the freshwater IJsselmeer with the Markermeer hived off later (see box p.151).

The Provos and the 1960s

The radical and youthful mass movements that swept through the West in the 1960s transformed Amsterdam from a middling, rather conservative city into a turbo-charged hotbed of **hippy action**. In 1963, one-time window cleaner and magician extraordinaire **Jasper Grootveld** won celebrity status by painting "K" – for *kanker* ("cancer") – on cigarette billboards throughout the city. Two years later, he proclaimed the statue of the *Lieverdje* ("Loveable Rascal") on the Spui (see p.52) the symbol of "tomorrow's addicted consumer" – since it had been donated to the city by a cigarette manufacturer – and organized large-scale gatherings there once a week. His actions enthused others, most notably **Roel van Duyn**, a philosophy student at Amsterdam University, who assembled a Left-wing-cum-anarchist movement known as the **Provos** – short for *provocatie* ("provocation"). The Provos participated in Grootveld's meetings and then proceeded to organize their own street "happenings", which proved to be fantastically popular among young Amsterdammers. The number of Provos never exceeded about thirty and the group had no coherent structure, but they did have one clear aim – to bring points of political or social conflict to public attention by spectacular means. More than anything, they were masters of publicity, and pursued their "games" with a spirit of fun rather than grim political fanaticism. The reaction of the police, however, was aggressive; the first two issues of the Provos' magazine were confiscated and, in July 1965, they intervened at a Saturday-night "happening", setting a pattern for future confrontations. The magazine itself contained the Provos' manifesto, a set of policies that later appeared under the title "**The White Plans**". These included the famously popular **white bicycle plan**, which proposed that the council ban all cars in the city centre and supply 20,000 bicycles (painted white) for general public use.

There were regular police-Provo confrontations throughout 1965, but it was the **wedding of Princess Beatrix** to Claus von Amsberg on March 10, 1966, that provoked the most serious unrest. Amsberg had served in the German army during World War II and many Netherlanders were deeply offended by the marriage. Consequently, when hundreds took to the streets to protest, pelting the wedding procession with smoke bombs, a huge swath of Dutch opinion supported them – to some degree or another. Amsberg himself got no more than he deserved when he was jeered with the refrain "Give us back the bikes", a reference to the commandeering of hundreds of bikes by the retreating German army in 1945. The wedding over, the next crisis came in June when, much to the horror of the authorities, it appeared that students, workers and Provos were about to combine. In panic, the Hague government ordered the dismissal of Amsterdam's police chief, but in the event the Provos had peaked and the workers proved far from revolutionary, settling for arbitration on their various complaints.

The final twist in the Provos tale was the formation of a splinter group called the **Kabouters**, named after a helpful gnome in Dutch folklore. Their manifesto described their form of socialism as "not of the clenched fist, but of the intertwined fingers, the erect penis, the escaping butterfly..." – appealing perhaps, but never a vote winner.

The 1970s and 1980s – and the squatters

In 1967, the Provos formally dissolved their movement at a happening in the Vondelpark, but many of their supporters promptly moved on to **neighbourhood committees**, set up to oppose the more outlandish development plans of the city council. The most hated scheme by a long chalk was the plan to build a **metro line** through the Nieuwmarkt to the new suburb of Bijlmermeer as this involved both wholesale demolitions and compulsory relocations. For six months, there were regular confrontations between the police and the protestors and, although the council eventually had its way, the scene was set for more trouble. In particular, the council seemed to many to be unwilling to tackle Amsterdam's acute **housing shortage**, neglecting the needs of its poorer citizens in favour of business interests. It was this perception that fuelled the **squatter movement**, which coalesced around a handful of symbolic squats. The first major incident came in March 1980 when several hundred police evicted squatters from premises on **Vondelstraat**. Afterwards, there was widespread rioting, but this was small beer in comparison with the protests of April 30, 1980 – the **coronation day of Queen Beatrix** – when a mixed bag of squatters and leftists vigorously protested both the lavishness of the proceedings and the expense of refurbishing Beatrix's palace in Den Haag. Once again there was widespread rioting and this time it spread to other Dutch cities, though the unrest was short-lived.

Now at its peak, Amsterdam's squatting movement boasted around ten thousand activists, many of whom were involved in two more major confrontations with the police – the first at the **Lucky Luyk** squat, on Jan Luykenstraat, the second at the **Wyers** building, when, in February 1984, the squatters were forcibly cleared to make way for a Holiday Inn, now the *Crowne Plaza Hotel* (see p.46). The final showdown – the **Stopera** campaign – came with the construction of the **Muziektheater/Stadhuis** complex on Waterlooplein (see p.98). Thereafter, the movement faded away, at least partly because of its repeated failure to stop the developers, who now claim, with some justification, to be more sensitive to community needs.

The 1990s and the rise of Pim Fortuyn

In the 1990s, Amsterdam's street protests and massive squats became an increasingly distant memory, but some of the old ideas – and ideals – were carried forward by the **Greens**, who attracted – and continue to attract – a small but significant following in every municipal and national election. One of the recurring political problems was that the city's finely balanced system of **proportional representation** brought little rapid change, often getting mired in interminable compromise and debate. The same is true **nationally**, where politics has long seemed a bland if necessary business conducted between the three main parties, the **Protestant–Catholic CDA** coalition, the **Liberal VVD** and the **Socialist PVDA**. However, the entire political class received a jolt in the national elections of May 2002 when a brand-new Rightist grouping – **Leefbaar Neederlands** (Liveable Netherlands) – led by Rotterdam's **Pim Fortuyn**, swept to second place behind the CDA, securing seventeen percent of the national vote. Stylish and witty, openly gay and a former Marxist, Fortuyn managed to cover several popular bases at the same time, from the need for law and order through to tighter immigration controls. Most crucially, he also attacked the liberal establishment's espousal of multiculturalism even when the representatives of minority groups were deeply reactionary, anti-gay and sexist. Politically, it worked a treat, but a year later Fortuyn was assassinated and his party rapidly unravelled, losing most of its seats in the general election of January 2003 (see below).

One of the reasons for Fortuyn's electoral success reflected the other shock to the Dutch system, which came with the publication of a damning report on the failure of the Dutch army to protect the Bosnian Muslims ensconced in the UN safe-haven of **Srebrenica** in 1995. Published in April 2002, the report told a tale of extraordinary incompetence; the UN's Dutch soldiers were inadequately armed, but still refused American assistance, and watched as Serb troops separated Muslim men and women in preparation for the mass executions, which the Dutch soldiers then did nothing to stop (though they were never involved). In a country that prides itself on its internationalism, the report was an especially hard blow and the whole of the PVDA-led government, under **Wim Kok**, resigned in April 2002.

The present

The general election of 2003 was a close-run thing, and there was certainly a revival in PVDA fortunes, but a **Rightist alliance** – consisting of the VVD, the CDA and the Lijst Pim Fortuyn (formerly Leefbaar Neederlands) – still managed to cobble together an administration under the leadership of **Jan Peter Balkenende**. In the event, this coalition proved most unstable, but Balkenende soldiered on (with different partners) until the national election of November 2006. This saw modest gains for the far right and left, but not enough to unseat Balkenende, who is now at the head of a majority CDA, PVDA and Christian Union (CU) administration. Superficially, therefore, and with Leefbaar Neederlands dead and gone (the party dissolved itself), it seems that normal political service has been resumed, but although the CDA and the PVDA are once again the largest parties, there is an uneasy undertow. In truth, Fortuyn's popularity pushed certain sorts of social debate, particularly on **immigration**, to the right and the situation got much worse – and race relations much tenser – when, in late 2004, the filmmaker **Theo van Gogh** was shot dead on an Amsterdam street by a Moroccan who objected to a film he had made – *Submission* – about Islamic violence against women. Shown on Dutch TV, the film was scripted by an MP, **Ayaan Hirsi Ali**, a Somali refugee and Dutch citizen, whose pronouncements on this same subject have been hard-hitting and headline-grabbing in equal measure: "But tell me" she was reported to have said in an interview with the UK's *Daily Telegraph* in December 2004, "why any Muslim man would want Islamic women to be educated and emancipated? Would a

Roman voluntarily have given up his slaves?". Unfortunately for Ali, she was engulfed by controversy of a different kind in 2006 when it turned out that her application for asylum had not been entirely truthful – and the ensuing furore created parliamentary panic. More generally, with polls indicating that many Dutch feel apprehensive, if not actually hostile, to the Muslims in their midst, it will take all of Balkenende's skills to keep the lid on the inter-communal pot. Other Netherlanders are voting with their feet: in 2005, 121,000 mostly middle-class Dutch citizens emigrated – the largest number ever.

National politics aside, March 2006 saw **municipal elections** in Amsterdam with the PVDA the runaway winners in terms of the popular vote, but still needing the support of another party – in this case, the leftist **GroenLinks** ("GreenLeft") – to form a majority administration. With the support of most Amsterdammers, the new city council will undoubtedly continue to cast the city as a dynamic, go-ahead metropolis – with the drugs, the prostitutes and the hippies as a by-line. More than anything else, redevelopment has become the name of the game, particularly amidst the old docklands bordering the River IJ. There have also been political rumblings about the Red Light District, with the mayor, for one, railing against gangsterism and money laundering, and others proposing to have the whole caboodle moved to the polders east of the city.

Dutch art

Designed to serve only as a quick reference, the following **outline** is the very briefest of introductions to a subject that has rightly filled volumes. Inevitably, it covers artists that lived and worked in both the Netherlands and Belgium, as these two countries have – along with Luxembourg – been bound together as the "**Low Countries**" for most of their history. For in-depth and academic studies, see the recommendations in "Books" on p.293.

Beginnings – the Flemish Primitives

Throughout the medieval period, **Flanders**, in modern-day Belgium, was one of the most artistically productive parts of Europe, and it was here that the solid realist base of later Dutch painting developed. Today, the works of these early Flemish painters, the **Flemish Primitives**, are highly prized, and although examples are fairly rare in the Netherlands, Amsterdam's Rijksmuseum has a healthy sample, though unfortunately many of them are not on display during the museum's refurbishment (see p.114).

Jan van Eyck (1385–1441) is generally regarded as the first of the Flemish Primitives, and has even been credited with the invention of oil painting – though it seems more likely that he simply perfected a new technique by thinning his paint with turpentine (at the time a new discovery), thus making it more flexible. The most famous of his works still in the Low Countries is the altarpiece in Belgium's Ghent Cathedral, which was revolutionary in its realism, for the first time using elements of native landscape in depicting biblical themes. Van Eyck's style and technique were to influence several generations of the region's artists.

Firmly in the Eyckian tradition were the **Master of Flemalle** (1387–1444) and **Rogier van der Weyden** (1400–64), one-time official painter to the city of Brussels. The Flemalle master is a shadowy figure; some believe he was the teacher of Van der Weyden, others that the two artists were in fact the same person. There are differences between the two, however; the Flemalle master's paintings are close to Van Eyck's, whereas van der Weyden shows a greater degree of emotional intensity in his religious works. Van der Weyden also produced serene portraits of the bigwigs of his day and these were much admired across a large swath of western Europe. His style, never mind his success, influenced many painters, one of the most talented of these being **Dieric Bouts** (1415–75). Born in Haarlem but active in Leuven, Bouts is recognizable by his stiff, rather elongated figures and horrific subject matter, all set against carefully drawn landscapes. **Hugo van der Goes** (d.1482) was the next Ghent master after van Eyck, most famous for the Portinari altarpiece in Florence's Uffizi gallery. After a short painting career, he died insane, and his late works have strong hints of his impending madness in their subversive use of space and implicit acceptance of the viewer's presence.

Few doubt that **Hans Memling** (1440–94) was a pupil of van der Weyden. Active in Bruges throughout his life, he is best remembered for the pastoral charm of his landscapes and the quality of his portraiture, much of which survives on the rescued side panels of triptychs. **Gerard David** (1460–1523) was a native of Oudewater, near Gouda, but he moved to Bruges in 1484, becoming the last of the great painters to work in that city, before it was outstripped by Antwerp, producing formal religious works of traditional bent. Strikingly different, but broadly contemporaneous, was **Hieronymus Bosch** (1450–1516), who lived for most of his life in the Netherlands, though his style is linked to that of his Flemish contemporaries. His frequently reprinted religious allegories are filled with macabre visions of tortured people and grotesque beasts, and appear at first faintly unhinged, though it's now thought that these are visual representations of contemporary sayings, idioms and parables. While their interpretation is far from resolved, Bosch's paintings draw strongly on subconscious fears and archetypes, giving them a lasting, haunting fascination.

The sixteenth century

At the end of the fifteenth century, Flanders was in economic and political decline and the leading artists of the day were drawn instead to the booming port of **Antwerp**, also in present-day Belgium. The artists who worked here soon began to integrate the finely observed detail that characterized the Flemish tradition with the style of the Italian painters of the Renaissance. **Quentin Matsys** (1464–1530) introduced florid classical architectural details and intricate landscapes to his works, influenced perhaps by the work of Leonardo da Vinci. As well as religious works, he painted portraits and genre scenes, all of which have recognizably Italian facets – and paved the way for the Dutch genre painters of later years. **Jan Gossaert** (1478–1532) made the pilgrimage to Italy too, and his dynamic works are packed with detail, especially finely drawn classical architectural backdrops. He was the first Low Countries artist to introduce the subjects of classical mythology into his paintings, part of a steady trend towards secular subject matter, which can also be seen in the work of **Joachim Patenier** (d.1524), who painted small landscapes of fantastical scenery.

The middle of the sixteenth century was dominated by the work of **Pieter Bruegel the Elder** (c.1525–69), whose gruesome allegories and innovative interpretations of religious subjects are firmly placed in Low Countries settings. Pieter also painted finely observed peasant scenes, though he himself was well connected in court circles in Antwerp and, later, Brussels. **Pieter Aertsen** (1508–75) also worked in the peasant genre, adding aspects of still life; his paintings often show a detailed kitchen scene in the foreground, with a religious episode going on behind. Bruegel's two sons, **Pieter Bruegel the Younger** (1564–1638) and **Jan Bruegel** (1568–1625), were lesser painters; the former produced fairly insipid copies of his father's work, while Jan developed a style of his own – delicately rendered flower paintings and genre pieces that earned him the nickname "Velvet". Towards the latter half of the sixteenth century highly stylized Italianate portraits became the dominant fashion, with **Frans Pourbus the Younger** (1569–1622) the leading practitioner. Frans hobnobbed across Europe, working for the likes of the Habsburgs and the Médicis.

Meanwhile, there were artistic rumblings in the province of Holland. Leading the charge was **Geertgen tot Sint Jans** (Little Gerard of the Brotherhood of St John; d.1490), who worked in Haarlem, initiating – in a strangely naive style – an artistic vision that would come to dominate the seventeenth century.

There was a tender melancholy in his work very different from the stylized paintings produced in Flanders, and, most importantly, a new sensitivity to light – and lighting. **Jan Mostaert** (1475–1555) took over after Geertgen's death, developing similar themes, but the first painter to effect real changes in northern painting was **Lucas van Leyden** (1489–1533). Born in Leiden, his bright colours and narrative technique were refreshingly novel, and he introduced a new dynamism into what had become a rigidly formal treatment of devotional subjects. There was rivalry, of course. Eager to publicize Haarlem as the artistic capital of the northern Netherlands, **Karel van Mander** (see p.146) claimed **Jan van Scorel** (1495–1562) as the better painter, complaining, too, of van Leyden's dandyish ways. Certainly van Scorel's influence should not be underestimated. Like many of his contemporaries, van Scorel hotfooted it to Italy to view the works of the Renaissance, but in Rome his career went into overdrive when he found favour with Pope Hadrian VI, one-time bishop of Utrecht, who installed him as court painter in 1520. Van Scorel stayed in Rome for four years and when he returned to Utrecht, armed with all that papal prestige, he combined the ideas he had picked up in Italy with those underpinning Haarlem realism, thereby modifying what had previously been an independent artistic tradition once and for all. Amongst his several students, probably the most talented was **Maerten van Heemskerck** (1498–1574), who duly went off to Italy himself in 1532, staying there five years before doubling back to Haarlem.

The Golden Age

The seventeenth century begins with **Karel van Mander** (1548–1606), Haarlem painter, art impresario and one of the few contemporary chroniclers of the art of the Low Countries. His *Schilderboek* of 1604 put Flemish and Dutch traditions into context for the first time, and in addition specified the rules of fine painting. Examples of his own work are rare – though Haarlem's Frans Hals Museum (see p.145) weighs in with a couple – but his followers were many. Among them was **Cornelius Cornelisz van Haarlem** (1562–1638), who produced elegant renditions of biblical and mythical themes; and **Hendrik Goltzius** (1558–1616), who was a skilled engraver and an integral member of van Mander's Haarlem academy. These painters' enthusiasm for Italian art, combined with the influence of a late revival of Gothicism, resulted in works that combined **Mannerist and Classical** elements. An interest in realism was also felt, but, for them, the subject became less important than the way in which it was depicted; biblical stories became merely a vehicle whereby artists could apply their skills in painting the human body, landscapes, or copious displays of food. All of this served to break religion's stranglehold on art, and make legitimate a whole range of everyday subjects for the painter.

In what is now the Netherlands (and this was where the north and the south finally diverged) this break with tradition was compounded by the **Reformation**; the austere Calvinism that had replaced the Catholic faith in the United (ie northern) Provinces had no use for images or symbols of devotion in its churches. Instead, painters catered to the burgeoning middle class, and no longer visited Italy to learn their craft. Indeed, the real giants of the seventeenth century – Hals, Rembrandt, Vermeer – stayed in the Netherlands all their lives. Another innovation was that painting split into more distinct categories – genre, portrait, landscape – and artists tended (with notable exceptions) to confine themselves to one field throughout their careers. So began the **Golden Age** of Dutch art.

Historical and religious painting

The artistic influence of Renaissance Italy may have been in decline, but Italian painters still had clout with the Dutch, most notably **Caravaggio** (1571–1610), who was much admired for his new realism. Taking Caravaggio's cue, many artists – Rembrandt for one – continued to portray classical subjects, but in a way that was totally at odds with the Mannerists' stylish flights of imagination. The Utrecht artist **Abraham Bloemaert** (1564–1651), though a solid Mannerist throughout his career, encouraged these new ideas, and his students – **Gerard van Honthorst** (1590–1656), **Hendrik Terbrugghen** (1588–1629) and **Dirck van Baburen** (1590–1624) – formed the nucleus of the influential **Utrecht School**, which followed Caravaggio almost to the point of slavishness. Honthorst was perhaps the leading figure, learning his craft from Bloemaert and travelling to Rome, where he was nicknamed "Gerardo delle Notti" for his ingenious handling of light and shade. In his later paintings, however, this was to become more routine technique than inspired invention, and though a supremely competent artist, Honthorst is somewhat discredited among critics today. Terbrugghen's reputation seems to have aged rather better; he soon forgot Caravaggio and developed a more individual style, his later, lighter work having a great influence on the young Vermeer. After a jaunt to Rome, Baburen shared a studio with Terbrugghen and produced some fairly original work – work which also had some influence on Vermeer – but today he is the least studied member of the group and few of his paintings survive.

Above all others, **Rembrandt** (1606–69) was the most original historical artist of the seventeenth century, also chipping in with religious paintings throughout his career. In the 1630s, the poet and statesman Constantijn Huygens procured for him his greatest commission – a series of five paintings of the Passion, beautifully composed and uncompromisingly realistic. Later, however, Rembrandt drifted away from the mainstream, ignoring the smooth brushwork of his contemporaries and choosing instead a rougher, darker and more disjointed style for his biblical and historical subjects. This probably contributed to a decline in his artistic fortunes and it is significant that while the more conventional Jordaens, Honthorst and van Everdingen were busy decorating the Huis ten Bosch near Den Haag for the Stadholder Frederick Henry, Rembrandt was having his monumental *Conspiracy of Julius Civilis* – painted for the new Amsterdam Town Hall – thrown out. The reasons for this rejection have been hotly debated, but it seems likely that Rembrandt's rendition was thought too pagan an interpretation of what was an important event in Dutch history – Julius had organized a revolt against the Romans, which had obvious resonance in a country just freed from the Habsburgs. Even worse, perhaps, Rembrandt had shown Julius to be blind in one eye, which was historically accurate but not at all what the city's burghers had in mind for a Dutch hero.

Finally, **Aert van Gelder** (1645–1727), Rembrandt's last pupil and probably the only one to concentrate on historical painting, followed the style of his master closely, producing shimmering biblical scenes well into the eighteenth century.

Genre painting

Often misunderstood, the term **genre painting** was initially applied to everything from animal paintings and still lifes through to historical works and landscapes, but later – from around the middle of the seventeenth century – came to be applied only to scenes of everyday life. Its target market was the region's burgeoning middle class, who had a penchant for non-idealized portrayals of common scenes, both with and without symbols – or subtly disguised details – making one moral point or another. One of its early practitioners was Antwerp's **Frans Snijders** (1579–1657), who took up still-life painting where Aertsen (see p.279) left off, amplifying his subject – food and drink – to even larger, more sumptuous canvases. Snijders also doubled up as a member of the Rubens art machine (see p.286), painting animals and still-life sections for the master's works. In Utrecht, Hendrik Terbrugghen and Gerard van Honthorst adapted the realism and strong chiaroscuro learned from Caravaggio to a number of tableaux of everyday life, though they were more concerned with religious works (see p.281), whilst Haarlem's Frans Hals dabbled in genre too, but is better known as a portraitist. The opposite is true of one of Hal's pupils, **Adriaen Brouwer** (1605–38), whose riotous tavern scenes were well received in their day and collected by, among others, Rubens and Rembrandt. Brouwer spent only a couple of years in Haarlem under Hals before returning to his native Flanders, where he influenced the inventive **David Teniers the Younger** (1610–90), who worked in Antwerp, and later in Brussels. Teniers' early paintings are Brouwer-like peasant scenes, although his later work is more delicate and diverse, including *kortegaardje* – guardroom scenes that show soldiers carousing. **Adriaen van Ostade** (1610–85), on the other hand, stayed in Haarlem most of his life, skilfully painting groups of peasants and tavern brawls – though his later acceptance by the establishment led him to water down the realism he had learnt from Brouwer. He was teacher to his brother **Isaak** (1621–49), who produced a large number of open-air peasant scenes, subtle combinations of genre and landscape work.

The English critic E.V. Lucas dubbed Teniers, Brouwer and Ostade "coarse and boorish" compared with **Jan Steen** (1625–79) who, along with Vermeer, is probably the most admired Dutch genre painter. You can see what he had in mind Steen's paintings offer the same Rabelaisian peasantry in full fling, but they go their debauched ways in broad daylight, and nowhere do you see the filthy rogues in shadowy hovels favoured by Brouwer and Ostade. Steen offers more humour, too, as well as more moralizing, identifying with the hedonistic mob and reproaching them at the same time. Indeed, many of his pictures are illustrations of well-known proverbs of the time – popular epithets on the evils of drink or the transience of human existence that were supposed to teach as well as entertain.

Leiden's **Gerrit Dou** (1613–75) was one of Rembrandt's first pupils. It's difficult to detect any trace of the master's influence in his work, however, as Dou initiated a style of his own: tiny, minutely realized and beautifully finished views of a kind of ordinary life that was decidedly more genteel than Brouwer's – or even Steen's for that matter. He was admired, above all, for his painstaking attention to detail; and he would, it's said, sit in his studio for hours waiting for the dust to settle before starting work. Among his students, **Frans van Mieris** (1635–81) continued the highly finished portrayals of the Dutch bourgeoisie, as did **Gabriel Metsu** (1629–67) – perhaps Dou's most talented pupil – whose pictures often convey an overtly moral message. Another pupil of Rembrandt's, though a much later one, was **Nicholas Maes** (1629–93), whose early works were almost entirely genre paintings, sensitively executed and again with an obvious didacticism. His later paintings show the influence of a more refined style of portraiture, which he had picked up in France.

As a native of Zwolle, well to the east of Amsterdam, **Gerard ter Borch** (1619–81) found himself far from all these Leiden/Rembrandt connections; despite trips abroad to most of the artistic capitals of Europe, he remained very much a provincial painter. He depicted the country's merchant class at play and became renowned for his curious doll-like figures and his ability to capture the textures of different cloths. His domestic scenes were not unlike those of **Pieter de Hooch** (1629–after 1684), whose simple depictions of everyday life are deliberately unsentimental, and have little or no moral commentary. De Hooch's favourite trick was to paint darkened rooms with an open door leading through to a sunlit courtyard, a practice that, along with his trademark rusty red colour, makes his work easy to identify and, at its best, exquisite. That said, his later pictures reflect the encroaching decadence of the Dutch Republic; the rooms are more richly decorated, the arrangements more contrived and the subjects far less homely.

It was, however, **Jan Vermeer** (1632–75) who brought the most sophisticated methods to painting interiors, depicting the play of natural light on indoor surfaces with superlative skill – and the tranquil intimacy for which he is now famous the world over. Another observer of the better-heeled Dutch household and, like de Hooch, without a moral tone, he is regarded (with Hals and Rembrandt) as one of the big three Dutch painters – though he was, it seems, a slow worker. As a result, only about forty paintings can be attributed to him with any certainty. Living all his life in Delft, to the south of Amsterdam, Vermeer is perhaps the epitome of the seventeenth-century Dutch painter – rejecting the pomp and ostentation of the High Renaissance to record quietly his contemporaries at home, painting for a public that demanded no more than that: bourgeois art at its most complete.

Portraits – and Rembrandt

Predictably enough, the ruling bourgeoisie of the United Provinces' mercantile society were keen to record and celebrate their success, and consequently portraiture was a reliable way for a young painter to make a living. **Michiel Jansz Miereveld** (1567–1641), court painter to Frederick Henry of Orange-Nassau in Den Haag, was the first real portraitist of the Dutch Republic, but it wasn't long before his stiff and rather conservative figures were superseded by the more spontaneous renderings of **Frans Hals** (1585–1666). Hals is perhaps best known for his "corporation pictures" – portraits of the members of the Dutch civil guard regiments that were formed in most of the larger towns during the war with Spain, but subsequently becoming social clubs. These large group pieces demanded superlative technique, since the painter had to create a collection of individual portraits while retaining a sense of the group, and accord prominence based on the relative importance of the sitters and the size of the payment each had made. Hals was particularly good at this, using innovative lighting effects, arranging his sitters subtly, and putting all the elements together in a fluid and dynamic composition. He also painted many individual portraits, making the ability to capture fleeting and telling expressions his trademark; his pictures of children are particularly sensitive. Later in life, however, his work became darker and more akin to Rembrandt's, spurred – it's conjectured – by his penury.

Jan Cornelisz Verspronck (1597–1662) and **Bartholomeus van der Helst** (1613–70) were the other great Haarlem portraitists after Frans Hals – Verspronck recognizable by the smooth, shiny glow he always gave to his sitters' faces, van der Helst by a competent but unadventurous style. Of the two, van der Helst was the more popular, influencing a number of later painters and leaving Haarlem as a young man to begin a solidly successful career as portrait painter to Amsterdam's burghers.

The reputation of **Rembrandt van Rijn** (1606–69) is still relatively recent – nineteenth-century connoisseurs preferred Gerard Dou – but he is now justly regarded as one of the greatest and most versatile painters of all time. Born in Leiden, the son of a miller, he was a boy apprentice to Jacob van Swanenburgh, a then quite important, though singularly uninventive, local artist. Rembrandt shared a studio with Jan Lievens, a promising painter and something of a rival, though now all but forgotten, before venturing forth to Amsterdam to study under the fashionable Pieter Lastman. Soon he was painting commissions for the city elite and became an accepted member of their circle. The poet and statesman Constantijn Huygens acted as his agent, pulling strings to obtain all of Rembrandt's more lucrative jobs, and in 1634 the artist married Saskia van Ulenborch, daughter of the burgomaster of Leeuwarden and quite a catch for a relatively humble artist. His self-portraits from this period show the confident face of security – on top of things and quite sure of where he's going.

Rembrandt would not always be the darling of the Amsterdam burghers, but his fall from grace was still some way off when he painted *The Night Watch* (see p.119), a group portrait often – but inaccurately – associated with the artist's decline in popularity. Indeed, although Rembrandt's fluent arrangement of his subjects was totally original, there's no evidence that the military company who commissioned the painting was anything but pleased with the result. More likely culprits are the artist's later pieces, whose obscure lighting and psychological insights took the conservative Amsterdam merchants by surprise, and his irascibility. Whatever the reason, his patrons were certainly not sufficiently enthusiastic about his later work to support both his taste for art collecting and his expensive house on Jodenbreestraat (see p.96), the result being that Rembrandt was declared bankrupt in 1656. Rembrandt died thirteen years later, a broken and embittered old man – as his last self-portraits show. Throughout his career he maintained a large studio, and his influence pervaded the next generation of Dutch painters. Some – Dou and Maes – more famous for their genre work, have already been mentioned. Others turned to portraiture.

Govert Flinck (1615–60) was perhaps Rembrandt's most faithful follower, and he was, ironically enough, given the job of decorating Amsterdam's new Town Hall after his teacher had been passed over. Unluckily for him, Flinck died before he could execute his designs and Rembrandt took over, but although the latter's *Conspiracy of Julius Civilis* was installed in 1662, it was discarded a year later for reasons that remain obscure. The early work of **Ferdinand Bol** (1616–80) was also heavily influenced by Rembrandt, so much so that for centuries art historians couldn't tell the two apart, though Bol's later paintings are readily distinguishable, blandly elegant portraits which proved very popular with the wealthy. At the age of 53, Bol married a wealthy widow and promptly stopped painting – perhaps because he knew how emotionally tacky his work had become. Most of the pitifully slim extant work of **Carel Fabritius** (1622–54) was portraiture, but he too died young, before he could properly realize his promise as perhaps the most gifted of all Rembrandt's students. Generally regarded as the teacher of Vermeer, he forms a link between the two masters, combining Rembrandt's technique with his own practice of painting figures against a dark background, prefiguring the lighting and colouring of Vermeer.

Landscapes

Aside from Pieter Bruegel the Elder (see p.279), whose depictions of his native surroundings make him the first true Low Countries landscape painter, **Gillis van Coninxloo** (1544–1607) stands out as the earliest Dutch landscapist. He imbued his native scenery with elements of fantasy, painting the richly wooded views he had seen on his travels around Europe as backdrops to biblical scenes. In the early seventeenth century, **Hercules Seghers** (1590–1638), apprenticed to Coninxloo, carried on his mentor's style of depicting forested and mountainous landscapes, some real, others not; his work is scarce but is believed to have had considerable influence on the landscape work of Rembrandt. **Esaias van der Velde**'s (1591–1632) quaint and unpretentious scenes show the first real affinity with the Dutch countryside, but while his influence was likewise considerable, he was soon overshadowed by his pupil **Jan van Goyen** (1596–1656). A remarkable painter, who belongs to the so-called "tonal phase" of Dutch landscape painting, van Goyen's early pictures were highly coloured and close to those of his teacher, but it didn't take him long to develop a marked touch of his own, using tones of green, brown and grey to lend everything a characteristic translucent haze. His paintings are, above all, of nature, and if he included figures it was just for the sake of scale. A long-neglected artist, van Goyen only received recognition with the arrival of the Impressionists, when his fluid and rapid brushwork was at last fully appreciated.

Another "tonal" painter, Haarlem's **Salomon van Ruysdael** (1600–70) was also directly affected by Esaias van der Velde, and his simple and atmospheric, though not terribly adventurous, landscapes were for a long time consistently confused with those of van Goyen. More esteemed is his nephew, **Jacob van Ruysdael** (1628–82), generally considered the greatest of all Dutch landscapists, whose fastidiously observed views of quiet flatlands dominated by stormy skies were to influence European landscapists right up to the nineteenth century. Constable, certainly, acknowledged a debt to him. Ruysdael's foremost pupil was **Meindert Hobbema** (1638–1709), who followed the master faithfully, sometimes even painting the same views as in his *Avenue at Middelharnis*.

Nicholas Berchem (1620–83) and **Jan Both** (1618–52) were the "Italianizers" of Dutch landscapes. They studied in Rome, taking back to the Netherlands rich, golden views of the world, full of steep gorges and hills, picturesque ruins and wandering shepherds. **Allart van Everdingen** (1621–75) had a similar approach, but his subject matter stemmed from his travels in Norway, which, after his return to the Netherlands, he reproduced in all its mountainous glory. **Aelbert Cuyp** (1620–91), on the other hand, stayed in Dordrecht all his life, painting what was probably the favourite city skyline of Dutch landscapists. He inherited the warm tones of the Italianizers, and his pictures are always suffused with a deep, golden glow.

Of a number of specialist seventeenth-century painters who can be included here, **Paulus Potter** (1625–54) is rated as the best painter of domestic animals. He produced a surprisingly large number of paintings in his short life, the most reputed being his lovingly executed pictures of cows and horses. The accurate rendering of architectural features also became a specialized field, in which **Pieter Saenredam** (1597–1665), with his finely realized paintings of Dutch church interiors, is the most widely known exponent. **Emanuel de Witte** (1616–92) continued in the same vein, though his churches lack the spartan crispness of Saenredam's. **Gerrit Berckheyde** (1638–98) worked in Haarlem soon after, but he limited his views to the outside of buildings, producing variations on the same townscapes. Nautical scenes in praise of the Dutch navy were, on the other hand, the speciality of **Willem van der Velde II** (1633–1707), whose melodramatic canvases, complete with churning seas and chasing skies, are displayed to greatest advantage in the Nederlands Scheepvaartsmuseum in Amsterdam (see p.108).

A further thriving category of seventeenth-century painting was the still life, in which objects were gathered together to remind the viewer of the transience of human life and the meaninglessness of worldly pursuits. Thus, a skull would often be shown alongside a book, pipe or goblet, and some half-eaten food. Two Haarlem painters dominated this field: **Pieter Claesz** (1598–1660) and **Willem Heda** (1594–1680), who confined themselves almost entirely to this type of painting.

Rubens and his followers

Down in the south, in Antwerp, **Pieter Paul Rubens** (1577–1640) was easily the most important exponent of the Baroque in northern Europe. Born in Siegen, Westphalia, he was raised in Antwerp, where he entered the painters' Guild in 1598. Two years later, he became court painter to the Duke of Mantua and thereafter he travelled extensively in Italy, absorbing the art of the High Renaissance and classical architecture. By the time of his return to Antwerp in 1608 he had acquired an enormous artistic vocabulary – and like his Dutch contemporaries (see p.281), the paintings of Caravaggio were to greatly influence his work. His first major success was *The Raising of the Cross*, painted in 1610 and displayed today in Antwerp cathedral. A large, dynamic work, it caused a sensation at the time, establishing Rubens' reputation and leading to a string of commissions that enabled him to set up his own studio.

The division of labour in Rubens' studio, and the talent of the artists working there (who included Anthony van Dyck and Jacob Jordaens – see opposite) ensured an extraordinary output of excellent work. The degree to which Rubens personally worked on a canvas would vary – and would determine its price. From the early 1620s onwards he turned his hand to a plethora of themes and subjects – religious works, portraits, tapestry designs, landscapes, mythological scenes, ceiling paintings – each of which was handled with supreme vitality and virtuosity. From his Flemish antecedents he inherited an acute sense of light, and used it not to dramatize his subjects (a technique favoured by Caravaggio and other Italian artists), but in association with colour and form. The drama in his works comes from the vigorous animation of his characters. His large-scale allegorical works, especially, are packed with heaving, writhing figures that appear to tumble out from the canvas.

The energy of Rubens' paintings was reflected in his private life. In addition to his career as an artist, he also undertook diplomatic missions to Spain and

England, and used these opportunities to study the works of other artists and – as in the case of Velázquez – to meet them personally. In the 1630s, gout began to hamper his activities, and from this time his painting became more domestic and meditative. Hélène Fourment, his second wife, was the subject of many portraits and served as a model for characters in his allegorical paintings, her figure epitomizing the buxom, well-rounded women found throughout his work.

Rubens' influence on the artists of the period was enormous. The huge output of his studio meant that his works were universally seen and also widely disseminated by the engravers he employed to copy his work. Chief among his followers was the portraitist **Anthony van Dyck** (1599–1641), who worked in Rubens' studio from 1618, often taking on the depiction of religious figures in his master's works that required particular sensitivity and pathos. Like Rubens, van Dyck was born in Antwerp and travelled widely in Italy, though his initial work was influenced less by the Italian artists than by Rubens himself. Eventually van Dyck developed his own distinct style and technique, establishing himself as court painter to Charles I in England, and creating portraits of a nervous elegance that would influence the genre there for the next 150 years. **Jacob Jordaens** (1593–1678) was also an Antwerp native who studied under Rubens. Although he was commissioned to complete several works left unfinished by Rubens at the time of his death, his robustly naturalistic works have an earthy – and sensuous – realism that is quite different and distinct in style and technique.

The eighteenth and nineteenth centuries

Accompanying the Netherlands' economic decline was a gradual deterioration in the quality and originality of Dutch painting. The subtle delicacies of the classical seventeenth-century painters was replaced by finicky still lifes and minute studies of flowers, or overly finessed portraiture and religious scenes, as in the work of **Adrian van der Werff** (1659–1722). Of the era's big names, **Gerard de Lairesse** (1640–1711) spent most of his time decorating a rash of brand-new civic halls and mansions, but, like the buildings he worked on, his style and influences were French. **Jacob de Wit** (1695–1754) continued where Lairesse left off, painting burgher ceiling after ceiling in flashy style. He also benefited from a relaxation in the laws against Catholics, decorating several of their (newly legal) churches. The eighteenth century's only painter of any real talent was **Cornelis Troost** (1697–1750) who, although he didn't produce anything stunningly original, painted competent portraits and some neat, faintly satirical pieces that have since earned him the title of "The Dutch Hogarth". Cosy interiors also continued to prove popular, and the Haarlem painter **Wybrand Hendriks** (1744–1831) satisfied demand with numerous proficient examples.

Johann Barthold Jongkind (1819–91) was the first important artist to emerge in the nineteenth century, painting landscapes and seascapes that were to influence Monet and the early Impressionists. He spent most of his life in France and his work was exhibited in Paris with the Barbizon painters, though he owed less to them than to van Goyen and the seventeenth-century "tonal" artists. Jongkind's work was a logical precursor to the art of the **Hague School**. Based in and around Den Haag between 1870 and 1900, this prolific group of

△ Van Gogh's *Irises*

painters tried to re-establish a characteristically Dutch national school of paint-ing. They produced atmospheric studies of the dunes and polders around Den Haag, nature pictures that are characterized by grey, rain-filled skies, windswept seas, and silvery, flat beaches – pictures that, for some, verge on the sentimen-tal. **J.H. Weissenbruch** (1824–1903) was a founding member, a specialist in low, flat beach scenes dotted with stranded boats. The banker-turned-artist **H.W. Mesdag** (1831–1915) did the same but with more skill than imagina-tion, while **Jacob Maris** (1837–99), one of three artist brothers, was perhaps the most typical with his rural and sea scenes heavily covered by grey, chasing skies. His brother **Matthijs** (1839–1917) was less predictable, ultimately tiring of his colleagues' interest in straight observation and going to London to design windows, while the youngest brother **Willem** (1844–1910) is best known for his small, unpretentious studies of nature.

Anton Mauve (1838–88) is better known, an exponent of soft, pastel land-scapes and an early teacher of van Gogh. Profoundly influenced by the French

Barbizon painters – Corot, Millet et al – he went to Hilversum near Amsterdam in 1885 to set up his own group, which became known as the "Dutch Barbizon". **Jozef Israëls** (1826–1911) has often been likened to Millet, though it's generally agreed that he had more in common with the Impressionists, and his best pictures are his melancholy portraits and interiors. Lastly, **Johan Bosboom**'s (1817–91) church interiors may be said to sum up the romanticized nostalgia of the Hague School; shadowy and populated by figures in seventeenth-century dress, they seem to yearn for the country's Golden Age.

Vincent van Gogh (1853–90), on the other hand, was one of the least "Dutch" of Dutch artists, and he spent most of his relatively short painting career in France. After countless studies of Dutch peasant life – studies which culminated in his sombre *Potato Eaters* (see p.121) – he went to live in Paris with his art-dealer brother Theo. There, under the influence of the Impressionists, he lightened his palette, following the pointillist work of Seurat and "trying to render intense colour and not a grey harmony". Two years later he went south to Arles, the "land of blue tones and gay colours", and, struck by the brilliance of Mediterranean light, his characteristic style began to develop. A disastrous attempt to live with Gauguin, and the much-publicized episode when he cut off part of his ear and presented it to a local prostitute, led to his committal in an asylum at St-Rémy. Here he produced some of his most famous, and most Expressionistic, canvases – strongly coloured and with the paint thickly, almost frantically, applied. Now one of the world's most popular – and popularized – painters, Amsterdam's Van Gogh Museum has the world's finest collection of his work (see pp.120–123).

Like van Gogh, **Jan Toorop** (1858–1928) went through multiple artistic changes, though he did not need to travel to do so; he radically adapted his technique from a fairly conventional pointillism through a tired Expressionism to Symbolism with an Art Nouveau feel. Roughly contemporary, **George Hendrik Breitner** (1857–1923) was a better painter, and one who refined his style rather than changed it. His snapshot-like impressions of his beloved Amsterdam figure among his best work and offered a promising start to the new century.

The twentieth century

Each of the major modern art movements has had – or has – its followers in the Netherlands and each has been diluted or altered according to local taste. Of many lesser names, **Jan Sluyters** (1881–1957) stands out as the Dutch pioneer of Cubism, but this is small beer when compared with the one specifically Dutch movement – **De Stijl** (The Style). **Piet Mondriaan** (1872–1944) was De Stijl's leading figure, developing the realism he had learned from the Hague School painters – via Cubism, which he criticized for being too cowardly to depart totally from representation – into a complete abstraction of form which he called Neo-Plasticism. Mondriaan was something of a mystic, and this was to some extent responsible for the direction that De Stijl – and his paintings – took: canvases painted with grids of lines and blocks made up of the three primary colours plus white, black and grey. Mondriaan believed this freed his art from the vagaries of personal perception, making it possible to obtain what he called "a true vision of reality".

De Stijl took other forms too; there was a magazine of the same name, and the movement introduced new concepts into every aspect of design, from painting to interior design and architecture. But in all these media, lines were kept simple, colours bold and clear. **Theo van Doesburg** (1883–1931) was a De Stijl co-founder and major theorist. His work is similar to Mondriaan's except for the noticeable absence of thick, black borders and the diagonals that he introduced into his work, calling his paintings "contra-compositions" – which, he said, were both more dynamic and more in touch with twentieth-century life. **Bart van der Leck** (1876–1958) was the third member of the circle, identifiable by white canvases covered by seemingly randomly placed interlocking coloured triangles. Mondriaan split with De Stijl in 1925, going on to attain new artistic extremes of clarity and soberness before moving to New York in the 1940s and producing atypically exuberant works such as *Victory Boogie Woogie* – named for the artist's love of jazz.

During and after De Stijl, a number of other movements flourished in the Netherlands, though their impact was not so great and their influence was largely local. The Expressionist **Bergen School** was probably the most localized, its best-known exponent **Charley Toorop** (1891–1955), daughter of Jan, developing a distinctively glaring but strangely sensitive realism. **De Ploeg** (The Plough), centred in Groningen, was headed by **Jan Wiegers** (1893–1959) and influenced by Ernst Ludwig Kirchner and the German Expressionists; the group's artists set out to capture the uninviting landscapes around their native town, and produced violently coloured canvases that hark back to van Gogh. Another group, known as the **Magic Realists**, surfaced in the 1930s, painting quasi-surrealistic scenes that, according to their leading light, **Carel Willink** (1900–83), revealed "a world stranger and more dreadful in its haughty impenetrability than the most terrifying nightmare."

Postwar Dutch art began with **CoBrA**: a loose grouping of like-minded painters from Denmark, Belgium and the Netherlands, whose name derives from the initial letters of their respective capital cities. Their first exhibition at Amsterdam's Stedelijk Museum in 1949 provoked a furore, at the centre of which was **Karel Appel** (b.1921), whose brutal Abstract Expressionist pieces, plastered with paint inches thick, were, he maintained, necessary for the era – indeed, inevitable reflections of it. "I paint like a barbarian in a barbarous age," he claimed. In the graphic arts, the most famous twentieth-century Dutch figure was **Maurits Cornelis Escher** (1898–1972), whose Surrealistic illusions and allusions were underpinned by his fascination with mathematics.

As for today, a vibrant contemporary art scene sustains an ambitious programme of temporary exhibitions at several public galleries, most notably De Appel (see p.77) and the Stedelijk Museum (see p.109), and nourishes about a dozen premier private/commercial art galleries (box, see p.221). Among modern Dutch artists, look out for the abstract work of **Edgar Fernhout** (1912–74) and **Ad Dekkers** (1938–74), the reliefs of **Jan Schoonhoven** (1914–94), the multimedia productions of **Jan Dibbets** (b.1941), the imprecisely coloured geometric designs of **Rob van Koningsbruggen** (b.1948), the smeary Expressionism of **Toon Verhoef** (b.1946), and the exuberant figures of **Rene Daniels** (b.1950) – to name just seven of the more important figures.

Books

Most of the following books should be readily available in bookshops or online, though you may have a little more difficulty tracking down those few titles we mention which are currently out of print, signified o/p.

Travel and general

A. Burton et al *Smokers Guide to Amsterdam.* Exactly what it says – a dope-smokers' guide to the city with no leaf unturned. There's an associated website too – ⓦwww.smokersguide.com. o/p

🏃 **Han van der Horst** *The Low Sky: Understanding the Dutch.* Thoughtful, thoroughgoing attempt to explain the Dutch mentality to the outside world, from the peripheral – herring eating and gardening – to weightier sections on attitudes to egalitarianism and conspicuous consumption. The best book of its type on the market.

Simon Kuper *Ajax, the Dutch, the War: Football in Europe in the Second World War.* Full marks for the idea, but the tying in of the Ajax football team to the broader themes of the book's title is a tad cumbersome in its execution. Nevertheless, some intriguing details – and disappointments – regarding the extent of collaboration during the German occupation.

Tim Webb *Good Beer Guide to Belgium & Holland.* Detailed and enthusiastic guide to the best bars, beers and breweries, including a strong showing for Amsterdam. A good read,

and extremely well informed to boot, though it's beginning to show its age – it was published in 2002. Nonetheless, it's the best book on its subject on the market.

David Winner *Brilliant Orange – The Neurotic Genius of Dutch Football.* Great title, great cover and great idea – zeroing in on the fine Dutch footballers of the 1960s and 1970s, including super-talented Johan Cruyff, and the way they – and their style of play – reflect Dutch culture and history. The problem is that sometimes the inferences and conclusions seem too obtuse, or at least unconvincing. Seven out of ten.

🏃 **Manfred Wolf (ed.)** *Amsterdam: A Traveler's Literary Companion.* Published by an independent American press, Whereabout Press, these anthologies aim to get to the heart of the modern cities they cover, and this well-chosen mixture of travel pieces, short fiction and reportage does exactly that, uncovering a low-life aspect to the city of Amsterdam that exists beyond the tourist brochures. A high-quality and evocative selection, and often the only chance you'll get to read some of this material in translation.

History and politics

Ayaan Hirsi Ali *Infidel: My Life.* This powerful and moving autobiography written by one of the Netherlands' most controversial figures, begins with Ali's harsh and sometimes brutal childhood in Somalia and then Saudi Arabia, where

– amongst other tribulations – her grandmother insisted she have her clitoris cut off when she was five. Later, in 1992, Ali wound up in the Netherlands at least partly to evade an arranged marriage. Thereafter, she made a remarkable transition from factory cleaner to MP, becoming a leading light of the rightist VVD political party and remaining outspoken in her denunciations of militant Islam (see p.276). Due to death threats, Ali was forced to go into hiding in 2004, only returning to parliament in 2005. She now lives in the USA.

Leo Akveld et al *The Colourful World of the VOC*. Beautifully illustrated, coffee-table sized book on the VOC – the East India Company. The subject is dealt with in a series of intriguing essays on the likes of the uses of Eastern spices, Indonesian fashion and furniture, rituals and beliefs. The only problem is that it is hard to get hold of outside of Amsterdam.

J.C.H. Blom (ed.) *History of the Low Countries*. Books on the totality of Dutch history are thin on the ground, so this heavyweight volume fills a few gaps, though it's hardly sun-lounge reading. A series of historians weigh in with their specialities, from Roman times onwards. Taken as a whole, its forte is in picking out those cultural, political and economic themes that give the region its distinctive character.

Mike Dash *Tulipomania*. An examination of the introduction of the tulip into the Low Countries at the height of the Golden Age – and the extraordinarily inflated and speculative market that ensued. There's a lot of padding and scene-setting, but it's an engaging enough read, and has nice detail on seventeenth-century Amsterdam, Leiden and Haarlem.

Pieter Geyl *The Revolt of The Netherlands 1555–1609* and *The Netherlands in the Seventeenth Century 1609–1648*. Geyl presents a detailed account of the Netherlands during its formative years, chronicling the uprising against the Spanish and the formation of the United Provinces. First published in 1932, it has long been regarded as the classic text on the subject, though it is a hard and ponderous read.

A. C. Grayling *Descartes: The Life and Times of a Genius*. One of the greatest philosophers of all time, René Descartes (1596–1650) was a key figure in the transition from medieval to early modern Europe. He also made key contributions to optics and geometry and, amongst his miscellaneous travels, spent time living in Amsterdam (see p.70). This crisply written, erudite biography deals skilfully with the philosophy – Grayling is himself a philosophy professor – and argues that Descartes was almost certainly a Jesuit spy acting on behalf of the Habsburg interest during his time here in Amsterdam.

Christopher Hibbert *Cities and Civilisation*. Includes a diverting chapter on Amsterdam in the age of Rembrandt. Hibbert, one of the UK's best historians, is always a pleasure to read.

Lisa Jardine *The Awful End of Prince William the Silent*. Great title for an intriguing book on the premature demise of one of the country's most acclaimed heroes, who was assassinated in Delft in 1584. At just 160 pages, the tale is told succinctly, but – unless you have a particular interest in early firearms – there is a bit too much information on guns.

Carol Ann Lee *Roses from the Earth: the Biography of Anne Frank*. Amongst a spate of recent publications trawling through and over the life of the young Jewish diarist, this is probably the best, written in a straightforward and insightful manner without sentimentality. Working the same mine is the same author's *The Hidden Life of Otto Frank* – clear, lucid and equally as interesting.

Geert Mak *Amsterdam: A Brief Life of the City*. First published in 1995, this infinitely readable trawl through the city's past is a simply wonderful book – amusing and perceptive, alternately tart and indulgent. It's more a social history than anything else, so – for example – it's here you'll find out quite why Rembrandt lived in the Jewish Quarter and why the city's merchant elite ossified in the eighteenth century. It's light and accessible enough to read from cover to cover, but its index of places makes it easy to dip into. Highly recommended.

🏃 **Geoffrey Parker** *The Dutch Revolt*. Compelling account of the struggle between the Netherlands and Spain. Quite the best thing you can read on the period. Also *The Army of Flanders and the Spanish Road 1567–1659*. The title may sound academic, but this book gives a fascinating insight into the Habsburg army that occupied the Low Countries for well over a hundred years – how it functioned, was fed and moved from Spain to the Low Countries along the so-called Spanish Road.

Simon Schama *The Embarrassment of Riches: An Interpretation of Dutch Culture in the Golden Age*. Long before his reinvention on British TV, Schama had a reputation as a specialist in Dutch history, and this chunky volume draws on a huge variety of archive sources. Also by Schama, *Patriots and Liberators: Revolution in the Netherlands 1780–1813* focuses on one of the less familiar periods of Dutch history and is particularly good on the Batavian Republic set up in the Netherlands under French auspices. Both are heavyweight tomes, and leftists might well find Schama too reactionary by half. See also Schama's *Rembrandt's Eyes* (below).

Andrew Wheatcroft *The Habsburgs*. Excellent and well-researched trawl through the family's history, from eleventh-century beginnings to its eclipse at the end of World War I. Enjoyable background reading.

Art and architecture

Svetlana Alpers *Rembrandt's Enterprise*. Intriguing 1988 study of Rembrandt, positing the theory – in line with findings of the Leiden-based Rembrandt Research Project – that many previously accepted Rembrandt paintings are not his at all, but merely the products of his studio. Bad news if you own one.

🏃 **Anthony Bailey** *A View of Delft*. Concise, startlingly well-researched book on Vermeer, complete with an accurate and well-considered exploration of his milieu.

R. H. Fuchs *Dutch Painting*. As complete an introduction to the subject – from Flemish origins to the present day – as you could wish for, in just a couple of hundred pages. First published in the 1970s. o/p

Walter S. Gibson *Hieronymus Bosch* and *Bruegel*. Two wonderfully illustrated Thames & Hudson titles on these two exquisite allegorical painters. The former contains everything you wanted to know about Hieronymus Bosch, his paintings and his late fifteenth-century milieu, while the latter takes a detailed look at Pieter Bruegel the Elder's art, with nine well-argued chapters investigating its various components.

H.L.C. Jaffé *De Stijl: Visions of Utopia*. A good, informed introduction to the twentieth-century movement and its philosophical and social influences. Well illustrated too. o/p

Melissa McQuillan *Van Gogh*. Extensive, in-depth look at Vincent's paintings, as well as his life and times. Superbly researched and illustrated; published by Thames & Hudson.

Simon Schama *Rembrandt's Eyes*. Published in 1999, this erudite work received good reviews, but it's very, very long – and often very long-winded.

Irving Stone *Lust for Life: the Life of Vincent Van Gogh*. Everything you ever wanted to know about van Gogh in a pop genius-is-pain biography.

🏃 **Mariet Westerman** *The Art of the Dutch Republic 1585–1718*. This excellently written, immaculately illustrated and enthralling book tackles its subject thematically, from the marketing of works to an exploration of Dutch ideologies – but unfortunately it's o/p. Also by Westerman is an all-you-could-ever-want-to-know book about *Rembrandt*.

Christopher White *Rembrandt*. White is something of a Rembrandt specialist, writing a series of books on the man and his times. Most of these books are expensive and aimed at the specialist art market, but this particular title is perfect for the general reader. Well illustrated plus a wonderfully incisive and extremely detailed commentary.

Frank Wynne *I was Vermeer: The Legend of the Forger who Swindled the Nazis*. Amsterdam's Han van Meegeren (see p.72) fooled everyone, including Hermann Goering, with his "lost" Vermeers, but in fact he painted them himself. This story of bluff, bluster and fine art is an intriguing tale no doubt, but Wynne's newly published book, though extremely well informed, is overly written and overly long. For more on van Meegeren, you might try **Maurice Moiseiwitsch**'s *The Van Meegeren Mystery* instead, though it's o/p and fairly hard to get hold of (it was published in 1964).

Literature

Tracey Chevalier *Girl with a Pearl Earring*. Chevalier's novel is a fanciful piece of fiction, building a story around the subject of one of Vermeer's most enigmatic paintings. It's an absorbing read, if a tad too detailed and slow-moving for some tastes, and it paints a convincing picture of seventeenth-century Delft, exploring its social structures and values. Has proved very popular.

Rudi van Dantzig *For a Lost Soldier*. Honest and convincing tale, largely autobiographical, that gives an insight into the confusion and loneliness of the approximately 50,000 Dutch children evacuated to foster families during World War II. The novel's leading character is Jeroen, an 11-year-old boy from Amsterdam who is sent to live in the countryside. During the Liberation celebrations, he meets an American soldier, Walt, with whom he has a brief sexual encounter; Walt disappears a few days later. Van Dantzig was the artistic director of the Dutch National Ballet until 1991. This was his debut novel. o/p

Anne Frank *The Diary of a Young Girl*. Lucid and moving, the most revealing book you can read on the plight of Amsterdam's Jews during the German occupation. An international bestseller since its original publication in 1947.

Nicolas Freeling *Love in Amsterdam*; *Dwarf Kingdom*; *A Long Silence*; *A City Solitary* (o/p); *Strike Out Where Not Applicable* (o/p). Freeling writes detective novels, and his most famous creation is the rebel cop van der Valk. These are light, carefully crafted tales, with just the right amount of twists to make them classic cops 'n' robbers reading – and with good Amsterdam (and Dutch) locations. London-born, Freeling still evokes Amsterdam (and Amsterdammers) as well as any writer ever has, subtly and unsentimentally using the city and its people as a vivid backdrop to his fast-moving action.

Etty Hillesum *An Interrupted Life: the Diaries and Letters of Etty Hillesum, 1941–43*. The Germans transported Hillesum, a young Jewish woman, from her home in Amsterdam to Auschwitz, where she died. As with Anne Frank's more famous journal, penetratingly written – though on the whole a tad less readable.

Richard Huijing (ed. & trans.) *The Dedalus Book of Dutch Fantasy*. A fun and artfully selected collection of stories containing contributions from some of the greats of Dutch literature, including a number whose work does not, as yet, appear in translation anywhere else. o/p

Arthur Japin *The Two Hearts of Kwasi Boachi*. Inventive re-creation of a true story in which the eponymous Ashanti prince was dispatched to the court of King William of the Netherlands in 1837. Kwasi and his companion Kwame were ostensibly sent to Den Haag to further their education, but there was a strong colonial subtext. Superb descriptions of Ashanti-land in its pre-colonial pomp. Also Japin's *Lucia's Eyes*, an imaginative extrapolation of a casual anecdote found in Casanova's memoirs and set for the most part in eighteenth-century Amsterdam.

Adrian Matthews *The Apothecary's House*. Amsterdam is perhaps the most compelling character in this recent thriller, in which local colour is often the winner over a sometimes creaky plot. At over 600 pages, it's a bit of a commitment, but it's a deliberately evocative and therefore interesting book to take with you on a visit to the city.

Sylvie Matton *Rembrandt's Whore*. Taking its cue from Chevalier's *Girl with a Pearl Earring* (see opposite), this slim novel tries hard to conjure Rembrandt's life and times, with some (limited) success. Matton certainly knows her Rembrandt onions – she worked for two years on a film of his life.

Sarah Emily Miano *Van Rijn*. Carefully composed re-creation of Rembrandt's milieu, based on the (documented) visit of Cosimo de Medici to the artist's house. As an attempt to venture into Rembrandt's soul it does well – but not brilliantly.

Marga Minco *The Fall*; *An Empty House*; *The Glass Bridge*; *Bitter Herbs*. The prolific Minco has written widely and well about the city's Jewish community, particularly during the German occupation. She herself was a Holocaust survivor, spending several years in hiding – unlike the rest of her family, who were dispatched to concentration camps where they all died. One of Minco's favourite hideaways was Kloveniersburgwal 49, which served as a safe house for various Dutch artists and later as the inspiration for *An Empty House*. Published in 1989, *Bitter Herbs* is her testament. All o/p.

Deborah Moggach *Tulip Fever*. At first Deborah Moggach's novel seems no more than an attempt to build a story out of her favourite domestic Dutch interiors, genre scenes and still-life paintings. But ultimately the story is a basic one – of lust, greed, mistaken identity and tragedy. The Golden Age Amsterdam backdrop is well realized, but almost incidental.

Marcel Moring *In Babylon*. Popular Dutch author with an intense style and thought-provoking, philosophical content. *In Babylon* has an older Jewish man and his niece trapped in a cabin in the eastern Netherlands and here they ruminate on their family's history. Moring's *Dream Room* is also gracefully nostalgic in its concentration on the family of Boris and his son, David, while Moring's latest novel, *Dis*, is set in the town of Assen, again in the east of the country, during the annual Dutch TT motorbike races.

Harry Mulisch *The Assault*. Set part in Haarlem, part in Amsterdam, this novel traces the story of a young boy who loses his family in a reprisal-raid by the Nazis. A powerful tale, made into an excellent and effective film. Also, *The Discovery of Heaven*, a gripping yarn of adventure and happenstance; *The Procedure*, featuring a modern-day Dutch scientist investigating strange goings-on in sixteenth-century Prague; and *Siegfried: a Black Idyll*, whose central question is whether a work of imagination can help to understand the nature of evil in general and Hitler in particular.

Multatuli *Max Havelaar: Or, The Coffee Auctions of the Dutch Trading Company*. Classic nineteenth-century Dutch satire of colonial life in the East Indies. Eloquent and intermittently amusing. If you have Dutch friends, they should be impressed (dumbstruck) if you have actually read it, not least since it's 352 pages long. For more on Multatuli, see p.66.

Cees Nooteboom *Rituals*. Nooteboom published his first novel in 1955, but only hit the literary headlines with this his third novel, in 1980. The central theme of all his work is the phenomenon of time; *Rituals* in particular is about the passing of time and the different ways of controlling the process. Inni Wintrop, the main character, is an outsider, a well-heeled, antique-dabbling "dilettante" as he describes himself. The book is almost entirely set in Amsterdam, and although it describes the inner life of Inni himself,

it also paints a strong picture of the city.

David Veronese *Jana*. A hip thriller set in the druggy underworld of Amsterdam and London.

Janwillem van de Wetering *Tumbleweed*; *Hard Rain*; *Corpse on the Dyke*; *Outsider in Amsterdam*. Offbeat detective tales set in Amsterdam and the provinces. Humane, quirky and humorous, Wetering's novels have inventive plots and feature unusual characters in interesting locations, though the prose itself can be a tad indigestible.

Jan Wolkers *Turkish Delight*. Wolkers is one of the Netherlands' best-known artists and writers, and this is one of his early novels, a close examination of the relationship between a bitter, working-class sculptor and his young, middle-class wife. A compelling work, at times misogynistic and even offensive, by a writer who seeks reaction above all. If you like it, try Wolkers' *Horrible Tango*. Both o/p.

Language

Language

Language

I t's unlikely that you'll need to speak anything other than English while you're in Amsterdam; the Dutch have a seemingly natural talent for languages, and your attempts at speaking theirs may be met with some bewilderment – though this can have as much to do with your pronunciation (Dutch is very difficult to get right) as their surprise that you're making an effort. Outside Amsterdam, people aren't quite as cosmopolitan, but even so, the Dutch **words and phrases** below should be the most you'll need to get by; also included is a basic **food and drink glossary**, though menus are nearly always multilingual; where they aren't, ask and one will almost invariably appear.

Dutch is a Germanic language – the word "Dutch" itself is a corruption of Deutsche, a label inaccurately given by English sailors in the seventeenth century, and indeed, although the Dutch are at pains to stress the differences between the two languages, if you know any German you'll spot many similarities. As for phrasebooks, the *Rough Guide to Dutch* is pocket-sized, and has a good dictionary section (English–Dutch and Dutch–English), as well as a menu reader; it also provides a useful introduction to grammar and pronunciation.

Pronunciation

Dutch is **pronounced** in much the same way as English. However, there are a few Dutch sounds that don't exist in English, which can be difficult to get right without practice.

Consonants

Double-consonant combinations generally keep their separate sounds in Dutch: *kn*, for example, is never like the English "knight". Note also the following consonants and consonant combinations:

j is an English y

ch and **g** indicate a throaty sound, as at the end of the Scottish word loch. The Dutch word for canal – *gracht* – is especially tricky, since it has two of these sounds – it comes out along the lines of *khrakht*. A

common word for hello is *Dag!* – pronounced like *daakh*

ng as in bring

nj as in onion

y is not a consonant, but another way of writing **ij**

Vowels and diphthongs

A good rule of thumb is that doubling the letter lengthens the vowel sound.

a is like the English apple

aa like cart

e like let

ee like late

o as in pop

oo in pope

u is like the French t**u** if preceded by a consonant; it's like w**oo**d if followed by a consonant

uu is the French t**u**

au and **ou** like h**ow**

ei and **ij** as in f**i**ne, though this varies strongly from region to region; sometimes it can sound more like l**a**ne

oe as in s**oo**n

eu is like the diphthong in the French l**eu**r

ui is the hardest Dutch diphthong of all, pronounced like h**ow** but much further forward in the mouth, with lips pursed (as if to say "**oo**").

Words and phrases

Basics

ja	yes
nee	no
alstublieft	please
(nee) dank u or bedankt	(no) thank you
hallo, dag or hoi	hello
goedemorgen	good morning
goedemiddag	good afternoon
goedenavond	good evening
tot ziens	goodbye
tot straks	see you later
Spreekt u Engels?	Do you speak English?
Ik kan je niet verstaan	I don't understand
vrouwen/mannen	women/men
kinderen	children
heren/dames	men's/women's toilets
Ik wil...	I want...
Ik wil niet... (+verb)	I don't want to...
Ik wil geen...(+noun)	I don't want any...
Wat kost...?	How much is...?

Travel, directions and shopping

Hoe kom ik in...?	How do I get to...?
Waar is...?	Where is...?
Hoe ver is het naar...?	How far is it to...?
ver/dichtbij	far/near
links/rechts	left/right
rechtdoor	straight ahead
luchthaven	airport
postkantoor	post office
postbus	postbox
postzegel(s)	stamp(s)
geldwisselkantoor	money exchange
kassa	cash desk
spoor or perron	railway platform
luchthaven	airport
loket	ticket office
hier/daar	here/there
goed/slecht	good/bad
groot/klein	big/small
open/gesloten	open/closed
duwen/trekken	push/pull
nieuw/oud	new/old
goedkoop/duur	cheap/expensive
heet or warm/koud	hot/cold
met/zonder	with/without
noord	North
zuid	South
oost	East
west	West

Signs and abbreviations

A.U.B.	*Alstublieft*: please (also shown as S.V.P., from French)	BG	*Begane grond*: ground floor
		BTW	*Belasting Toegevoegde Waarde*: VAT

LANGUAGE — Words and phrases
L
300

geen toegang	no entry	**open**	open
gesloten	closed	**T/M**	*Tot en met:* up to and including
ingang	entrance	**toegang**	entrance
K	*kelder:* basement	**uitgang**	exit
let op!	attention!	**V.A.**	*vanaf:* from
heren/ dames	men's/women's toilets	**Z.O.Z.**	please turn over (page, leaflet, etc)

Useful cycling terms

band	tyre	**trapper**	pedal
lek	puncture	**pomp**	pump
rem	brake	**stuur**	handlebars
ketting	chain	**kapot**	broken
wiel	wheel	**fietspad**	cycle path

Days of the week

zondag	Sunday	**vandaag**	today
maandag	Monday	**morgen**	tomorrow
dinsdag	Tuesday	**morgenochtend**	tomorrow morning
woensdag	Wednesday	**jaar**	year
donderdag	Thursday	**maand**	month
vrijdag	Friday	**week**	week
zaterdag	Saturday	**dag**	day
gisteren	yesterday		

Months of the year

januari	January	**juli**	July
februari	February	**augustus**	August
maart	March	**september**	September
april	April	**oktober**	October
mei	May	**november**	November
juni	June	**december**	December

Time

hour	uur	3.30	half vier
minute	minuut	3.35	vijf over half vier
What time is it?	Hoe laat is het?	3.40	tien over half vier
It's…	Het is…	3.45	kwart voor vier
3.00	drie uur	3.50	tien voor vier
3.05	vijf over drie	3.55	vijf voor vier
3.10	tien over drie	8am	acht uur 's ochtends
3.15	kwart over drie	1pm	een uur 's middags
3.20	tien voor half vier	8pm	acht uur 's avonds
3.25	vijf voor half vier	1am	een uur 's nachts

Numbers

When saying a number, the Dutch generally transpose the last two digits: for example, €3.25 is *drie euros vijf en twintig*.

0	nul		19	negentien
1	een		20	twintig
2	twee		21	een en twintig
3	drie		22	twee en twintig
4	vier		30	dertig
5	vijf		40	veertig
6	zes		50	vijftig
7	zeven		60	zestig
8	acht		70	zeventig
9	negen		80	tachtig
10	tien		90	negentig
11	elf		100	honderd
12	twaalf		101	honderd een
13	dertien		200	twee honderd
14	veertien		201	twee honderd een
15	vijftien		500	vijf honderd
16	zestien		525	vijf honderd vijf en twintig
17	zeventien		1000	duizend
18	achttien			

L

LANGUAGE | Food and drink

Food and drink

Basics

boter	butter		pindakaas	peanut butter
boterham/broodje	sandwich/roll		sla/salade	salad
brood	bread		slagroom	whipped cream
dranken	drinks		smeerkaas	cheese spread
eieren	eggs		stokbrood	French bread
gerst	barley		suiker	sugar
groenten	vegetables		vis	fish
honing	honey		vlees	meat
hoofdgerechten	main courses		voorgerechten	starters/hors d'oeuvres
kaas	cheese		vruchten	fruit
koud	cold		warm	hot
nagerechten	desserts		zout	salt
peper	pepper			

Starters and snacks

erwtensoep/snert	thick pea soup with bacon or sausage		patat/friet	chips/French fries
			soep	soup
huzarensalade	potato salad with pickles		uitsmijter	ham or cheese with eggs on bread
koffietafel	light midday meal of cold meats, cheese, bread, and perhaps soup			

Meat

biefstuk (hollandse)	steak		kip	chicken
biefstuk (duitse)	hamburger		kroket	spiced veal or beef in hash, coated in breadcrumbs
eend	duck			
fricandeau	roast pork			
fricandel	frankfurter-like sausage		lamsvlees	lamb
gehakt	mince		lever	liver
ham	ham		ossenhaas	beef tenderloin
kalfsvlees	veal		rookvlees	smoked beef
kalkoen	turkey		spek	bacon
karbonade	a chop		worst	sausages

Fish

forel	trout		oesters	oysters
garnalen	prawns		paling	eel
haring	herring		schelvis	haddock
haringsalade	herring salad		schol	plaice
kabeljauw	cod		tong	sole
makreel	mackerel		zalm	salmon
mosselen	mussels			

Vegetables

aardappelen	potatoes		rijst	rice
bloemkool	cauliflower		sla	salad, lettuce
bonen	beans		stampot andijvie	mashed potato and endive
champignons	mushrooms		stampot boerenkool	mashed potato and cabbage
erwten	peas			
hutspot	mashed potatoes and carrots		uien	onions
knoflook	garlic		wortelen	carrots
komkommer	cucumber		zuurkool	sauerkraut
prei	leek			

Cooking terms

belegd	filled or topped, as in *belegde broodjes* (bread rolls topped with cheese, etc)	geraspt	grated
		gerookt	smoked
		gestoofd	stewed
doorbakken	well-done	half doorbakken	medium-done
gebakken	fried/baked	Hollandse saus	hollandaise (a milk and egg sauce)
gebraden	roasted		
gegrild	grilled	rood	rare
gekookt	boiled		

Indonesian dishes and terms

ajam	chicken	nasi rames	a *rijsttafel* on a single plate
bami	noodles with meat and vegetables	pedis	hot and spicy
		pisang	banana
daging	beef	rijsttafel	assortment of spicy dishes served with plain rice
gado gado	vegetables in peanut sauce		
goreng	fried	sambal	hot chilli-based sauce
ikan	fish	sate	meat on a skewer
katjang	peanut	satesaus	peanut sauce to accompany meat grilled on skewers
kroepoek	prawn crackers		
loempia	spring rolls	seroendeng	spicy, shredded and fried coconut
nasi	rice		
nasi goreng	fried rice with meat/chicken and vegetables	tauge	bean sprouts

Sweets and desserts

appeltaart/ appelgebak	apple tart or cake	pannenkoeken	pancakes
		pepernoten	Dutch ginger nuts
drop	Dutch liquorice, available in *zoet* (sweet) or *zout* (salted) varieties; the latter an acquired taste	poffertjes	small pancakes/fritters
		(slag)room	(whipped) cream
		speculaas	spice- and cinnamon-flavoured biscuit
gebak	pastry		
ijs	ice cream	stroopwafels	waffles
koekjes	biscuits	taai-taai	spicy Dutch cake
oliebollen	traditional sweet sold at New Year – similar to a doughnut	vla	custard

Fruits and nuts

aardbei	strawberry	hazelnoot	hazelnut
amandel	almond	kers	cherry
appel	apple	kokosnoot	coconut
appelmoes	apple purée	peer	pear
citroen	lemon	perzik	peach
druiven	grape	pinda	peanut
framboos	raspberry	pruim	plum/prune

Drinks

anijsmelk	aniseed-flavoured, warm milk		kopstoot	beer with a *jenever* chaser
appelsap	apple juice		melk	milk
bessenjenever	blackcurrant gin		met ijs	with ice
chocomel	chocolate milk		met slagroom	with whipped cream
warme chocolade melk	hot chocolate		pils	Dutch beer
citroenjenever	lemon gin		proost!	cheers!
droog	dry		sinaasappelsap	orange juice
frisdranken	soft drinks		thee	tea
jenever	Dutch gin		tomatensap	tomato juice
karnemelk	buttermilk		vruchtensap	fruit juice
koffie	coffee		wijn	wine
koffie verkeerd	coffee with warm milk		(wit/rood/rosé)	(white/red/rosé)
			vieux	Dutch brandy

Glossary

Abdij Abbey

Amsterdammertje Phallic-shaped bollard placed in rows alongside many Amsterdam streets to keep drivers off pavements – and out of the canals.

Begijnhof Similar to a hofje (see below), but occupied by Catholic women (begijns) who led semi-religious lives without taking full vows.

Beiaard Carillon chimes

Belfort Belfry

Beurs Stock exchange

Botermarkt Butter market

Brug Bridge

BTW Belasting Toegevoegde Waarde – VAT (sales tax)

Burgher Member of the upper or mercantile classes of a town, usually with certain civic powers

Gasthuis Hospice for the sick or infirm

Geen toegang No entry

Gemeente Municipal, as in Gemeentehuis (town hall)

Gerechtshof Law Courts

Gesloten Closed

Gezellig A hard term to translate – something like "cosy", "comfortable" and "inviting", all in one – but a term which is often said to lie at the heart of the Dutch psyche. A long, relaxed meal in a favourite restaurant with friends is *gezellig*; grabbing a quick snack is not. The best brown cafés ooze *gezelligheid*; Kalverstraat on a Saturday afternoon definitely doesn't.

Gilde Guild

Gracht Canal

Groentenmarkt Vegetable market

Grote Kerk Literally "big church" – the main church of a town or village.

Hal Hall

Hijsbalk Pulley beam, often decorated, fixed to the top of a gable to lift goods, furniture etc. Essential in canal houses whose staircases were – and mostly still are – narrow and steep; *hijsbalken* are still very much in use today.

Hof Courtyard

Hofje Almshouse, usually for elderly women who could look after themselves but needed small charities such as food and fuel; usually comprising a number of buildings centred around a small, enclosed courtyard.

Huis House

Ingang Entrance

Jeugdherberg Youth hostel

Kasteel Castle

Kerk Church

Koning King

Koningin Queen

Koninklijk Royal

Kunst Art

Lakenhal Cloth hall: the building in medieval weaving towns where cloth would be weighed, graded and sold.

Markt Central town square and the heart of most Dutch communities, normally still the site of weekly markets.

Mokum A Yiddish word meaning "city", originally used by the Jewish community to indicate Amsterdam; now in general usage as a nickname for the city.

Molen Windmill

Nederland The Netherlands

Nederlands Dutch

Omgang Procession

Paleis Palace

Plein A square or open space

Polder An area of land that has been reclaimed from the sea.

Poort Gate

Raadhuis Town hall

Randstad Literally "rim-town", this refers to the urban conurbation that makes up much of Noord- and Zuid-Holland, stretching from Amsterdam in the north to Rotterdam and Dordrecht in the south.

Rijk State

Schepenzaal Alderman's Hall

Schone kunsten Fine arts

Schouwburg Theatre

Sierkunst Decorative arts

Spionnetje Small mirror on a canal house enabling the occupant to see who is at the door without descending the stairs.

Spoor Train station platform

Stadhuis The most common word for a town hall.

Stedelijk Civic, municipal

Steeg Alley

Steen Stone

Stichting Institute or foundation

Straat Street

Toegang Entrance

Toren Tower

Tuin Garden

Uitgang Exit

V.S. Verenigde Staten "United States"

Vleeshuis Meat market

Volkskunde Folklore

VVV Tourist information office

Waag Old public weighing-house, a common feature of Dutch towns.

Weg Way

Wijk District

Art and architecture glossary

Ambulatory Covered passage around the outer edge of the choir of a church.

Apse Semicircular protrusion, usually at the east end of a church.

Art Deco Geometrical style of art and architecture popular in the 1930s.

Art Nouveau Style of art, architecture and design based on highly stylized vegetal forms, especially popular in the early part of the twentieth century.

Balustrade An ornamental rail, running, almost invariably, along the top of a building.

Baroque The art and architecture of the Counter-Reformation, dating from around 1600 onwards. Distinguished by extreme ornateness and by the complex but harmonious spatial arrangement of interiors.

Carillon A set of tuned church bells, either operated by an automatic mechanism or played on a keyboard.

Caryatid A sculptured female figure used as a column.

Chancel The eastern part of a church, often separated from the nave by a screen (see "rood screen"). Contains the choir and ambulatory.

Classical Architectural style incorporating Greek and Roman elements – pillars, domes, colonnades, etc – at its height in the seventeenth century and revived, as Neoclassical, in the nineteenth.

Diptych Carved or painted work on two panels. Often used as an altarpiece – both static and, more occasionally, portable.

Expressionism Artistic style popular at the beginning of the twentieth century, characterized by the exaggeration of shape or colour; often accompanied by the extensive use of symbolism.

Flamboyant Florid form of Gothic.

Fresco Wall painting – durable through application to wet plaster.

Gable The triangular upper portion of a wall – decorative or supporting a roof – which is a feature of many Amsterdam canal houses. Initially fairly simple, they became more ostentatious in the late seventeenth century, before turning to a more restrained if imposing classicism in the eighteenth and nineteenth centuries.

Genre painting In the seventeenth century the term "genre painting" applied to everything from animal paintings and still lifes through to historical works and landscapes. In the eighteenth century, the term came to be applied only to scenes of everyday life.

Gothic Architectural style of the thirteenth to sixteenth centuries, characterized by pointed arches, rib vaulting, flying buttresses and a general emphasis on verticality.

Grisaille A technique of monochrome painting in shades of grey.

Misericord Ledge on a choir stall on which the occupant can be supported

while standing; often carved with secular subjects (bottoms were not thought worthy of religious subject matter).

Nave Main body of a church.

Neoclassical A style of classical architecture (see above) revived in the nineteenth century, popular in the Low Countries during and after the Napoleonic occupation.

Neo-Gothic Revived Gothic style of architecture popular between the late eighteenth and nineteenth centuries.

Pediment Feature of a gable, usually triangular and often sporting a relief.

Pilaster A shallow rectangular column projecting, but only slightly, from a wall.

Renaissance The period of European history marking the end of the medieval period and the rise of the modern world. Defined, amongst many criteria, by an increase in classical scholarship, geographical discovery, the rise of secular values and the growth of individualism. Began in Italy in the fourteenth century. Also refers to the art and architecture of the period.

Rococo Highly florid, light and intricate eighteenth-century style of architecture, painting and interior design, forming the last phase of Baroque.

Romanesque Early medieval architecture distinguished by squat, heavy forms, rounded arches and naive sculpture.

Rood screen Decorative screen separating the nave from the chancel. A rood loft is the gallery (or space) on top of it.

Stucco Marble-based plaster used to embellish ceilings, etc.

Transept Arms of a cross-shaped church, placed at ninety degrees to nave and chancel.

Triptych Carved or painted work on three panels. Often used as an altarpiece.

Tympanum Sculpted, usually recessed, panel above a door.

Vault Arched ceiling or roof.

Travel
store

UK & Ireland

Britain
Devon & Cornwall
Dublin **D**
Edinburgh **D**
England
Ireland
The Lake District
London
London **D**
London Mini Guide
Scotland
Scottish Highlands
& Islands
Wales

Europe

Algarve **D**
Amsterdam
Amsterdam **D**
Andalucía
Athens **D**
Austria
Baltic States
Barcelona
Barcelona **D**
Belgium &
Luxembourg
Berlin
Brittany & Normandy
Bruges **D**
Brussels
Budapest
Bulgaria
Copenhagen
Corfu
Corsica
Costa Brava **D**
Crete
Croatia
Cyprus
Czech & Slovak
Republics
Denmark
Dodecanese & East
Aegean Islands
Dordogne & The Lot
Europe
Florence & Siena
Florence **D**
France
Germany
Gran Canaria **D**
Greece
Greek Islands

Hungary
Ibiza & Formentera **D**
Iceland
Ionian Islands
Italy
The Italian Lakes
Languedoc &
Roussillon
Lanzarote &
Fuerteventura **D**
Lisbon **D**
The Loire Valley
Madeira **D**
Madrid **D**
Mallorca **D**
Mallorca & Menorca
Malta & Gozo **D**
Menorca
Moscow
The Netherlands
Norway
Paris
Paris **D**
Paris Mini Guide
Poland
Portugal
Prague
Prague **D**
Provence
& the Côte D'Azur
Pyrenees
Romania
Rome
Rome **D**
Sardinia
Scandinavia
Sicily
Slovenia
Spain
St Petersburg
Sweden
Switzerland
Tenerife &
La Gomera **D**
Turkey
Tuscany & Umbria
Venice & The Veneto
Venice **D**
Vienna

Asia

Bali & Lombok
Bangkok
Beijing

Cambodia
China
Goa
Hong Kong & Macau
Hong Kong
& Macau **D**
India
Indonesia
Japan
Kerala
Laos
Malaysia, Singapore
& Brunei
Nepal
The Philippines
Rajasthan, Dehli
& Agra
Singapore
Singapore **D**
South India
Southeast Asia
Sri Lanka
Taiwan
Thailand
Thailand's Beaches
& Islands
Tokyo
Vietnam

Australasia

Australia
Melbourne
New Zealand
Sydney

North America

Alaska
Baja California
Boston
California
Canada
Chicago
Colorado
Florida
The Grand Canyon
Hawaii
Honolulu **D**
Las Vegas **D**
Los Angeles
Maui **D**
Miami & South Florida
Montréal
New England
New Orleans **D**
New York City

New York City **D**
New York City Mini
Guide
Orlando & Walt
Disney World® **D**
Pacific Northwest
San Francisco
San Francisco **D**
Seattle
Southwest USA
Toronto
USA
Vancouver
Washington DC
Washington DC **D**
Yellowstone & The
Grand Tetons
Yosemite

Caribbean
& Latin America

Antigua & Barbuda **D**
Argentina
Bahamas
Barbados **D**
Belize
Bolivia
Brazil
Cancún & Cozumel **D**
Caribbean
Central America
Chile
Costa Rica
Cuba
Dominican Republic
Dominican Republic **D**
Ecuador
Guatemala
Jamaica
Mexico
Peru
St Lucia **D**
South America
Trinidad & Tobago
Yúcatan

Africa & Middle East

Cape Town & the
Garden Route
Dubai **D**
Egypt
Gambia
Jordan

D: Rough Guide
DIRECTIONS for
short breaks

Available from all good bookstores

www.roughguides.com

Information on over 25,000 destinations around the world

- **Read** Rough Guides' trusted travel info
- **Access** exclusive articles from Rough Guides authors
- **Update** yourself on new books, maps, CDs and other products
- **Enter** our competitions and win travel prizes
- **Share** ideas, journals, photos & travel advice with other users
- **Earn** points every time you contribute to the Rough Guide community and get rewards

Avoid Guilt Trips

Buy fair trade coffee + bananas ✓
Save energy - use low energy bulbs ✓
- don't leave tv on standby ✓
Offset carbon emissions from flight to Madrid ✓
Send goat to Africa ✓
Join Tourism Concern today ✓

Slowly, the world is changing.
Together we can, and will, make a difference.

Tourism Concern is the only UK registered charity fighting exploitation in one of the largest industries on earth: people forced from their homes in order that holiday resorts can be built, sweatshop labour conditions in hotels and destruction of the environment are just some of the issues that we tackle.

Sending people on a guilt trip is not something we do. We know as well as anyone that holidays are precious. But you can help us to ensure that tourism always benefits the local communities involved.

Call 020 7133 3330
or visit **tourismconcern.org.uk** to find out how.

A year's membership of Tourism Concern costs just £20 (£12 unwaged) - that's 38 pence a week, less than the cost of a pint of milk, organic of course.

Fighting Exploitation in Tourism

TourismConcern

NOTES

NOTES

NOTES

Small print and

Index

A Rough Guide to Rough Guides

Published in 1982, the first Rough Guide – to Greece – was a student scheme that became a publishing phenomenon. Mark Ellingham, a recent graduate in English from Bristol University, had been travelling in Greece the previous summer and couldn't find the right guidebook. With a small group of friends he wrote his own guide, combining a highly contemporary, journalistic style with a thoroughly practical approach to travellers' needs.

The immediate success of the book spawned a series that rapidly covered dozens of destinations. And, in addition to impecunious backpackers, Rough Guides soon acquired a much broader and older readership that relished the guides' wit and inquisitiveness as much as their enthusiastic, critical approach and value-for-money ethos.

These days, Rough Guides include recommendations from shoestring to luxury and cover more than 200 destinations around the globe, including almost every country in the Americas and Europe, more than half of Africa and most of Asia and Australasia. Our ever-growing team of authors and photographers is spread all over the world, particularly in Europe, the USA and Australia.

In the early 1990s, Rough Guides branched out of travel, with the publication of Rough Guides to World Music, Classical Music and the Internet. All three have become benchmark titles in their fields, spearheading the publication of a wide range of books under the Rough Guide name.

Including the travel series, Rough Guides now number more than 350 titles, covering: phrasebooks, waterproof maps, music guides from Opera to Heavy Metal, reference works as diverse as Conspiracy Theories and Shakespeare, and popular culture books from iPods to Poker. Rough Guides also produce a series of more than 120 World Music CDs in partnership with World Music Network.

Visit www.roughguides.com to see our latest publications.

Rough Guide travel images are available for commercial licensing at www.roughguidespictures.com

Rough Guide credits

Text editors: Natasha Foges, Andy Turner
Layout: Dan May
Cartography: Amod Singh
Picture editor: Nicole Newman
Production: Aimee Hampson
Proofreader: Jan McCann
Cover design: Chloë Roberts
Photographer: Mark Thomas, Anthony Cassidy, Tim Draper, Neil Setchfield
Editorial: London Kate Berens, Claire Saunders, Ruth Blackmore, Polly Thomas, Alison Murchie, Karoline Densley, Andy Turner, Keith Drew, Edward Aves, Nikki Birrell, Alice Park, Sarah Eno, Lucy White, Jo Kirby, Samantha Cook, James Smart, Natasha Foges, Roisin Cameron, Emma Gibbs, Joe Staines, Duncan Clark, Peter Buckley, Matthew Milton, Tracy Hopkins, Ruth Tidball; **New York** Andrew Rosenberg, Steven Horak, AnneLise Sorensen, Amy Hegarty, April Isaacs, Ella Steim, Anna Owens, Joseph Petta, Sean Mahoney
Design & Pictures: London Scott Stickland, Dan May, Diana Jarvis, Mark Thomas, Jj Luck, Chloë Roberts, Nicole Newman, Sarah Cummins; **Delhi** Umesh Aggarwal, Ajay Verma, Jessica Subramanian, Ankur Guha, Pradeep Thapliyal, Sachin Tanwar, Anita Singh, Madhavi Singh, Karen D'Souza
Production: Aimee Hampson, Vicky Baldwin
Cartography: London Maxine Repath, Ed Wright, Katie Lloyd-Jones; **Delhi** Jai Prakash Mishra, Rajesh Chhibber, Ashutosh Bharti, Rajesh Mishra, Animesh Pathak, Jasbir Sandhu, Karobi Gogoi, Amod Singh, Alakananda Bhattacharya, Swati Handoo
Online: New York Jennifer Gold, Kristin Mingrone; **Delhi** Manik Chauhan, Narender Kumar, Rakesh Kumar, Amit Kumar, Amit Verma, Rahul Kumar, Ganesh Sharma, Debojit Borah
Marketing & Publicity: London Liz Statham, Niki Hanmer, Louise Maher, Jess Carter, Vanessa Godden, Vivienne Watton, Anna Paynton, Rachel Sprackett; **New York** Geoff Colquitt, Megan Kennedy, Katy Ball; **Delhi** Reem Khokhar
Editorial Coordinator: Emma Traynor
Manager India: Punita Singh
Series Editor: Mark Ellingham
Reference Director: Andrew Lockett
Publishing Coordinator/PA: Helen Phillips
Publishing Director: Martin Dunford
Commercial Manager: Gino Magnotta
Managing Director: John Duhigg

Publishing information

This ninth edition published August 2007 by
Rough Guides Ltd,
80 Strand, London WC2R 0RL
345 Hudson St, 4th Floor,
New York, NY 10014, USA
14 Local Shopping Centre, Panchsheel Park,
New Delhi 110017, India
Distributed by the Penguin Group
Penguin Books Ltd,
80 Strand, London WC2R 0RL
Penguin Group (USA)
375 Hudson Street, NY 10014, USA
Penguin Group (Australia)
250 Camberwell Road, Camberwell,
Victoria 3124, Australia
Penguin Books Canada Ltd,
10 Alcorn Avenue, Toronto, Ontario,
Canada M4V 1E4
Penguin Group (NZ)
67 Apollo Drive, Mairangi Bay, Auckland 1310,
New Zealand

Cover concept by Peter Dyer.
Typeset in Bembo and Helvetica to an original design by Henry Iles.
Printed in Italy by LegoPrint S.p.A
© Martin Dunford/Phil Lee/Rough Guides, 2007
No part of this book may be reproduced in any form without permission from the publisher except for the quotation of brief passages in reviews.
344pp includes index
A catalogue record for this book is available from the British Library
ISBN: 9781-84353-809-7

1   3   5   7   9   8   6   4   2

Help us update

We've gone to a lot of effort to ensure that the ninth edition of **The Rough Guide to Amsterdam** is accurate and up to date. However, things change – places get "discovered", opening hours are notoriously fickle, restaurants and rooms raise prices or lower standards. If you feel we've got it wrong or left something out, we'd like to know, and if you can remember the address, the price, the time, the phone number, so much the better. We'll credit all contributions, and send a copy of the next edition (or any other Rough Guide if you prefer) for the best letters. Everyone who writes to us and isn't already a subscriber will receive a copy of our full-colour thrice-yearly newsletter. Please mark letters: **"Rough Guide Amsterdam Update"** and send to: Rough Guides, 80 Strand, London WC2R 0RL, or Rough Guides, 345 Hudson St, 4th Floor, New York, NY 10014. Or send an email to **mail@roughguides.com** Have your questions answered and tell others about your trip at
www.roughguides.atinfopop.com

Acknowledgements

Martin Dunford would like to thank Natasha Foges for casting her patient and watchful eye over things, Phil and Karoline for being such delightful co-authors, and Caroline, Daisy and Lucy for everything else.

Phil Lee would like to thank his editor, Natasha Foges, for her good humour and thoroughness during the preparation of this new edition of Amsterdam. Special thanks also to Els Wamsteeker of Amsterdam's ATCB; Suzanne Kuijer of the Netherlands Board of Tourism; Suzanne Morton-Taylor and Malijn Maat for their help with all sorts of queries; and co-authors, Martin Dunford and Karoline Densley.

Karoline Densley would like to thank the following people for their time; Sanne Oomens, Tamara Tong Sang, Xaviera Hollander, Daniëlle Bouwman, Alieke Keizer, Maaike Arwert, Suzanne Morton, Elard Diekman, Marieke Pronk, Kerstin Anthoni, Pieter Visser and Stephan van Egmond. A special thanks to Marcel van Woerkom for allowing me into his wonderful home, to Marvin for the conversation, the staff at The Dylan who always make me feel welcome, and my co-authors, Martin and Phil, and Natasha for her fine editing. Lastly, thanks to Martin Thomas for his patience, home hub and the football.

The editor would like to thank cartographer Amod Singh for a great set of maps, Nicole Newman for tireless picture research, Dan May for his layout skills, and Jo Kirby for her helpful advice.

Readers' letters

Thanks to all the readers who have taken the time to write in with comments and suggestions (and apologies if we've inadvertently omitted or misspelt anyone's name):

Joachim Allgaier; Gio Alzapiedi; Caroline Baurdoux; Maarten Bax; Christel de Boer; Diederik von Bonninghausen; Chris Booth; Bram Bos; Howard Bourne; Anna Broisma; David Buckley; Dick Butler; Sarah Clayton; Brian Clapp; Martin Christlieb, Lyndsey Daley; Nathalie Delorme; Julian Dorling; Francine van de Duin; Michael Farr; Eep Francken; David Fraser Jenkins; Annette Gahlings; Jeroen Gerlag; Steve Graham; Francis Groves; Karin Grunewald; Maarten van der Gulik; Lesley Hall; Annmarie Hanlon; Graham Heaney; Maartje Heerkens; Frederik Hemmes; Dominic Herrington; Jeff Hobbs; Lynn Horton; Diana den Houdijker; Zane Katsikis; Michael Kirby; Peter de Koning; Leo Lacey; Natali Lekka; Richard Lim; Wendy Lloyd; Marit Lokhorst; Jonas Ludvigsson; Malijn Maat; Betty Anne McCall; Jenny McCubbin; Craig MacDonald; Caroline McElwee; Dolores Mateo; Edward Mayor; Lera Miles; Norman Miller; Alison Morley; John Morton; Bernadette and Michael Mossley; Leann Nelson; Judith Orford; Jill Pearson; Bill Paton; Nick Reeves; Fiona Rempt; Lesa Rollo; Nienke Rozendaal; Bobby Russell; Carolien Selderijk; Nigel Sandford; Toby Screech; Johanna Sleeswijk; Hilary Smith; K. Tan; Matthew Teller; Dunya Verwey; Anna Vidou; Ronald Walgreen; Clare Webster; Susan Webster; Christel van Weezep; Paul Weston; B. White; J. Wood; Karen Woods; Alison Young; Liz Young.

Photo credits

All photos © Rough Guides except the following:

Things not to miss
07 Koninklijk Paleis © Martin Dunford
13 Secret door in the Anne Frank Huis © Anne Frank Huis
19 Rijksmuseum © Rijksmuseum
20 Queen's Day © Martin Dunford

Black and whites
p.46 View of Damrak from Beurs Van Berlage © Nicole Newman
p.159 Alkmaar cheese market © Koen Suyk/epa/Corbis
p.201 Yamazoto © Yamazoto
p.236 Albert Cuypmarkt © Andy Marshall/Alamy
p.244 Amsterdam Pride © Michel Porro/Getty Images
p.260 Queen's Day © Martin Dunford

p.262 Man smoking giant marijuana joint during Cannabis Cup © Jeffrey L. Rotman/Corbis
p.266 Map of Amsterdam 1662 © Visual Arts Library (London)/Alamy
p.288 Irises, 1890 by Vincent van Gogh © Bridgeman Art Library

Colour section: The Golden Age
The Night Watch, c. 1642 by Rembrandt van Rijn © Collectie Rijksmuseum Amsterdam
The Managers of the Haarlem Orphanage, 1663 by Jan de Bray © Frans Hals Museum/Bridgeman Art Library
The Feast of St Nicholas, c. 1665–1668 by Jan Steen © Collectie Rijksmuseum Amsterdam
Nineteenth-century tulip illustration © Corbis

SMALL PRINT

Index

Map entries are in colour.

Map symbols

maps are listed in the full index using coloured text

-----	Chapter division boundary	♦	Point of interest
	Motorway	ⓘ	Information office
	Major road	⊠	Post office
	Minor road	🄿	Parking
	Pedestrianized road	◉	Accommodation
....	Tunnel	⚘	Garden
	Railway	⊙	Statue/memorial
- - -	Footpath	✡	Synagogue
	Waterway	⌖	Church
— —	Ferry route		Building
⊠—⊠	Gate	☐	Market
⏝	Bridge	⬭	Stadium
▬	Boat		Cemetery
✈	Airport		Park/National park
Ⓜ	Metro station		Beach

Concertgebouw

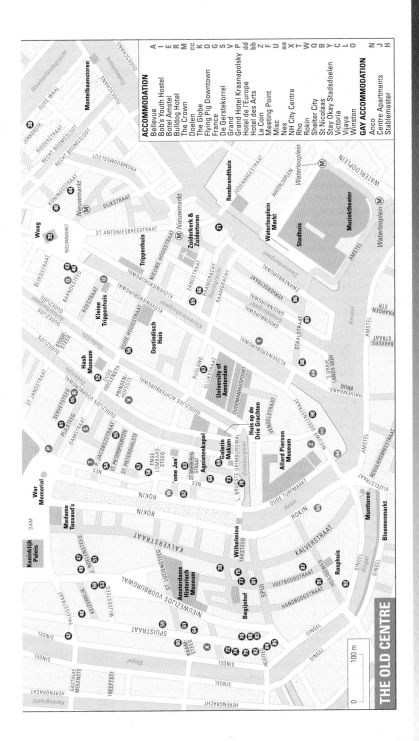

ACCOMMODATION

Bellevue	A
Bob's Youth Hostel	I
Botel Amstel	E
Bulldog Hotel	R
The Crown	M
Doelen	cc
The Globe	K
Flying Pig Downtown	D
France	G
De Gerstekorrel	S
Grand	V
Grand Hotel Krasnapolsky	P
Hotel de l'Europe	dd
Hotel des Arts	bb
Le Coin	Z
Meeting Point	F
Misc	U
Nes	aa
NH City Centre	X
Rho	T
Rokin	W
Shelter City	Q
St Nicolaas	B
Stay Okay Stadsdoelen	Y
Victoria	C
Vijaya	L
Winston	O

GAY ACCOMMODATION

Anco	N
Centre Apartments	J
Stablemaster	H

THE OLD CENTRE

0 ___ 100 m

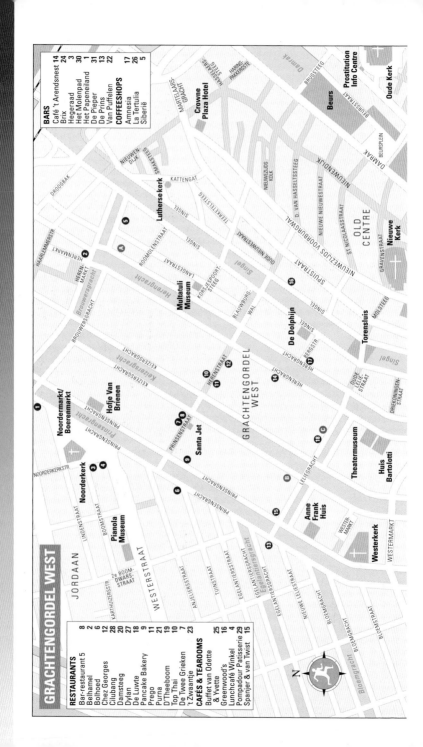

GRACHTENGORDEL WEST

RESTAURANTS
Bar-restaurant 5	8
Belhamel	2
Bolhoed	6
Chez Georges	12
Cilubang	28
Damsteeg	20
Dylan	27
De Luwte	18
Pancake Bakery	9
Prego	11
Purna	21
D'Theeboom	19
Top Thai	10
De Twee Grieken	7
't Zwaantje	23

CAFÉS & TEAROOMS
Buffet van Odette & Yvette	25
Greenwood's	16
Lunchcafé Winkel	4
Pompadour Patisserie	29
Spanjer & van Twist	15

BARS
Café 't Arendsnest	14
Brix	24
Hegeraad	3
Het Molenpad	30
Het Papeneiland	1
De Pieper	31
De Prins	13
Van Puffelen	22

COFFEESHOPS
Amnesia	17
La Tertulia	26
Siberië	5

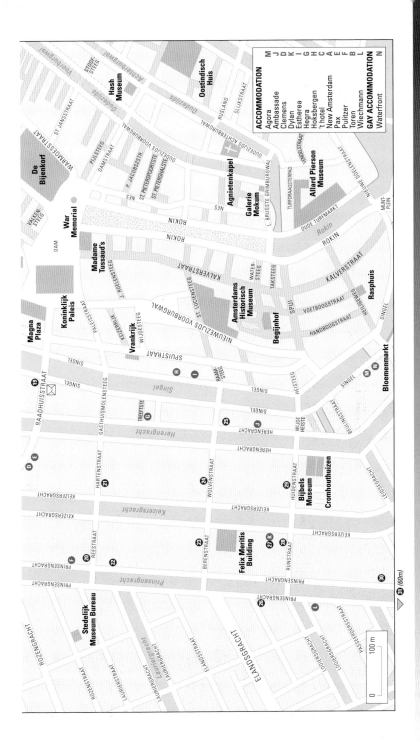

ACCOMMODATION
Agora — M
Ambassade — J
Clemens — D
Dylan — K
Estherea — I
Hegra — G
Hoksbergen — H
't hotel — C
New Amsterdam — A
Pax — E
Pulitzer — F
Toren — B
Wiechmann — L
GAY ACCOMMODATION
Waterfront — N

De Bijenkorf
Hash Museum
Oostindisch Huis
Magna Plaza
Koninklijk Paleis
War Memorial
Madame Tussaud's
Agnietenkapel
Galerie Mokum
Allard Pierson Museum
Amsterdams Historisch Museum
Vrankrijk
Beginhof
Rasphuis
Bloemenmarkt
Stedelijk Museum Bureau
Felix Meritis Building
Bijbels Museum
Crombouthuizen

Rokin
ROKIN
KALVERSTRAAT
KALVERSTRAAT
NIEUWEZIJDS VOORBURGWAL
OUDEZIJDS VOORBURGWAL
OUDEZIJDS ACHTERBURGWAL
Voorburgwal
Achterburgwal
SINGEL
HERENGRACHT
KEIZERSGRACHT
PRINSENGRACHT
ELANDSGRACHT
ROZENGRACHT
LAURIERGRACHT
LIJNBAANSGRACHT
RAADHUISSTRAAT
SPUISTRAAT
SPUI
DAM
WARMOESSTRAAT

0   100 m

↘ (60m)

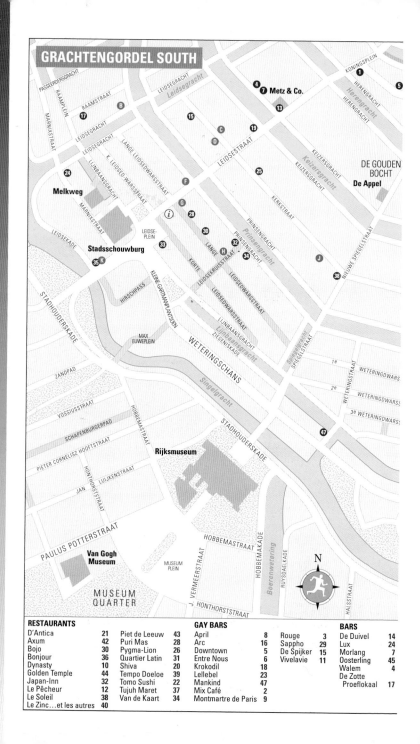

GRACHTENGORDEL SOUTH

Metz & Co.

DE GOUDEN BOCHT

De Appel

Melkweg

Stadsschouwburg

LEIDSE-PLEIN

MAX EUWEPLEIN

Rijksmuseum

Van Gogh Museum

MUSEUM PLEIN

MUSEUM QUARTER

N

RESTAURANTS				GAY BARS					BARS	
D'Antica	21	Piet de Leeuw	43	April	8	Rouge	3		De Duivel	14
Axum	42	Puri Mas	28	Arc	16	Sappho	29		Lux	24
Bojo	30	Pygma-Lion	26	Downtown	5	De Spijker	15		Morlang	7
Bonjour	36	Quartier Latin	31	Entre Nous	6	Vivelavie	11		Oosterling	45
Dynasty	10	Shiva	20	Krokodil	18				Walem	4
Golden Temple	44	Tempo Doeloe	39	Lellebel	23				De Zotte	
Japan-Inn	32	Tomo Sushi	22	Mankind	47				Proeflokaal	17
Le Pêcheur	12	Tujuh Maret	37	Mix Café	2					
Le Soleil	38	Van de Kaart	34	Montmartre de Paris	9					
Le Zinc…et les autres	40									

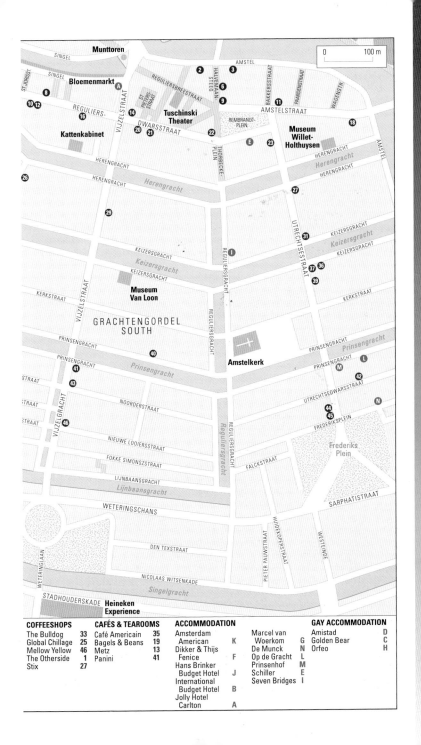

COFFEESHOPS

The Bulldog	33
Global Chillage	25
Mellow Yellow	46
The Otherside	1
Stix	27

CAFÉS & TEAROOMS

Café Americain	35
Bagels & Beans	19
Metz	13
Panini	41

ACCOMMODATION

Amsterdam American	K
Dikker & Thijs Fenice	F
Hans Brinker Budget Hotel	J
International Budget Hotel	B
Jolly Hotel Carlton	A
Marcel van Woerkom	G
De Munck	N
Op de Gracht	L
Prinsenhof	M
Schiller	E
Seven Bridges	I

GAY ACCOMMODATION

Amistad	D
Golden Bear	C
Orfeo	H

THE JORDAAN AND WESTERN DOCKLANDS

0   200 m

& Realeneiland

Westerpark

HAARLEMMERWEG

HAARLEMMERWEG

NASSAU-
PLEIN

HAARLEMER-
PLEIN

Prinsen-
eiland   WESTERDOK

Westerdok

Haarlemerpoort

The Movies

SCHEEPVAARTS-
BUURT

PALMGRACHT

PALMSTRAAT

WILLEMSSTRAAT

GOUDSBLOEMSTRAAT

LINDENGRACHT

Noordermarkt/
Boerenmarkt

JORDAAN   Noorderkerk

LINDENGRACHT

LINDENSTRAAT

BOOMSTRAAT

Hofje Van
Brienen

Karthuizer-
hofje

Pianola Museum

WESTERSTRAAT

ANJELIERSSTRAAT

TUINSTRAAT

EGELANTIERSSTRAAT

EGELANTIERSGRACHT

Anne
Frank Huis

LELIESTRAAT

LELIEGRACHT

Greenpeace
HQ

Theater-
museum

Nieuwe
Kerk

Westerkerk

Homo-
monument

WESTERMARKT

Magna
Plaza

Koninklijk
Paleis

BLOEMGRACHT

BLOEMSTRAAT

COC

RAADHUISSTRAAT

ROZENGRACHT

Stedelijk
Museum Bureau

REESTRAAT   HARTENSTRAAT

Amsterdams
Historisch
Museum

ROZENGRACHT

LAURIERSTRAAT

LAURIERGRACHT

DA COSTA
PLEIN

ELANDSSTRAAT

BERENSTR.   WOLVENSTRAAT

ELANDSGRACHT

De Looier
Market

KINKERSTRAAT

Melkweg

Stadsschouwburg

N

ACCOMMODATION

Acacia	C
Johanna's B&B	A
Mark's Studio	B
The Shelter Jordaan	D
Van Onna	E

BARS		RESTAURANTS	
Chris	24	Albatros	14
Dulac	3	Bordewijk	10
Finch	7	Burgers Patio	17
De Kat in de Wijngaert	6	Capri	9
Nol	13	Cinema Paradiso	12
De Reiger	22	Claes Claesz	16
't Smalle	18	Da Noi	2
De Tuin	15	Divan	27
CAFÉS & TEAROOMS		Duende	5
Arnold Cornelis	28	De Eettuin	17
Festina Lente	30	De Gouden Reael	1
COFFEESHOPS		Himalaya	8
Barney's Breakfast Bar	4	Jur	19
Bronx	11	Rakang Thai	29
Paradox	25	Semhar	21
GAY BAR		De Vliegende Schotel	23
Saarein	26	Yam Yam	20

THE OLD JEWISH QUARTER AND EASTERN DOCKLANDS

ACCOMMODATION
Adolesce — B
Arena — E
Fantasia — C
Intercontinental Amstel — D
Lloyd — A

GAY ACCOMMODATION
Liliane's Home — F

BARS
11 — 11
Brouwerij Het IJ — 1
De Druif — 8
De Groene Olifant — 15
Odessa — 2
De Sluyswacht — 9

CAFÉ
De Hortus — 13

COFFEESHOP
Pollinator Company — 14

RESTAURANTS
éénvistwéévis — 6
Greetje — 4
Klimanjaro — 7
King Solomon — 12
Koffiehuis van de Volksbond — 10
Lloyd — A
Rosario — 5
Vorbij Het Einde — 3

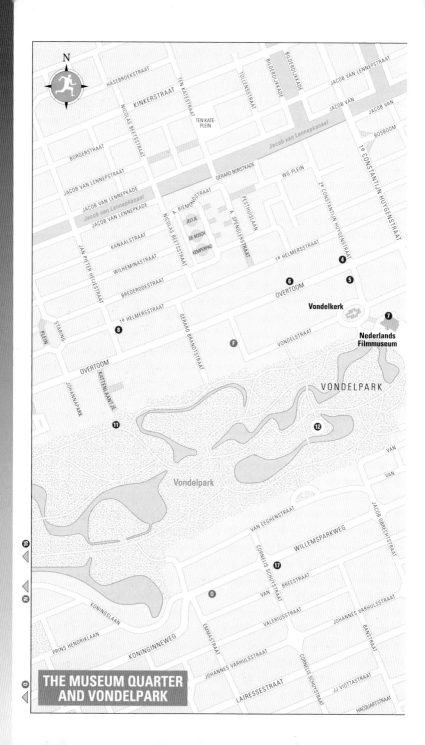

THE MUSEUM QUARTER
AND VONDELPARK

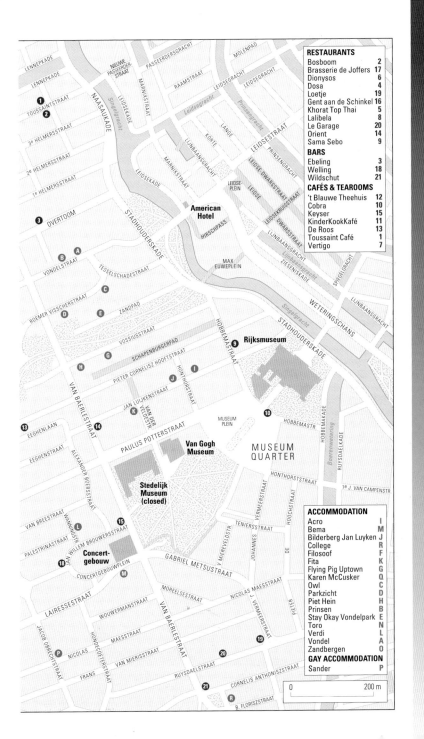

RESTAURANTS

Bosboom	2
Brasserie de Joffers	17
Dionysos	6
Dosa	4
Loetje	19
Gent aan de Schinkel	16
Khorat Top Thai	5
Lalibela	8
Le Garage	20
Orient	14
Sama Sebo	9

BARS

Ebeling	3
Welling	18
Wildschut	21

CAFÉS & TEAROOMS

't Blauwe Theehuis	12
Cobra	10
Keyser	15
KinderKookKafé	11
De Roos	13
Toussaint Café	1
Vertigo	7

ACCOMMODATION

Acro	I
Bema	M
Bilderberg Jan Luyken	J
College	R
Filosoof	F
Fita	K
Flying Pig Uptown	G
Karen McCusker	Q
Owl	C
Parkzicht	D
Piet Hein	H
Prinsen	B
Stay Okay Vondelpark	E
Toro	N
Verdi	L
Vondel	A
Zandbergen	O

GAY ACCOMMODATION

Sander	P

AMSTERDAM TRAMS, BUSES AND THE METRO

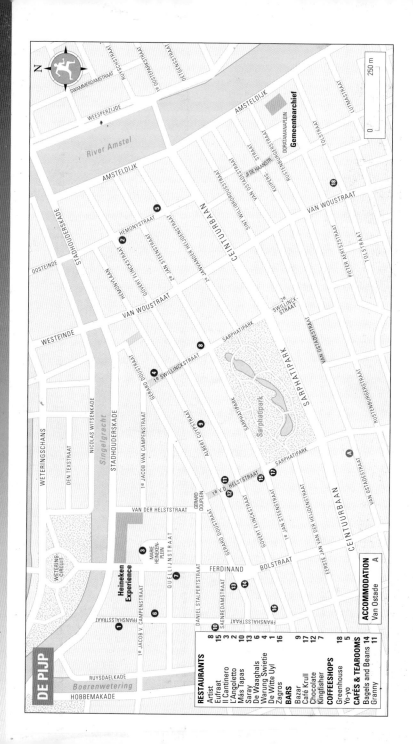

DE PIJP

N

River Amstel

Gemeentearchief

ACCOMMODATION
Van Ostade   A

RESTAURANTS
Artist	8
Eufraat	15
Il Cantinero	3
L'Angoletto	2
Más Tapas	10
Saray	13
De Waaghals	6
Warung Swietie	4
De Witte Uyl	1
Zagros	16

BARS
Bazar	9
Café Krull	17
Chocolate	12
Kingfisher	7

COFFEESHOPS
Greenhouse	18
Yo-yo	5

CAFÉS & TEAROOMS
Bagels and Beans	14
Granny	11

0   250 m